Scribner Handbook of English

FOURTH EDITION

FOURTH EDITION

SCRIBNER
HANDBOOK
of ENGLISH

ALBERT H. MARCKWARDT
Professor of English • Princeton University

FREDERIC G. CASSIDY
Professor of English • University of Wisconsin

NEW YORK · CHARLES SCRIBNER'S SONS

PREFACE

TO THE FOURTH EDITION

MORE than twenty-five years' experience with the *Scribner Handbook of English* has demonstrated the soundness of its fundamental approach, namely that there is no workable substitute for an objective presentation of the facts of the language. The present edition maintains this basic philosophy.

Throughout this period it has been a source of satisfaction to the authors to see how often their conclusions relative to specific usages and their general approach to the treatment of certain language problems have appeared elsewhere.

The present edition retains the same organization as the preceding, keeping separate those portions devoted to the stimulation of self-expression and those calculated to aid the student in adhering to standards of acceptability in writing. A complete student paper has been included as an example of writing done from an outline and employing correct documentation.

Certain chapters have undergone extensive revision, reflecting some changes in teaching practices. The chapter on the dictionary is no longer keyed to a single work; any of the excellent desk dictionaries now available may be used in connection with it. The treatment of footnotes and bibliography has been changed in accordance with the tendency toward standardization, due largely to the wide acceptance of *The MLA Style Sheet*. Illustrative examples have been brought up to date at many points, and sections devoted to exercise materials have been enlarged and increased in number. A new method of diagraming will be found in Appendix I.

We are grateful to Dr. Rose Marie Rogers, Philip Moe, and Charles S. Underhill for their excellent contributions to this edition.

ALBERT H. MARCKWARDT
FREDERIC G. CASSIDY

CONTENTS

CONTENTS

3. THE SENTENCE

4. THE WORD

Part Two: STANDARDS OF MODERN WRITING

5. THE DICTIONARY

6. *GRAMMAR*

7. *PUNCTUATION AND MECHANICS*

8. *SPELLING*

9. *USAGE*

Part Three: THE LONG PAPER

CONTENTS

SCRIBNER
HANDBOOK
of ENGLISH

FOURTH EDITION

PART ONE

EFFECTIVE WRITING

ALL of us use language constantly. We have been using it ever since we were small children. We employ it to satisfy the simplest necessities of our lives, to secure food, clothing, and shelter. At the other extreme language serves us as the vehicle for the expression of ideas as abstract and complex as the theory of relativity, and as beautiful as those contained in a lyric by Rossetti or a sonnet by Edna St. Vincent Millay.

Most of us, however, are neither physicists nor poets. We spend at least part of our daily lives in business following various trades, or in the professions. We use language for making explanations, analyzing situations, or discussing the relative merits of one procedure or another. To be successful, these language activities demand precision and forcefulness. Consequently we must all learn to express ourselves clearly and effectively.

In college too you will find that clear and effective expression is a daily necessity. Often it constitutes the difference between a brilliant and an average recitation. It is an equally important factor in reading and laboratory reports, term papers, and examinations.

The kind of writing that we most often need to do is called *exposition* or *expository writing*. To "expose" something is to set it forth or to explain it. Directions for mixing and applying the newest type of lacquer are exposition. So too is an account of the various interacting parts of the United Nations organization. You may explain why corn is detasseled in growing the hybrid seed or how the meter of a sonnet suits the expression of its ideas. You may set forth the merits of one or another type of labor union or sales campaign. All these are examples of exposition.

Chapter I contains some practical suggestions for expository writing.

I. The Whole Theme

1. CHOOSING A SUBJECT

a. Choose a subject within your range of experience.

IF you are like most readers, you get satisfaction out of the feeling that a writer obviously knows his subject. Even if it is something he has imagined, he manages to make it seem real. When you set about writing, remember this: limit yourself to subjects in which you have some experience—otherwise you are almost certain to blunder and produce something naive or unintentionally funny.

It would hardly be wise to attempt the description of an ocean voyage if you have never taken one. If you have never seen the inside of a factory, you had better not attempt to write about industrial problems (even with the help of reference materials) or, if you have never gone beyond the Hudson River, to write about the difficulties of Middle Western farmers.

This does not rule out imagination in the choice of a subject. With proper caution you may be able to portray the world as it may be in the year 2000, to describe the United States at the present time if the South had won the Civil War, to picture the changes that might come about if a woman were to win the Presidency. But since, to be successful, such imaginative subjects must give the effect of plausibility, they depend quite as much on the amount of real experience or knowledge you can bring to them.

In any event, do not choose a subject unless you have a real interest in it or (in the case of a research paper) genuinely want to find out more about it. If you are "not interested in anything at all," you do not belong in college. If you want to stay in college, be prepared to enlarge your range of interests.

b. Be constantly on the lookout for suggestions for theme subjects.

Most of us, teachers as well as students, encounter every day—every hour, almost—enough material to suggest dozens of themes. Unfortunately we do not observe closely, nor do we give our imaginations sufficient play over what we do observe. The apparently uneventful happenings of a single day may, as in James Joyce's *Ulysses*, be developed into a long novel. Percy Marks in a discussion of the same point once listed sixteen possible theme subjects arising from a student's walk down town. His list included such diversified subjects as "College Slang," "A Popcorn Machine," and "Is Lying Ever Justified?" A glance at the "Talk of the Town" section of *The New Yorker* magazine will illustrate the exceptional ingenuity of its authors in selecting random subjects for comment and discussion. In a single issue, for example, there were

1. A commentary on the fact that the new Air Force Academy cadet's uniform includes a sword.
2. An account of the plans made by a Scottish charitable society in New York for its 200th anniversary banquet, with Scottish dishes and entertainment.
3. A visit to a convention of security analysts, members of a new profession who advise corporations on investments and who feel that their prestige is rising.
4. The story of a former child-prodigy pianist who is returning to the concert stage after several years' eclipse.
5. The anecdote of a salesgirl who thinks that a synthetic fabric has come from a fur-bearing animal.

6. A description of the meeting of a motor-scooter club, with one member's thoughts about its purposes and plans.

7. The troubles of a woman caught in an automatic elevator which she does not know how to operate.

Readers look forward eagerly every week to this department, largely because its authors recognize that many of the trivial and commonplace incidents of everyday life have story material in them. Conversations, group discussions, any situation where there may be a conflict of opinion or desires are also likely to provide a fruitful source of subject matter. Above all, write on something that interests you.

c. Limit your subject so that you may treat it adequately in the space at your disposal.

The length of your essay or theme will usually be specified when it is assigned. In four pages or two thousand words, you cannot possibly expect to say much about such subjects as "Experimentation in the Modern Drama," "Television Broadcasting," "Mechanization in the Home," or "Post-Khrushchev Russia." These are far too broad for a short theme: you would have space only for the most general, therefore empty and pointless, statements.

A single aspect of one of these subjects, however, would be entirely appropriate, especially if you have had direct experience or knowledge of it. Limiting the second subject given in the list above, you might arrive at such subjects as "What Television Does Best," "How the Picture Tube Works," "Radio Versus Television as Media," "Censorship of Television," "Working in a Television Studio," "How I Would Run My Own TV Show," "Television as a Career," "The Technical Aspects of UHF." After choosing a properly limited subject for your theme, you should be ready to begin developing it.

5

Limit the following topics sufficiently for treatment in less than one thousand words:

Magazine Advertising	Campus Society
Sports	Chief Justice Warren
Viet Nam	Political Parties
Uranium	Debating
Labor Relations	The Constitution

2. GATHERING YOUR IDEAS; YOUR AUDIENCE

Much of the work of a successful composition must be done before the first word of the theme itself is ever written. After properly limiting the subject, think it through and write down every idea about it, every fact or opinion that comes to mind. You will not necessarily want to use all of these points, but you do need to consider the possibilities fully.

Besides the subject you must consider the reader. No writer is ever operating in a vacuum. Even one who thinks he is writing merely to get something off his chest—to express ideas or emotions that are pressing on him—is writing tacitly for himself or for people like himself. Most writers have a definite kind of reader in mind. People who submit their articles to periodicals are regularly told: Study our current publication and note the kind of public we aim at; if you want us to publish your work, write for our established clientele; or if you have written for one particular kind of audience, submit your work to the periodical that this audience reads. Literary agents do not waste postage sending articles of one type to magazines of another.

A student writing an essay must think of the reader too. Should he aim his essay at other students, at the teacher, at the general public? The way he handles his subject will depend in part on his audience; it cannot be ignored.

Now let us suppose you have chosen the limited subject of "Censorship of Television" and you want to aim your remarks at the more thoughtful members of the TV audience. Your preliminary list of rough ideas or topics might look something like this:

1. Censorship of crime programs
2. Undesirable commercials
3. Government censorship
4. Censoring matters of sex
5. Where the churches come in
6. Political censorship
7. Control of programs by sponsors
8. Censorship by the public
9. Things that ought to be outlawed
10. The status quo is satisfactory
11. Censorship and the Bill of Rights
12. How much censorship?
13. Penalties for illegal telecasts
14. Programs that need censoring now

These topics have been set down in the haphazard order in which they might first occur to you. Reading this list over, you discover that it is miscellaneous indeed. Some items are matters of fact, some matters of opinion; some could be treated neutrally, others would force you to take sides. Any of the possible approaches may be fit for expository treatment, but they dare not be confused. You must choose one and stick to it.

Let us suppose you decide to examine the subject objectively rather than to argue for one point of view. Returning to your list you notice that topics 9, 10, 11, 12, and 14 would be likely to involve you in argument. You decide to discard them. What you have done, described formally, is *classification*, the process of sorting out individual items in a class (here, *topics that have occurred to me on the subject of "Censorship of Television"*) into mutually exclusive (no topics in both subclasses) and exhaustive (no topics omitted from both subclasses) subclasses (here, *topics that would require taking sides and topics that would not . . .*) according to a basis (*potentiality for involving me in argument*). Further classification of the members of the remaining subclass on the basis of *tendency to assume censorship to exist* leads you to discard topic 13 (the only member of the subclass of topics which *do* assume censorship to exist). The remaining items (1-8), you notice, all suggest things which might play a part in the act of censorship (the defining characteristic of the remaining, homogeneous class). On the basis of *part played in the act of censorship* you divide this class into two subclasses: *things that might be censored* (containing topics 1, 2, 4, and 6) and *sources that might apply censorship* (containing topics 3, 5, 7 and 8). Tabulated and simplified for closer parallelism, these look like this:

Things that might be censored:

      Crime   Sex
      Commercials   Politics

Sources that might apply censorship:

      Government   Sponsors
      Churches   The public

Upon further thought you add *treatment of minority groups* under *things* and *producers* under *sources*.

If a classification is to be rigorous, the sorting must be done on a single basis. Shifting from one basis to another before completing a classification results in cross-classification. For example, suppose after setting up the first subclass tabulated above you had shifted your attention to the basis *potentiality for being harmed by censorship*. Applying this might have given you, as your second subclass, *things that might be harmed by censorship* (members: crime, politics, producers, the public). Your two subclasses would not have been mutually exclusive or exhaustive.

Your next step, planning the organization of the theme, will lead you to do further classification to decide how to order the topics and the details used to develop each topic.

3. SEQUENCE OF THOUGHT

Different subjects will require somewhat different treatment, but there must be some kind of orderly sequence if your presentation is to be effective. Here are several ways of attaining orderly sequence:

Arrange ideas or events in chronological order.

During the Pliocene period, which lasted at least six million years and terminated with the onset of the glacial epoch, perhaps a million years B.C. . . . Before the end of the glacial period, perhaps 25,000 years ago. . . . After the final glacial retreat, perhaps not more than eight to ten thousand years ago. . . .

Present things according to their relative physical position.

Since the brass goods industry in Connecticut's Naugatuck valley demands a high percentage of skills, the logical place for our examination to begin is Thomaston. . . . This accords very neatly with the situation in Baltimore. . . . In Greenville, South Carolina, it is the same story over again. . . .

9

Begin with a general statement and proceed to specific details.

Rivalries have often existed between groups or certain social, economic, or racial orders within the same region. . . . When the Anglo-American civilization struck the Spanish culture in the Southwest. . . . The English colonists came into contact with a French civilization in Canada. . . . New England Puritans met and mingled with the German settlers of the Old Northwest. . . .

These examples illustrate only a few of the possible plans of organization. There are many others: you might proceed from *cause* to *effect*, follow an *order of development*, go from the *abstract* or *general* to the *concrete* or *specific*, from the *familiar* to the *unfamiliar*, from the *more* to the *less important*—whatever appears to suit your subject best. Each of these plans of organization is a classification of some kind, and you should be aware that the best organization is likely to be the classification that has been made on the basis most relevant to the purpose of your essay.

Sometimes the plan of organization is quite easy to decide upon, as when you follow a manufacturing process from the raw materials to the finished product, or the progress of a battle from dawn to dark. Sometimes one order is nearly as good as another (but not as *any* other), and the "best" is a matter of opinion. Whatever order you choose, the important thing is to have a plan and then to follow it through from beginning to end.

EXERCISE II

1. Write a list of topics for one of the theme subjects listed below, using the chronological order.
2. Write a similar list with another subject, using the familiar-to-the-unfamiliar order.

3. Do the same using the general-to-specific order.

4. Write a theme using the list of topics you have worked out under 1, 2, or 3. (Length to be assigned.)

5. Make preliminary plans for themes on any two of the subjects which you have not used in answering 1, 2, or 3.

> Circling "The Square"
> Off-Campus Pleasures
> Knitting a Ski Sweater
> The Ideal Summer Trip
> When I Was Very Young
> Our Underpopulated Areas
> A Visit to the Dentist
> How to Use Sour Milk
> Politics in the Home Town
> Exploring Caves
> The American Drug Store
> On Being Social Chairman
> A Lost Art

4. THE OUTLINE

The chief argument in favor of outlining is that it forces you to *build* your theme rather than merely to jumble it together out of casual or misfitting bits. Outlining will give your essay structure, shape and balance, and direction in its development; and as a result, your theme will express your ideas more effectively.

In the present theme, "Censorship of Television," the topics you had tentatively listed in the first category concern crime, commercials, sex, politics, and treatment of minorities. What is the preferable order for presenting these? You decide that crime and sex are most closely associated; treatment of them on television may offend in much the same ways—against good taste, morality, respect for law.

Treatment of minority groups and censorship in political matters are rather different: our form of society and government, the Bill of Rights, loyalty and patriotism are involved. As for commercials, you suddenly realize that these are a vehicle, like the programs themselves—they are not on a par with such topics as crime, sex, treatment of minorities, and politics. You therefore decide to have only these four topics under the first heading, and in the order given.

In the second category your problem is much simpler. Here you might place your groups in the order in which they are likely to become involved in censorship: first, the sponsors and producers, who may prevent a show or portions of a show from being aired; next, the public, which may respond directly to a show; finally, the churches and the government.

You now have an *undeveloped outline*. To develop it you need to put under each topic and in an orderly sequence the details with which you will explain, illustrate, or attempt to demonstrate your points. Your *developed outline* may look something like this:

I. Aspects of television that may call for censorship:

    A. Crime
        1. The number of crime shows is very high.
        2. Criminal methods are realistically depicted.
        3. The criminal is seen in a favorable light.
        4. Crime shows affect our thinking.

    B. Sex
        1. Sex is associated with crimes of violence.
        2. Sex shows affect our thinking.

    C. Treatment of minorities and politics
        1. There may be unfair treatment of minorities.
        2. There may be partisan and propagandistic abuses.

II. Where censorship may originate:

  A. The sponsors and producers
    1. Sponsors may be over- or under-cautious.
    2. Sponsors' interests are not those of the public.
    3. Producers are largely under the sponsors' control.

  B. The public
    1. Letters may be unrepresentative or misguided.
    2. Opinion polls may be inaccurate.

  C. The churches
    1. Moral attitudes differ among denominations.
    2. The power of censorship may arouse disagreement among them.

  D. The government
    1. Some people want social legislation to control TV.
    2. Others want television as free as the press and movies.
    3. The FCC already exerts control over TV programming.

III. Summary

A short essay may not absolutely require an outline. But if you are going to do without one, the only satisfactory procedure is to write the first draft immediately after choosing the subject, when you are still in the heat of your enthusiasm for it. After the first draft is written, subject it to a number of thorough revisions. But never confuse a first draft, or merely a fresh copy, with a revised, finished essay. (Your instructor will not do so!)

Upon examination this second process turns out to be not so very different from working from an outline. The first draft, supposedly written at a fever pitch of creative energy, is little more than *gathering your ideas,* as described in **T2**. Careful revision will result in proper *sequence of thought,* as described in **T3**. The student should attempt to write both with and without an outline, to see the appropriateness of both methods. (For further discussion of outlining, see Chapter XII.)

EXERCISE III

Choose any one of the subjects listed and set down whatever ideas it suggests. Organize and revise these into a theme outline. The suggested subjects may be limited or modified to conform to your own experience.

> What Makes a Good Dance Band
> A Freshman Is Born
> Athletic Scholarships
> Impractical Education
> I Am All Mixed Up
> A Foreign Student I Have Met
> Making My Own Budget
> My Life in a Factory
> Having Fun in College
> Lost in the Library
> My Parents Decided
> "Getting There Is Half the Fun"

5. THE THESIS SENTENCE

Whether or not you use an outline, you should precede any expository writing by setting down clearly, in a single, specific, and complete statement just what idea you intend to develop in your essay. As one teacher has put it, "the student will never learn to write until he is able to make the leap from what he wants to *talk about* to what he wants to *say*." Here is a rather important distinction.

You have already decided that censorship of television is to be your subject—"what you want to talk about." You have chosen and arranged your ideas and even put down the details that you will use. Now you must make explicit your thesis, the summary statement of whose truth you will inform or seek to convince your reader—"what you want to say." This statement must include only what belongs and exclude what does not belong to your subject. For your subject, the thesis sentence might be something like this:

The enormous and increasing power of television over the mass of our population has led many people to consider the possibility of censorship: the things it may be advisable to censor and the people or organizations that might be the censors.

The thesis sentence need not be the opening one; but it is always wise, somewhere near the beginning of the essay, to indicate its scope and purpose with such a sentence.

EXERCISE IV

Write a thesis sentence for one of the subjects listed in Exercise III, and suggest, briefly, what sort of supporting detail would be needed to make that thesis seem plausible.

6. BEGINNING THE COMPOSITION

The student knows that no matter how inauspiciously any theme of his may begin, the instructor is duty bound to wade through it to the end. This is not true of writing done apart from the college class. The opening of any piece of writing, be it a novel, an essay, an advertisement, or even a letter of application for a position, must be arresting. If it starts in a dull or uninteresting fashion, if it does not catch the attention of the reader, it may remain unread.

The following methods of securing your reader's attention may be used singly or in combination:

a. State briefly and simply the central purpose of what you are planning to write about.

(See the thesis sentence just given in the preceding section.)

b. Introduce concrete details that the reader may easily grasp.

1. Begin with some vivid description.

When the thermometer drops rapidly and the wind begins to run with a seeping sound and to slice at your neck above the collar, you know that tomorrow the skating will be good.

2. Begin with an incident.

This afternoon I watched a squirrel on our front lawn collecting acorns and burying them. For a time he carried them one by one to some cache; but now he was burying each where he found it without bothering to mark the spot.

3. Introduce one or more characters.

Imagine if you can the New York of 1953. A young man who has just served in the Korean War is laying siege to the city desks of the metropolitan papers. He has good legs, but his past record includes nothing more substantial than having been expelled from college and having worked during vacations on a small city paper upstate and on a Hearst-owned Chicago paper.

c. Start with something that gives the impression of conversation.

1. Begin with a fragment of dialogue.

"Could you inform, please, where is International Club?"
"The International Center?"
"Center, yes, kindly —"
"Why, yes. I'm going right by. I'll show you."
This was my first meeting with Saito Hirazumi, who later became my laboratory partner.

> 2. Begin with a quotation, direct or indirect, of what someone else has said.

"We have no iron curtain," a highly placed Russian diplomat is reported to have said; "it is an invention of our enemies."

> 3. Ask a question or a series of questions.

Is there such a thing as modern biography? Can one name a year in which suddenly the old biography ceased to exist and modern biography came into being? And if so, what is the difference between old and modern biography?

d. Employ the element of unexpectedness.

> 1. Make a statement that arouses curiosity.

If a man were literally to "eat like a bird," he would have to consume approximately forty pounds of food each day.

> 2. Put the reader in suspense.

Have you ever thought you were absolutely alone in a house—and then something began to go tap-tap in the basement?

> 3. Parody a familiar quotation.

In medieval society there was a place for everybody, and everybody was expected to be in his place.

> 4. Make a paradoxical statement.

If you stop to think about it, you probably know very few people who have ever seen the sun.

EXERCISE V

1. Examine the beginnings of ten articles, using several of the following, or comparable magazines: *Harper's*, *The Reporter*, *Fortune*, *The New Yorker*, *Newsweek* (not picture or story magazines). What devices are used to gain the reader's attention? If a beginning does not employ any of the methods listed above, frame your own brief, generalized description of the method employed. (This may be assigned for oral or written presentation.)

2. Do the same with any one book by each of the following authors: Sir Walter Scott, W. M. Thackeray, Thomas Hardy, Mark Twain, Sinclair Lewis, John Galsworthy, John Steinbeck, R. L. Stevenson, William Faulkner, Clarence Day, Ernest Hemingway.

3. Examine in any single issue of a large Sunday newspaper both the news stories and the articles in the magazine section. How do these begin?

4. Employing the devices mentioned, write beginning sentences for each of the theme subjects listed in Exercise II. (The number may be specifically assigned.)

7. DEFINING TERMS

When writing an explanatory or argumentative theme, or any other kind in which you have to introduce terms that may be unfamiliar to your reader (or unfamiliar in the special sense that you intend), be certain that you define all such terms at the beginning. If you were seeking to prove that isolationism was a greater menace to America than Communism, you could not begin your argument until you had made perfectly clear what was meant by *isolationism* and *Communism*.

In a theme dealing with present educational trends in American universities you would have to explain what you meant by the *humanities* and an *integrated curriculum;* in a theme dealing with governmental policies you might have to define such terms as *AEC, OEO, tight money.*

Briefly, a definition is usually a statement that a noun (the term defined) has the same meaning as another noun or group of words. You are already familiar with dictionary or *lexical* definitions, definitions that simply record usage or the meanings that many users of the nouns give to them. Two other kinds of definition that you may want to use are *stipulative* definitions, which indicate determination to give certain meanings to certain nouns ("in this paper, I shall by 'senior citizen' mean 'a citizen at least seventy years of age who is retired or semi-retired' "), and *persuasive* definitions, which are intended to persuade the reader to change an opinion ("the *true* meaning of 'democracy' is 'belief in social equality' ").

8. CONNECTING THE PARTS

There would be little point in drawing a map of some territory if you were the only one who could interpret it. So it is with the organization of your composition. Make this so clear that your reader will be able to follow your plan in a single reading.

The following devices may be employed to couple one division of a theme to another:

a. Use word and phrase connectives.

Many serious-minded persons are urging us to prohibit strikes and lockouts. . . .

While the justifications for this proposal are persuasive, it has the limitation that . . .

Moreover, the very nature of the process of compulsory arbitration . . .

To sum up, it is extremely probable . . .

Connecting words and phrases may be sorted according to the functions they perform. Some useful ones follow, in a more or less descending order of formality:

1. Those which show that a similar, supplementary point is being made: *Furthermore, moreover, in like manner, and so again, in addition, next, again.*
2. Those which show that a contrasting point is being made: *On the contrary, nonetheless, nevertheless, despite this, in spite of this, on the other hand, however, yet, still, but, while.*
3. Those which show relationships of space, time, or importance: *Hitherto, foremost, formerly, in particular, beyond, above, around.*
4. Those which show the stages in your argument or in your marshaling of evidence: *Initially, at the outset, to begin with, from the start; up to now, so far; in sum, in conclusion, lastly, finally, after all.*

b. Repeat a portion of the preceding division.

Clearly, if there is any substitute for war, it must lie in the *pacific settlement of controversies* out of which wars grow . . .

As against these policies based upon power, the intermittent suggestion of securing *pacific settlement* by using among nations the agencies worked out in the domestic policy of civilized states . . .

From its beginning the United States has had an attitude favoring the *pacific settlement of international controversies* . . .

c. Use key words and phrases to show the proposed development of your argument, repeating them at the beginning of each division.

We shall discuss the *present status* of the securities market, the *causes* for the prevailing conditions, and whatever *remedies* seem to suggest themselves. . . .

At *present* the *status* of . . .
Turning now to the *causes* . . .
What are the *remedies* which may improve . . .

d. Number your division.

Of the details of that lesson, we can name and illustrate *three* of some technical importance . . .

The *first* is oneness of tone or pitch . . .
Let me approach a *second* and more specific agent of unity . . .
In the third place, the modern craftsman has learned . . .

The writer must be careful to avoid tiresome and repetitious division numbers or key words. Connectives should do their work unobtrusively, showing the reader the pattern or order of the theme without calling attention to themselves.

e. Use pronouns to refer to people or things mentioned in an earlier sentence.

The delinquent, rather than being a rebel, is . . .

He is afraid to do things alone and feels really secure only when *he* does things with a gang of *his* friends . . .

f. Use parallel sentence structure.

Development of the space program will be of benefit to the American citizen in several ways.

It will benefit science by providing . . .
It will benefit the economy both through increased . . .
It will benefit the security of the United States . . .

g. Arrange your sentences in an orderly sequence.

Effective linking of sentences can be achieved by using such orderly sequences as arrangement of ideas or events in chronological order and presentation of things according to their relative physical position (see **T3**).

EXERCISE VI

1. Examine a number of magazine articles (for example, those read for Exercise V), and make a list of the connectives which you find in each.

2. Supply appropriate connecting sentences for the lists of topics you worked out in Exercise II.

9. CONSISTENCY

Consistency is that quality which gives the reader a sense of a harmoniously planned composition in which the parts form an organic whole. In practice this means that when writing, and especially when revising, you must keep always in mind a sense of the total essay. (Here is the great value of an outline, which insures that the subject has been thought through.) Do not begin to write until you know pretty clearly what you intend to say—not, of course, every detail, but the general pattern and the main parts. This sense of the whole will help you to avoid straying, to integrate your theme.

a. Maintain the same physical point of view throughout.

If you were attempting to give your reader some notion of the buildings and business establishments which were clustered about the public square in your home town, you would scarcely jump from one side of the square to the other six or seven times in your account.

FAULTY: The house which Doctor King has just built is a model of compactness and economy of space. It consists of a dining room, living room, and kitchen on the first floor; three bedrooms and a bath on the second. The stair is enclosed, as it used to be in original colonial houses, and there is no waste passage around it. The kitchen region of the house ingeniously includes an inside entry and a breakfast alcove. The bedrooms all have plenty of closet space, and there is cross-ventilation in each of them as well as useful wall space for furniture. The living room is sixteen by twenty-eight feet and is reached through a small entryway which has a lavatory adjoining.

REVISED: The house which Doctor King has just built is a model of compactness and economy of space. It consists of a dining room, living room, and kitchen on the first floor; three bedrooms and a bath on the second. The living room is sixteen by twenty-eight feet and is reached through a small entryway which has a lavatory adjoining. The kitchen region of the house ingeniously includes an inside entry and a breakfast alcove. The stair is enclosed, as it used to be in original colonial houses, and there is no waste passage around it. The bedrooms all have plenty of closet space, and there is cross-ventilation in each of them as well as useful wall space for furniture.

b. Maintain the same chronological point of view throughout.

In describing a process or telling a story it is important to relate the stages or events in the order in which they occurred. A skillful writer may at times choose to relate a comparatively recent event before he tells some things which happened earlier, but for the less experienced one it is preferable to adhere to a straight chronological order.

FAULTY: Three months ago I began the study of Latin and at present I am beginning to read small selections from Cæsar. The declensions and verb forms seemed hard at first, but now my chief difficulty is the word order. That is not my first experience with a foreign language, since I studied French for two years when I was in high school. I am gradually becoming accustomed to the vocabulary, but expect to have difficulty as I come upon more new words.

23

REVISED: My first experience with a foreign language was in high school, where I studied French for two years. Three months ago I began the study of Latin. At first the declensions and verb forms seemed difficult, but now, as I am beginning to read small selections from Cæsar, my chief difficulty is with word order. I am gradually becoming accustomed to the vocabulary, but I expect to have difficulty as I come upon more new words.

c. Maintain the same grammatical point of view throughout.

Inexperienced writers and speakers frequently confuse the reader or hearer by shifting without cause from singular to plural, from active to passive, or in other ways. The whole point of grammatical agreement is to avoid such inconsistency. (For a full treatment see Chapter VI, especially G9 and G11; see also Chapter II, ¶11.)

One glaring type of fault, the confusion of pronouns, will suffice for illustration here. Notice the shift from personal *you* to impersonal *one*, and from singular *he*, *himself* to plural *those*, *their*.

FAULTY: *You* may be liberal essentially in four ways, namely with respect to social, economic, political, and religious matters. If *one* is liberal in each of these four fields, *he* may call *himself* a *liberal* in the true sense of the word. . . . In short, liberals are *those people* who are willing to give *their* serious thought to those proposals which may further human progress.

REVISED: *One* may be liberal essentially in four ways, namely with respect to social, economic, political, and religious matters. If *one* is liberal in each of these four fields, *he* may call *himself* a *liberal* in the true sense of the word. . . . In short, a liberal is *one* who is willing to give *his* serious thought to those proposals which may further human progress.

d. Maintain the same tone throughout.

If you were listening to a humorous story, you would consider it jarring if the teller inserted in the middle of it a serious reflection on the virtues of thrift, and then went back to finish his story. Avoid such breaks in your own writing.

If you are writing a formal composition, don't become cheaply witty or colloquial. If you are writing in an emotional mood, don't suddenly become satirical. One or two ill-chosen words are enough to mar consistency of tone.

FAULTY: This is but one side of a well-organized student work plan. In addition to the advantages to the student which I have mentioned, there are those which are enjoyed by the corporation. The principal one is undoubtedly the infusion of new blood into the corporation, since it is necessary for every corporation to remain young and healthy if it is to survive. Of course every corporation needs some *old-timers* who *know the ropes*, but that is not enough to keep a company going.

Notice that this is not a condemnation of the expressions *old-timer* and *know the ropes*. In another setting (informal) they might be wholly appropriate. But here they suddenly change the tone from the prevailing formal one and introduce a mixed metaphor: knowing the ropes has nothing to do with infusion of new blood. (What expressions might be more appropriate?)

Conversely, one or two words that are too dignified or artificial may spoil the flavor of a vigorous but simply written passage:

FAULTY: The hardest problem that a foreign student has to face at the beginning of the school year is that of finding a room. He may have to look for a long time before he will find a landlady who will take him in. There are several reasons for this. The lady of the house may be afraid that she will be unable to rent the rest of her rooms if it becomes known that a foreigner is *residing at her domicile*.

10. EFFECTIVENESS

You have noticed, perhaps a little enviously, that some of your acquaintances can tell a story or express an opinion so effectively that everyone listens. There are also effective writers, writers who arrest and hold the interest of their readers.

How does one become an effective writer? The answer lies partly in the personality of the writer, but there are a few useful principles which may be consciously applied.

a. Use concrete illustrations whenever possible.

You have only to leaf through the advertisements of any magazine to see what is meant by the use of concrete illustrations. Compare the two examples which follow and note the difference in the effect achieved by the appeal to the senses and the imagination.

INEFFECTIVE: John was unsuccessful as a student partly because of his inability to concentrate on his work and partly because he could always be persuaded to neglect his studies in favor of some trifling amusement.

EFFECTIVE: John was an unsuccessful student, but not for lack of intelligence or good intentions. He learned easily enough what he heard or was told, but his note-taking at lectures and his application to textbooks was far from regular. In occasional accesses of resolution he would go to classes, sit down firmly, take out notebook and pencil, and inscribe a few lines. Then some easy distraction would catch him—a phrase left on the blackboard, a bird flying past the window, two girls whispering, almost anything—and John would forget all else. It was the same at the dormitory: his radio, the fellows down the hall, the need to go out for a smoke; so his books would remain unread. John's good brain and bursts of good will were not enough to overcome a lack of concentration and of the power to resist trifling amusements.

The use of illustrative incidents to make a point or idea clear is always an effective device. Lincoln was given to using simple and homely figures to drive home a point. His well-known comment about the danger of swapping horses midstream is effective because it puts an idea in terms of an incident, even though the incident itself is not told.

b. Vary your style to avoid monotony.

1. Do not use sentences that are too much alike in length or construction—for example, be sure they do not all begin with the subject, that not all are simple sentences, and so on.

WEAK: I offer as an example my own father. My father's parents had little money. They provided a grade school education for their children. Then the children were forced to shift for themselves. My father had two brothers. Today he has achieved success in his field and is considered equal to those around him. His brothers are still where they were when they finished school. They all had the same opportunities, the same intelligence. Perhaps they had even more intelligence. However, he had initiative and a desire for success. They had none.

BETTER: I offer the experience of my father and his two brothers as an illustration of this point. Their parents had little money and were able to give the children only a grade school education. Beyond the eighth grade, the children were forced to shift for themselves. My father has achieved success in his field and is considered equal to those around him, while the brothers are still where they were when they finished school. All three had the same opportunities, the same intelligence; possibly the unsuccessful brothers were even more intelligent than my father. However, he had initiative and a desire for success where they had none.

In some cases, of course, you will want to repeat a sentence pattern for the sake of rhetorical emphasis, clarity, or coherence (see discussion of parallel sentence structure,

S9c). In fact, the use of variety for the sake of variety alone is a common fault of writers and is one that you should be careful to avoid (see discussion of elegant variation, **W6f**). Striking a proper balance between variety and repetition is not an easy thing to do, but you should be aware that, if properly used, both can be aids to good expression.

2. You will sometimes find dialogue and direct quotation helpful means of avoiding monotony.

WEAK: Long before I had the notion of attending a university for the purpose of educational advancement, I had the curiosity to ask some of the older men with whom I worked what a college education meant to them. I was frequently told that college training was not an absolute essential in acquiring intellectual and cultural training. Most of my co-workers, however, seemed to value most highly the social contacts and friendships which they had made in college.

BETTER: Long before I had the notion of attending a university, I had the curiosity to ask some of the older men with whom I worked what a college education meant to them. The typical answer was that of a man who is recognized as a successful person intellectually, financially, and socially:

"If you have sufficient energy and real interest in the cultural and intellectual aspects of life, you can educate yourself nearly as well at the Public Library as you would at college. But you would miss the thing that after fifteen years means most to me from having gone to college: the social contacts and friendships built up while I was there."

3. Use (but don't overuse) questions and explanations.

WEAK: The same holds true for professors and students. Of course, it is impossible to expect an equality between professors and students because the former are more learned and are here to teach the less learned, but the student body should be given equal rights among themselves, and these rights should be respected by the professors. When I say equality among the students I do not mean absolute equality, because I believe that their rights should be equally respected and justice equally dispensed. There can be no justice when superficialities are allowed to enter into the weighing of the worth of an individual.

BETTER: Should not all students be treated equally by their professors? Should any distinctions be made among the student body? I believe we will agree that equal rights are due to all and these rights ought to be respected by the faculty. Yet some professors show a degree of favoritism to certain students. What are the reasons? Sometimes the student's personality especially appeals; there may be a similarity of ideas that attracts the professor's attention. Or perhaps the student has an eagerness not shown by the rest of the class; he immediately grasps the point which the professor is trying to make, while others merely sit through the hour.

c. Use the active voice in general; save the passive voice for those places where it is effective.

The passive is useful when the identity of the actor is unknown, or when one has some reason for withholding it. The small boy tells his mother, in the passive, "The window was broken," either because he does not know who broke it, or because he does not want to say, in the active, "I broke it," or "Steve broke it."

Another use for the passive is to avoid excessive reference to oneself, with the egotism or boastfulness which some people associate with this. Compare:

ACTIVE: The situation was critical. I saw that there was one thing to do, and I did that as well as I could in the circumstances. I assure you I did my best.

PASSIVE: The situation was critical. Only one thing could be done, and that was done as well as the circumstances permitted. You may be assured that the best possible was done.

29

The directness and force of the active generally make it more desirable. The passive is easily overused, and then may give the effect of detachment or avoidance of actualities. Notice the difference in effectiveness here:

PASSIVE: The ball was advanced six yards by Jones, the quarterback.
ACTIVE: Jones, the quarterback, advanced the ball six yards.

d. Strive for proportion in your composition.

1. Omit everything that does not contribute definitely to the purpose of your theme.

2. Give each idea the space it deserves, no more. The introduction and conclusion should be shorter than the body of the theme. Give less space to subordinate ideas and the most space to the most important phases of your theme.

(See Chapter II, ¶8, for illustrations of this principle applied to the individual paragraph.)

11. ENDING THE THEME

Many a good theme is spoiled by a clumsy ending. The writer may be too obvious, he may run off the track, he may trail away to nothing. Student themes in particular sometimes seem to end merely because the assigned number of words have been written, or because the writer collapsed from fatigue. Yet it is a psychological fact that the reader is most strongly impressed with the last thing he has read. Thus an effective conclusion is quite as important as a striking beginning.

There is no one right way to end a theme; the choice must depend on the writer's purpose. Nonetheless, there should usually be some attempt, direct or implicit, to summarize the content or the argument, or to leave the main point sticking in the reader's mind. Some of the most useful ways of concluding are the following:

1. After a formal argument, you may restate what you have proved.
2. You should end an emotional or persuasive piece of writing strongly or intensely.
3. You may end with a rhetorical question.
4. You may end with a question or remark which opens for the reader the further implications of the subject.
5. Occasionally you may find an abrupt break effective.
6. You may find irony or paradox effective sometimes.

The short theme needs little formal conclusion. Nothing is gained by merely repeating the points just discussed—in fact, this is patently inexpert. Take the trouble to find some effective way of finishing. (See Chapter II, ¶12b, for illustrations of effective and ineffective conclusions of individual paragraphs.)

EXERCISE VII

1. Study the conclusions of ten magazine articles and classify them according to type.
2. Study the conclusions of ten newspaper articles. Do they differ in type from the magazine articles?
(You may use the same articles you read in connection with Exercises V or VI, or others in similar publications.)

12. WRITING THE TITLE

A good title should suggest the limits of your subject.

The title is a sort of promise to the reader. If it promises more than the theme gives, the reader will feel cheated; if less, he still has a right to feel misled. When you finish writing a theme, look back to your title and make certain that it does not promise too much or too little. Some writers write the title last.

A good title is always applicable.

Usually, in expository and argumentative writing, the title tells exactly what the selection is about or what it sets out to do. For imaginative types of writing a title that hints is frequently more striking than one which merely labels. *Ariel*, the title of a biography of the poet Shelley, is effective not because it announces that that particular book is a life of Shelley, but rather because it indicates in a single, superbly chosen word just what conception the author had of his subject.

A good title should be short.

A count of the number of words in the titles of sixty essays contained in a modern collection gives an average of five. Of the sixty essays, there were two with titles containing eight words; none was longer than this. A short title impresses by its conciseness and can be remembered with ease. A lively phrase is usually to be preferred to a clause.

Keep the title of the theme separate from the opening sentence. The meaning of the first sentence should not depend on a reference to the title.

FAULTY: *Economics and Morality*. Many people believe that these two forces are inevitably bound together.
BETTER: *Economics and Morality*. Many people believe that economics and morality are inevitably bound together.
OR: *Two Related Forces*. Many people believe that there is an inevitable relationship between economics and morality.

EXERCISE VIII

From the book review section of the New York *Times* or other metropolitan newspaper, choose ten books which have just appeared. Read the reviews and form an idea of the contents of the book. In each case decide whether the title of the book is appropriate and appealing, and point out the factors which do or do not make it so.

(This exercise may be assigned for written or oral presentation.)

13. THE FINISHED THEME

We have now followed the preparation of a theme through several stages: first, choosing the broad subject of television and limiting it to censorship of television; next, gathering ideas and putting them in order, making an outline, and writing a thesis sentence. We have also considered a number of problems which arise in the actual composition of any theme. Now the theme itself is given below. (The paragraphs are numbered for reference.) After you have read it, use Exercise IX to help you to analyze it.

ARE WE SEEING TOO MUCH?

1. Television, to most people, is no more than an amusement, something to relax with after the day's work is over. But is this really all it is? The more we see of this amusement the more we realize that it has enormous potentialities—in fact, its power for good or ill over the mass of our people has led many to wonder whether we do not need some form of control—in a word, censorship. Three subjects that continually come up on television might at present call for censorship: crime, sex, and politics.

2. By far the greatest amount of time is now allotted to programs involving crime in some form, all the way from children's

shows to those for adults based on real cases. Many of these come at the hours of the maximum audience and can hardly be avoided. They show crimes of violence—shootings, beatings, knifings and all the rest—with complete realism. Some almost amount to courses of study in criminal techniques. Police techniques for combating crime are shown also, it is true, but too often the criminal is the real hero, the "dumb cop" is made fun of, and the crook is defeated by his own mistake, not by the superiority of the forces of law. The kind of treatment may well produce a cynical attitude in which crime is regarded as inevitable and public opposition to it is weakened.

3. Inextricably mixed with the crime on many programs is sex, since the motive is often some rivalry over a woman—or, for that matter, a man. But even without the crime, the picture tubes display a great deal of embracing, kissing, and other physical contact, to say nothing of what showmen call "leg art." If it were art there might be no objection, but this is usually no more than an excuse for simple sexual excitation. The daily diet of sex on television cannot fail to produce a preoccupation with it—something which is hardly desirable and might well call for some censorship.

4. In politics, too, television presents certain obvious dangers. Dictatorial governments use it, along with the press and radio, frankly as an organ of propaganda. Even in a democratic country it might all too easily be perverted to the same ends by falling under partisan control. It could then be used against minorities of any kind, racial, religious, political, or be made the mouthpiece of some powerful individual or clique. Again, the way to prevent this, as some people feel, is through censorship.

5. But it is one thing to consider censorship of television and quite another to decide how to apply it. Who are to be the censors?

6. At present it is the sponsor who, although negatively, exerts the most censorship. The sponsor's single purpose is to sell his

product to the largest possible body of purchasers. He therefore seeks only to keep the public satisfied. But since the ignorant or stupid man's dollar is as good as any other, the sponsor is likely to pay undue attention to his likes and dislikes. Sponsors are extremely sensitive to adverse opinion, to organized objectors and all sorts of pressure groups. Some become timorous and avoid any kind of thoughtful program; others sail as close to the winds of sensation and excitement as they dare. Very few will risk a truly adult program. Under the circumstances it is clear that the sponsor is hardly the man to set up as a satisfactory censor. No more so the producer, who, as an artist, is not likely to reflect conventional attitudes, and whose daily bread, in any case, is in the sponsor's hands.

7. The public is an active force in writing letters to the broadcasters about what they do and especially do not like. Yet this is rather haphazard: those who make the effort to write are not necessarily representative of the entire public, nor are their criticisms always valid. And though the broadcasters try to compensate through professional public-opinion polls, these have often proved inaccurate. The public, in any case, is an amorphous force without any special direction or control, and in itself is hardly fitted for the role of censor.

8. Some feel that the churches, being directly concerned with public morality, could act as censors, as to some extent they now do indirectly. Others point out that there is so wide a variation of attitudes among the churches on this matter that to give them the power of censorship would only arouse disagreement within their ranks and make it very difficult for them to find common ground or to act effectively.

9. What about government control? This already exists in regard to foods, drugs, utilities, transportation, and other areas in which the entire public is concerned. Some people feel that, in the spirit of preventive medicine, government should control television through social legislation. Others make the comparison rather with radio and the press, considering television a medium

of public information which must be as free as possible. Yet others point to the dangers of government censorship that already exist in the control exerted over TV programming by the Federal Communications Commission.

10. The question then remains: Does television, with all its defects and potentialities, need a greater degree of censorship? If present forces are inadequate, what new ones would be desirable, and what should their duties be? The thoughtful viewer, at least, when he turns the dial off for the day, cannot but wonder whether in some respects we may be seeing too little, and in others perhaps too much.

EXERCISE IX

1. How appropriate is the title? Does it arouse interest? (See **T12**.)

2. Which method of beginning has been used? Are two or more combined? (See **T6**.)

3. Is the thesis sentence appropriately placed? (See **T5**.)

4. What paragraphs correspond to the numbered points in the developed outline? (See **T4**.)

5. What connections do you find between the parts? (See **T8**.)

6. Do you find any inconsistencies of tone or point of view? (See **T9**.)

7. What examples of effectiveness do you find? (See **T10**.)

8. Is the conclusion satisfactory? (See **T11**.)

II. The Paragraph

INTELLIGENTLY and skillfully employed, the paragraph can be an aid in setting forth the organization of your ideas and the development of your thought. It is necessary, therefore, to find out what the paragraph is and how it is put together.

1. HISTORY OF THE WORD PARAGRAPH

Paragraph came originally from the Greek, formed from the prefix *para* ("by the side") and *graphos* ("written"). It referred to a symbol or character, now usually written ¶, which indicated the end of one section or part of a narrative or discourse, and the beginning of a new one. It was generally placed in the margin or at the beginning of the line as a guide to the eye.

Later the term *paragraph* came to be applied to written matter which was introduced by the mark ¶. Then indentation became established as the accepted mode of marking a section of written matter. Finally the symbol ¶ ceased altogether to be used for this purpose.

This bit of history tells us several important things about the paragraph. Most significant of all is the fact that the paragraph signals the reader, telling him in effect that the indented sentence begins a new division of the complete text before him and that the material between any two indentations, judged in terms of the whole, constitutes a subdivision or a single unit.

Basically, the paragraph is a device of the written language. We talk in sentences much as we write in sentences, the period as a point of punctuation in writing corresponding to the turn of the intonation and the pause which mark the end of a spoken sentence. There is nothing equally tangible in speech corresponding to the break in the line which concludes one paragraph or the indentation which begins the next. Thus paragraphing becomes a matter of the increased regard for logic and structure which differentiates writing from informal talk.

2. SOME EXAMPLES OF CONTEMPORARY PARAGRAPHS

Before taking up in detail some of the problems you will encounter in paragraphing your own writing, let us examine some paragraphs from contemporary writing to see how they are put together and what they contribute to an understanding of the selections of which they are a part.

a. Dialogue

William Malet came to the chamber door and said: "Lord Duke, the Earl would speak with you. He says it is an urgent matter."

"Bid him wait," said William.

Malet went out, very pale.

"It is now or never, brother," said Odo. "God sent him to your hands." HOPE MUNTZ, *The Golden Warrior*

b. Narration

In the morning Ken arranged with a man to take us on to Chalco, and that afternoon the man and his helper arrived with donkeys. We had a heap of supplies—kerosene, gasoline, canned milk, canned vegetables, army cots, clothing, books—and it took at least an hour to tie them on the donkeys.

It was five o'clock that afternoon by the time we left with the three riding and eight pack animals. The heat of the day was over and the country was beautiful. Ahead of us, as far as I could see, was range after range of mountains, and here and there a trail disappeared in the distance.

The animal I was riding was a small horse, and he didn't like associating with donkeys. If one came close to him, he bared his teeth and dived for him. As long as it was light I didn't mind that he kept ahead of the pack, but later I wasn't pleased to be in the lead. After dark when I could see neither Florrie nor Ken, my only connection with human beings was the whistle with which the animal drivers urged their animals on. I had never thought the whistle of a strange man could be a comforting sound, but that one was.

We stopped for the night in the Aztec village of San Fernando. It had an inn which had more room for the donkeys than it did for us. Ken slept on the counter of its little store, and Florrie and I had the bedroom. The bed was a board shelf built out from the wall, with a straw mat laid over the top—no covers, no mattress, no pillow. As we rolled up in our blankets, I heard the animals munching their corn outside, and then, almost immediately, I was asleep.   EUNICE V. PIKE, *Not Alone*[1]

c. Description

Across the hall was the sitting room, smaller, cozier, with easier chairs, bookcases, a tall brass lamp, a gas stove in the corner (fireplaces had not yet come back except as tiled ornaments for the hall, where, of course, no one ever used them), and an air of comfort and usability. Here the family sat and friends were entertained (company went into the parlor). Here were the magazines, the books to be read, the cat, the dog, and the children studying after supper. This was the heart of the home.

The dining room, again, was formal, family portraits on the wall, a china cupboard out of which glinted what never was used even on the grandest occasion. Morning sun in the dining room was one of the specifications, as important as the sideboard and the serving table. The pantry was built up to the high ceiling in tiers of shelves and closets on and in which

[1] Used by permission of Moody Press, Moody Bible Institute, 820 N. Lasalle Street, Chicago 10, Illinois.

were kept that incredible clutter of household china and glass which every family seemed to accumulate. There was a drawer labeled 'Cake,' another 'Bread,' and a lead-lined sink with cock-roach poison on the edges. The kitchens sprawled—coal stoves, laundry tubs, tables for baskets, tables for rolling dough, hooks and closets for a forest of tinware, and so on out into the shed with its tables and bins and closets. And in the cellar more bins, more shelves, a cold room, and a bricked-in furnace as big as a funeral vault.

The main stairs followed a curving serpent of black walnut to a long upstairs hall off which opened vast bedrooms. The bathroom was here (often the only one) with doors in at least two directions, accessible to all. The parents' room would be an upstairs sitting room also, with a desk somewhere spilling with small change and account books, and at the farther end a vast walnut bed whose back rose to the ceiling, a cliff of pol-ished veneer topped by a meaningless escutcheon. Other mon-umental pieces of black walnut flanked it at either side, and at the foot was a crib for the smallest child, or a green plush sofa for naps. HENRY SEIDEL CANBY, American Memoir[1]

d. Exposition

1. American culture is predominantly material, its thought and its standards quantitative. The normal American tends to compute almost everything in numbers, even qualitative things such as religion or art. He takes pride in statistics of population growth, automobile production, magazine circulation, and col-lege enrollment, and is inclined to put a financial value on objects of public interest—houses, or bridges, or works of art— not because he is primarily interested in money but because money furnishes the most convenient quantitative yardstick. He is proud when his company builds the highest office-building, or his city the most miles of boulevard, or his college the largest stadium.

This passion for quantity is looked upon as naive, even as vulgar, by outsiders; it has given acute pain to such different

[1] Reprinted by permission of Houghton Mifflin Company.

critics as Matthew Arnold, Knut Hamsun, and de Madariaga. Yet it has certain advantages. Oftentimes quantity is meaningless, but oftentimes, too, it contributes directly to human welfare and happiness. The American wants the highest standard of living, and knows that telephones and libraries and boulevards contribute to that standard. Only rarely does he delude himself that twenty thousand students at the State University guarantee a higher standard of education than five thousand students at Oxford, but at the same time he is prepared to maintain that two million students in colleges and universities do make for a more enlightened citizenry than, say, one hundred thousand. He is not to be dissuaded from his pride in keeping twenty-seven million boys and girls in his public schools or in the handsome buildings he commonly provides for them.

His respect for numbers contributes to the maintenance of the two-party system, and to a more cheerful acquiescence in majority decisions than is to be found in many other countries. It may even be argued that there is a connection between majority—or quantitative—rule and economic and social progress. It is suggestive that the section of the country where minority control is indulged has made least material progress, and least progress in social and intellectual tolerance. Nor is the quantitative standard wholly without significance in international relations. The American can fight when outnumbered —witness the history of the Confederacy—but prefers to fight with the largest numbers and the best equipment, and the ability of America to muster large numbers and produce superior equipment is a basic consideration in world affairs.

HENRY STEELE COMMAGER, *Portrait of the American*[1]

2. One of the odd effects of the importance which each of us attaches to himself is that we tend to imagine our own good or evil fortune to be the purpose of other people's actions. If you pass in a train a field containing grazing cows, you may sometimes see them running away in terror as the train passes. The

[1] From *Years of the Modern*, edited by John W. Chase, copyright 1949. Reprinted by permission of Longmans, Green & Co., Inc.

cow, if it were a metaphysician, would argue: "Everything in my own desires and hopes and fears has reference to myself; hence by induction I conclude that everything in the universe has reference to myself. This noisy train, therefore, intends to do me either good or evil. I cannot suppose that it intends to do me good, since it comes in such a terrifying form, and therefore, as a prudent cow, I shall endeavor to escape from it." If you were to explain to this metaphysical ruminant that the train has no intention of leaving the rails, and is totally indifferent to the fate of the cow, the poor beast would be bewildered by anything so unnatural. The train that wishes her neither well nor ill would seem more cold and more abysmally horrifying than a train that wished her ill. Just this has happened with human beings. The course of nature brings them sometimes good fortune, sometimes evil. They cannot believe that this happens by accident. The cow, having known of a companion which had strayed on to the railway line and been killed by a train, would pursue her philosophical reflections, if she were endowed with that moderate degree of intelligence that characterizes most human beings, to the point of concluding that the unfortunate cow had been punished for sin by the god of the railway. She would be glad when his priests put fences along the line, and would warn younger and friskier cows never to avail themselves of accidental openings in the fence, since the wages of sin is death. By similar myths men have succeeded, without sacrificing their self-importance, in explaining many of the misfortunes to which they are subject. But sometimes misfortune befalls the wholly virtuous, and what are we to say in this case? We shall still be prevented by our feeling that we must be the center of the universe from admitting that misfortune has merely happened to us without anybody's intending it, and since we are not wicked by hypothesis, our misfortune must be due to somebody's malevolence, that is to say, to somebody wishing to injure us from mere hatred and not from the hope of any advantage to himself. It was this state of mind that gave rise to demonology, and the belief in witchcraft and black magic. The witch is a person who injures her neighbors from sheer hatred, not from any hope of gain. The belief in witchcraft, until about the middle of the seventeenth century, afforded a most satisfying outlet for the delicious emotion of self-righteous cruelty. There was Biblical warrant for the belief, since the Bible says: "Thou shalt not suffer a witch to live." And on this ground the Inquisition punished not only witches, but those who did not believe in the possibility of witchcraft, since to disbelieve it was heresy. Science, by giving some insight into natural causation, dissipated the belief in magic, but could not wholly dispel the fear and sense of insecurity that had given rise to it. In modern times, these same emotions find an outlet in fear of foreign nations, an outlet which, it must be confessed, requires not much in the way of superstitious support.

BERTRAND RUSSELL, *Unpopular Essays*[1]

3. All of our women had some amount of leisure time during which they engaged in a variety of activities. Most often reported was their active or passive participation in cultural and creative activities such as art, music, and the crafts. Sports were an important attraction, and all of the group spent some time in social activities.

The women reported on their leisure-time activities in many ways: "I read to keep alive above the neck." "Reading restoreth my soul." "I can become totally engrossed in art; it requires no other participants." A former English major, now at home caring for two children, commented: "Writing seems to give life some meaning." A mother of four who engaged in swimming, reading, drama, attendance at concerts, writing poetry, remarked: "These are my rewards for being good."

Some responses were more unusual. A newly married writer said: "Being romantically in love, all leisure activities—including even some conventional hobbies—have centered around the act of love and the spirit of loving." A mother of two who had stopped working, said: "The many pressures of jobs and civic activities resulted for me in such constant activity that I often felt I lacked the chance to grow within and to achieve the kind of personal

[1] Reprinted by permission of Simon and Schuster, Inc. and Allen & Unwin, Ltd.

development I would have liked—reading, thinking, 'being' instead of 'doing.' Now with more leisure I am intrigued with the challenge of growth and use of leisure creatively."

Some were caustic: "With five children?!" Another, with two children and a full-time job, wrote: "I do not know what is meant by leisure time. I swim. Occasionally, I have bowled. Primarily I read, sew, garden, work, iron, mend, clean during leisure hours. Sometimes I sleep."

Leisure-time activities appear to play much the same role in the lives of these educated women as for other women. They help to fill time, they provide opportunities for self-development, and they are an arena for family enrichment.

ELI GINZBERG et al., *Life Styles of Educated Women*[1]

In the foregoing pages we have six illustrations of the ways in which authors deal with the paragraph. We are interested in how these paragraphs are organized and how much they contain. Consider them in the light of the following questions:

1. Do all the paragraphs deal with but a single or central idea—are they unified in content?

2. In any of the examples, do two or more successive paragraphs treat the same idea?

3. How do these examples compare in length?

4. How do they compare in the number of sentences they contain?

3. ORGANIZATION AND CONTENT

We shall find it convenient to discuss the example paragraphs in order. Example a was included primarily to illustrate the use of paragraphing in a passage containing dialogue

[1] From *Life Styles of Educated Women* (New York: Columbia University Press, 1966), pp. 71-72. Reprinted by courtesy of Columbia University Press.

or conversation. Here indentation is used primarily to signal a change of speaker. We shall see later (Chapter XIII, **MS3**) that practice is not wholly uniform and that certain complexities may be encountered in material of this sort, but the general principle is evident.

Example *b* is narrative. The four paragraphs, covering the events of a single day, are organized on a chronological basis. The first covers the activities of the morning and early afternoon—arranging for the trip and packing the donkeys. The second paragraph gets the company on its way, by late afternoon. The third describes travelling in the darkness of evening, and in the fourth we learn how they passed the night.

The organization of the descriptive example *c* is equally self-evident. In this word picture of a typical American house of the 1890's, the first quoted paragraph describes the principal living room of the house, the second proceeds to the dining room, pantry, kitchens, and cellar, and the third takes us to the second floor.

It is unmistakable that with examples *b* and *c*, *each paragraph makes a unified contribution to a larger whole.*

Such a unity is easy to grasp and to observe when we write about events and things: narration and description. Exposition, which is often the basis of a freshman English course, deals rather with facts and ideas. Here the unity is less likely to have a physical correlate and tends to become more abstract; as a consequence, practices in paragraphing tend to be more diverse.

For this reason three examples of expository paragraphs are included under *d*. Reread them carefully, noting to what extent they are unified, whether they treat of one topic or more than one, and whether the topic under discussion is fully developed in the one paragraph.

When read by itself, Mr. Russell's paragraph (2) seems

to be capable of division into three or possibly four parts. The putative reaction of the cow to the train, constituting the first seven sentences, might very well be set off by itself. The next six sentences make a direct application of this situation to human psychology and seem likewise to constitute a unit. The remaining nine sentences, dealing with the special problem of misfortune befalling the wholly virtuous, could either stand as a single final unit, or the portion devoted to witchcraft might be separated from it.

Such a conclusion, however, is based upon an examination of this paragraph only, leaving the broader context and the development of Russell's argument entirely out of consideration. Actually the title of this particular essay is "Ideas That Have Harmed Mankind." It begins by dividing the misfortunes of mankind into two major classes: those inflicted by environment and those inflicted by other people. In the latter category are false beliefs arising from superstition, from envy, and from pride. Seen in this light, the paragraph in question is merely one of four treating various kinds of religious or superstitious beliefs. Consequently, though the contents of this paragraph are capable of division into smaller units, there is logical justification for keeping the paragraph together as a whole.

Conversely, the short paragraphs from *Life Styles of Educated Women* (3) seem to be merely items in a list, one which might as well have been arranged in some other way without much affecting the presentation of the information. One might argue here that since all we have is a series of short citations expressing a variety of opinions, they could have been presented in a single paragraph as a unified block. The author, however, or perhaps the copy editor, evidently had an eye to the appearance of the paragraph on the page. Paragraphs in the entire book from which this selection was taken are relatively short and make for quick, easy reading. The factual generally dominates;

there is no complicated analysis calling for a sustained or closely knit organization. *Thus, again, what constitutes a unit or topic depends not only upon the actual facts and ideas set forth but on their relationship to the whole.* (It depends also, of course, upon what is said in the paragraph itself—in a topic sentence, say—about the unifying idea of the paragraph.)

Of the three expository examples, Mr. Commager's (1) seems to strike a happy medium. His first paragraph explains the tendency of the average American to compute almost everything in numbers, the second asserts that at times this tendency results in certain contributions to human welfare, and the third makes a connection between majority rule and social and economic progress. It is not easy to break up any one of these into smaller pieces, nor can we justifiably argue that any two—or all three—should be combined.

4. LENGTH

Paragraph length, though in itself perhaps not supremely important, is in a sense a by-product of paragraph organization and content. The twenty-two sentences of the paragraph by Bertrand Russell which we have examined in some detail contain precisely six hundred words. This is taken from a printed book. In contrast, all five paragraphs of the example from *Life Styles of Educated Women* contain a total of just three hundred and twenty words (though the number of sentences, twenty, is about the same.

Although here we have just shown a passage from a modern book that contains very short paragraphs, generally it is true that newspaper paragraphs are shorter than those in magazines or books and that paragraphs in magazines are often shorter than those in books. In college composition classes the general limits of the paragraph are often defined as ranging between one hundred and three hundred words; newspaper style-books generally place the maximum limit of the paragraph at one hundred words and the average at sixty or thereabouts.

Paragraph length then is extremely variable, usually depending upon the kind of material that is written and the medium in which it appears. Possibly the hasty and highly factual character of newspaper writing will result in shorter paragraphs, since topics are seldom completely developed.

If we remember that the paragraph is essentially a guide to the eye, another reason for the variations in paragraph length suggests itself. The newspaper is printed in small type, set in narrow columns averaging about six words to the line and nine lines, or a little more than fifty words, to the column inch. A paragraph of two hundred and fifty words would then require about five column inches. Without question, readers would find material so printed fatiguing to the eye. Magazines, on the other hand, while they often employ the narrow columns, invariably use larger type and can admit longer paragraphs. Books, using large type and a page-wide line, can afford to be least concerned about length.

In student papers, or in the informal writing of the average person, factors such as the size of the paper, the size of the handwriting, whether the manuscript is handwritten or typewritten, all play a part in determining paragraph length.

5. *STANDARDS OF PARAGRAPHING*

In summary we may conclude:

1. Paragraphing is a visual aid to the reader, breaking up the solidity of a page or column of type.

2. The length of the paragraph may vary with the mechanics of writing or publication.

3. The length and organization of the paragraph will vary according to the subject treated.

4. Effectively employed, the paragraph will reveal the writer's concept of the organization and ordering of his subject matter.

This last is, of course, the most important. Most of the writing that you do will be judged by your instructors. Whether the class is in the social sciences or in English, the one thing your instructors will be especially interested in is your capacity to think. Are you able to organize your ideas? Are you capable of logical analysis?

The answers to these questions will rest in no small part upon your ability to write paragraphs that will correspond in each instance to the introduction of a unit in thought or the development of an idea. In this way you can demonstrate your powers of organization and logical analysis.

Write from an outline. You will have less trouble with paragraphing than if you depend upon the inspiration of the moment.

6. UNITY WITHIN THE PARAGRAPH

a. Limit yourself to a single topic or one aspect of a topic within a paragraph.

Your paragraph should show singleness of purpose.

NOT UNIFIED: Many different types of drums are used by the savage tribes of Africa. The largest of these could be classified as a bass drum. These were used to beat the time for the native singers and dancers when the tribes were called together for battle and religious ceremonies. Up to the present day bass drums play an important part in marching bands, symphonic bands, dance orchestras, and symphonic orchestras. In concert bands and symphonic bands a huge, double-tension bass drum, which produces a tremendous amount of volume, is used because the instrumentation is so great. In marching bands a smaller type of double-tension bass drum that is used is called a Scotch bass drum. This is played with two sticks that can be swung over the drum and in circular motions with the aid of leather thongs.

The writer of this student theme has included two topics within a single paragraph: (1) the use of the drum among the African natives, and (2) its present use among Western peoples.

REVISED: Many different types of drums have been used by savage tribes in Africa. The largest of these could be classified as bass drums. They were used to beat time for native singers and dancers when the tribes were called together for battle or for religious ceremonies.

In America and Europe at the present time, drums play an important part in marching, concert, and symphonic bands, dance orchestras, and symphonic orchestras. Concert bands and symphonic bands and orchestras employ a huge, double tension bass drum which produces the tremendous volume necessary to meet the demands of the instrumentation. Marching bands use a smaller type of double-tension bass, called a Scotch bass drum. This is played with two sticks that can be swung over the drum or in circular motions with the aid of leather thongs.

Here is another example:

NOT UNIFIED: Hospital work is amazingly interesting. I never realized before that in medicine one meets such a variety of people. Perhaps I will study to be a social worker as a result of my work this summer. The type of people I saw this summer gave me an excellent idea of how the other half lives. If by being a social worker, I could better living conditions for such needy people, I would study it in a minute. Sometimes I wonder if they really can be helped. The majority of the patients I saw were not the type to appreciate any assistance given them without pay. They seemed to think that the city owed them a living. Perhaps this attitude is not prevalent among all needy people. I don't know. If it is, in my estimation they deserve no help from anyone. I rather imagine that there are some very deserving of help who don't receive any at all. It is these people whom I would like to help.

This concluding paragraph of a paper entitled "My First

Job" is badly mixed. The writer has not clarified in her own mind her ideas on what her summer's experience meant. She says first that she would gladly become a social worker if by so doing she could help people like those she met in the hospital, but in almost the next breath she expresses doubt, questioning whether or not they deserve help. Her last two sentences say something still different.

The paragraph contains at least three ideas, each of which could be amplified to a degree.

1. Hospital work is interesting because one comes into contact with all types of people. Among these are the needy.

2. Some of the needy do not appreciate what is done for them. Others, some of whom receive no help at all, are really deserving.

3. I should like to help this last group to better their living conditions. If I could convince myself that by becoming a social worker I would be able to give such help, I would adopt this as a vocation.

b. Remember that paragraph length is related to coherence.

While overlong paragraphs make the most interesting material seem dull and long-winded, paragraphs that are too short give an impression of incoherence. They suggest that the writer has not sufficient mental stamina to develop a thought completely.

Short paragraphs may be used tellingly in a narrative when an effect of haste, excitement, indignation, or any strong emotion is desired. Do not use them in a deliberative or reflective composition.

NOT UNIFIED: Reuther and the automobile industry. These great opponents are foremost in the minds of people who believe the automobile industry is the key to our prosperity.

Reuther represents an organization in this country aimed at protecting a large part of America's millions of factory workers.

The Big Three, manufacturers of most of our automobiles, have been seeking to regain their independence of labor, and so have come into conflict with the UAW and its leader.

Notice that all four sentences might be more profitably combined into a single paragraph.

NOT UNIFIED: The old-fashioned idea that college is an unnecessary luxury is now fading in the minds of most people. The demand for high-school and college diplomas has increased greatly, for an education is needed even in many of the simpler fields.

The persons who considered college unimportant in the past, with the growth of their families have come to see the importance of a college education and all that it offers.

NOT UNIFIED: Government, as it exists today, plays a large role in the life of the private individual. It is certainly an indispensable institution. There are two reasons for this. First it gives protection. Our police departments, fire departments, health services, and many other government institutions are absolutely necessary for the maintenance of a successful community, and not only a successful community but a livable one. The same is true of the external protection governments maintain in the form of an army, navy, and merchant marine.

Secondly, government offers, or rather controls, institutions for the betterment of society as a whole, such as schools, aid for the poor, and protection for various groups such as farmers.

The writer of the last two paragraphs has reached a broad conclusion based on two sets of facts. Two courses are open to him: he may paragraph his conclusion separately and then give a paragraph to each of the sets of facts upon which it is based; or he may place all the material, conclusion and reasons, in a single paragrph. Either of these is preferable to placing the conclusion and the first set of facts in one paragraph and paragraphing the second set of facts separately.

EXERCISE I

A. Break up these passages into shorter, unified paragraphs:

1. The most difficult fear to overcome, so far, has been fear of the sea. Our first attempt to take the boy into the sea was at the age of two and a half. At first, it was quite impossible. He disliked the cold of the water, he was frightened by the noise of the waves, and they seemed to him to be always coming, never going. If the waves were big, he would not even go near to the sea. This was a period of general timidity; animals, odd noises, and various other things caused alarm. We dealt with fear of the sea piecemeal. We put the boy into shallow pools away from the sea, until the mere cold had ceased to be a shock; at the end of the four warm months, he enjoyed paddling in shallow water at a distance from waves, but still cried if we put him into deep pools where the water came up to his waist. We accustomed him to the noise of the waves by letting him play for an hour at a time just out of sight of them; then we took him to where he could see them, and made him notice that after coming in they go out again. All this, combined with the example of his parents and other children, only brought him to the point where he could be near the waves without fear. I am convinced that the fear was instinctive; I am fairly certain there had been no suggestion to cause it. The following summer, at the age of three and a half, we took the matter up again. There was still a terror of going actually into the waves. After some unsuccessful coaxing, combined with the spectacle of everybody else bathing, we adopted old-fashioned methods. When he showed cowardice, we made him feel that we were ashamed of him; when he showed courage, we praised him warmly. Every day for about a fortnight, we plunged him up to the neck in the sea, in spite of his struggles

53

and cries. Every day they grew less; before they ceased, he began to ask to be put in. At the end of a fortnight, the desired result had been achieved: he no longer feared the sea. From that moment, we left him completely free, and he bathed of his own accord whenever the weather was suitable—obviously with the greatest enjoyment. Fear had not ceased altogether, but had been partly repressed by pride. Familiarity, however, made the fear grow rapidly less, and it has now ceased altogether. His sister, now twenty months old, has never shown any fear of the sea, and runs straight in without the slightest hesitation.

BERTRAND RUSSELL, *Education and the Good Life*[1]

2. That evening we were busily occupied completing catalogues and other written work. The camp was very still and Ben and Bassi had long since departed into the blackness of the night with the shotguns and the torch. A shot rang out some distance away and was followed almost immediately by a quick left and right. After a short pause there came further firing. Suddenly I developed a keen desire to see the spoils and decided to slip out of camp and join the hunt. Taking the spare torch, I crept away unobserved and was soon weaving my way among the trees and creepers in the direction from which the occasional shots still rang out. When I was some distance from the position of the last shot fired, I entered an area where a considerable number of animals were noisily moving through the trees above me, apparently shifting from the centre of danger. I shone the beams of the torch upwards in the hope of catching a glimpse of them. When I did so my whole inside gave a clutch with excitement and delight as I gazed upward, for suspended from a branch almost directly above me was an animal of the most curious though unaccountably loveable appearance. This statement may sound mad, but to those whose childhood was spent among Teddy bears it may perhaps be intelligible. It was upside down, with an eager little round face peering down over its back at me. So low down was it, indeed, that I could only watch

[1] Reprinted by courtesy of the Liveright Publishing Corporation.

fascinated while it licked its pink nose with a tiny pink tongue to match. The rest of the body was compact, brown and woolly. It blinked at me in the glaring light and then began laboriously clambering forward in the direction of the tree trunk, still suspended upside down like a sloth. A presumably natural urge prompted me to attempt a climb so that I could come to closer quarters with this adorable little toy of the forest and perhaps even capture it. The climb was not an easy one, though it was a miracle that there were any branches at all to allow of an ascent. This was difficult, as I had to keep the torch beam on the animal all the time so that it would not disappear among the tangled foliage, and the whole procedure evolved into a race between myself and the potto (for that was what it was) to reach the angle between the branch and the trunk. Most unfortunately I got there first.

IVAN SANDERSON, Animal Treasure[1]

B. Combine these paragraphs into longer and more unified paragraphs:

1. In the United States, where I had been returned by President Quirino at the beginning of 1952 with the portfolio of Ambassador to Washington added to my role as permanent delegate to the United Nations, I received disturbing reports of the growing tension between Quirino and Magsaysay. The political duckling that Quirino had nourished was developing into an eagle.

The reports grew more disturbing through the year and into 1953. Magsaysay increased in stature and success. The President commented more than once, "This man Magsaysay is getting too ambitious."

Magsaysay was ambitious. He knew there were many gaps in his political knowledge. But he was willing to learn. He had an open mind and would listen to many people and to all sides.

He made speeches in behalf of the Mindanao project and land

---

[1] Reprinted by courtesy of the Viking Press, Inc.

reform, and they were simple, pungent speeches that drove straight to the hearts of the people.

He would say things like this: "I am proud to be a Filipino. We are a great people. With the right leadership and with the guidance and assistance of the United States this country can grow to be the head of a family of democratic nations in this part of the globe."

All that he was saying and doing was in behalf of the psychological warfare that was regaining the confidence of the people in their democracy. It was his contribution to the information sources being thrown open to the people by way of speeches, pamphlets, loyalty meetings, broadcasts, conferences, and rallies.

Everything was being done to win the great mass of the people completely away from the dangerous trend that had threatened for a time to wrest freedom from one of the few countries in Asia that was still free.

CARLOS P. ROMULO, *Crusade in Asia*[1]

2. Although the times of Stalinist terror are long since gone, a certain feeling of fear persists among the Russians.

Innocent people no longer are arrested and exiled, but less radical measures are still practiced to punish cases of "unorthodoxy" such as sustained close contact with Western foreigners. The most common of these measures are demotion in rank, temporary dismissal from a job, and suspension or expulsion in the case of university students.

However there are no fixed classifications for such "crimes," and no written punitive code. Many Russians are willing to take a chance, particularly the younger generation raised in the post Stalin era.

Several times I tried to ask my Russian friends whether they were subjecting themselves to any danger by associating with me. Some of them expressed genuine surprise that such a thought could even occur to me. Some laughed it off uneasily. And one

[1] Copyright 1955 by Carlos P. Romulo. Reprinted from *Crusade in Asia* by Carlos P. Romulo by permission of The John Day Company, Inc., publisher.

young research scientist told me frankly that too close a contact with me might harm his career.

Despite all the cold war tensions the young Soviets are surprisingly unprejudiced in their attitude toward the average American. One reason is, I think, the fact that the Soviet press, vicious though it may be, never lumps all Americans together. In all its attacks on the United States, it uses terms such as the "White House" or the "Pentagon" to show that the ordinary people are not responsible for the actions of their government.

My friends at the University of Moscow were avidly curious about the United States. Their interests lay mainly in non political areas such as art, literature, education, customs, habits and so on.

The system of higher education in the USSR is oriented towards training specialists in various fields. Having completed his high school education, a young Russian can study for four to six years in a specialized institute or a particular university department of his choice. He must abide by the prescribed curriculum, and is not allowed to take courses for credit in other departments. A diploma from a university or an institute guarantees its holder an adequate job in his field.

The Soviet state does not force its youth to go into this or that profession. Choosing a profession is entirely a matter of individual inclinations and capacities.

I found that in my department of the university very little freedom of expression was allowed. The literature students had to do a prodigious amount of reading of the primary sources, but for interpretation they had to resort to party line textbooks and critical works. The lecturers also abided by the official line and seldom expressed their personal opinions.

In seminars and small discussion groups the same air of orthodoxy prevailed. Many students had their own ideas and interesting opinions but they knew better than to voice them in front of teachers. Unorthodox opinions resulted in lowering of grades, and a consequent reduction of the stipend. There is a minimum stipend for all, but it can vary in proportion to the level of the academic record.

Together with everybody else, I had to take the final oral examinations, but as a Western foreigner I was treated most diplomatically and allowed to express any opinions I pleased.[1]

IRINA SHAPIRO, *U.S. Student Detects Fear, Loyalty in Russia*

7. THE TOPIC SENTENCE

Just as the central idea of a whole composition is often crystallized in a single thesis sentence, so in writing that is primarily argumentative or expository, each paragraph often contains a sentence or statement which gives the gist of that particular division of the whole composition. In speaking of the paragraph, we call such a sentence the *topic sentence*. A topic sentence may announce the topic to be treated, or it may summarize the contents of the paragraph. Though it usually comes at or near the beginning, it may come anywhere in the paragraph. In the paragraphs which follow, the topic sentence appears in italics.

TOPIC SENTENCE FIRST:

A more popular and lasting basis of a humorous story is the theme of mistaken identity. Mr. Jones is mistaken for Mr. Brown, whereupon all things may happen. This is especially the case if the two people confused are really of utterly different categories—if an Egyptologist is mistaken for a plumber or a bishop gets mixed up with a janitor, or a lunatic at large is mistaken for all sorts of people.   STEPHEN LEACOCK, *How to Write*[2]

TOPIC SENTENCE LAST:

I well remember a conversation I had with a friend with whom I had been working in a wartime government agency which was

[1] From the Sacramento Bee, March 11, 1962. Reprinted by permission of United Press International.

[2] Copyright 1934, by Dodd, Mead & Company.

about to dissolve. She had had a position of real responsibility and had executed her manifold duties with apparent ease and vigorous good sense. We were talking about what we would be doing next. "You know," she said, "it sounds absurd, and I'm ashamed to admit it, but the kind of job I really want is to be that invaluable assistant to a man who is doing something I believe in. I'd work like a nailer, and I'd be so tactful that he wouldn't know how much he depended on me, but I want him to make the final decisions." She paused a minute and then said reflectively, "I think it's the kind of job most women really want." I may confess that her words gave me a real shock, but I believe that she uttered a profound truth. *I believe that a great many women have an essentially low opinion of their own powers, that they are possessed by a feeling of humility that is at the same time touching and infuriating.*

AGNES ROGERS, "The Humble Female"
Harper's Magazine, March 1950[1]

Upon occasion a paragraph will begin with a topic sentence which is repeated or completed at the end.

By a strange perversity in the cosmic plan, the biologically good die young. Species are not destroyed for their shortcomings but for their achievements. The tribes that slumber in the grave-yards of the past were not the most simple and undistinguished of their day, but the most complicated and conspicuous. The magnificent sharks of the Devonian period passed with the passing of the period, but certain contemporaneous genera of primitive shellfish are still on earth. Similarly, the lizards of the Mesozoic era have long outlived the dinosaurs, which were im-measurably their biologic betters. Illustrations such as these could be endlessly increased. *The price of distinction is death.*

JAMES HODGDON BRADLEY, *Patterns of Survival*[2]

[1] Copyright, 1950, by Harper & Brothers. Reprinted from *Harper's Magazine* by Special Permission.

[2] Reprinted by permission of the author and of Grune and Stratton, Inc.

Practiced writers can and do produce paragraphs without topic sentences. This is particularly true of narrative and descriptive writing. In your own writing, however, especially when its purpose is expository or argumentive, you will find it more orderly to build most of your paragraphs around a topic sentence.

The parts of your outline will frequently suggest the topic sentences. By all means avoid slavish repetition of the phrases of the outline; you do not want the skeleton to show through the flesh. Try to introduce each point in an interesting way and vary the position of the topic sentences. In fact, the place of the topic sentence should be dictated by the way in which you are developing the basic idea of the paragraph and whether it better fits your purpose to make an initial announcement or to produce a climactic conclusion.

Since topic sentences very often take the form of generalizations (general statements or propositions of fact), you should be careful not to weaken your argument by using an *unwarranted generalization* as a topic sentence. An unwarranted generalization is a proposition of fact about a class of things that is weakly supported by concrete examples or evidence. "All college athletes are poor students," for example, is an unwarranted generalization if the only supporting example you have given is "My roommate in college is on the varsity basketball and track teams, and his grades have been borderline for the past three years." Though the example you have given does offer *some* support of the generalization, as evidence it is weak and inconclusive. Your roommate may not be representative of most athletes; besides, even if he did not spend so much time in sports his grades might be no better. Obviously you will need much more evidence about the academic ability of college athletes before you can offer your generalization. (See ¶13c.)

EXERCISE II

A. Select the topic sentence in each of the following paragraphs:

1. If, as I have said, the things already listed were all we had to contribute, America would have made no distinctive and unique gift to mankind. But there has been also the *American dream*, that dream of a land in which life should be better and fuller and richer for every man, with opportunity for each according to his ability or achievement. It is a difficult dream for the European upper classes to interpret adequately, and too many of us ourselves have grown weary and mistrustful of it. It is not a dream of motor cars and high wages merely, but a dream of a social order in which each man and each woman shall be able to attain to the fullest stature of which they are innately capable, and be recognized by others for what they are, regardless of the fortuitous circumstances of birth or position. I once had an intelligent young Frenchman as guest in New York, and after a few days I asked him what struck him most among his new impressions. Without hesitation he replied, "The way that everyone of every sort looks you right in the eye, without a thought of inequality." Some time ago a foreigner who used to do some work for me, and who had picked up a very fair education, used occasionally to sit and chat with me in my study after he had finished his work. One day he said that such a relationship was the great difference between America and his homeland. There, he said, "I would do my work and might get a pleasant word, but I could never sit and talk like this. There is a difference there between social grades which cannot be got over. I would not talk to you there as man to man, but as my employer."

JAMES TRUSLOW ADAMS, "The American Dream"[1]

---

[1] Reprinted by permission of Atlantic Monthly Press (Little, Brown & Co.).

2. Their popularity was a result of the changing social and economic scene. A century earlier it would not have been possible. The increased leisure and generally higher standard of living of the laboring masses in the first instance made possible the role of these diversions in modern life, but equally important was the new attitude toward amusement which was itself born of this economic progress. By the opening of the twentieth century, recreation had become fully accepted in this country as a natural right of people of whatever social status. The concept of democracy coalesced with the profitable economy of mass production to flood the land with moving pictures, automobiles, and radios. It was not by accident that in no other country of the world did any comparable diffusion of these new means of amusement take place among the masses of the people.

FOSTER R. DULLES, *America Learns to Play*[1]

3. The great need still is to make our cities and towns much better places for family life, and especially for women and children. In his report, Professor Buchanan advocated a policy of designing the town's primary road system to create what he calls 'environmental areas'. In this way, housing neighbourhoods would be clearly defined, and only traffic having business in them would enter them. This would make them safer, more peaceful, more humane, as they are in the new towns we are building. The same thing was said twenty years ago by Lewis Mumford, the authority on city design and change. Writing about the post-war plans for Britain, he said that our largest cities, to become fine cities must first become country towns. What he meant was that we must open them out to provide the houses, the parks, the shops and the schools in a series of separate communities together making up the single entity of the city. And the city could then hold an even richer store of cultural, recreational, and educational facilities. The surest way to destroy the city is to allow it to become more congested with people, vehicles, and buildings.

WYNDHAM THOMAS, "City Centres Die at Six"[2]

[1] Reprinted by permission of Appleton-Century-Crofts, Inc.

[2] From *The Listener*, LXXI (February 13, 1964). Reprinted by permission of the author.

4. Again the plainest diet seems the fittest to be preceded by the grace. That which is least stimulative to appetite leaves the mind most free for foreign considerations. A man may feel thankful, heartily thankful, over a dish of plain mutton with turnips, and have leisure to reflect upon the ordinance and institution of eating; when he shall confess a perturbation of mind, inconsistent with the purposes of the grace, at the presence of venison or turtle. When I have sate at rich men's tables, with the savoury soup and messes steaming up the nostrils, and moistening the lips of the guests with desire and a distracted choice, I have felt the introduction of that ceremony to be unseasonable. With the ravenous orgasm upon you, it seems impertinent to interpose a religious sentiment. It is a confusion of purpose to mutter out praises from a mouth that waters. The heats of epicurism put out the gentle flame of devotion. The incense which rises round is pagan, and the belly-god intercepts it for his own. The very excess of the provision beyond the needs, takes away all sense of proportion between the end and means. The giver is veiled by his gifts. You are startled at the injustice of returning thanks—for what?—for having too much, while so many starve. It is to praise the Gods amiss.

CHARLES LAMB, "Grace Before Meat"

B. Supply topic sentences for each of the following:

1. It is true, of course, that a genius may, on certain lines, do more than a brave and manly fellow who is not a genius; and so, in sports, vast physical strength may overcome weakness, even though the puny body may have in it the heart of a lion. But, in the long run, in the great battle of life, no brilliancy of intellect, no perfection of bodily development, will count when weighed in the balance against that assemblage of virtues, active and passive, or moral qualities, which we group together under the name of character, and if between any two contestants, even in college sport or in college work, the difference in character on the right side is as great as the difference of intellect or strength the other way, it is the character side that will win.

THEODORE ROOSEVELT, *The Strenuous Life*[1]

[1] Reprinted by permission of Appleton-Century-Crofts, Inc.

2. Thus it was left to the white man to recover this lost Indian history. Yet this was only one of many puzzles the New World offered as a challenge to European intelligence. On a more material level it offered opportunity, wealth and adventure. All the old families of white America, whose traditions made our culture what it is, are the descendants of explorers and adventurers whose legends are so deeply rooted in our scheme of life that the first thing one of us thinks of doing when he attains a little leisure is to go off on an expedition. Great popular award and acclaim go to the explorer who finds something new. To discover dinosaur eggs is more popular than to lead an army to victory. And how the mystery of the Indian stirs one! The first white scholars in Europe and America assumed that the Indian came from the Old World. After Russian explorers in the north Pacific Ocean made it clear that Alaska almost touched the mainland of Asia, wise men said the Indian came from that continent. You will find such statements in the oldest books upon the subject. In 1739 a great portrait painter named Smibert came to Boston to paint the colonial governors. He had painted at the Russian Court and so was familiar with the Siberians who appeared there from time to time. When Smibert saw Indians he pronounced them Mongolians. From that day to this, notwithstanding the intensive research of specialists, everything points to a Mongoloid ancestry for the Indian. Even the oldest human bones found in America have been pronounced Mongoloid. So one question is answered: the first man to discover America came from Siberia. This may not be the final answer, but since nothing to contradict it has been discovered since 1492 we must accept it as the best answer.

CLARK WISSLER, Indians of the United States[1]

C. Write a paragraph developing one of the following topic sentences:

1. Writing makes an exact man.
2. A game is never lost until the final whistle blows.

[1] Copyright 1940 by Doubleday & Company, Inc.

3. The newspaper is the poor man's university.
4. Architecture is frozen music.
5. The evil that men do lives after them.
6. A jammed landing gear does not leave one much choice.
7. The noise of the machines was terrific, but not without variety.

8. SELECTION OF MATERIAL

a. Do not omit material that is relevant, especially facts or assumptions which form important links in your general presentation.

Here is a portion of a student composition which tells about a visit to a county jail. The writer intended the four paragraphs to deal with (1) the type of prisoners, (2) their behavior, (3) their activities, and (4) their living conditions. Only in the last of these paragraphs has the writer filled out his outline by providing sufficient illustrative material.

The prisoners are in jail for various reasons and for various lengths of time. The main charges are drunkenness, fighting, and forgery. The minors are mostly runaways or car thieves. Men usually outnumber the women, and colored people outnumber the white people.

The matron said that most of the prisoners do not cause much trouble. A few, however, waste much of her time by asking such useless questions as, "What time is it?" Others are very co-operative and as a result are allowed to sit on the jail lawn. Only very violent ones are guarded. The men but not the women are locked in their sleeping quarters at night.

The prisoners spend their days working, reading, playing cards, or smoking. County male prisoners work on the roads and colored women do odd jobs such as cooking and working in the yard. No organized recreation is provided, but church is conducted every Sunday.

The living conditions of the prisoners are not entirely unsatisfactory. The colored women stay in one cell block which has four rooms with four beds in a room. The white women are kept in two rooms with four beds to a room. The men are housed in cell blocks which have twenty-four beds. Prisoners receive three meals a day—breakfast at six, dinner at twelve, and coffee and cake at six. They are fed in aluminum pans and cups with only spoons as utensils. Knives and forks are not permitted because they might injure themselves or others with them. Luxuries such as cigarettes, cokes, and candy may be obtained from a portable store. Medical service is provided by two local doctors for any prisoner who is sick or injured.

Sometimes what is lacking in a paragraph is not so much a matter of factual detail as an explanation, a concept, or an assumption that is needed to clarify the course of the author's thought. Observe the following paragraph in its original form and subsequent revision:

FAULTY: Where do our rules of grammar come from? How can anyone determine what is right and what is wrong? The English grammarian is a scientist; he must derive his rules in exactly the same manner that any scientist, working in any field, arrives at his conclusions. These general conclusions are the rules of grammar.

REVISED: Where do our rules of grammar come from? How can anyone determine what is right and what is wrong? The English grammarian is a scientist; he must derive his rules in exactly the same manner that any scientist, working in any field, arrives at his conclusions. *He must first observe the behavior of whatever he is studying, in this instance the English language; he must then classify the results of his observation; and when this is done, he may draw certain general conclusions.* These general conclusions are the rules of grammar.

   b. Exclude facts or statements which do not contribute (1) to the purpose for which you have designed the paragraph or (2) to the conclusion you are attempting to reach.

FAULTY: The modern automobile has proved its value to the

American people both for usefulness and pleasure. Think of the amount of business and the number of businesses which depend on motor transportation. Think of the distances we have to cover in so large a country and how inaccessible much of our population would be if it were not for cars. Of course there are other means of transportation, and we all have our preferences. Some prefer trains, and some would rather fly. The Sunday drive, too, is a great American institution, taking us to see our friends and getting city people out into the country for a healthful change.

REVISED: The automobile has proved its value to the American people for both usefulness and pleasure. Think of the amount of business and the number of businesses which depend on motor transportation. Think of the distances we have to cover in so large a country and how inaccessible much of our population would be if it were not for cars. Thanks to them, too, the Sunday drive has become a great American institution, taking us to see our friends and getting city people out into the country for a healthful change.

EXERCISE III

Exclude from the following paragraph whatever material you consider superfluous:

More than ever before youth should be the object of our solicitude. All over the world the enthusiasm of youth, the restlessness of the parent reflected in the young, the flaming desire of boys and girls to spring to the relief of their distressed families, all have brought about a new problem which we must solve. Our youth eagerly, anxiously are seeking new opportunity. Despite temporary limitations, they will find their goal if we but preserve to them the thing rightfully theirs—the opportunity and the means for a sound education. Would that we fathers and mothers gathered here today had been afforded the same opportunity as the present-day youth. At this point I feel it incumbent upon me to address a word to both boys and girls and their parents in relation to the vital and evergrowing need for vocational education. Each year there has been graduated in the past and will continue to be graduated in the future a very large number of students from your high school here in Stonington. Many of these young boys and girls are fortunate enough to have both the means and the inclination to matriculate further and obtain college degrees, and many also have neither the means nor the inclination to pursue a college education. It is to the latter group that I speak today, because I have experienced an increasing concern for the future welfare of these boys and girls. I cannot urge too strongly, therefore, these boys and girls and their parents to take advantage of every opportunity for vocational training that will be afforded in this fine new institution, the new Stonington High School. It is quite true that we have in this great country of ours today an increasing number of unemployed, but the basic reason for this unemployment is the lack of training on the part of our youth. And so I say to those of you who do not plan to attend universities and seek professions, equip yourselves for your future, at any cost. You have before you some of the most revolutionary industries of the age still in their infancy: computer, space technology, and electronics, industries almost unheard of when most of our boys and girls were babies. And to the parents I say have your children take advantage of the splendid opportunities afforded in these industries to make their future secure and the future of the fine families they will contribute to their communities.

9. SEQUENCE OF THOUGHT

Present your ideas in the most logical order.

If the purpose of your paragraph is to develop an idea, you can do it most effectively by means of an organizational plan. In treating a number of events, you may find that the most orderly way to present them may be to arrange them chronologically. If your concern is with a question of cause and effect, a clear-cut distinction between the two is imperative. A logical order is one which enables the reader to follow your thinking and to grasp—and, you may hope, to agree with—the point you are presenting. (See also Chapter I, **T3**.)

FAULTY: In any country or age architecture is limited by the building materials which are available. In turn these various materials give rise to different types of construction. Wood must be held together through beams jointed into framing; stone must be assembled in blocks; clay is held by continuous aggregation. In forest country wood will, of course, be the chief material. If the country is rocky, stone buildings will be developed. In open country without trees or stone, the builders often resort to clay for material.

REVISED: In any country or age the nature of the architecture is determined by the building materials which are available. In a forest country wood will, of course, be the chief material. If the country is rocky, stone buildings will be developed. In a country that is without trees or stone, the builders often resort to clay for material. In turn these various materials give rise to different types of construction. Wood must be held together through beams jointed into framing; stone must be assembled in blocks; clay is held together by continuous aggregation.

EXERCISE IV

These sentences have been intentionally disarranged. Put them in their proper order in a paragraph.

(1) Of course there is nothing new about this. (2) Farmers in this country too, in the days before rural electrification became a reality, used wind motors for pumping water. (3) Such projects present difficult engineering problems. (4) We refer to the use of wind for power production. (5) But only in the past decade have schemes for commercial power production by wind engaged the planners of public utilities. (6) In the windswept areas of Holland windmills have for centuries added their picturesque silhouettes to the landscape. (7) The exploitation of climatic "income" has also spread in another direction. (8) To adjust the variable wind to the variable load is so complicated that many engineers have rejected the scheme as impractical.

(9) Economical power production, however, is based on maintaining proper levels for the fluctuating load requirements. (10) The wind in most localities is quite variable in direction and intensity.

10. CONNECTION

Connect your material in such a way that the relation of the various elements of the paragraph to one another will be clear.

Use the devices which were suggested in Chapter I, **T8.** Observe these connectives:

While I do not believe in *these* restrictive measures and paying for not raising crops, I decided it was no worse than the rest of the bill and I would let it go by without too much objection. *However*, when I began to inquire about the bill and put the question to its author as between early rose and late rose potatoes, I found it did not apply. I found it was not the early or late variety that counted, but where the potatoes were raised. *For example*, potatoes raised in Pennsylvania would receive the 4-cent rate, but over the state line in Maryland the bonus would be 6 cents. *This* extra pay of 2 cents a bushel would be forthcoming to all who danced to the fiddler, and all of the way south from the Pennsylvania and Maryland state line as far as our domain extends, *this* 6-cent rate would prevail.

11. CONSISTENCY

Avoid unnecessary shifts in person, number, and tense.

Reread the paragraphs illustrating consistency in Chapter I, **T9.** Notice the following paragraphs:

UNNECESSARY SHIFT IN PERSON: When men feel patriotic toward their country, they feel that the only way for that country to exist and to become great is through having an army. Although such is not so widely the case in the United States, one sees it throughout

Europe where conditions are different. Here, we feel that we are quite safe from invasion by our neighbors and that we can become great economically. In Europe, however, many large competing countries are close together, countries which have no love for each other. To be patriotic means to love your country, to love your country means to want to protect it, and certainly plenty of protection is needed by European countries.

UNNECESSARY SHIFT IN NUMBER: In adjusting myself to fraternity life, I have been faced with a number of problems. The chief of these is maintaining an open mind. One of the first things to consider is the fellows that we are associated with and their ideas. In many cases they may have very little initiative of their own and just let the other fellow do their thinking for them. This soon becomes a habit and is passed on to the new member.

UNNECESSARY SHIFT IN TENSE: The best movie produced in the last few years, in my opinion, is *Dr. Strangelove, or How I Learned to Stop Worrying and Love the Bomb*, in which Peter Sellers starred. In it he plays the part of Dr. Strangelove (one of three roles that he plays) with something close to perfection. He and Sterling Hayden, who assumed the role of a mad SAC general, keep the audience in uproarious laughter. The result was one of the funniest films that Peter Sellers has ever made.

12. EFFECTIVENESS

a. A clear and concisely worded topic sentence contributes to the effectiveness of a paragraph.

Reread ¶7 (on the *topic sentence*).

b. Pay particular attention to the beginning and ending of your paragraphs to avoid unemphatic or inconclusive writing.

INEFFECTIVE BEGINNING: I shall attempt to discuss the free recreational facilities provided by the city. A city as large as New York with its millions of inhabitants needs literally hundreds of parks, playgrounds, and swimming pools.

INEFFECTIVE CONCLUSION: Sometimes young people wanted more exciting recreation, turning to petty thievery, which in later years could turn them into criminals. As a result of these poorer children trying to find excitement, juvenile delinquency became a great problem. Children were sent to reform schools, where some of them turned into hardened criminals. Perhaps it seems far-fetched to some that all the above-mentioned things result from a lack of recreational facilities, but it has happened. Of course there have been other factors involved.

INEFFECTIVE BEGINNING AND CONCLUSION: Perhaps I could refer to a very good example by going back to the days when Napoleon was running rough-shod over Europe. Since the then-divided German states were too near to his own country, it was only natural that the great French general should war with them. At the time, the citizens of the various German states were getting along none too well among themselves. There was no sense of unity; they did not think of themselves as a single nation. However, the threat of Napoleon threw them together for mutual protection, and they no longer thought of themselves as separate states. They became patriotic Germans. Furthermore, was it not also natural for them to become militaristic under such circumstances?

EFFECTIVE BEGINNING AND CONCLUSION: Perhaps the men of genius are the only true men. In all the history of the race there have been only a few thousand real men. And the rest of us—what are we? Teachable animals. Without the help of the real men, we should have found out almost nothing at all. Almost all the ideas with which we are familiar could never have occurred to minds like ours. Plant the seeds there and they will grow; but our minds could never spontaneously have generated them.

ALDOUS HUXLEY, *Young Archimedes and Other Stories*[1]

The whole swing of American style, for a quarter century past, has been toward greater and greater freedom in the use of essentially national idioms. The tart admonitions of English purists—as, for example, in the *Literary Supplement* of the Lon-

[1] Reprinted by courtesy of Harper & Row, Publishers, Inc.

don *Times*—are no longer directed solely or even mainly to writers who need apology at home: the offenders now include many of the best we have yet produced. And they begin to get the understanding and approval of a larger and larger fraction of intelligent Englishmen.

H. L. MENCKEN, *Supplement One, The American Language*[1]

All the English teachers in the country are trying to get their pupils to discover the varied relationships of ideas, and to range their ideas in the proper order of subordination. Hemingway is just as strenuously working to reduce all ideas to a single order of relationship, the conjunctive coördinate relationship, in which no one item is subordinated to any other. It is the great leveling democracy of the *and*. Both Hemingway and the English teachers have their reasons. The teachers are concerned with the logical structure of thought and with hoping to raise their pupils a few degrees in their level of understanding. The writer of fiction is concerned with the aesthetic projection of images. The understanding spirals back upon itself and ties itself in subtle knots that will hold the thought firm. But the writer of fiction is telling a story, and he wants it to flow and not be lost in eddies of logic.

JOSEPH WARREN BEACH, *American Fiction, 1920–1940*[2]

c. Vary sentence structure to avoid monotony.

For additional material on varying sentence structure, reread Chapter I, T10b.

FAULTY: These men know that they will receive their government checks. These checks represent buying power for the purchase of goods, although the men can buy little with the checks. Therefore the workers have little or no incentive to work, so they accomplish little towards real efficiency. On the other hand the worker in a society of equals will have no security as to a pay check. His

---

[1] Reprinted by permission of Alfred A. Knopf, Inc.
[2] Reprinted by permission of The Macmillan Company.

security will depend upon the quality of his work and cooperation with other men.

IMPROVED: These men know that they will receive their government checks, representing purchasing power, although not much can be bought with them. Therefore, having little or no incentive to work, such laborers scarcely attain what may be called real efficiency. In a society of equals, on the other hand, there is no such security as a pay check for a worker. Instead, the quality of his work and the extent of his cooperation with others determine his security.

d. Repetition of sentence structure may sometimes make a paragraph more emphatic.

For additional material on repetition of sentence structure, reread Chapter I, **T10b**, and see Chapter III, **S9c**.

This standpoint establishes for us a certain scale of values. In every aspect of knowledge and of living, the test of life holds. It accounts for our pleasures and our antipathies. The test of life was with us a racial thought, wordless and needing no definition or giving of reasons. It was that test of life which, instinctively I think, guided us to distrust civic civilization and uphold the rural ideal in art, life and letters, to dislike religion in our rational moments, to play with Buddhism but never quite accept its logical conclusions, and to hate mechanical ingenuity. It was that instinctive trust in life that gave us a robust common sense in looking at life's kaleidoscopic changes and the myriad vexatious problems of the intellect which we rudely ignored. It enabled us to see life steadily and see life whole, with no great distortions of values. It taught us some simple wisdom, like respect for old age and the joys of domestic life, acceptance of life, of sex and of sorrow. It made us lay emphasis on certain common virtues, like endurance, industry, thrift, moderation and pacifism. It prevented the development of freakish extreme theories and the enslaving of man by the products of his own intelligence. It gave us a sense of values, and taught us to accept the material as well as the spiritual goods of life. It taught us that, after all is said and done, human happiness is the end of all knowledge. And we arrange ourselves to make our lives happy on this planet, under whatever vicissitudes of fortune.   LIN YUTANG, *My Country and My People*[1]

EXERCISE V

1. Analyze the paragraphing in the leading editorial in your newspaper for any selected day. Notice the length and unity of the paragraphs, the sequence of ideas, the way in which they are connected, and the devices used to make them forceful.

2. Apply a similar analysis to essays in such magazines as *Harper's*, the *Atlantic Monthly*, *Fortune*, etc.

3. Apply paragraph analysis to a novel you have recently read.

13. KINDS OF PARAGRAPH DEVELOPMENT

In writing a paragraph you are attempting to develop an idea. Consequently you cannot content yourself with an unplanned collection of sentences. You must have a plan or method.

It is true that writers, intent upon what they have to say, are seldom conscious of the exact pattern or organization they follow in writing a particular paragraph. The structure of the paragraph depends upon the nature of the topic and the purpose of the writer at that particular point.

Yet a knowledge of the various ways in which a paragraph can be developed will prove helpful both in suggesting possible lines of presentation and in detecting faulty structure.

There is nothing mysterious about the types of paragraph development. They are not even peculiar to the paragraph as a unit. They are simply the usual logical procedures which a skillful writer employs to explain, to clarify, to persuade,

---

[1] Reprinted by permission of the John Day Co.

and to convince. The following paragraphs illustrate how good authors use various means of paragraph development.

a. Definition

We have, then, in attempting to make more precise our *definition of socialism*, to avoid relating it in our minds to any utopian picture of the future. We can say that socialists seek the common ownership and collective control of the means of production and exchange; but we cannot say that this involves either the "nationalization" of all industries or some particular way of managing them. There are many possible forms of common ownership—nationally by the state, locally by municipalities or similar bodies, and locally or nationally by quasi-public trusts, guilds or corporations acting on behalf of the public. There are also many possible forms of administration—directly by state or municipal departments, by specially constituted boards or commissions of experts, or by representative bodies of producers or consumers or of both. All these forms of ownership and administration have had advocates among socialists, and many socialist plans embody features from several of them, or allow for diversity of experiment in different cases. Nor can it even be assumed that socialists wish all the means of production to be publicly owned. If the vital and basic industries and services were under public control, many socialists would be ready to leave smaller enterprises largely in private hands.

G. D. H. COLE, in *Encyclopædia Britannica* (14th ed.)[1]

b. Exemplification

The statement of a general truth or principle is followed by a number of specific facts which support it.

In any tree, however live and growing, the substance composing trunk and branch is inert and lifeless matter. The heartwood of a tree, the heaviest and solidest part, extending a considerable distance from the centre, is dead in every sense of the word. Its tubes

---

[1] Reprinted by courtesy of *Encyclopædia Britannica*.

no longer convey the sap upward, because their walls have become thickened and filled with lignin. In them there is not even the semblance of vital activity. From the heartwood outward to a point very near the surface we find the water-conveying structure consisting of long tubes; and these tubes are mere conduits, inert and lifeless. They serve a useful purpose in conveying the water upward, but they are not themselves alive. At first, when they were being built, there were live cells working inside of them, little bags of protoplasm; but, once they were completed, the live tenants disappeared. Interspersed among these tubes is tissue which still contains protoplasm, but it is not alive in the sense that it can grow or reproduce itself.

CHARLES D. STEWART, "The Tree as an Invention"[1]

c. Generalization

A number of specific facts are presented, and a general conclusion is drawn from them.

It is a matter of course that a familiar piece of music, whether a tune you heard in your childhood or a symphony you have studied, cannot come to you otherwise than charged with associations. Herein lies a meaning of music, a meaning which technical language cannot define, yet which it would be stupid to deny. Even in music which we hear for the first time the suggestion of familiar things plays upon us continually, and with meaning. They may be things not personally but only racially familiar. The timbre of voices, the sound of instruments surely act upon us in this way. For whom could the music of bagpipes be only a sequence of sounds, their fine melodic variations only patterns in tonal design. The difference between the oboe and the flute is far more than the difference in the order of their partial tones. Each instrument is inseparable from associations that run back perhaps thousands of years. So it is with the trumpet, the drum, the guitar, and in fact, with most instruments. I cannot hold that those have less enjoyed music, have even perhaps less understood it, whose memory has

[1] Reprinted by courtesy of the author.

drifted from their listening, whose imagination has conjured visions athwart the sound.

LELAND HALL, "The Power of Music,"
Harper's Magazine, May 1933[1]

d. Cause to Effect

The most fateful mistake Venezuela made when she appeared on the political stage was beyond doubt the adoption of a regime of tolerance. The law codes by which our magistrates were guided were not designed to teach them the practical science of government. They were the compilation of certain amiable visionaries who, with an imaginary republic in mind, aimed for political perfection, and assumed the perfectibility of mankind. As a result, we had philosophers for leaders, philanthropy for legislation, dialectics for policy, and sophists for soldiers.

JULES MANCINI, "Bolivar's First Campaign," in
The Green Continent, ed. by German Arciniegas[2]

e. Effect to Cause

Unhappily, too, Thompson's verse is certainly fatiguing to read, and one of the reasons why it is so fatiguing is that the thought that is in it does not progress; it remains stationary. About the fragile life which cries somewhere in its center he builds up walls of many colored bricks, immuring his idea, hiding it, stifling it. How are we to read an ode of many pages in which there is no development, not even movement? Stanza is heaped upon stanza, page is piled upon page, and we end where we began. The writer has said endless things about something but never the thing itself. Poetry consists in saying the thing itself.

ARTHUR SYMONS, *Dramatis Personae*[3]

---

[1] Reprinted by courtesy of *Harper's Magazine*.

[2] Reprinted by permission of Alfred A. Knopf, Inc.

[3] Copyright 1923. Used by special permission of the publishers, the Bobbs-Merrill Company, Inc.

f. Comparison and Contrast

A European, when he first arrives, seems limited in his intentions, as well as in his views; but he very suddenly alters his scale; two hundred miles formerly appeared a very great distance; it is now but a trifle; he no sooner breathes our air than he forms schemes, and embarks in designs he never would have thought of in his own country. There the plenitude of society confines many useful ideas, and often extinguishes the most laudable schemes, which here ripen into maturity. Thus Europeans become Americans.

HECTOR ST. JOHN DE CRÈVECOEUR,
Letters from an American Farmer, III

g. Elimination

This method develops what the subject is not and finally what it is.

This brings us to another kind of thought which can fairly easily be distinguished from the three kinds described above. It has not the usual qualities of the reverie, for it does not hover about our personal complacencies and humiliations. It is not made up of the homely decisions forced upon us by everyday needs, when we review our little stock of existing information, consult our conventional preferences and obligations, and make a choice of action. It is not the defense of our own cherished beliefs and prejudices just because they are our own—mere plausible excuses for remaining of the same mind. On the contrary, it is that peculiar species of thought which leads us to change our mind.

JAMES HARVEY ROBINSON, *The Mind in the Making*[1]

14. PARAGRAPHING QUOTED MATERIAL

See Chapter XIII, **MS3**.

[1] Reprinted by courtesy of Harper & Row, Publishers, Inc.

CHAPTER **III. The Sentence**

THE sentence, more than anything else, is the basic unit of language. It may consist of a single word, or it may run on for a hundred or more words if the idea to be expressed is complex. But whatever its length, it gives the hearer or reader a sense of relative completeness or independence as it stands.

In speaking or writing our native tongue we unconsciously put words into sentence patterns which, like the words themselves, are characteristics of the language. Sentence patterns differ from one language to another, as you discover the moment you try to translate Latin, French, German; and each particular language has its own stock upon which its users may draw. Without thinking consciously about it, we know that *I have* means one thing and *Have I* means another, or that *John kissed Susan* and *Susan kissed John* are not exactly equivalent.

The variety of ways in which a speaker or writer is able to express himself—the responsiveness and adaptability of his thoughts—depends to a very great extent on the sentence patterns which he has at his command. Every native user of English has known the basic patterns since early childhood, but all of us can increase our range and our control—and must, if we are to write better.

1. SPEECH AND WRITING

Morning, Mary.
Hello, Bill! Well, how'd you do on the exam?
Not too badly—made my B.
You *didn't!* Were you relieved?

Was I relieved! Means my scholarship'll be renewed, that's all. Now I can quit worrying about a loan or a summer job.

Say, that's fine. So now you can celebrate.

I'm planning to. In fact, Mary—

Yes?

Well, the Winter Carnival dance is next Saturday night, and I thought maybe—

Well?

How about it? Eight o'clock, informal.

Well, I wasn't planning anything else—

It's a date then. O.K.?

O.K.

Great! See you Saturday. So long!

This piece of conversation, though perhaps not an example of elegance, will be recognized as typical. Actually, it was spoken, and was directed to the ear; here it has been written down, and is directed to the eye. As a result, certain features of sound have been translated into terms of sight. Most obvious is the use of *punctuation* to show pauses (commas), hesitation (dashes), emphasis (italics, exclamation marks).

Less obvious, though always present and essential to meaning, are features of the voice. Emphasis comes chiefly from *volume*: Mary speaks more loudly when she says *didn't* (which is emphatic also to indicate irony); Bill reduces the volume, speaks a little softly when he begins to make his invitation, and says *Mary*—. The difference between a question and an exclamation lies chiefly in *pitch*: the pitch drops at the end of every exclamation, and usually rises at the end of each question. The phrase *Were you relieved?* clearly demands an answer, since the voice rises in pitch at the end; but *Was I relieved!* though grammatically in the form of a question, is clearly not one, since the pitch of the voice falls definitely at the end. So with *O.K.* which is first a question, then an answer, with rising and then falling pitch. These features of voice, though essential to meaning, are inadequately indicated in writing.

There are still other features of the voice which punctuation fails altogether to show. A playwright is often forced to give directions in the script, such as "in a whisper," "softly," "fiercely"; a narrative writer quoting dialogue frequently adds, "he growled," "she sighed," "said he with a shrug." For in speech we face each other, we react visibly, we make gestures, our voices go up and down, fast and slowly, loudly and softly. The words alone do not have to carry the burden.

In writing, apart from the help which punctuation can give, the words and sentence patterns must do all the work. The shades of facial expression, gesture, and intonation are lacking; a substitute must be supplied. This is done through more careful choice of words than we make in ordinary talk, greater variety in the sentence patterns, and other such means.

If we look again at the conversation of Mary and Bill, we see that it is very limited in the range of patterns. There are greetings and exclamations (*Morning; Great; So long*), abbreviations (*made my B; See you Saturday*), fragments (*In fact, Mary—; I thought maybe—*), answers that are incomplete without their questions (*Not too badly—; I'm planning to*). These would seldom appear in writing except as imitations of speech. There are also, however, many of the "relatively complete utterances" which are the staple of both spoken and written language (*How'd you do on the exam?; the Winter Carnival dance is next Saturday night; It's a date then*). Speech has a considerable proportion of the fragments and abbreviations; writing depends almost wholly on the "relatively complete utterances," in a great many variations.

It should be noticed further that the informality of this conversation lies not only in its words, but in its structure. The conversation is obviously made up as it goes along; there is no deliberate phrasing. Something is said, then (often by afterthought) it is supplemented with something more (*Say, that's fine. So now you can celebrate. How about it? Eight o'clock, informal.*).

The main difference between the sentences of speech and writing should now be evident.[1] Certainly, not all informal speech is as elementary as the sample (though by far the greatest part of our use of language is of this kind, as we shop and eat and chat with our friends, exchanging opinions and giving information about our doings and plans). But even when ideas are being discussed, or some serious point argued, the same basic situation prevails. Gestures, volume, pitch, tone of voice are still present to aid the words; the speakers still stop and start as the expression comes more or less fluently; they still speak in fragments as they interrupt one another, repeat things for emphasis and continuity, rephrase them as they find a better way.

Much of the same process may go on inside us before we write, but it should not show in the finished product. Those trials which prove to be errors may be left aside, and we may present to our reader only the best statement of our thought of which we are capable. It will differ considerably from the uneven, irregular, somewhat haphazard thing that is conversation. For we will have had the time to choose those words and sentence patterns which will make up for the absent shadings of voice and gesture, will avoid unnecessary repetitions, give a tighter, deliberate structure to the expression, and make it far more effective.

---

[1] Not only the sentences but the words used in conversation may differ from those of good writing. See Chapter IV, W6f-g.

2. STRUCTURE OF THE SENTENCE

The vast majority of sentences turn out, when we examine them, to have a basic structure which we may call the conventional one. They are made up of two related parts called a *subject* and a *predicate*.[1] What with variations and combinations of this basic structure, the English language has developed a wide range of sentence patterns suiting the different requirements of expression. (It is obvious that vigorous, rapid expression will call for one kind of sentence structure, thoughtful and deliberate expression another, and so on. The writer must choose whatever structure suits his purpose best.) There are also a few sentence patterns in which the basic structure is incomplete, the subject or the predicate part having been reduced in some way—even eliminated. Such less-than-full sentences, nevertheless, are an established feature of the language. We shall first consider regular or full sentences and later the reduced ones.

3. SIMPLE SENTENCES

A simple sentence has only one subject-predicate combination. For example:

Dogs	bark.
Dogs	are quadrupeds.
Subject	**Predicate**

Notice how the subject and predicate are related through their meaning. If English is our native tongue, our language sense makes us recognize these as normal, grammatical statements. Analyzing them, we discover that the subject identifies *who* or *what* does what the predicate states and that the predicate gives *a specific piece of information* about the subject's action. Without changing this basic pattern of rela-

[1] When the verb of the predicate is in the imperative mood—that is, when it is expressing a command or a request—the subject is usually omitted. See Chapter VI, G5b.

tionship between the subject and predicate we may amplify each in various ways. First the subject:

Dogs	bark.
Simple Subject	**Predicate**
Dogs and foxes	bark.
Compound Subject	
The dogs on the farm	bark.
Simple Subject	
Angry dogs and foxes	bark.
Compound Subject	

Then the predicate:

Dogs	bark.
Subject	**Simple Predicate**
Dogs	run and bark.
	Compound Predicate
Dogs	run all over the farm.
	Simple Predicate
Dogs	run around and bark angrily.
	Compound Predicate

Or both:

Dogs and foxes	run around and bark.
Compound Subject	**Compound Predicate**

All of the above sentences are *simple* because, though the subject or predicate may have one or more parts, there is only one subject-predicate relationship in each sentence. A subject-predicate group is also called a *clause*; thus one may say that a *simple sentence* has one clause. Other kinds of sentences (*compound*, *complex*, and combinations of these) are made by uniting two or more clauses in various ways. (A *phrase*, in traditional terminology, is any group of words having less than the minimum requirements of a clause.) But before coming to these other kinds of sentences, we must examine further the nature of the predicate.

a. The English language requires a "finite" verb as the core or basis of the predicate.

Without a finite verb (see Glossary of Grammatical Terms, page 260) the utterance would not be "relatively complete" in effect. The finite verb may stand by itself (a simple verb), as:

Dogs *bark*.	Birds *sing*.	Cars *go*.	**Present**
Dogs *barked*.	Birds *sang*.	Cars *went*.	**Past**

Or it may be the first of a related series called a *phrasal verb*.[1] Some common examples are the following:

(Subject)	Finite Verb	Infinitive	Past Participle	Present Participle	
(Dogs)	are			barking.	**Present Progressive**
(Dogs)	were			barking.	**Past Progressive**
(Dogs)	are		stolen.		**Present Passive**
(Dogs)	were		stolen.		**Past Passive**
(Dogs)	have		been	barking.	**Present Perfect Progressive**
(Dogs)	had		been	barking.	**Past Perfect Progressive**
(Dogs)	have		barked.		**Present Perfect**
(Dogs)	had		barked.		**Past Perfect**

(For uses of the infinitive, see the next tabulation.)

[1] In a phrasal verb, the finite verb and the infinite forms (infinitives and participles) which follow it, except the last word in the phrasal verb, are traditionally called *auxiliary verbs*; the last is called the *main verb*. These terms refer to the fact that the main verb expresses chiefly meaning, whereas the auxiliaries express chiefly the grammatical structure. *Be, have, do* and their forms, are one class of auxiliaries; the modals are another. They may be used separately or together. The phrasal verb in modern English may comprise as many as four auxiliary forms functioning with the main verb.

One small group of finite verbs, the *modals* (Mod.), functioning in the phrasal verb, allows English to express a number of relationships of emotional orientation or attitude which exist between the subject and the action of the verb. These relationships depend on the meaning of the modal itself: for example, *intention* and the like are expressed with *shall* and *will*; *obligation* is expressed with *ought* and *must*; *potentiality* is expressed with *can*, *dare*, and *may*; *necessity* is expressed with *need*. Some examples are the following:

(Subject)	Finite Verb	Infinitive	Past Participle	Present Participle
(Dogs)	will	bark.		
(Dogs)	would	bark.		
(Dogs)	need	to bark.		
(Dogs)	ought	to be		barking.
(Dogs)	must	be	exercised.	
(Dogs)	may	have	been	barking.
(Dogs)	might	have	been	barking.

As anybody who knows English will recognize, the parts of a phrasal verb must come in the order shown in the tabulation. And as these examples show, the phrasal verb may include an *infinitive* (with or without *to*), a *past participle*, a *present participle*,[1] and various combinations of these forms; but the essential element is the finite verb. To omit it from any of the phrasal verbs above will either

---

[1] The *infinitive* is formally marked by *to* preceding it, except in a small list of modals. The *present participle* is formally marked by ending with -*ing*. The *past participle* is formally marked by ending with -*ed* regularly; but with irregular verbs it is formally marked in other ways, as by internal vowel change (*swam*), by suppletion (*went*), etc. Though we meet these forms (as a group called *verbals*) as components of the phrasal verb, they can also function in other contexts as equivalents of nouns or adjectives. For these functions see the next section, S3b.

change the grammar and meaning radically (as, *Dogs can bark* becoming *Dogs bark*) or will produce a less-than-complete utterance (as, *Dogs barking, Dogs stolen, Dogs been barking.*)[1]

The use of the phrasal verb in English makes possible a highly subtle and varied series of expressions which grammars of the past often ignored and modern grammarians are just beginning to study. There is even evidence of the growth of patterns new both as to meaning and form.[2]

Constructions of the kind we have just been looking at have only a subject, usually a noun or pronoun ("*Dogs* bark," "*Who* cares") and a verb ("Dogs *bark*," "Who *cares*"). However, many verbs require a third element to complete the thought and give meaning to the verb:

Jane was	INCOMPLETE
Ruth bought	INCOMPLETE
He considered this	NOT NECESSARILY COMPLETE

When such verbs are completed by another element, the third element is called a *complement*. Note that the first parts of *complement* and *complete* are the same.

Jane was *a good student*.	(*subject complement*)
Ruth bought *a new dress*.	(*direct object*)
He considered this *a wise move*.	(*object complement*)

---

[1]Such utterances, it is true, are sometimes possible in the context of speech: "What did you hear?" "Dogs barking." Or, "All safe?" "I'm not sure. Dogs been barking." (This last is an abbreviation for "[The] dogs [have] been barking.") But these are not appropriate to expository writing.

[2]For example, *am* and *have* followed by the infinitive can express obligation as effectively as *ought*. Compare: "I *am* to go"; "I *have* to go"; "I *ought* to go."

The phrase *be able*, composed of verb and adjective, has become equivalent to the basic meaning of *can* and may function like it in most respects.

Note that the *subject complement* refers to the subject, and that the *object complement* refers to and completes the meaning of the *direct object* (the word designating the person or thing thought of as undergoing, or being directly affected by, the action of the verb). Here, the *dress* is the thing that Ruth *bought*, and *this* is the matter that he *considered*. Not all verbs can take objects: *was* does not indicate action; going back further, dogs do not *bark* anything—they simply bark.[1] (See Chapter VI, **G5g**, for a discussion of *linking verbs*.)

> **b. The participles and infinitive, when not combined with an auxiliary verb, function as adjectives or noun respectively, and are often used to introduce additional details into the sentence.**

THUS: *Dogs do not bite* is a complete, simple sentence; but we may want to give further detail, so we say:

Barking   dogs   do not bite.
Participial Adjective

And similarly:

A dog,   stolen   from the farm,   was found   in the city.
      Participial   **Adverb Phrase**   **Adverb Phrase**
      Adjective

To call   with all the force   at one's command   is unnecessary.
Infinitive   **Adverb Phrase**   **Adjective Phrase**
Noun Use

One may pile up these modifying phrases almost indefinitely (though, of course, this is easily overdone). For example, the following is still, in terms of its basic structure, a *simple sentence*, though it is anything but simple in terms of the information given. Try to separate the subject, the

---

[1] A verb that takes a direct object is called *transitive*; one that takes no object is *intransitive*.

predicate, and the modifying phrases, and decide what each phrase modifies.

Dogs, barking lustily on the farms in the dead of night at the approach of strangers with unfamiliar scents, and growling in their kennels for the protection of their masters asleep in their homes, do not bite at the calves of the intruders but snap at their ankles.

EXERCISE I

Select the subject, the finite verb, and complement (if there is one) in each of the following sentences.

EXAMPLES: The horse galloped.
   Subject, *the horse*; verb, *galloped*.
   The foundation appeared unstable.
   Subject, *the foundation*; verb, *appeared*; subject complement, *unstable*.

1. We were certain of good results.
2. The box contained several letters.
3. A gold watch was found on the floor.
4. They elected Jones secretary.
5. Only the brave deserve the fair.
6. The directory will surely be printed.
7. Hundreds of thousands crowded the streets of the old city.
8. Even the prosperous citizens wore old suits and battered hats.
9. The waves tossed and churned.
10. Not a creature was stirring, not even a mouse.

4. COMPOUND SENTENCES

A compound sentence is so called because it is compounded or made up of what, if separate, would be simple sentences. We may want to keep separate the two simple sentences *Dogs run* and *Rabbits hop*; or we may want to indicate some closer relationship between them and may therefore convert them into a compound sentence, joining them in some way. There are two chief ways of joining these ideas: by using a coordinating conjunction (see Chapter VI, G8) or by placing them side by side with a semicolon between.[1] Occasionally some mark other than a semicolon may be used (see **S8e**). For example:

a. Dogs run	and **Conjunction**	rabbits hop.
b. Dogs run	but **Conjunction**	rabbits hop.
c. Dogs run	; **Semicolon**	rabbits hop.
d. Dogs run	; **Semicolon**	rabbits hop ; snakes slide. **Semicolon**
e. Dogs run	and **Conjunction**	horses trot ; rabbits hop. **Semicolon**

Notice the variations in these compound sentences: a, b, and c have two clauses each; d and e have three clauses each. There is no theoretical limit to the number of clauses which may be in a compound sentence. (Practically, we seldom have use for more than three, since with more the sentence becomes unwieldy or monotonous.) Sentences a and b use conjunctions alone; c and d use semicolons alone; e combines both.

What differences, of use to a writer, are produced by these various combinations? Apart from the difference in meaning introduced by and, but, or the other conjunctions, the chief thing gained is the holding together of the parts so that the reader becomes aware of the relation between them. In b, c, and d, this is a relation of contrast. In a there is simply addition. In e the similar ideas of the first two

[1] Obviously this refers to their written form. In speech we gain the effect of these two statements' being joined or closely related by what our voice does: the pitch rises slightly or is sustained through a slight pause, but does not fall definitively until the end of the last statement.

clauses are combined, then this group is contrasted with the third clause.

EXERCISE II

A. Which of the following are simple sentences, and which are compound? Which have compound subjects or predicates?

1. Butter and eggs with toast and jam make a fine breakfast.
2. The choice of swimming or drowning lay before him.
3. Jack paddled; Mary sang and played the mandolin.
4. The grass is growing, but meantime the horse is starving.
5. Take it or leave it.
6. On the contrary, and despite his efforts, the court ruled unfavorably for his client.

B. Examine the following passages (from a short story and an editorial) and decide where simple and compound sentences have been well used, or where one type would do better than the other. (Note, in the second, the use of the colon.)

And so the long afternoon wore on. But there was no change. The boat continued to rise upon the swells. The sea, blue and relentlessly glittering in the sun, rose and fell. The boat rose and fell with it. The men knew the desperation of monotony and then lapsed into dullness. The sea rose and fell. Bjorn still lay back against his thwart; his head bobbed loosely. His eyes stared. But still instinctively, or by the course of custom, his right hand grasped the tiller.

Democracy is not the same thing as equalitarianism. Equalitarianism is impossible. No two men are literally born equal. Nor can they be made equal. There is no physical equality. Some are strong. Some are weak. There is no economic equality: some have all they need; others have not enough. It will never be possible to have equality in these things. Nor would it be desirable, but there are some things in which equality is both possible and desirable. And these democracy seeks to achieve.

5. COMPLEX SENTENCES

In a compound sentence, as we have just seen, the clauses are of approximately equal importance and can, if the sentence is broken up, stand separately. But in combining clauses we often need to show that one is more important than the other, and here we use the *complex sentence*. For example:

> The dogs bark loudly.   The dogs live on the hill.

Here we have two simple sentences. As they stand, they are given about the same importance. So they would be too if they came in the opposite order, or if they were made into a compound sentence.

But if we want to suggest that the dogs' barking is more important (for our present meaning) than the place where they live, we may write a complex sentence:

> The dogs *that live on the hill* bark loudly.

Here the first sentence has become the *main* or *independent clause* (since it could still stand alone); and the second, with the change of a word, has become the *dependent* or *subordinate clause* (and cannot, in this form, stand alone). The subordinate clause has been *embedded* into the main clause.

Or, on the other hand, if we want to give more importance to the place where the dogs live than to their barking, we may *embed* the first statement into the second:

> The dogs *that bark loudly* live on the hill.

The word *that*, in each case, has taken the place of *dogs* in the subordinate clause; it depends for its meaning on its

93

antecedent in the main clause (here, *dogs*), and thus connects the two clauses, putting them in the desired relation of unequal value.

There are three kinds of words used in English subordination: 1. The *relative* pronoun; 2. Certain *adverbs*; 3. *Subordinating conjunctions*.

1. The *relative* pronoun. The *that* just used above is an example; others are *who, whose, whom, which, what,* etc. For example (the subordinate clauses italicized):

> a. I do not know *who was there.*
> b. It does not matter *whose hat you took.*
> c. Choose the partner *whom you prefer.*
> d. *Which he chose* is immaterial.
> e. He did not say *what he wanted.*

Note that in *d* and *e* the independent clause is not complete without the dependent, which in *d* is the subject of *is*, and in *e* is the object of *say*.

Note also that very frequently in speech, and often in writing, there occurs the so-called "omitted relative construction."[1] For example, sentence *c* above could omit the relative *whom* and still be perfectly acceptable (though less formal) English. In such a construction, obviously, meaning is possible because the two clauses are side by side. If anything except the relative came between, it would break the connection. This construction is often useful when a writer is seeking fluency rather than strict formality.

2. Certain *adverbs*: *when, where, how, why, whenever,* etc. These connect the clauses by introducing the subordinate clause and modifying a word in the main clause.

---

[1] This designation is misleading, since it implies that the relative *ought* to be present, or that the construction is less than complete without it. Yet this has never been the case; this construction has been in good and constant usage from Anglo-Saxon times forward.

For example:

> a. Dogs bark *when(ever)* *they smell* a fox.
> b. *Wher(ever)* *they found water*, they made their camp.
> c. *How you did it* does not matter.
> d. He did not say *why he had come*.

Note again that in c and d the subordinate clause is necessary to complete the main clause.

3. The *subordinating conjunctions: since, because, unless*, etc. (See Chapter VI, **G8**.) For example:

> a. *Since the clock was late*, I missed my train.
> b. He likes a bungalow *because there are no stairs*.
> c. *Unless this catch is released*, the trigger will not move.

Complex sentences are valuable because they allow the writer to differentiate easily the more important and the less important parts of his thought. (See also **S9d**.)

EXERCISE III

A. Make complex sentences from the following pairs of simple sentences, first subordinating a of each to b, then b to a. (You will have to supply conjunctions and to change the italicized pronouns and adverbs.)

1a. I will not come.	b. He is angry.
2a. Lincoln was great.	b. Lincoln understood kindliness.
3a. He felt like a fool.	b. He apologized.
4a. Nothing seems to matter.	b. You are tired.
5a. She needs encouragement.	b. Her voice is good.
6a. He works *there*.	b. He eats *there*.
7a. You must accept *that*.	b. You deserve *that*.

B. Convert the following comparatively weak sentences into complex ones which put the parts into an effective relationship. (You may add necessary subordinating words.)

1. He will come in June and we will begin to build.
2. Eskimos live in ice houses but they keep as warm as anybody.
3. The vote must be heavy or we will not win.
4. The new director came to dinner today; I met him last week.
5. The rain began coming through the top and we patched it.

6. COMBINATIONS OF COMPOUND AND COMPLEX

Compound and complex sentence structures may be combined in a number of different ways. Examples of the main types follow:

a. The dog barks, and the cat purrs *when her fur is rubbed*.

b. The dog barks *when a stranger comes*, but the cat, *who is timid*, runs into a corner.

c. The dog, *who has guarded the house ever since we left it*, always barks *when a stranger comes*.

In *a*, a simple clause is coordinated by *and* with a complex element; in *b*, two complex elements of equal rank are coordinated with *but*; in *c*, there is only one independent clause, to which two other clauses are subordinated, the first of which itself has a dependent clause.

Entire books have been written in simple sentences—as they have, too, in words of one syllable. But this is a special feat of simplification, by no means necessary or desirable in general. Such writing is more simple even than everyday conversation; it becomes colorless and repetitious, and annoys the intelligent reader with its kindergarten style. The writer who does not "write down" in this way will find the compound and complex sentences and their combinations of great value. And, what is more, if the simple sentence is not overused it will be the more effective when it *is* used: by contrast with the more involved sentences it will gain sharpness, decisiveness, force.

EXERCISE IV

Examine the following passage from a story by Henry James for his use of sentences. a. Which kinds has he used? b. Try to separate the passage into clauses and to rewrite these as simple sentences only. What do you discover?

I must confess that I had spent much of the interval in wondering what the disagreeable thing was that my charming friend's disagreeable cousin had been telling her. The "Belle Cuisinère" was a modest inn in a shady by-street, where it gave me satisfaction to think Miss Spencer must have encountered local color in abundance. There was a crooked little court where much of the hospitality of the house was carried on; there was a staircase climbing to bedrooms on the outer side of the wall; there was a small, trickling fountain with a stucco statuette in the midst of it; there was a little boy in a white cap and apron cleaning copper vessels at a conspicuous kitchen door; there was a chattering landlady, neatly laced, arranging apricots and grapes into an artistic pyramid upon a pink plate. I looked about, and on a green bench outside of an open door labeled *Salle à Manger*, I perceived Caroline Spencer. No sooner had I looked at her than I saw that something had happened since the morning. She was leaning back on her bench, her hands were clasped in her lap, and her eyes were fixed upon the landlady, at the other side of the court, manipulating her apricots.

But I saw she was not thinking of apricots.

HENRY JAMES, "Four Meetings"

7. SUMMARY

The conventional requirements of the written sentence may be stated as follows:

a. A sentence must contain at least one subject-predicate sequence, or independent clause.

See S3. Further:

1. The predicate must contain a finite verb. (*Dogs bark*, not *Dogs barking.*) See **S3a.**

2. Dependent clauses must not be treated as sentences; they cannot stand alone. (*They came in when it rained*, not *They came in. When it rained.*) See **S8d.**

b. If two or more subject-predicate sequences are put into a sentence, they may be connected in various ways. If of about equal importance, they should be coordinated (compound sentence); if of unequal rank, the less important should be subordinated (complex sentence); or coordination and subordination may be combined.

See **S4–6.**

EXERCISE V

Classify the following sentences as simple, compound, or complex, and in each of the complex sentences select the independent subject-predicate sequence (or *clause*) and those which are dependent. (Do not confuse modifying phrases with clauses.)

1. The shoes and stockings were of the same color.

2. This color, which was an unusual shade, was guaranteed not to fade.

3. The stockings were of finest silk, and the shoes had soles of heavy leather.

4. The booklet will tell you how to take delightful pictures in your home.

5. She excels in short-story writing and has just finished a novel.

6. The plan for the house grew and grew.

7. Anyone who can understand the natures of those three men can understand mine.

8. I leave it, nevertheless, in its former condition, and I do not

now write unadvisedly, and think it wrong to cancel my previous statement; but it must not so remain without a few added words.

9. Lastly, let us return to the lines respecting the power of the keys, because now we can understand them.

10. Neither does a great nation send its poor little boys to jail for stealing six walnuts; and allow its bankrupts to steal their hundreds of thousands with a bow; and its bankers, rich with poor men's savings, to close their doors; and large landed estates to be bought by men making their money by going with armed steamers up and down the China seas, selling opium at the cannon's mouth.

11. When men are rightly occupied, their amusement grows out of their work, as the color petals out of a fruitful flower; when they are faithfully helpful and compassionate, all their emotions become steady, deep, perpetual, and vivifying to the soul as the natural pulse to the body.

12. I speak, therefore, of good novels only, and our modern literature is particularly rich in types of such.

13. Well read, indeed, these books have serious use, being nothing less than treatises on moral anatomy and chemistry; studies of human nature in the elements of it.

14. I suppose few people reach the middle or later period of their age without having, at some moment of change or disappointment, felt the truth of those bitter words, and been startled by the fading of the sunshine from the cloud of their life, into the sudden agony of the knowledge that the fabric of it was as fragile as a dream, and the endurance of it as transient as the dew.

15. And this is right; but it is a pity that the accuracy insisted on is not greater and required to a serious purpose.

16. He was obviously a great artist.

17. I believe that they will come when the play is over.

18. Our friends left early, but we were sorry to see them go.

19. The destination of the ship was the west coast of Africa, then a favorite cruising and training ground for the navy.

20. When our instincts warn us to be cautious, they are often overridden by our enthusiasms, and disaster results.

8. *UNCONVENTIONAL SENTENCES*

There are ways of expression widely used by good authors which do not conform to the requirements just summarized, but which are still acceptable in standard prose writing. It is now time to consider these. We are not referring here to experimental or highly individualistic writing such as some modern authors have produced; however interesting, that is outside the scope of this book. Yet it might be pointed out that Gertrude Stein, James Joyce, and others have not written in less conventional manners because they *could not* write standard prose, but because they felt that their literary purpose demanded a special medium.

In college composition courses the purpose is different. One primary aim of the writer is to demonstrate his command of the formal, standard language—a medium which, by the way, will generally be found quite adequate to what he has to say, as it has been to many minds before his. This does not mean that he should merely imitate the giants of the past any more than that he should imitate the experimenters of today. Pope's dictum is an excellent one for the beginner:

> Be not the first by whom the new is tried,
> Nor yet the last to lay the old aside.

Not till the student has mastered standard prose, and still finds it inadequate to his purposes, is he ready for exploration outside its boundaries.

The word *unconventional*, then, refers here to the grammar of the sentences considered, not to their acceptability as standard English. They lack some things required by the conventional sentence, or they contain more than it may. Many of them are characteristic of speech and appear in writing when it imitates or tries to reproduce speech:

a. Exclamations and commands

Get it. Quick! Ouch! One round trip to Chicago. Ham on rye.

b. Questions

Why not? Who? What of it?

Others appear in formal writing for purposes of emphasis or economy:

c. Transitional phrases at the beginning of a new section of a composition

To proceed to the next issue. So much for the cause: now for the cure.

Nothing would be gained by saying *"Let us* proceed" . . . or "Now *we are ready* for the cure," etc.)

d. Words or phrases set off within a connected argument, exposition, or narrative:

But nowhere was there a tree or even a bush big as a garden lilac. And no water for the lightening canteens.

MARI SANDOZ, Cheyenne Autumn

At the very instant when they seemed absolutely impossible, smug, self-sufficient, sure they were right, they pulled something like this. Were willing to admit they had been wrong—and he remembered his own fights with his father, that ended in his father's beating him . . .

MAY SARTON, Birth of a Grandfather

It quite literally provided only "a suggestive starting point," and no more than that was promised in the various convention talks and panel discussions and NCTE journal articles during the decade after Fries' *Structure*. With one exception. [New paragraph:] The exception was a paper read. . . .

College English, January, 1965

Philosophy was widely thought to be more pleasing in dialogue form than in direct exposition. Thus Chaucer's *Melibee*.

CHARLES MUSCATINE, *Chaucer and the French Tradition*

These examples contain less than the conventional minimum requirements of the sentence, hence they are *sentence fragments*. Nevertheless, when skillfully used, they are acceptable.

While some sentence fragments can be justified, others clearly result simply from hasty writing or careless proofreading:

Having painstakingly examined the fabric for flaws and the wood for cracks.

All I ask the right to be heard.

My brother, who was in charge of the commissariat and forgot to buy salt.

So far we have seen only examples containing less than the conventional minimum requirements of the sentence; the following group contains more than the conventional maximum.

e. Short coordinate clauses closely connected in thought and separated only by commas.

These are usually used when the writer wishes to show contrast, to move rapidly between associated thoughts, or to make less of a separation than would be made by a colon or semicolon. When this is done inappropriately, or done through carelessness, and therefore makes a bad connection, a *comma splice* is produced—that is, the clauses seem merely spliced together with commas, rather than well connected with colons or semicolons. This is one of the chief signs of slovenly writing.

The following are examples of the *comma splice*:

He told me about it, however I did not believe him.

He did not seek to prove that the accident was an "act of God," of that he was convinced, but he wanted to collect the insurance.

Most of the work is now done, the rest I will finish next year.

In unskillful writing even the comma is sometimes left out between independent clauses; the results are *run-to-gether* or *fused* sentences.

Note by contrast the following successful uses of this kind of comma-splice structure:

Elizabeth was flushed and beautiful from the heat of the oven, and the sight of her overwhelmed me, she was so much lovelier than all my yearning dreams of her in absence had been.

KENNETH ROBERTS, *Northwest Passage*

Man fixed the association of colors with grief and gladness, he made ornaments the insignia of office, he ordained that fabric should grace the majesty of power.

AGNES REPPLIER, *Americans and Others*

The beautiful big valve lit up, the motor whirred.

RICHARD HUGHES, *In Hazard*

Note that just because they are unconventional, sentences like these are conspicuous and should therefore be used sparingly. Though some conservative writers avoid them, they are established in standard usage. Handled skillfully, they should not be objectionable and are added resources to the writer. But do not use them unless you are prepared to justify their use.

EXERCISE VI

Prove that you have mastered the requirements of the conventional sentence by revising these sentences from student themes. *a.* Which are *comma splices, run-together* sentences, and *fragments*? *b.* Put the sentences into conventional sentence form. c. After considering each carefully, do you think any might be justified in its present form? Explain.

1. Supposing that a child has ideas. For building a toy.

2. This sort of person is injuring himself to the extent that he is becoming decidedly narrow-minded, he is not able to find things out for himself.

3. One can easily see this by looking at the different types of government there are in the world. The United States with her democracy, Russia with her communism, Spain with her fascism.

4. From Robinson's essay, "On Various Kinds of Thinking," I find that I am very normal in my thinking in respect to reveries, practical decisions, and rationalizing, these are insignificant however, to creative thought, a type of progressive thinking.

5. After many hardships as a result of which the brother, guides, and woman were killed.

6. The top office said, "Cut out half your organization by June 30." We did just that in a period of a month. Twenty branch companies wiped out like trees in a forest fire.

7. The wealthy have control of all the necessities, industries, and political powers of the community and compel the poor to do their bidding. Yet how could or how can we remedy this, the author of "A Plea for Equality" says this inequality leads in the end to revolution.

8. Under the present conditions of environment and education in the slums, the poor have an excuse for not improving their conditions, they do not receive a fair opportunity.

9. I think that it has been a long time since men have been moved by these ideals. Except, perhaps, the ideal of the family which has lasted longer than the others.

10. Some of the men who were leaders in the strike movement are sorry now that they were mixed up in it. They find they are getting more work to do. That the boss is getting tougher.

11. When a person does things because his grandfather and his grandfather before him did them. Or in other words his life is ruled by custom.

12. There are many different types of people in this world

Some that are easy to get along with and others that are not so easy to get along with.

13. I would not say that rational thinking is altogether harmful, however, it remains to be seen that creative thought is much more advantageous.

14. It is by this sort of demonstration that new members are gained. A practice which is definitely undemocratic.

15. It isn't because my environment, parents, or contact with other people prevent it in fact, they encourage it. It isn't because of time I have had a sufficient quantity of it.

9. WRITING GOOD SENTENCES

As has been suggested, the types of sentences you use should depend on the kind of writing you are doing. A literary purpose will call for a wider variety of sentences, more closely adapted to the nuances of idea and emotion, than everyday expository prose will demand. But no matter where, a short, sharp sentence will differ in effect from a long, deliberate one; a compact one from a loose one; a slow or heavy one from a smooth, rapid one.

The independent clause, always the basic unit of expression, may be used by the skillful writer as a skeleton to be fleshed out in a variety of ways, as he needs to add details to the bare statement, keeping them organically related to it. Let us follow the process through which a writer might go in choosing, from many possibilities, the kind of sentence he can best use. Perhaps he begins with two simple sentences whose relationship is not apparent:

> Man is the most perverse of creatures. Man is the most intelligent of creatures.

He first tries to show the relationship by means of the word *but*, and makes a compound sentence:

> Man is the most intelligent of creatures, but he is the most perverse.

This balances well, yet it strikes him that the words *he is* are unnecessary. He therefore omits them and has a simple sentence with a compound complement. The result now seems to him a little too obvious; he does not want to moralize so much as to show the paradox. If he merely puts the two facts side by side, he will make his point. So he changes *but* to *and*, and has this:

> *Man is the most intelligent of creatures, and the most perverse.*

This pleases him, but to make sure that he is not overlooking something better, he tries it as a complex sentence:

> *Though man is the most intelligent of creatures, he is the most perverse.*

Clear enough, but still rather more obvious than he wants. He tries it as a simple sentence with a participial modifier:

> *Man, having the most intelligence, is yet the most perverse of creatures.*

This seems somewhat affected, and the rhythm is clumsy. He amends the participial modifier to an appositional construction:

> *Man, the most intelligent of creatures, is yet the most perverse.*

That corrects the rhythm, but not the affectation, so he returns to his third attempt, with its brevity and easy movement; he substitutes a dash for the comma to point up the paradox slightly, and has, as a final epigrammatic result:

> *Man is the most intelligent of creatures—and the most perverse.*

This process, as we have followed it, is very laborious, and certainly one could not apply it to the writing of every sentence in a college theme! But first, it is not necessary for every sentence—only for those which, as the student revises his first draft, seem not to suit their context or his intention. And second, the actual process of revision is not as laborious as it appears in this text. The mind works rapidly, and with practice a writer sees the problem more quickly and solves it efficiently. The solution which this writer arrived at may not please everyone; such things are to some extent questions of opinion. But the important matter is that the student be aware of the variety of ways in which he may manipulate his sentences and that he improve steadily in adapting his choice to his purpose.

So much for the positive side. On the negative, there are certain tendencies common to inexperienced writers which it would be well to be aware of and to avoid. The rest of this chapter is given to a discussion and illustration of the chief things to do and to avoid in order to write good sentences.

a. Correctness

Before thinking of writing *well*, you must be sure you are writing *correctly*. In English, as in any living language, certain things are unequivocally right or wrong; certain others vary with circumstances; and a few, being in the process of change, cannot be flatly legislated about. For the latter two kinds, refer to the Glossary of Usage (Chapter IX). For the first, refer to the Grammar (Chapter VI). In English grammar there are rules of *concord:* singular subjects must be used with singular verbs, plural with plural; reference words must agree with their antecedents in certain ways. (See Chapter VI, **G9–13.**) Though these are not strictly matters of sentence writing, errors in them are so frequent that some examples may be given here.

1. Be sure that subject and verb agree in number.

Remember that a compound subject is plural. (See also Chapter VI, **G9a**.)

WRONG: Robinson's ideas on creative thinking seems to be more for the future and provide no solution for our present needs.

RIGHT: Robinson's ideas on creative thinking seem to be more for the future and provide no solution for our present needs.

WRONG: Desire for profit is one of the things that encourages economic activity.

RIGHT: Desire for profit is one of the things that encourage economic activity.

WRONG: In contrast to these fine qualities was his appearance and habits of cleanliness.

RIGHT: In contrast to these fine qualities were his appearance and habits of cleanliness.

WRONG: The international situation is one of the factors that has been engaging our attention.

RIGHT: The international situation is one of the factors that have been engaging our attention.

OR: The international situation is one factor that has been engaging our attention.

2. See that the antecedent of every pronoun is unmistakably clear.

Pronouns may be made to refer most clearly to their antecedents by being placed close to them. Sometimes even placing the antecedent close to the pronoun will still not make a satisfactory sentence, and the whole sentence or passage will have to be revised so that only one noun remains as a plausible antecedent. Make sure that the words *former, latter, other* are unmistakable in their reference. (See also Chapter VI, **G9b**.)

FAULTY: Most manufacturers put several pads of rubber on the frame where the body is bolted on, and this filters out the noises. Also to take care of vibration from the engine, it is mounted on rubber.

REVISED: To filter out noises, most manufacturers put several pads of rubber between frame and body where these are bolted together. Moreover, to eliminate vibration, they mount the engine on rubber.

FAULTY: With a policy of internationalism, it gives the United States a chance to keep abreast of other nations in scientific, commercial, and cultural advancement. Without this we would undoubtedly fall far behind in matters of this sort.

REVISED: A policy of internationalism will give the United States a chance to keep abreast of other nations in scientific, commercial, and cultural advancement. Without such a policy we would undoubtedly fall far behind.

FAULTY: Had it not been for his ability to influence the students and the other members of the faculty, his dream of a great university would never have been realized.

REVISED: Had it not been for his ability to influence the students and his colleagues on the faculty, his dream of a great university would never have been realized.

3. Avoid shifts in the person of pronouns.

(See Chapter I, T9, on *logical point of view*; see also Chapter II, ¶11.)

WRONG: It feels as if I have left all the things I love behind and have come to a place where no one even notices your presence.
RIGHT: It feels as if I have left behind all the things I love, and have come to a place where no one even notices my presence.
OR: You feel as if you have left behind all the things you love, and have come to a place where no one even notices your presence.

4. Avoid inconsistencies in the tenses of verbs.

(See Chapter II, ¶11; see also Chapter VI, G11.) Notice that the first example illustrates a frequent type of error.

WRONG: If he would have known the day before, he would have been able to leave in time.

RIGHT: If he had known the day before, he would have been able to leave in time.

WRONG: If every army private stops and asks *why* every time an order is given him, not much would be accomplished.

RIGHT: If every army private stopped and asked *why* every time an order was given him, not much would be accomplished.

OR: If every army private stops to ask *why* every time an order is given him, not much is accomplished.

WRONG: The interests of the majority have been satisfied, or in a few cases tried to have been satisfied.

RIGHT: The interests of the majority have been satisfied or, in a few cases, the attempt has been made to satisfy them.

Similar failures of concord, occurring particularly with collective nouns, indefinite pronouns, and case forms of pronouns, are more extensively treated in Chapter VI. See also *parallelism*, S9c.

b. Clear Modification

A *modifier* is any element which, added to another word, alters its meaning somewhat without changing it basically. The term includes adjectives, adverbs, or any word, phrase, or clause that functions like an adjective or adverb.

In English sentences, phrasal and clausal modifiers (particularly adverbial ones) have a certain freedom of movement. We may say:

> A man must work *to be elected*,   OR
> *To be elected*, a man must work,   OR
> A man, *to be elected*, must work.

A clause (such as *wherever he may be*) may behave similarly. Which position the writer chooses for his modifier will depend on several things—clarity, emphasis, rhythm, etc.—which become ever more important for him to attend to as he puts more clauses together. The misplacing of modifiers often leads to clumsiness, even to ambiguity.

1. In general, avoid the insertion of modifiers between subject and verb, and between verb and object.

FAULTY: Lord Bryce, to describe and explain democracy, has given illustrations from six countries.
REVISED: To describe and explain democracy, Lord Bryce has selected six countries as illustrations.

FAULTY: He must decide, within a couple of weeks, on a fraternity of which all in his estimation have a great many faults.
REVISED: Within a couple of weeks he must decide on a fraternity, though all, in his estimation, have a great many faults.

2. In general, place subordinate clauses near the words they modify.

FAULTY: This does not mean that the children should be neglected and made to do everything for themselves, as many modern parents think.
REVISED: This does not mean, as many modern parents think, that the children should be neglected and made to do everything for themselves.

FAULTY: I secured an office job soon after I was out of high school, which lasted throughout the summer.
REVISED: Soon after I was out of high school, I secured an office job which lasted throughout the summer.

3. Place phrases as near as possible to the words they modify; if they are independent, place them at one of the extremities of the sentence.

FAULTY: His warmth, personality, and sincerity made, in my opinion, Albert Schweitzer the truly great man he was.
REVISED: In my opinion, his warmth, personality, and sincerity made Albert Schweitzer the truly great man he was.

FAULTY: In the city children frequently play ball in the streets where traffic is heavy. Records show how many children are killed each year through this practice by automobiles.
REVISED: Records show how many children are killed by automobiles each year because of this practice.

4. Place participial, gerund, and infinitive phrases where they will cause no ambiguity; or convert them to finite verbs.

(See Chapter VI, **G5b.2** and **G5d**, for definitions of these terms.)

FAULTY: When visiting Mr. Thomas not long before he left us, he compared himself to Oliver Wendell Holmes' "last leaf."
REVISED: When I was visiting Mr. Thomas not long before he left us, he compared himself to Oliver Wendell Holmes' "last leaf."

FAULTY: Returning to Robinson's essay, we find that the author deplores this credulous acceptance without questioning either source or correctness.
REVISED: Returning to Robinson's essay, we find that the author deplores a credulous acceptance of ideas which questions neither their source nor their correctness.

The faulty sentences just given are not clear because they have *dangling* or misrelated modifiers. This means that the modifier, in each case, hangs loosely—what it is intended to modify is either not clear or not expressed. In the first, who was *visiting*? In the second, who is *questioning*? This information must be given to the reader through proper placing of the modifier or through use of some other method of expression. As might be expected, this kind of loose modification often occurs in speech. But in writing, the ambiguity which it produces must be carefully avoided.

The following points may be observed about dangling modifiers:

Certain participial phrases (equivalent to adverbs) have become idiomatic without the noun or pronoun subject being expressed, since it is felt to be either self-evident or unimportant.

EXAMPLE: Even allowing for hasty preparation, this definition involves a contradiction of terms.

EXAMPLE: Generally speaking, the election indicated widespread dissatisfaction.

Ambiguity seldom results when the participial construction is followed by a possessive or pronominal adjective.

EXAMPLE: In learning to write, your first problem is to clarify your own ideas.

EXAMPLE: Having given this warning, one's duty to the reader is done.

Danger of ambiguity arises when the participial phrase includes nouns or pronouns which may be confused with the subject of the clause.

FAULTY: Questioning the validity of his belief, he at once gives substantial evidence of its incorrectness.

(Notice that here we do not know whether *his* and *he* refer to the same person or to two people.)

REVISED: Questioning the validity of Wright's belief, Smith at once gives substantial evidence of its incorrectness.

The greatest ambiguity comes when the subject of the clause seems to be (but is not) the subject of the participle.

FAULTY: Opening the door, the picture window becomes visible.

This is a ridiculous statement; the window cannot open the door.

REVISED: Opening the door, you can see the picture window.
OR: As you open the door, you can see the picture window.
OR: When the door is opened, the picture window can be seen.

One of the writer's first concerns must be to avoid confused, ambiguous, or loose expression. The participial or gerund phrase is often a source of danger; but, used carefully, it can be a valuable resource by which the writer may achieve compactness and economy.

5. Avoid placing a clause, phrase, or word modifier between two parts of a sentence when it is not clear to which part the modifier is intended to apply. This is often called a "squinting construction" because it seems to look two ways at once.

FAULTY: I was told when it was noon the boat would sail.
REVISED: I was told that the boat would sail when it was noon.
OR: When it was noon, I was told the boat would sail.

FAULTY: Students who fail in nine cases out of ten have defective reading ability.
REVISED: In nine cases out of ten, students who fail have defective reading ability.

FAULTY: The automobile involved in the accident today was found to have defective brakes.
REVISED: The automobile involved in the accident was found, today, to have defective brakes.
OR: The automobile involved in today's accident was found to have defective brakes.

6. When a single-word modifier might be understood to apply to more than one element of the sentence, place it so that no uncertainty of meaning will arise.

This situation develops with such qualifying adverbs as *merely, nearly, just, almost, hardly, even, scarcely, quite,* etc., which might modify either the verb or any secondary word or phrase in the predicate. Such adverbs commonly occur before the verb in informal or spoken language.

INFORMAL: We just had enough time to catch the train.
FORMAL: We had just enough time to catch the train.

INFORMAL: Our team didn't even score once.
FORMAL: Our team did not score even once.

7. The adverb only is a special case among single-word modifiers.

It may often be interpreted either as an adjective, modifying the subject, or as an adverb, modifying the verb.

EXAMPLE: I only had five dollars.

This sentence is, of course, never understood to mean *I and no one else had five dollars*, and in the form quoted it is common both in written and spoken English.

A second type of construction occurs when *only* modifies a clause or phrase introduced by the verb.

EXAMPLE: Its expression can only be caught by side glimpses.

As here, *only* is frequently found before the main verb, both in spoken and written English, even though not entirely clear.

When you are puzzled about the position of *only*, or any other adverb for that matter, the important thing is to leave no question as to the exact meaning of your sentence. Remember, here, the differences between spoken and written English. A sentence such as "I can only believe what I have been told" could, in spoken English, clearly indicate the function of *only* through word stress:

I can only *believe* what I have been told. (*Only* modifies *believe*. I can only *believe* it; I cannot disbelieve it or put it to a test. I must accept it on faith.)

I can only believe *what I have been told*. (*Only* modifies *what I have been told*. I can believe only this and nothing more.)

The writer, lacking the aid that word stress gives to

meaning, compensates for it by placing the adverb where its function as a modifier will be clearly evident.

I can only believe what I have been told. (*Only* modifies *believe.*)

I can believe only what I have been told. (*Only* modifies *what I have been told.*)

EXERCISE VII

Revise the following sentences so that the modification is clear:

1. A person in a steel plant only works eight hours a day for five days a week except those who hold higher positions.
2. The colonists have not offered to pay for the land, but have chosen to take it by force, a principle which I oppose greatly.
3. Having been raised in an atmosphere of religion, the natural trend of thought for my mind would be religious.
4. Liberty is that state in which every one is able to do as he desires with only the restraint of his conscience.
5. The time for graduation comes, and I do not care particularly about entering the profession. I could secure a position with many companies because of my knowledge of law.
6. Looking over the past few weeks, though I know I'm undoubtedly silly, I realize that a great many of my thoughts were centered around these lectures.
7. They have taken away the power over the tariff from the House of Representatives and the Senate, which has been surrendered to the Secretary of State.
8. Also on most campuses there are places of religious interest of almost any denomination.
9. Although in reading one of his books there may appear to be a doubtful light cast on one of the chief characters, he may be assured that it will be quite satisfactorily erased before its completion.
10. We do ever so many things as a matter of course without thinking about them just because those before us did them.

11. The treatment at the time for consumption was no air; in winter her windows were sealed with paper; and copious doses of opium.

12. Many shows on television this season in my opinion should be considered among the best in television.

13. For example, when entering an elevator, the oldest graduate waiting to return on duty, though she may have only arrived like the group of others, as the elevator reaches the floor, has supreme preference, while younger graduates and students who undoubtedly have more work to accomplish may be kept waiting for ten or fifteen minutes.

14. Unlike the average young person of today, my favorite author is a nonfiction writer.

15. The player who is offside in the end harms only his own team.

c. Clear Parallelism

When things are to be compared, contrasted, or shown as similar, the parts of the sentence should be constructed alike, so that the parallel in the grammar may make clear the parallel in the content.

1. Make certain that related or parallel elements such as begin . . . end, do . . . don't, possible . . . impossible **are treated consistently.**

FAULTY: This starts him on a ring career, and ends up, of course, being world champion.
REVISED: This starts him on a ring career, and he ends, of course, as the world champion.
OR: This starts him on a ring career, which brings him in the end, of course, to the world championship.

FAULTY: It tries or does get people to thinking what they believe or don't believe about the government and its projects.
REVISED: It tries—with some success—to get people to think about what they believe and what they don't believe concerning the government and its projects.

117

2. When two parallel constructions govern a single sentence element, avoid placing the single element between the two that are parallel.

FAULTY: This sort of inequality cannot be abolished because of its very nature and should not be nullified by a class of false leaders.

REVISED: Because of its very nature, this sort of inequality cannot be abolished and should not be nullified by a class of false leaders.

3. Make certain that correlatives (either . . . or, neither . . . nor, both . . . and, not only . . . but also) **are followed by elements in the same construction.**

FAULTY: When they do go to church, it is only because they have to go, and not of their own desire.

REVISED: When they do go to church, it is only because they have to go, and not because they want to.

FAULTY: The book was not only well-written but amused me.

REVISED: The book was not only well-written but amusing.

Avoid the ambiguity that results from placing not only . . . but **as in the following sentence:**

FAULTY: Charles Dickens lends not only a melancholy air to his novels, but through his humorous characters brings forth some of the more likeable of human traits.

REVISED: Charles Dickens not only lends a melancholy air to his novels, but brings forth, by means of his humorous characters, some of the more likeable of human traits.

Though the reason is . . . because **is common in speech, in writing its redundancy should be avoided by using instead** the reason is . . . that.

EXAMPLE: The *reason* he came *was because* he wanted to see his father.

REVISED: The *reason* he came *was that* he wanted to see his father.

EXAMPLE: Just *because* you do not like him *is no reason* to condemn him.
REVISED: The fact *that* you do not like him *is no reason* to condemn him.

The use of *because* is best justified when *reason* is separated from *is* by long sentence elements. In such situations *because* emphasizes the causal relationship being expressed.

EXAMPLE: *The* chief *reason* why it seems so dismal an absurdity to send a task force to the area *is because* it could only serve. . . .

4. In formal writing it is customary to repeat introductory words before parallel sentence elements.

This applies to prepositions, articles, conjunctions, *to* before the infinitive, and at times even to auxiliary verbs.

LESS FORMAL: Labor was organizing itself in America and England.
MORE FORMAL: Labor was organizing itself *in* America and *in* England.

LESS FORMAL: The singular and plural of the past tense were not always based on the same principal part.
MORE FORMAL: *The* singular and *the* plural of the past tense were not always based on the same principal part.

LESS FORMAL: We were allowed to remain and attend the special service.
MORE FORMAL: We were allowed *to* remain and *to* attend the special service.

LESS FORMAL: We were notified that they were ready and would enter the stage at once.
MORE FORMAL: We were notified *that* they were ready and *that* they would enter the stage at once.

119

EXERCISE VIII

Revise the following sentences wherever necessary so that parallel constructions are clear and consistent.

1. We of television do not hope to compete with newspapers in the richness of detail which they can afford. We can only bring history as it happens—and the experience of hearing an English prime minister make history is a thrill that it can never bring.

2. Every trivial plan or trip that the President makes or does gets in the newspapers.

3. Persuasion often is as effective, sometimes more, as physical force.

4. His greatest assets and possibly the biggest reason for his popularity is his democratic ideas.

5. However, everyone has a position and is much happier than they were under the old feudal system.

6. On this day one is supposed to rest, attend services, and above all not to write.

7. Not only does it create a restful feeling, but also a carefree mood.

8. I may say that while some people deny it, the fact is that the early potato is perishable. While some people disagree with this statement, it is a fact, and they are taken off the market before your potatoes come in.

9. Every state needs prestige among other ones that compose the civilized world. Prestige is nothing more than having all the other states admiring your social system.

10. As a general rule, the program or artist with the greatest following is considered superior for no other reason than that of its fan mail, while an actually better program may be held in considerably less esteem.

d. Effectiveness

One thing every writer must learn is to put himself in the place of the reader. What is in the writer's mind can never be understood until he expresses it. And though it may seem clear to him, who knows his own thought best, the real test lies in his making it clear to another. He should therefore remember that the clarity and effectiveness of his ideas depend heavily upon their *combination* and their *sequence*.

1. Avoid a long series of coordinate clauses all connected by the conjunctions but **and** and; **they may become monotonous.**

FAULTY: In past days aristocratic women could be recognized by their clothes, but now the great majority of women have been educated in their tastes and a great many women today dress very well and still they could not be called aristocratic.

REVISED: In past days aristocratic women could be recognized by their clothes. Today the great majority of women have become educated in their tastes, and a great many of them dress very well. Yet these women could not therefore be called aristocratic.

2. Avoid a series of involved dependent and independent clauses which confuse the reader. Break them up.

FAULTY: Although I had often imagined that my work in the U.S. Forestry Service would be an aid to society, I see now the difference between aiding society and bettering society, and that I can better society only through creative thinking, which I must learn.

REVISED: Before now I had often imagined that by working in the U.S. Forestry Service I would be aiding society. Now I am able to see the distinction between aiding society and bettering society. I can better society only through creative thinking, a power which I must develop.

3. Avoid compound sentences which contain clauses having little or no logical relationship with one another.

FAULTY: The Scotch are a thrifty race and they are not musically inclined.

Note that, unless you are implying that thrifty peoples are unmusical, showing some relationship between thrift and musical inclination, these ideas are not sufficiently close to be placed in a coordinate relationship.

REVISED: The Scots are a thrifty race. They are not musically inclined.

FAULTY: Shelley was a poet of the Romantic School and he went to Italy for his health in 1812.
REVISED: Shelley, a Romantic poet, went to Italy for his health in 1812.

4. Avoid illogical and incomplete comparisons.

ILLOGICAL: In college, the teachers are less friendly than high school.
IMPROVED: The teachers in college are less friendly than those in high school.

ILLOGICAL: I like Edward Albee's plays better than Tennessee Williams.
IMPROVED: I like Edward Albee's plays better than Tennessee Williams'.

INCOMPLETE: The users of this toothpaste have 30% fewer cavities.
COMPLETE: Users of this toothpaste, after a one-year testing period, have 30% fewer cavities than the users of any other leading toothpaste.

INCOMPLETE: The dorm proctor gives me a harder time than Jim.
COMPLETE: The dorm proctor gives me a harder time than he does Jim.

5. Use grammatical subordination to place ideas in their proper relationship.

FAULTY: Their parents have always helped them decide matters, so that the children depend upon other people too much.

Note that the second clause, containing the idea which the writer is trying to emphasize, is grammatically subordinate to the first. This is "upside-down subordination." The sentence will be more logical if the second clause is made the chief or independent clause.

REVISED: Since their parents have always helped them decide matters, the children depend upon other people rather than upon themselves.

6. Unless you wish to express a rapid tempo and tense feeling, avoid a series of short, simple sentences, all built on the same pattern.

WEAK: These television programs include all types of entertainment. Not all of these are serious or educational. In fact, some of them are humorous.
BETTER: All types of entertainment, humorous as well as serious or educational, are included in these television programs.

WEAK: Of course, this question is a matter of opinion. My opinion is divided.
BETTER: Of course, this is a question (or matter) of opinion— and mine is divided.

7. To make a sentence more effective, place important words at the beginning, or out of their common position.

COMMONPLACE: They find now that their early training becomes valuable to them.
BETTER: Their early training, they now find, becomes valuable to them.
OR, *if the time element is the important thing:* Now it is that their early training becomes valuable to them.
OR: Now it is that they discover the value of their early training.

Before beginning a sentence with a conjunction, consider whether it will weaken or strengthen your writing. Certain conjunctions placed at the beginning of a sentence tend to make the whole statement sound like an afterthought.

WEAK: Many famous plays and motion pictures are presented on this program. Also famous people from all walks of life are interviewed between the acts.

BETTER: Many famous plays and motion pictures are presented on this program. Famous people from all walks of life are interviewed between the acts.

Some writers consciously use a conjunction at the beginning of a sentence as a strengthening device, usually to point a contrast. (This is easily overdone.)

EXAMPLE: And the delegation of legislative powers to be exercised by the executive department is the same delegation of congressional powers that all Democrats and leaders in Congress previously condemned as vicious legislation, unwarranted, and dangerous to our form of government.

8. Items in series should be so arranged that the strongest or most important item comes at the end.

WEAK: The news which is distributed over the radio is unbiased, accurate, and up-to-date.

BETTER: The news which is distributed over the radio is up-to-date, accurate, and unbiased.

WEAK: The game was close; the weather was good; the crowd was enthusiastic.

BETTER: The weather was good; the crowd was enthusiastic, the game was close.

9. Parallelism or balance in sentence structure may aid in making a sentence more effective.

WEAK: I do say that they bring into the limelight all of the organization's numerous faults and keep the good that it has done in the background.

BETTER: I do say that they bring into the limelight all of the faults of the organization and keep in the background all the good that it has done.

10. A sentence can often be made more effective by using a periodic structure, one in which the main clause is not completed until the end.

Avoid placing a weak or inconclusive statement or word at the end of the sentence.

WEAK: A Sunday-night presentation is assured of a fair chance to gain a listening public because of all the people who congregate around their television sets that evening.
BETTER: Because of all the people who congregate around their television sets on Sunday evening, a program given on that night is assured of a fair chance to gain a listening public.

A few final words about sentences:

In the foregoing section we have had to deal with sentences in isolation. But the student must never forget that in writing they go in groups. No effective writing can possibly be done by merely joining a string of sentences together, however good each may be individually. Every sentence in a composition is a part of the larger whole and must be considered as such, especially during the process of revision.

In the formal writing of the past, sentences were longer and more elaborate than they tend to be today. Modern style is on the whole more rapid and direct: proportionally more simple sentences are used, a good many compound ones, fewer complex ones. In fact, for the contemporary taste, the periodic sentence, in which the meaning is suspended until the end, is easily overused. Nevertheless, the more elaborate sentences have their place; with them a compact and highly integrated style may be achieved; without them, indeed, intellectual writing would be much weakened.

Nobody can tell you exactly how many of the various kinds of sentences are desirable in given circumstances;

this is a matter of judgment which can be learned only through reading successful writing and aiming at similar effects oneself.

REVIEW EXERCISE

Revise each of the following sentences. Be able to point out the principles of sentence structure which have been violated.

1. Madame Récamier, after years of close association, was with him, old and blind when he died.

2. The world and times are constantly changing, and with the new times comes photography.

3. Also the world as a whole should benefit by this wise teaching.

4. Children whose parents look after them and do many things for them often cannot do their own thinking.

5. Rex Harrison, who plays the part of the phonetician Professor Higgins, tries to teach a cockney flower girl about the ways of the English upper class when they go to the races at Ascot.

6. My last few summers have been spent working as cashier and salesgirl in a small specialty shop, which was considered a part of the necessary practical experience I must have in order to understand the inner working of my chosen vocation.

7. If no member of the Board was heard, it was because they did not care to be heard.

8. Neither of these give a very complete nor accurate picture of the profession whose school I plan to enter and major in however.

9. If many of the citizens of the country felt as this man does, it would be relatively simple, with a lack of law and order, for someone to set up a tyranny, according to the conservatives.

10. This is a surrender of legislative powers no less and no more than the surrender made by the Republican administration and Congress, and which all Democrats condemned in the name of Jefferson and Jackson, as a dangerous invasion of the Constitution, and would open the way for abuse.

11. After getting up in the morning to face an hour and a half ride to work, and after this ride to endure a hot, stuffy office, isn't my idea of a life profession.

12. Each of Iago's subjects seems to be more pliable than the other, only one does it knowingly whereas the others work right into his plans unknowingly.

13. Only recently has the average student, the independent, been given a place on the class election ballot, and even at that his number has been small when compared to the ratio of independents to fraternity men.

14. The night of the formal dinners arrived. The girls made a lovely appearance in their formals, and as we gazed at them we realized we wanted to someday be a part of all these grand persons about us.

15. Space travel does not appeal to me at all because of the thought of getting to the moon.

16. It was good-bye night for the boys at Alpha Zeta Psi fraternity yesterday as Tommy Welch's brothers formally dined him and sent him back to Hennepin University, an engraved studio clock to remind him of the days he spent with them.

17. In the Senate Commerce Committee, in connection with maritime affairs, we have heard of many such disputes.

18. They built this project, and after they had it built they did not know what to do with the people that were to live in it, notwithstanding the fact, as I called attention through several other communications, that good houses were remaining vacant in that vicinity.

IV. The Word

1. WORDS

WE speak and write in sentences, but words are the stuff of which they are made. Throughout all history words have fascinated vast numbers of people. When the Old English poet set about the composition of a poem, he was said to "unlock his word hoard." Robert Louis Stevenson was called a word-smith and the poet, William Morris, spoke of himself as a word-spinner. The Gospel of St. John begins with the statement, "In the beginning was the Word," which again serves as an index of importance, irrespective of how the clause is to be interpreted.

In our modern society words continue to have a powerful influence. They play a great part in prompting us to buy and sell, to vote, to go to church, to choose our friends. Wars are threatened and fought to the tune of slogans and propaganda. It is not too much to say that the peace of the world and the well-being of any society depend not only upon the responsible use of words but also upon their critical reception and comprehension.

Aside from this, words are important to everyone in his role as an individual. In his recent book, *The Origins and Development of the English Language* (New York, 1964), Thomas Pyles has put the case very succinctly: "The fact is that, if we are going to be able to talk about anything very far beyond our day-to-day, bread and butter living, if we are going to associate in an easy manner with cultivated people, if we are going to read books which such people have found to be important and significant, then we must have at our command a great many words that the man in the street and the man with the hoe neither know nor use." There is, moreover, a high degree of personal satisfaction in being able to use words effectively. The fluent speaker and the exact writer are admired for their ability to express their thoughts and feelings easily and precisely.

2. OUR VARIOUS VOCABULARIES

The English language has a very large stock of words. The larger dictionaries generally record about half a million, and there are in addition other words which, for various reasons, are not included. At the same time this extensive word stock or lexicon poses certain problems for anyone who attempts to improve his mastery of it. In the first place, it consists of two quite distinct classes of words, *popular* and *learned*; and these are somewhat more sharply divided than is the case in many languages.

The popular words are those which we use in ordinary conversation. We have learned them from members of our family, our playmates, and others with whom we associate every day. For the most part they have to do with our daily activities, with the ordinary things of life. Everyone knows them and uses them all of the time. They are of the people, and for this reason they are called *popular*. At the same time the English language includes a large number of words which most of us learn from books, lectures, or possibly the formal conversation of educated speakers. We use such words rarely in the intimate conversations of the family circle or on the other informal occasions which for the most part fill our days. The following quotation from Greenough and Kittredge's *Words and Their Ways in English Speech* will serve to illustrate the two types:

We may describe a girl as "lively" or as "vivacious." In the first case, we are using a native English formation from the familiar noun "life." In the latter, we are using a Latin derivative which has precisely the same meaning. Yet the atmosphere of the two words is quite different. No one ever got the adjective "lively" out of a book. It is a part of everybody's vocabulary. We cannot remember a time when we did not know it, and we feel sure that we learned it before we were able to read. On the other hand, we must have passed several years of our lives before learning the word "vivacious." We may even remember the first time we saw it in print or heard it from some grownup friend who was talking over our childish heads. Both "lively" and "vivacious" are good English words, but "lively" is popular and "vivacious" is learned.[1]

Thus, the popular vocabulary consists of short words, usually of native words, words which have many meanings. For the most part, the learned vocabulary contains longer words, words of foreign origin, often though not necessarily somewhat more specific in their meanings.

Another way of looking at the English lexicon is to recognize the distinction between what is called a *passive* or *recognition* vocabulary and an *active* or *use* vocabulary. The recognition vocabulary comprises those words which we recognize on seeing or hearing them but which we do not ordinarily employ. The use vocabulary includes those words which we regularly use in speaking or writing. The recognition vocabulary is by far the larger. According to some estimates, it is about three times the size of the use vocabulary.

3. *IMPROVING DICTION*

Diction means the use of words. Good diction involves the choice of the best available words for the speaker's or writer's purpose. Success in these choices often makes the difference between merely passable writing and good writing.

[1] J. B. Greenough and G. L. Kittredge, *Words and Their Ways in English Speech* (New York, 1901), p. 19. Reprinted by permission of the Macmillan Company.

As a writer, you want to take hold of your reader, to capture his interest, to make him read willingly, even eagerly and with pleasure. How is this to be done? First of all you must make sure that you do not drive your reader away. If you bore him, annoy him, confuse or disappoint him, he is all too likely to shy away from your writing. You will hold him only if your writing is fresh, clear, and attractive. The words you choose to employ are important in developing these qualities.

The most frequent difficulties which students have with respect to diction arise from three causes:

1. Their stock of words is too scanty.
2. Words which they do have are not always accurately employed.
3. Words are used in violation of canons of taste and style.

4. ACQUIRING MORE WORDS

We have already seen that the English language contains a large number of words divided into two quite well-defined layers, the learned and the popular. It is also evident that the total lexicon of the language is much larger than that of any person who speaks or writes in it. Every speaker has a recognition and a use vocabulary, the first of these more extensive than the second. Anyone who wants to develop a larger vocabulary must work within this context, giving particular attention to three phases of it:

1. He must increase the range and extent of his recognition vocabulary.
2. He must transfer words from his recognition to his use vocabulary.
3. He must develop the ability to form new words when the occasion demands, particularly by taking advantage

of the rich supply of word-forming elements in the language.

We may best begin by asking ourselves how we have learned the words we already know, even when we were not trying consciously to add to our stock of them. Generally we do so through reading or hearing them and then coming to some conclusion about them from the context in which they appear. Suppose you were to hear someone say, at different times in the course of the day, "Turn on the spauntler," "The spauntler isn't working," "I must buy a new spauntler." Though you did not see the object referred to, you would immediately begin to work out, from just the words themselves, some understanding of the new term. Your first guess might be that a spauntler was a device of some kind to control—what? Electricity, gas, water? Or perhaps that it was an appliance—a shower, a stove, a musical instrument? Now if you could know the physical context (living room, back yard, basement, bedroom), that would limit the possibilities; or if you could know what happened when the spauntler was turned on. Then at last you hear the statement, "Since the spauntler was broken, her hair was wet and she was late for the party." Now you feel fairly certain that a spauntler is a hair-dryer.

We learn by the same process with words in print. In this sentence, for example, one meets a word for the first time: "He was sedulous in paying court to the people." Since *paying court to the people* implies a certain deliberate self-application, one may surmise that *sedulous* is closely related. Later, one comes upon a reference to "the Algonquin Indians, of whose language he had been so sedulous a student,"—and again the context suggests application or diligence. And then one reads in Robert Louis Stevenson's famous account of how he taught himself to write, "I have played the sedulous ape to Hazlitt, to Lamb, to Wordsworth." By now one may be relatively sure that *sedulous,* clearly an adjective, implies application of a constant or repeated kind. Consulting the dictionary, one finds given as synonyms *assiduous, persistent.*

Since words usually have more than one shade of meaning, you will need to meet a new word a dozen or more times before feeling that your grasp of it is not one-sided. Further, a word should become firmly fixed in your recognition vocabularly before it is transferred to the active vocabulary. This will take little time for some words, much more for others. If your newly-acquired word has an atmosphere of familiarity and ease about it, you will soon begin to employ it both in speech and in writing. If it is a long word, an unusual word, a learned word, or one which you do not use very often, it will remain passive in your mind provided you do not forget it entirely.

Students are often advised to look up in the dictionary all unfamiliar words encountered in reading; record such words in a notebook or card index; and then put them to use as quickly as possible. An excellent plan—except that scarcely anyone ever follows it long enough.

It is all very well to say, "Look up every word you don't know," but suppose one finds in the course of his reading a passage like the following:

Yet Keats was a born genius if there ever was one. It is perhaps only additional proof of the authenticity of this genius that it ripened, did not spring spontaneously into maturity. Certainly it should be regarded as a pre-eminent quality of true genius to utilize and transform to its own purposes the rich resources of the world in which it resides, to accomplish, in the words of Coleridge, a reconciliation between the inner world of thought and feeling and the outer world of fact and substance. Precocity flames up in a brief moment, and, drawing only from within, quickly burns itself out; but genius, growing with what it feeds on, its natural powers reinforced through union with congenial elements from without, glows with increasing warmth until it reaches its full potential strength.[1]

In this passage of about ordinary difficulty you might be uncertain of six words: *authenticity, spontaneously, pre-eminent, utilize, reconciliation,* and *precocity.* If you were to follow literally and conscientiously the instructions usually given, you would have to look up all six words, a task which not only would increase the reading time of the paragraph by perhaps four minutes but would break the train of thought six times.

Yet it is evident that even if you were unfamiliar with all six words, all except *precocity* would be quite clear from context. Instead of looking up all six words, concentrate upon *precocity,* the one word which does need explanation if the sentence in which it occurs is to mean anything.

Examine this one word thoroughly. Note that it is formed from the adjective *precocious,* that it comes from Latin *prae* + *coquere,* "to cook or ripen beforehand"; that an adverb, *precociously,* and another noun, *precocious-ness,* may be formed from the same stem. Notice also that the slang phrase *half baked,* used to describe a rather stupid or perhaps quixotic individual, makes use of the same figure of speech as *precocious.* If a single difficult word is thus carefully studied, there is a greater likelihood that it will remain in your memory longer than any six words hastily looked up.

Learn to recognize words from context. You will make some mistakes; everyone does. Look up only those words which are necessary to the meaning. When you do look up a word, work carefully. Get everything your dictionary offers. Interest yourself in these words. Become word-conscious in a wholesome, not in a picayunish manner.

[1] John Keats, "Introduction," *Complete Poems and Selected Letters,* ed. C. D. Thorpe (New York: Doubleday Doran, 1935), p. xv. Reprinted by courtesy of the publisher.

The other usual admonition is keep a notebook in which you list new words which swim into your consciousness. "Use a word three times and it is yours." The difficulty here is that we can't always manufacture situations in which our newly-acquired words can be used. We are then in the position of Leora in Sinclair Lewis' *Arrowsmith*: after an afternoon spent reading about modern painting to impress her husband's associates, she found herself unable to maneuver the evening's conversation in that direction. Suppose we do discover for ourselves the words *atavistic*, *ontology*, and *recrudesce*. Finding even one normal conversation in which any of these could be used will not be easy; three situations, that the word might be "ours," would require patent manufacture!

It is here that writing comes to our aid. In writing we can choose the subject, as Leora could not, which will allow us to use our newly-acquired words. This has to be done with caution, of course; we must be quite sure of the word and use it with reasonable ease. It must not, for example, stick out as the lone polysyllable in an otherwise plain piece of writing.

But the surest way to acquire new words is to acquire new knowledge, especially through wide reading. Expand mentally and your vocabulary will expand. Increase the range of topics on which you write, and your command of words will improve.

5. EXACT USE OF WORDS

In the character Mrs. Malaprop, the dramatist Richard Brinsley Sheridan created one of the most amusing figures on the English stage. Although her name is derived from the French *mal apropos*, such gems as "an allegory on the banks of the Nile" and "a nice derangement of epitaphs" suggest that inaccuracy rather than inappropriateness was her principal problem. She knew a great many words but was totally confused about their meaning. Effective diction is first of all a matter of selecting those words which will express the intended meaning as clearly and precisely as possible.

a. Do not confuse words that are more or less alike in sound but have a different meaning or use.

The following list contains some of the words frequently confused in this way:

accept, to receive.
except, to leave out, reject.

affect, to act or produce an effect upon, to influence.
effect, verb: to bring to pass, execute, accomplish.

allusion, an indirect reference.
illusion, an unreal or misleading image, a deceptive appearance.

already, adverb: They had *already* gone.
all ready, separate words, a pronoun and an adjective: They were *all ready* to go.

altogether, adverb: They lost *altogether* too many sales.
all together, separate words, a pronoun and an adjective: Our seats are *all together* in the first row.

alumnus, a male graduate (plural, *alumni*).
alumna, a female graduate (plural, *alumnae*). (See dictionary for pronunciation.)

censor, as a noun: an overseer of morals and conduct, sometimes official; as a verb: to subject to censorship; to ban (in part or wholly).
censure, verb: to blame, condemn.

compose, to form by putting together, to constitute, to dispose in proper form.
comprise, to comprehend or include.

contemptible, worthy of contempt.
contemptuous, expressing contempt.

continual, a close or unceasing succession or recurrence: *continual* interruptions.

continuous, an uninterrupted continuity: a *continuous* murmur.

council, an assembly summoned for consultation, or the deliberation itself.

counsel, the advice given as a result of deliberation, or one who gives advice.

credible, worthy of belief, capable of being credited.

creditable, praiseworthy.

decided, unquestionable, clear cut, free from doubt: a *decided* change.

decisive, having the power of deciding or terminating a controversy, conclusive: *decisive* proofs.

effective, impressive, striking; emphasizing the actual production of an effect: an *effective* manner.

effectual, fulfilling an intended purpose; looking backward to a purpose having been fulfilled: an *effectual* retort.

emigrate, to leave a place or country.

immigrate, to come to a country to take up residence there.

flaunt, to wave, show off, display brazenly.

flout, to treat with contempt.

found, to place or base on something for support.

founder, to fall or sink down, fail, miscarry.

human, belonging or relating to man, characteristic of man.

humane, kind, benevolent, having feelings and inclinations creditable to man.

imply, to express indirectly, to hint at: He *implied* that he did not favor the measure.

infer, to derive by reasoning or implication: From the substance of his speech we *inferred* that he was displeased.

indefinite, having no exact or known limits or reference.

infinite, without limits, unbounded.

later, opposed to *earlier*, referring primarily to time.

latter, opposed to *former*, referring primarily to order, in which one of two things is mentioned.

livid, discolored, as bruised flesh; ashy gray.

vivid, bright in color.

loose, to unbind, untie, undo.

lose, to fail to keep, maintain, or sustain something.

luxuriant, exuberant or profuse in growth or display: *luxuriant* whiskers.

luxurious, pertaining or ministering to luxury: *luxurious* upholstery.

malicious, proceeding from ill will, dictated by malice.

malignant, having an evil influence, characterized by intense and active ill will.

manly, having qualities pertaining or becoming to a man.

manual, of or pertaining to the hands.

observance, act or practice of observing a rule or custom, or the customary act itself.

observation, the act or result of attentively considering or marking a fact or occurrence.

practicable, capable of being put into practice or action.

practical, pertaining to or manifested in practice; opposed to *theoretical*, *ideal*, or *speculative*.

precipitous, steep, like a precipice.

precipitate, adj.: rushing steeply downward, headlong, rash.

propose, to offer for consideration or adoption.

purpose, to intend.

rigid, stiff, inflexible; as, a rigid (unchangeable) rule.

rigorous, strict, severe; as, a rigorous (harsh) application of a law.

statue, a likeness of a person or animal, sculptured in solid substance.

stature, height.

statute, a law or act of a government or corporate body.

transfer, to convey from one place, person, or thing to another.
transform, to change the form, shape, appearance of.

venal, capable of being obtained for money; mercenary; open
   to bribery.
venial, capable of being forgiven.

Other pairs of words, confused because of similarity in
spelling rather than through likeness of pronunciation, are
treated in Chapter VIII, **Sp15.**

b. Discriminate carefully between synonyms.

Many pairs of words are synonymous in some, but not
in all, of their senses.

The meaning of words is based upon human experience.
In the United States the word *football,* when it is used
without a modifier of some sort, means *Rugby,* because that
is the common form of the game here. In England the un-
modified term means what we call *soccer,* a shortened form
of Association Football. Thus the word *football* means one
thing to an American and something else to an Englishman
primarily because their experiences with it differ, although
the two meanings do have something of a common element.

This ambiguity is true of much of our vocabulary. Because
of variability of experience, no one word means exactly the
same to all people, nor is it likely that there are any absolutely identical synonyms. Words often overlap in meaning, but they do not coincide.

Synonyms may lend variety and novelty to one's writing,
but they must be used exactly:

FAULTY: The tribute paid to the heroes was an excellent piece
of *inscription.*
REVISED: The tribute paid to the heroes was an excellent piece
of *writing.*

It is clear that the student meant to say that this tribute was an excellent piece of *writing*, using the word *writing* in a sense synonymous with *composition*. *Writing*, in another of its meanings, is synonymous with *inscription*; but that does not make *inscription* synonymous with *composition*, as the student consciously or subconsciously assumed.

FAULTY: Colleges and universities *take up* a part of the graduates of our high schools.
REVISED: Colleges and universities *absorb* a part of the graduates of our high schools.

Here the synonyms have even less in common. Of the five meanings of *absorb* given in the *Oxford Dictionary*,[1] two might be represented satisfactorily by *take up*; of the twenty-six meanings of *take up* given in the same dictionary, again only two could be represented by *absorb* as a synonym.

Another respect in which synonyms often differ is in what they *connote* (that is, in the suggestions or associations that cluster about them). Two words may have virtually the same *denotation* (that is, all that strictly belongs to the definition of the word) but rather different *connotations* —for instance, *proud* and *haughty*. Both of these words denote a quality of character or action implying a feeling of superiority, yet *proud* is frequently used in favorable, *haughty* almost always in unfavorable, senses. Carelessness about connotations leads to incongruity, contradiction, and inadvertent humor; good writing sometimes depends almost more on the connotations of words than on their denotations.

It is generally better to repeat a word than to use a synonym for its own sake—especially when the word may say exactly what you want, while the synonym may alter

[1] *The Oxford English Dictionary*, James A. H. Murray, et el., 1933.

the meaning. Nevertheless, repetition can become excessive and tiresome. To avoid this, consult the dictionary: a large one will discriminate at some length between synonyms, while even a small one will list some. There are also good dictionaries of synonyms available, and with caution one may get help from a thesaurus. The latter, however, merely gives synonyms and antonyms without explaining their differences of connotation or usage. As alternatives for the noun *cheat*, for example, one finds *deceiver, dissembler, sophist, snake in the grass, fraud, swindler, impostor, quack, charlatan*. Obviously these would not fit all contexts equally; they have different shades of meaning, some are formal, some informal—even slangy. A thesaurus gives you a miscellany to choose from; guide your choice, if necessary, with definitions from the dictionary.

EXERCISE I

A. Consult your dictionary for the distinction in meaning between each of the following pairs of frequently confused words, and be able to use each word in a sentence:

ability—capacity	contemptible—contemptuous
addicted to—subject to	exceptional—exceptionable
allude—refer	definite—definitive
anxious—eager	ingenious—ingenuous
avenge—revenge	noted—notorious
avocation—vocation	noteworthy—notable
climactic—climatic	proposition—proposal
respectful—respectable—respective	

B. Fill in the blanks with the words most appropriate to the context:

1. The doctor was certain that a long vacation would _____ a cure. (affect, effect)
2. We had to admit that Peter's explanation of his lazi-

ness was entirely _____, even if we didn't approve. (credible, creditable)

3. Although the invitation was very urgent, Elizabeth was not prepared to _____ it. (accept, except)

4. The lecturer was exasperated by the _____ interruptions. (continual, continuous)

5. The speaker made an _____ to the Twenty-Third Psalm. (allusion, illusion)

6. I meant to _____ that he did not believe me. (imply, infer)

7. According to the will, the property of the _____ was divided into four parts. (deceased, diseased)

8. All the contestants then returned to their _____ schools. (respectable, respective)

9. It was a _____ effort, indicating a mean and petty spirit. (contemptible, contemptuous)

10. The _____ made by the visiting expert were of considerable help to us in our work. (observances, observations)

C. Improve the wording of each of the following sentences by making substitutions for the italicized words:

1. We must recognize the difference between common and *statue* law.

2. The author of the article was severely *censored* for overlooking many of the essential facts.

3. The sky at sunset was *livid* with many rich colors.

4. It is said that habits make our lives and *wield* us to our destiny.

5. It was *all ready* six o'clock and the train had not yet arrived at the station.

6. Clear enunciation, a fine choice of words, excellent grammar, and a complete and thorough knowledge of the topic chosen for discussion *compose* the qualities of a good news commentator.

7. It was an *ingenuous* device for removing the impurities from crankcase oil.

8. He has retired now, but *formally* he was the president of a large manufacturing company and director of a bank.
9. Practical thinking was the kind of mental activity that was *cultured* most during my high-school course.
10. When he was elected, he began to *flaunt* those who disagreed with him.

c. Use nouns and verbs concretely and specifically. Avoid hazy or general terms.

Certain words in the language may be characterized as all-purpose terms. They have—or originally had—precise meanings, but they have come to be used in vague or hazy senses. Although such terms do serve a function, they are too often chosen when a writer is in a hurry, when he has not taken the time to think of the term which precisely fits the meaning or situation he has in mind. At times they result in wordiness, as in "A further type of situation that needs to be taken into consideration is the economy of production factor." This sentence says nothing more than, "We must also consider economy of production."

Be especially careful in your use of the following general or classifying terms:

angle	instance	regard
aspect	manner	situation
case	matter	style
factor	phase	thing
fashion	point	type
feature	problem	way
field	question	

FAULTY: Questions which they have never before had to face will arise, and they must know how to combat these *things*.
REVISED: Questions which they have never before had to face will arise, and they must know how to solve such *problems*.

FAULTY: Another *phase* of writing studied in fourth-year English was poetry.

REVISED: Another *form* of literature studied in fourth-year English was poetry.

FAULTY: Therefore, to create a community which will satisfy each of its members, certain set rules cannot be put down and religiously carried out, for they would be sure to *go against* someone.

REVISED: Therefore, to create a community which will satisfy each of its members, certain set rules cannot be put down and religiously carried out, for they would be sure to *harm* or *dissatisfy* someone.

d. Avoid the use of overemphatic words.

In the first example, the adjective and adverb almost contradict each other, giving a ludicrous effect.

FAULTY: In the world of today the superstitions of yesterday are *somewhat extinct*.

REVISED: In the world of today the superstitions of yesterday are *no longer current*.

FAULTY: One example will *prove* my point.

REVISED: One example will *support* my point.

FAULTY: A person with a truly open mind has an attribute that will be of *eternal* use to him.

REVISED: A person with true open-mindedness has an attribute that will be of *lifelong* use to him.

It is a normal tendency to want to express our feelings and reactions emphatically. At one point in time or another the speakers and writers of English have fixed upon certain words to indicate their approval or their disapprobation. As with the classifying terms discussed in the preceding section, this has resulted in a less precise meaning of the terms which are so used. For example, the word *nice* at one time in its history meant *foolish*; then it came to be used to indicate a minute degree of discrimination. *Fine* originally meant *finished*, then *brought to perfection, free from impurity*, and finally *superior*. Now both of these words are used to indicate varying degrees of general approval (a *fine* day, a *nice* book, a *fine* performance, a *nice* garden, etc.). Obviously no amount of emphasis upon word history could restore these to their original meanings, nor is it particularly desirable that they be restored. The language needs some very general words of approval. They are necessary to the informality of conversation.

A number of other words, however, undergoing the same processes to which *nice* and *fine* were subjected, have not yet gone the whole way. Use them with caution. Particularly are they out of place in formal or serious writing, because they suggest a certain poverty in the writer's diction. The reader is likely to think that he has no more precise or exact terms at his command.

Use the following words in your writing only when they are strictly appropriate:

amazing	magnificent
awful, -ly	mighty
dreadful	phenomenal
elegant	splendid
fierce	terrible, -ly
grand	tremendous
horrid	weird
lovely	wonderful

e. Include all the words necessary for the completion of a suggested relationship.

FAULTY: We should not say that the young people are no longer *moved* by their *country*.

REVISED: We should not say that the young people are no longer *moved* by *love* for their *country*.

Strictly speaking, a physical entity or thing does not *move* us; an emotion, feeling, or idea does.

FAULTY: His administration has poured millions of dollars into the spoils system for political *cohorts*.

REVISED: His administration has poured millions of dollars into the spoils system for political *patronage*.

OR: His administration has poured millions of dollars into the spoils system for the *benefit of his cohorts*.

f. Be sure your words are in proper agreement with others in the sentence.

The following are examples of common failures in word correspondence:

1. Noun-verb relationships, chiefly subject-verb, and verb-object

FAULTY: I shall try in every way to *carry out* the *statements* I have previously set forth.

REVISED: I shall try in every way to *carry out* the *resolutions* I have previously set forth.

OR: I shall try in every way to *explain* the *statements* I have previously made.

Notice that the meaning of the original sentence is not wholly clear because a *statement* is not carried out. Substitute for *statement* something which can be carried out; replace the verb *carry out* by some other verb which can logically govern the object *statement*.

FAULTY: Americanism is the *act* of *being* a good citizen who obeys the laws of the land, and who defends his country in times of invasion.

REVISED: Americanism is the *state* of *being* a good citizen who obeys the laws of the land, and who defends his country in times of invasion.

OR: Americanism includes such *acts* of good citizenship as *obeying* the laws of the land and *defending* the country in times of invasion.

The noun *act* implies that some activity is to follow,

whereas the participle *being* which it governs suggests a passive condition. We may change *act* to *state*, a word logically compatible with *being*, or we may omit *being* and use the less neutral verbs *obey* and *defend*.

2. Adjective-noun relationships

FAULTY: The masses of American citizens have shown an *irrefutable* loyalty to him.
REVISED: The masses of American citizens have shown an *unquestionable* (*undeniable*) loyalty to him.

An adjective not logically appropriate to the noun it modified was chosen. A loyalty may be *denied* or *questioned*; it is not *refuted*.

3. Adverb-verb relationships

FAULTY: During the past few months his popularity has *increasingly* diminished.
REVISED: During the past few months his popularity has *rapidly* (*progressively*) diminished.

The fault here is in the contradiction latent in the words *increase* and *diminish*.

4. Verb-verb relationships

FAULTY: If war propaganda can maintain the spirit, so can the spirit of making a new and better society *hold* the people *to agree* with the centralized authority.
REVISED: If war propaganda can maintain the spirit, so can the spirit of making a new and better society *lead* the people *to agree* with the centralized authority.

We cannot be *held* to agree with something, although we can be *held to* an agreement. We can be led or induced to agree with it—or we can be held *to obey* or *in obedience to* something.

5. Parallel situations involving any parts of speech

FAULTY: It would be foolish for the employers to *lower* the very standard of labor they have helped to *increase*.

REVISED: It would be foolish for the employers to *lower* the very standard of labor they have helped to *raise*.

FAULTY: He kills the man and goes on trial for his life, *outwardly* calm, *inside* sad and discouraged.

REVISED: He kills the man and goes on trial for his life, *outwardly* calm, *inwardly* sad and discouraged.

6. APPROPRIATE USE OF WORDS

A word used in a specific situation may be wholly clear as to meaning but still may jar the reader because it seems out of place, conveys the wrong tone, much as if a girl were to wear costume jewelry on a tennis court. The positive side of good diction may be summed up in a single word: appropriateness. Every word is used in a context, grammatical, stylistic, even physical. The author, if he knows what he is about, is seeking to produce a certain effect upon a certain kind of reader. What words will produce this effect? Is he trying to be familiar, literary, chatty, impressive? He must choose his diction accordingly.

Consider the following:

> The poor fish fell for that stale gag.
> The silly fellow was fooled by that old trick.
> Simpletons are deceived by outworn devices.
> Springes to catch woodcocks!

All four expressions say virtually the same thing—but with what a difference! The first is altogether slangy; the second, informal and conversational; the third, literary and sententious; the fourth, highly connotative to those who catch the allusion and recall Polonius's advice to his daughter given in his characteristic manner.[1] In each case the diction makes each phrase appropriate to a very different situation. The student must consciously make himself aware of such differences and suit his own words to his purpose.

The faults to avoid will be dealt with in detail in the following pages; the improvements to seek are, of course, their opposites.

a. Use words in the part-of-speech function in which they normally serve.

FAULTY: Whenever forestry is mentioned to the average uninformed citizen, his immediate reaction is to *vision* a raging forest fire.

REVISED: Whenever forestry is mentioned to the average uninformed citizen, his immediate reaction is to *visualize* a raging forest fire.

FAULTY: To the man of today, the idea of thinking has become more and more *loathe*.

REVISED: To the man of today, the idea of thinking has become more and more *loathsome*.

Note that in the first sentence the noun *vision* was transformed into a verb, while in the second, the verb *loathe* was made to serve as an adjective.

It is true, of course, that many words in English often serve as any one of several parts of speech. (This aspect of the language is dealt with in somewhat greater detail on page 204.) You should not assume, however, that the function of any word may be shifted at will; such shifts, unskillfully made, are often awkward or inappropriate.

b. Avoid words of your own invention that are not otherwise current.

The moment a word enters our active vocabulary it is no longer an isolated mental phenomenon; it is subject to

---

[1] *Hamlet*, Act 1, scene iii, line 115.

all the inflectional and derivational patterns we normally employ. For example, suppose we have just become actively aware of the words *precocious* and *precocity*. If there should arise a situation in which more than one *precocity* was involved, it would not be necessary for us to have learned the plural, *precocities*, as a separate fact. By the process of analogy we would automatically form the plural of this word by fitting it to the general pattern of all the regularly formed plurals that we already know.

This tendency goes farther than mere inflection. If we know the adjective *precocious* and a situation arises which calls for the use of an adverb with this meaning, we again automatically apply the *-ly* adverb pattern to the adjective, thus creating what is for us a new word, *precociously*. All languages grow and adapt themselves to new situations through the employment of such inflectional and word-forming patterns. But at times our creative instincts do betray us, and we form nonexistent words. This is often the result of putting together word-forming elements in a unique combination:

FAULTY: From the tone of this paper one is apt to believe me critical of these tendencies of *undemocracy*.
REVISED: From the tone of this paper one is apt to believe me critical of these *undemocratic* tendencies.

FAULTY: The best way to distinguish rationalized thinking from *irrationalized* thinking is simply to question statements made in defense of a particular idea.
REVISED: The best way to distinguish rational thinking from *irrational* thinking (or rationalized thinking from that which is not rationalized) is simply to question statements made in defense of a particular idea.

It is interesting to see how these unique words came to be formed. Beginning with *democrat*, one may form the adjectives *democratic* and *undemocratic* and then proceed to an abstract noun which is the antithesis or opposite of *democracy* by forming it on the pattern of the adjective *undemocratic*. The attempt is laudable enough; the only difficulty is that the word *undemocracy* just doesn't exist. In the same manner *irrationalized* results from a blending of the *rational-rationalize* and the *rational-irrational* patterns.

There is no intention here of condemning the formation of new words. New words there will be and must be, so long as the language is alive. Quite often they are coined to meet special situations, to name new inventions or developments of human knowledge. Such words as *ionosphere*, *heliport*, *gobbledygook*, *genocide* originated in this way. As a student, however, you had better bend your efforts toward acquiring the words that exist already and leave the coinage of new ones to the experienced writer.

EXERCISE II

Improve the diction of the following sentences by selecting another word for the one italicized. Explain why each italicized word is open to criticism.

1. He did everything possible to prevent a *dissolvement* of the company.

2. The type of movie varies in accord with the changes in world *politicalism*.

3. These changes have taken place because of the public's *nonacceptance* of certain types of pictures and its overwhelming interest in other types.

4. This class *predominates* our society by virtue of its economic power.

5. Thinking for yourself develops *independability*.

6. In *refute* to the argument that the state should be the chief end, many people believe that individuality will be destroyed.

7. If he feels *unjustice* has been done, he has a right to appeal to the State Tenure Commission.

8. This shows how popular and *wanted* color-TV is.

9. I, too, have been one to look very *disgustingly* at the clock at that early hour in the morning.

10. When I asked several of my close associates what they were really thinking about, they confessed that they were just *reverieing*.

11. He has lost a certain quality which to me makes life more *cherishable*.

12. Whenever a nation keeps a large standing army, it is clearly demonstrating an *unpeacelike* spirit.

13. The plan to recognize this little nation was put into writing and *initialized* by the President.

14. John's greatest fault is his *cowardness*.

15. The store was robbed last week, but the owner *suspicions* the janitor.

16. The Congress is seeking *finalization* of several of the temporary agencies.

17. History and its *relating* subjects have always interested me.

18. In this manner the frequent strikes tied up the operation of the factory and, in some cases, of an entire industry by stopping the output of some *manufacturing* necessity.

19. A strike is usually the fault of some one individual who spreads the feeling of *uncontentedness* among the workers.

20. The word "co-operative" always has a great *connoting* effect on me, arousing my sympathy, support, and approbation.

c. Use the preposition appropriate to each word or situation.

(See also Chapter VI, G7.)

The correct use of prepositions is a difficult matter in almost any language. This is especially true of English, where we say, for example, *at noon, in the evening, on Wednesday, in July, on July first*—all to express the same general relationship. Such phrases are *idioms*, expressions native to the language that cannot be analyzed either according to the meanings of the words that make them up or according to the general grammatical rules of the language. Since idioms commonly contain prepositions, it is important to learn which prepositions are appropriate in these expressions. You have already mastered hundreds of prepositional phrases such as those mentioned, which you write or speak with absolute ease and without even thinking about them. There are others, however, which are likely to give you trouble.

Observe the prepositions used with the following words. In no instance do they represent all the possible prepositional constructions which may follow the word in question, but rather those which are likely to be of greatest use to you. When in doubt about other similar expressions, consult your dictionary.

accord with
accordance with
according to

accused by (a person)
accused of (a deed)

agree in (an opinion, a characteristic)
agree on (a plan, a matter)
agree to (a proposal)
agree with (a person)
agreeable to

angry at, about (a happening, a situation)
angry with, at (a person)

argue against, for (a measure, a policy)
argue with (a person)

authority on (a topic, subject)
authority of, for (acting in a certain way)

comply with
conform to
conformity with

contend against (an obstacle)
contend for (a principle, a prize)
contend with (a person)

correspond to (things)
correspond with (persons)

desire for
desirous of

differ about (a question)
differ, different from (something else)
differ with (a person)

disagree with
dissent from

identical with
independent of
inferior to
in search of
jealous of
listen to

part from (a person)
part with (property, possession)

profit by
repent of
sensitive to
separate from
stay at home
superior to

treat of (a subject)
treat with (someone): to negotiate

unmindful of

wait at (a place)
wait for (a person)
wait on (a customer)

EXERCISE III

A. Consult your dictionary for the preposition or prepositions which may be appropriately used with the following words, and be able to use each expression in a sentence:

abhorrent	compare	oblivious
absolve	desist	preferable
acquiesce	inseparable	reconcile
acquit	mastery	repugnant
collide	meddle	subscribe

B. Improve the wording of each of the following sentences by making substitutions for the italicized words. Be able to explain what principle has been violated in each instance:

1. The industrial equality to which I refer hinges directly *with* several conditions.
2. One can concentrate on helping his own kind or country *much easier* and with better results than upon improving the state of the world in general.
3. There is also the *point* of self-satisfaction which cannot be overlooked.
4. Although our Constitution guarantees us life, liberty and the pursuit of happiness, it does not *ascertain* to us the privileges of a college education.
5. The *world* is becoming more and more *specialized*.
6. Sometimes the pendulum swung forward, sometimes *in reverse*.
7. Herein has education been *lacking* in that it has too frequently approached the subject without going beneath the surface.
8. Some sort of work is almost always done, whether it be in the *form* of a job, school, or something different.
9. It is believed that the serum, rushed from Chicago by army plane and *instituted* at once, was the saving factor.
10. Almost never does idle speculation lead to any practical *phase* because it revolves about the ego.

11. His speaking voice and his pleasing personality *lead* a pathway to millions of people in this country.

12. If a teacher has the *good will of prestige*, he need not be particularly well trained in his subject.

13. He kidnapped the other members of the airplane.

14. It is usually very restful to drop *on* a large, comfortable chair.

15. One of the greatest secrets behind his efficiency is his mastery *over detail*.

d. Avoid the use of jargon.

Two preceding portions of this section (**W6a** and **W6oc**) have dealt with matters of grammatical appropriateness, situations where the reader would be jarred because of a part of speech used in an unconventional way or a preposition that fails to fit. Inappropriateness quite as often stems from stylistic causes. A skillful writer maintains a consistent tone; he does not mix styles. He uses words which are in keeping with his subject matter, with the purpose or occasion for which he is writing, and with the expectations of the readers for whom he is writing.

The term *jargon* is to be understood here as the technical vocabulary of a science, art, profession, trade, sect, or other special group. All such groups have their special vocabularies, vocabularies that are quite justifiable when they are used by the psychologists, structural steel workers, or circus roustabouts for whom they have special or useful meanings.

It is the jargon of the professions and of business which the inexperienced writer is most often tempted to use in situations which do not call for such specialized terminology. When he does so, it often appears that he is trying to make the trivial seem important and that he is using long, technical sounding terms where an everyday word would be more expressive and immediately comprehensible. Moreover, the novice often uses the specialized language incorrectly.

Here are two examples of jargon incompetently used:

FAULTY: The types of pictures the public enjoys are widely distributed, and *those to which it has no reflex* are taken off the market.

FAULTY: He whizzed into the stadium in a long, low, convertible Lincoln, with Secret Service men on all sides, and cordons of police *before and aft.*

Notice the writer has confused *reflex* with *reaction*, although he means a negative reaction rather than *no* reaction. In the second sentence the expression should be *fore and aft;* the writer also has failed to note that this is always used in respect to parts of a ship and that it can scarcely be applied to a part *outside* the automobile itself.

Legal language must employ such terms of reference as *above, above-mentioned, below, said, same.* They are out of place in writing that is at all dignified and imaginative. For *above* it is well to substitute *preceding* or *foregoing* and to use these words adjectivally, not pronominally. For *below,* substitute *following;* for *said* and *same,* use the personal and demonstrative pronouns.

FAULTY: For the *above* reasons, Russia has shown herself to be the aggressor.

REVISED: For the *foregoing* reasons, Russia has shown herself to be the aggressor.

FAULTY: In order to understand the term "democracy," let us examine the definition of *the same* advanced by Bryce.

REVISED: In order to understand the term "democracy," let us examine Bryce's definition of *it.*

Other terms common in commercial usage which may arouse antagonism are *contact* used as a verb, *line* meaning a *field of endeavor* or *occupation, balance* for *remainder, favor* for *letter* or *communication, know-how* for *technical knowledge.*

157

FAULTY: It seems to me that there is no greater field in the teaching *line* than that of English.

REVISED: It seems to me that there is no more promising field in the teaching *profession* than English.

e. Avoid the inappropriate use of slang.

Slang is not jargon, it is not profanity, it is not provincial language, nor does it consist of violations of the rules of grammar. That is to say, *flunk, damn, reckon,* and *hain't* are not slang.

Much of it is metaphor heightened to the point of grotesqueness. *Gilt-edged* for *valuable* is basically a metaphor derived from the appearance of negotiable securities. *Pass* (or *cash*) *in your chips* for *to die* is a figure derived from a poker game.

Another form of slang is the result of shortening or clipping words. *Bus* for *omnibus, cab* for *cabriolet, mob* for *mobile vulgus* all started out in this fashion, but in the course of time became wholly accepted in standard formal usage, as they are today. Such words as *ad, auto, phone, copter, exam, gent, gym, prof,* and *taxi* are more recent shortenings and have acquired varying degrees of respectability. Still other forms taken by slang include intentional mispronunciations such as *wiff* for *wife* and the intentional addition of endings as in *sweetie.* Even this is by no means a complete account, for it has omitted the so-called counterwords such as *swell* and *lousy,* which develop from a desire for emphasis, but soon wear thin from frequent use.

Much slang, particularly of the metaphorical kind, arises from the praiseworthy desire for effectiveness. But through exaggeration and overuse it soon loses its freshness and spontaneity.

Avoid slang in your written compositions: much of it is ephemeral; it acquires and then loses its currency so quickly that in a very short space of time much of it is no longer understood; a few slang words become a part of the standard language and cease to be recognized as particularly strange, emphatic, or effective. Again, slang is out of keeping with serious thought or formal writing. Born of a desire for very strong emphasis, it suggests a lack of reasoned restraint, flippancy at the expense of good manners.

EXAMPLES:

The judgment of the members of the Supreme Court is by no means infallible. Many of the justices were appointed not because of their legal knowledge or experience but because of political *pull.*

Undoubtedly the chief reason for the conversational effectiveness of many individuals is their inherent ability to *dish it out.*

Shall he endure four years of a *brain-cracking* premedical course only to be refused permission to enter the overcrowded medical schools?

In general, use slang only when it is appropriate, when it is not merely the easy, lazy-man's choice. Slang words are usually to be put in quotation marks. (Do not overuse them.)

f. Try to use fresh, lively expressions. Avoid triteness, euphemisms, and elegant variation.

You may have just discovered *acid test* and *aching void,* but they have long been hackneyed through overuse. If you cannot think of something original, use the simple factual statement. Avoid clichés. The following list contains some of those commonly heard:

abreast of the times	captain of industry
as luck would have it	checkered career
bathed in tears	Dame Fortune
bitter end	dazed condition
breakneck speed	depths of despair
budding genius	epic struggle

159

ere long
filthy lucre
green with envy
Hand of Justice
in the last analysis
last but not least
mantle of snow
motley throng
nipped in the bud
paramount issue
psychological moment
replete with interest
slow but sure
soul of honor
thereby hangs a tale
the weaker sex
wee small hours
words fail to express
wreak havoc

Avoid such trite statements as the following:

He is a person of *high ideals*.
I came to college to *broaden* myself.
The greatest boon that college can give you is to *develop your personality*.
This teacher constantly held up before his pupils the *finer side of life*.

Euphemism is the attempt to designate an unpleasant fact or idea by using what seems a somewhat less offensive term. Thus, we say *prevaricate* for *lie*, *pass away* for *die*, *intoxicated* for *drunk*. When this device is overused, the language seems artificial. Closely connected with euphemism is the use of a labored terminology to upgrade quite ordinary occupations. Thus, office girls become *receptionists*, janitors are known as *custodians* or *maintenance engineers*, and file clerks are disguised as *research consultants*. Euphemism is one form of flowery language which young writers mistakenly feel is a mark of good writing. Born of the wholly praiseworthy effort to get away from the commonplace, such diction tends to be either trite or extravagant.

Avoiding the repetition of a word because variety for its own sake is mistakenly believed to be a virtue may result in *elegant variation*, another form of flowery language. Sports writers strain for terms which may be used to indicate the defeat of one team by another; as a consequence we get everything from *pound, clobber,* and *swamp* on the one hand to *squeak by, edge,* and *shade* on the other. At its worst, elegant variation not only makes writing sound pompous, focusing attention on the writer's ingenuity with synonyms, but also takes away from the possible effect that might have been created had repetition of the key word in a passage been used. Compare the following:

POOR: *Labor,* despite disclaimers from the lazy, is a tonic for most people. Having an *occupation* seems almost a precondition of happiness for some kinds of people, and the man without a *business* is poor in both pocket and spirit. Thus, *working* itself gives purpose to people's lives.

IMPROVED: W*ork,* despite disclaimers from the lazy, is a tonic for most people. Having *work* to do seems almost a precondition of happiness for some kinds of people, and the man without *it* is poor in both pocket and spirit. Thus, *working* itself gives purpose to people's lives.

The motive for flowery writing is understandable, but the effort becomes too obvious. This is equally true when we find that *budding genius* is applied to any reasonably intelligent person, that every table set for luncheon or dinner is *groaning* if not a *groaning board,* and that the ordinary policeman on the beat is characterized as a *minion of the law.*

g. Avoid a mixture of colloquial and formal literary language.

In Chapter V, page 187, dictionary definitions are cited to show that the term *colloquial* means *pertaining to conversation* and that, properly used, it is in no sense a term of condemnation.

The relationship between literary and colloquial English is frequently likened to that between formal evening wear and business clothes. A business suit with turndown collar and four-in-hand tie would be out of place at a formal reception, just as a white tie and tails would inspire comment in a business office. This comparison is apt, but it does not go far enough. First of all, it should be pointed out that of the two garments, the business suit is undoubtedly the more useful—it is worn every day, while formal evening wear is reserved for special occasions. In the same way, our writing and speaking is informal and colloquial more often than it is formal and literary. Recall that the wing collar, now one of the distinguishing marks of formal attire, was once worn with a business suit; and that styles in both tail coats and business suits vary from year to year. So, too, words which are now considered limited to one level of language can change their status.

What the student must guard against most is an incongruous mixture of the two styles. A white dress vest would be out of place with tweeds, as would a flowered necktie with a dinner coat.

EXAMPLES:

As far as I can *figure out*, Freshman Week was designed by the authorities to be hurried and confusing, half fun and half work.

They were well informed on *most* any topic that came up for discussion.

When he was in high school, he spent his after-school hours and his evenings *doing* the advertising for his father's theatre.

Once we *suspicion* another of reading our minds, we immediately assume the defensive.

h. Avoid mixed or inappropriate figures of speech.

We are all familiar with the man who smelled a rat, saw it floating in the air, and felt that he must nip it in the bud. Be careful also not to slip from figurative language to literal language before the figure has been carried out to its logical conclusion.

EXAMPLES:

A foothold seems to have been established in the minds of many of our people, and that foothold seems to hang upon one word—growth.

Yet they knew that there would be hurdles ahead as the spirit of Americanism passed from one hand to another. If a man is to open his mind to other people, he must first unlock the barriers of prejudice.

The New Yorker magazine regularly reprints mixed figures of speech as one source of incongruous and inadvertent humor. An example:

BLOCK THAT METAPHOR!

A relative quiet is likely to settle over the political battlefield until the Republican convention. That will be the kickoff for the G.O.P. Its candidates will jump out of the trenches, so to speak, and be met head-on by Democrats who have tasted blood and are in no mood to be routed.

From the Portland [Maine] *Press Herald*

EXERCISE IV

A. Improve the wording of the following sentences:

1. I studied early and late but still lack the seed for any brilliant advance in the course.
2. He tries to find points that will carry out or continue his ideas.
3. This epidemic of nonthinkers has been present as long as man.
4. Naturally and inevitably, it is necessary that she take every other subject that is in any way connected with her major field of specialization.

5. When the cooler weather had come, and the epidemic was at its worst, I took to my home to rest up for more hard labor of the coming fall.

6. Ere long there came a swarm of locusts which devoured all the crops.

7. It may be of greater advantage to the sorority to rush the first three weeks of school, but it is a decided disadvantage to the freshmen to have to make such an important decision in such a short time.

8. Some student, perhaps, through the study of literature will open up that spark of genius which we all hear so much about.

9. I do feel, however, that future years must bring a complete reversal of our present economic system so that the mass of people will become much happier and have better means of existence.

10. The ironical part of the entire situation is that parents and relatives who had grieved for loved ones lost in the wars were once more bearing their kin to the grim and gray business of war.

11. It is conceivable that mankind has failed to unite into a friendly brotherhood.

12. The prime requisite to my personal well-being is that necessary requirement which consumes, or should consume, at least eight hours of our daily living—namely, sleep.

13. When the President was inaugurated, his whole heart was seemingly out for the mass majority, the laborer.

14. Each of the two boys was so inseparably suited for the throne that even the prince's father didn't recognize the difference between his own son and the pauper lad.

15. She did all her tasks with tender care, especially that of tending the garden.

B. The following passages, by using vague, superfluous and hackneyed expressions (often referred to as *deadwood*), are much longer than need be for what they have to say (95 words, 97 words). How far can you condense them without loss of meaning? Blue-pencil them as an editor might, then rewrite them. How many words have you used?

The question is as to whether or not it will be possible or feasible to do this. It has been doubted by those most intimately concerned in the matter. Because of the fact that these experts, who in the nature of things ought to have worthwhile opinions on the subject, are uncertain about the probable outcome themselves, we must proceed with caution. We must not undertake to do that which may, for aught we know to the contrary, have disastrous results and lead in the final analysis to unforeseen consequences of a most undesirable nature.

Somewhere in the annals of fisticuffs he seems to recall that formerly he once read the autobiography of this man's life. He has searched and hunted throughout the entire realm of sportdom in an unrewarded effort to find this narrative again, but so far his examination has been in vain. However, as he says, if at first you don't succeed, try, try again; and with unlimited persistence he has set about the thankless task of inspecting yet once more the halls of fame of athletic greats in the hope of tracking his elusive quarry to its lair.

7. ECONOMY

Good diction is accurate; it is appropriate to its purpose. It is also efficient and concise. You want your words to count, every one of them as far as possible. You do not want to waste them, to repeat yourself, to use vague expressions which require further explanation. Effective diction is that which hits the mark directly.

Wordiness is a common fault of inexperienced writers. It has been called by many names: *prolixity, pleonasm, redundancy, tautology*. No matter what the term may be, it all boils down to needless repetition. This makes reading a chore and the reader impatient. To use three words in place of one in order to get your theme up to the minimum wordage set for the assignment deceives no one, least of all the instructor. Excess verbiage will not cloak a scantiness of ideas.

a. Avoid the use of coordinate synonyms which merely repeat one another.

FAULTY: With the *deeds* and *doings* of these pioneers of science still retained firmly in my mind, I have decided to enter the field of medicine.

REVISED: With the *accomplishments* of these pioneers of science still retained firmly in my mind, I have decided to enter the field of medicine.

FAULTY: Therefore we must differentiate *definitely* and *distinctly* between amateurs and semi-professionals.

REVISED: Therefore we must differentiate *clearly* between amateurs and semi-professionals.

b. Avoid the use of modifiers which repeat an idea already implicit or present in the word modified.

FAULTY: In the last decade movie production has advanced *forward* with great strides.

REVISED: In the last decade movie production has advanced with great strides.

FAULTY: He was the *completely* perfect example of a smart young man.

REVISED: He was the *complete* example . . . or, He was the *perfect* example. . . .

c. Avoid the use of qualifying adjectives and adverbs which contribute little to meaning or which weaken the expression.

FAULTY: My station is a *rather* typical *one*, consisting of a low-powered transmitter and a seven-tube receiver.

REVISED: My station is typical; it consists of a low-powered transmitter and a seven-tube receiver.

FAULTY: Why is it that poems always have to be enriched by *such* colorful adjectives and phrases?

REVISED: Why is it that poems always have to be enriched by colorful adjectives and phrases?

Such implies, of course, that certain specific illustrations have already been cited; in this case there were none.

d. When the simple word is sufficient to give the desired meaning, do not add prefixes and suffixes.

FAULTY: Reverie is a pleasant *preoccupation* and is also conducive to progress.

REVISED: Reverie is a pleasant *occupation* and is also conducive to progress.

FAULTY: Moreover, this idea is so firmly *affixed* in our minds that probably nine out of ten persons would refuse to accept the scientist's findings.

REVISED: Moreover, this idea is so firmly *fixed* in our minds that probably nine out of ten persons would refuse to accept the scientist's findings.

FAULTY: It was a very plain door, with few *ornamentations* on it.

REVISED: It was a very plain door, with few *ornaments* on it.

Attaching word-forming elements (prefixes and suffixes) is such a common phenomenon that it tends to become a habit with us. It is true that the words *affix* and *ornamentation* do exist. In the sentences given, the simple words are more economical and in better taste.

Quite frequently clumsiness in diction results from the addition of noun suffixes to words that already have corresponding abstract nouns. Avoid *virtuousness, cruelness, annoyingness, summarization;* use *virtue, cruelty, annoyance, summary.*

As you become more familiar with the meaning and uses of prefixes and suffixes, and with the derivations of the words you use, you will develop a feeling for the right word.

EXERCISE V

1. Examine the list of prefixes and suffixes below and form several (no more than ten) words from each.

2. What does each contribute to the meaning of the word to which it is added?

3. Observe to what part or parts of speech each is added and what part of speech the result is.

To illustrate, let us examine the suffix -*ness*, in such derivative formations as *blackness, holiness, coldness, hardness.* Note that this suffix is added to adjectives, and converts them into abstract nouns. It means *state or condition of being;* e.g., *hardness*—state or condition of being hard.

SUFFIXES

-aceous, -acious	-fy	-let	-tude
-craft	-ish	-ment	-ward
-dom	-ile	-ory	-wise

PREFIXES

amphi-	homo-	neo-	retro-
bene-	hyper-	ob-	sur-
contra-	mal-	pan-	under-
dia-	multi-	pseudo-	with-

e. Avoid wordy and cumbersome transitions.

Very often writers use more words than necessary in connecting one sentence or one paragraph to another. Suppose you have written, "Tax reform is an essential part of the legislative program this year." Now you want to give some reasons to justify your general statement.

FAULTY: This is true because of the fact that property taxes have increased to the point that they have become an unreasonable burden.

REVISED: Clearly, property taxes have become an unreasonable burden.

Next, you want to mention some other possible forms of taxation.

FAULTY: Because of this it is logical to conclude that if present state services are to be maintained, either an income tax or a sales tax must be imposed.

REVISED: Consequently, if present state services are to be maintained, either an income tax or a sales tax must be imposed.

You may also want to suggest that this conclusion is not universally maintained.

FAULTY: In considering this situation we must also take into account the fact that people are generally reluctant to accept new forms of taxation.

REVISED: Nevertheless, people are generally reluctant to accept new forms of taxation.

EXERCISE VI

The following groups of sentences contain violations of the principles of diction which have been discussed in various parts of the chapter. Revise each of the sentences.

(A) 1. The majority of people feel that the profits that are secured by the few should be curtailed and divided more evenly among the people who do the manly labor.

2. It hasn't gone far enough underneath the surface; it hasn't snatched the fundamentals, and it has not brought them to the light of a blinded people.

3. If this be the purpose of an education, an education seems to be a way of becoming above the average man.

4. Another influential feature in the building up of stories on false foundations was the feudal system.

5. If a certain actor can play a particular part well, he is typed as that particular kind until he finds himself actually enjoying his screen roles.

6. Disregard all signs of good or bad luck, and do not let them make a particle bit of difference in the planning of your life.

7. This time, though, there was no great responsibility, there was no rush, there were no new people to meet, and then too, the weather was swell.

8. If the people of a nation or state do not believe in the system, they are going to try to agitate reform.

9. I have found working very helpful to me, however, in understanding the value of money-making to put me through school, and hope to take all the advantages set before me.

10. The answer to the question of defining a highbrow person, group, or place, is one which requires considerable distinction, separation, and investigation.

11. After many weeks of hardships on location or filming of said picture, the actors usually return to Hollywood for a period.

12. Localization of concentration is one way of securing satisfactory results.

13. More and more parents have been considering it important to send their children to college, so that they may become not only cultured but specialized as well.

14. It might seem that Dickens exaggerated his malicious characters, and this may be true, but he has not failed in his errand.

15. I vigorously believe that the movies of today, and even those of yesterday, were produced to fulfill a public desire.

16. If troops are sent, a great number will be needed to guard the immense holds of some of our American companies which have property all over the Near East.

(B)   1. Although this hatred is most pronounced in Russia, in certain other countries people are sort of antagonistic against foreigners.

2. In other words, you must be eligible in your studies to be able to partake in any activities.

3. If one contrasts other forms of government with democracy, he will find that property rights have a dominant place in a democracy.

4. I will be better able to uphold a better position when I go forth with the knowledge I have gained.

5. To err is human, but I will put the question plainly "Can you name anyone who could steer us through this difficulty any better?" True enough, some snags were struck, but we managed to eke by.

6. The result of this unity of people, all united by a sense of duty toward the church, is an organization that has endured through the ages, and has never been disbanded, even through the most trialing conditions.

7. It is truly a crime how low the intelligence of the average voter is about democracy.

8. He too has certain prerequisites in choosing his friends.

9. This fellow wrote of his travels and his accomplishments so vividly that you could imagine yourself on the trip with him.

10. There is so much that should not be known that I censure my letters very carefully.

11. Journalism then is a powerful agency with ability to do great good or even greater harm.

12. During a revolution on one of the rich houses in the North his wife found a bag of jewels.

13. From the beginning of their childhood, the poor class of people has few chances of acquiring courage and intelligence, because of their environment and their parental standing.

14. Now I realize that receiving a letter from friends at home seems to comfort you and soothen your feelings.

(C) 1. As for his personal life, he is probably well fixed and can live as he usually does.

2. I read Salinger's books with a fiendish delight.

3. This is true of most all athletics that involve a team.

4. When it first came into general use, the radio could not offer such a wide variety of programs as is now presented for an ever-enlarging audience.

5. The reaction of a person after having seen this picture is very depressing.

6. This type of thinking is more or less of a habit, and since habits can be broken, this can also be substituted by an open-minded thinking.

7. The Fascist doctrines were origined by the industrialists.

8. Labor in summer time is always hard, but yet last summer the weather was passable. It was plenty cool, and only once or twice did it really boil.

9. The poor boy was not much different from the rich, and

he adjusted himself to his new environment with the same speed that the rich boy was forced to assume his new environment.

10. During the war we either did not take part in many important traditions or did away with them altogether.

PART TWO

STANDARDS OF MODERN WRITING

EFFECTIVENESS in writing is not easily reduced to a set of rules. The features and devices of language which make for effectiveness may vary considerably, depending upon the effect which the writer wishes to produce and the audience he has in mind. The writer has all the resources of the English language at his command. From among these he chooses the particular words, the groupings of words, and the organization of ideas which he believes will produce the effect that he is seeking.

The English language itself, however, has its own patterns of structure, its own conventions which underlie the various resources available to the skilled writer. If he does not observe certain of these patterns, confusion will result and no one will understand what he is trying to say. If the writer or speaker violates certain of the conventions of the language, he runs the risk of being marked as ignorant or uncultivated by his audience, and his language detracts attention from the material that he wishes to communicate.

The first part of this book was concerned with the basic questions of composition: the planning of the whole and the effective command of the various kinds of units or parts. This portion of the text will deal with the more mechanical and conventional considerations. Fortunately, these can be reduced to rather definite rules. When you have mastered these rules so thoroughly that they have become a part of your unconscious speech and writing habits, you will have acquired a mastery of the standard forms of present-day English.

V. The Dictionary

THE preceding chapter has shown us the importance of words in language and communication. We have seen how easily they can be misused and misapplied and how unfortunate the consequences may be.

At a conservative estimate, the English language has at least half a million words; the number increases every year. Clearly no one person knows everything there is to be known about all the words in English or in any other language. Dictionaries have been compiled for most of the modern languages as a help and a convenience. Speakers of English are particularly fortunate in that several excellent and complete dictionaries of the language are available.

In order to deal with words competently, one must be able to use a dictionary intelligently. The teacher, the lawyer, the professional writer—anyone who does any amount of speaking or writing—must learn this skill. They all have dictionaries on their desks for ready reference. It is even more important for those who are just becoming acquainted with the vast resources of the English language—students in college English courses.

Your first responsibility is to own a reliable and adequate dictionary which will always be at hand. You must then learn how to use it, to get everything out of it that you need, and above all to interpret its information correctly.

1. KINDS OF DICTIONARIES

Dictionaries may be divided into two classes: the extensive unabridged works, usually found in schoolrooms and libraries, and the condensed treatments which are within

fac·tor (fak′tər) *n.* **1.** One of the elements or causes that contribute to produce a result. **2.** *Math.* One of two or more quantities that, when multiplied together, produce a given quantity. **3.** *Biol.* The unit of heredity; gene. **4.** *Physiol.* An element important in metabolism and nutrition, as a vitamin, enzyme, or hormone. **5.** A person or organization that undertakes to finance the operations of certain companies, as textile firms, accepting receivables as collateral. **6.** One who transacts business for another on a commission basis; a commission merchant. **7.** *Scot.* An agent who manages an estate; a bailiff or steward. **8.** *U.S.* In some States, a garnishee. **— Syn.** See DOER. **—** *v.t. Math.* To resolve into factors. Abbr. *fac.* [< L, maker < *facere* to make] **— fac′tor·ship** *n.*

ABRIDGED[1]

the means of the average student. In the condensed versions the rare uses of a word are frequently omitted and the definitions are not so fully illustrated, but these smaller works will satisfy a large portion of your needs. Here are two definitions of the word *factor*, one from an abridged dictionary and one from an unabridged version. They illustrate the difference both in fullness and manner of treatment found in the two types of dictionaries.

a. Unabridged Dictionaries

Of the unabridged dictionaries, those furnishing the most accurate and recent information are

The Oxford English Dictionary. 13 vols. and Supplement. Oxford: Clarendon Press, 1888–1933. A corrected reissue appeared in 1933. The original issue bears the title *A New English Dictionary*.

The Shorter Oxford English Dictionary. 2 vols. Oxford: Clarendon Press, 1933. The 3rd edition, with corrections and revised addenda, was published in one volume in 1955.

Webster's New International Dictionary of the English Language. Springfield, Mass.: G. & C. Merriam Co., original copyright 1934; latest 1957.

Webster's Third New International Dictionary. Springfield, Mass.: G. & C. Merriam Co., 1961.

¹**fac·tor** \'faktə(r) *also* -ˌtȯ(ə)r *or* -ȯ(ə)\ *n* -s [ME *factour*, fr. MF *facteur*, fr. L *factor*, maker, doer, fr. *factus* + *-or*] **1 :** a person that acts or transacts business for another **:** AGENT, DEPUTY: as **a :** a commercial agent who sells or buys goods for others on commission **:** CONSIGNEE; *esp* **:** one permitted to buy and sell in his own name and entrusted with the possession and control of goods — compare BROKER **b** *now chiefly Scot* **:** a steward or bailiff of an estate; *also* **:** one appointed by law to have charge of forfeited or sequestered property **c :** an employee of the former East India Company of Britain that ranked above a writer and below a merchant **d :** the agent in charge of a trading post of the Hudson's Bay Company who adds to the usual duties of a factor the care of the company's territory and often exercises a quasi police control of the surrounding region **e :** a commercial banker or finance company specializing in financial services to producers and dealers (as the discounting of accounts receivable) **2** *obs* **a :** PARTISAN, ADHERENT **b :** a maker, author, or doer of anything **3 a :** something (as an element, circumstance, or influence) that contributes to the production of a result **:** CONSTITUENT, INGREDIENT ⟨people and people's doings are the essential ∼ —I.J.C.Brown⟩ ⟨such ∼s as availability of adequate power, transportation, and a labor source must be considered in appraising an industrial site⟩ ⟨hereditary predisposition, malnutrition, and overexertion are common ∼s in the development of many diseases⟩ **b** *or* **factor of production :** a good or service (as land, labor, or capital) used in the process of production **c :** one of the elements determined in job evaluation to be essential to a job (as skill and training required, effort demanded, responsibility and working conditions involved) — called also *job factor* **4 a :** GENE **b :** a presumed equivalent of a gene (as a plasmagene) ⟨some authorities recognize more than one kind of cytoplasmic ∼⟩ **5 a :** any of the numbers, quantities, or symbols in mathematics that when multiplied together form a product **b :** the number by which a given time is multiplied in photography to give the complete time for exposure or development **c :** a number that converts by multiplication the weight of one substance into the chemically equivalent weight of another substance — called also *gravimetric factor* **6 :** a substance (as a hormone or vitamin) promoting or functioning in a particular physiological process; *esp* **:** such a substance of which the exact nature or mode of action is unknown ⟨the role of extrinsic ∼s in blood formation⟩ **syn** see ELEMENT
²**fac·tor** \-ˌtə(r)\ *vb* **factored; factored; factoring** \-t(ə)riŋ\ **factors** *vt* **1 :** to resolve into factors **:** FACTORIZE **2 :** to act as factor for ⟨∼ed his cousin's estate after he got out of the army⟩ ∼ *vi* **:** to act as a factor esp. in discounting accounts receivable ⟨∼ing in connection with automobile installment accounts is a big business today⟩

UNABRIDGED²

New Standard Dictionary of the English Language. New York and London: Funk & Wagnalls, original copyright 1913; latest 1963.

The Random House Dictionary of the English Language. New York: Random House, 1966.

Of these more extensive works, the most important for the scholar is the *Oxford English Dictionary.* It is the product of more than fifty years of research. Particularly valuable are the illustrative citations which are given for every meaning of every word. For the general user, the Webster dictionaries listed above are the most convenient source of information on the language.

b. Abridged Dictionaries

Here is a list of some abridged or condensed dictionaries:

Webster's Seventh New Collegiate Dictionary. Springfield, Mass.: G. & C. Merriam Co., 1965.

The American College Dictionary. New York: Random House, original copyright 1947; latest 1966.

Standard College Dictionary. New York and London: Funk & Wagnalls, 1963. Text edition published by Harcourt, Brace & World, Inc.

Thorndike-Barnhart Comprehensive Desk Dictionary. Garden City, New York: Doubleday & Co., original copyright 1951; latest 1965.

Webster's New World Dictionary of the American Language. College Edition. Cleveland: The World Publishing Co., original copyright 1953; latest 1966.

2. LEARNING ABOUT YOUR DICTIONARY

Capable artisans usually take pride in their tools and know a great deal about them. A cabinetmaker will value a set of chisels of a particular make. A draftsman will prize his case of drawing pens and can often tell fascinating stories about their history and uses. In short, a skilled craftsman knows his tools.

As one who is learning the craft of word usage, your first task is to make the acquaintance of your own dictionary. One place to begin is with what is often called the *front matter*. This includes the title page, preface, and table of contents. Titles, for example, are not bestowed at random. They are intended to tell you something about the purpose, scope, and contents of the work. To label a dictionary *International* suggests something about its coverage; to label it a dictionary of the *American Language* implies something quite different. It is well to know who edited your dictionary, what sort of help he had in his staff and advisers, and above all to learn from the table of contents just what kinds of information the book will supply.

Many dictionaries include a section of specimen entries to show the many kinds of information that the dictionary entries themselves contain. The specimen entry facsimile reprinted on pages 182–83 should be helpful to you as you read **D3–8**.

The list of dictionaries given in the foregoing section usually distinguishes between the original and the latest copyright dates. This is important because the original copyright date shows when the current edition was compiled or revised. The last date given is that of the most recent printing. Dictionary publishers are able to make minor changes from one printing to another, but it is only when a dictionary is re-edited that its entire content is reconsidered and thoroughly revised.

EXERCISE I

By referring to the prefatory parts of your dictionary, answer as many of the following questions as you can:

1. What is the precise title? What does it suggest about the purpose and scope of your dictionary?

2. Who is the editor?

3. What is the name of the publisher?

4. What are the earliest and most recent copyright dates (see the back of the title page)? When was your particular volume printed? When was it edited?

5. Is the editorial staff named? Was there an advisory committee or board? A group of specialists who served as consultants?

6. What kinds of information does the preface contain?

7. Note the table of contents. Aside from the preface and the main portion of the dictionary, what special sections are there?

8. On which of the following points could you get information by turning to a special section of your dictionary?

    a. The location and size of Slippery Rock State College.

    b. The number of rods in a furlong.

    c. The symbols for the signs of the zodiac.

    d. The form to be used in addressing a letter to your congressman.

    e. The meaning of *stet* as a proofreader's mark.

    f. The uses of the hyphen.

    g. The names of the principal biographical dictionaries in English.

    h. Words that rhyme with *entrap*.

3. MEANING

The earliest dictionaries were compiled primarily for the purpose of explaining the "hard words" in the language. Definition is still a basic function of the dictionary. (See the discussion of definition in Chapter I, **T7**.) Here one word of caution must be given. When you consult the dictionary for the meaning of a word, be careful to read *all* the definitions. Do not stop with the first; it may not be the one you want or need.

The following illustration shows how necessary it is to

read all of the definitions: In an old play, written more than three hundred years ago, there is the following line: "Such a crafty spy I have caught. . . . Brought him to the court and in the porter's lodge *dispatched* him." The word *dispatched* is not wholly clear and we consult one of the unabridged dictionaries to get help. The first meaning given is *to send off or away.* Certainly this meaning does not make sense in the context we have. A second meaning is *to put to death.* This is a plausible interpretation, but we see that on the next page or so this same character bobs up again, and evidently he was not killed; we have not yet found the right meaning. A number of other definitions such as *to settle a piece of business quickly, to consume or devour, to start promptly for a place,* are all out of the question. Finally we come to one which reads *to put out of the way, to stow away.* This, from all appearances, fits the case. The spy had been placed in the porter's lodge for safe-keeping.

Remember that the other definitions are just as important as the first and that you must keep on applying the various definitions until you find one that exactly fits the context.

EXERCISE II

A. Find, in your abridged dictionary, the definition which properly applies to the italicized word in each of the following sentences:

1. The books on sale at the fair were there on *consignment.*
2. In many of its relations, hydrogen *demeans* itself much like a metal.
3. My watch is *fast.* She was *fast* asleep.
4. Everyone is familiar with the common *phenomenon* of a piece of metal being eaten away by rust.
5. It was not then certain if the gun was *unloaded.*

SPECIMEN ENTRIES

The numbers preceding the page numbers refer to sections in *The Plan of This Dictionary.*

fingerbreadth

fin·ger·breadth (fing′gər-bredth′, -bretth′) *n.* The breadth of a finger, from ¾ inch to one inch.

fin·ger·ing (fing′gər·ing) *n.* **1.** The act of touching or feeling with the fingers. **2.** *Music* **a** The action or technique of using the fingers in playing an instrument. **b** The notation indicating what fingers are to be used.

fin·ick·y (fin′i·kē) *adj.* Excessively fastidious or precise; fussy; exacting: also spelled *finicky.* [< FINE¹ + -ICAL]

fis·sile (fis′sal) *adj.* **1.** Capable of being split or separated into layers. **2.** Tending to split. [< L *fissilis* < *findere* to split] — **fis·sil·i·ty** (fi·sil′ə·tē) *n.*

fis·si·ped (fis′ə·ped) *adj.* Having the toes separated: also **fis·sip·e·dal** (fi·sip′ə·dəl, fis′i·ped′l), **fis·si·pe·di·al** (-pē′dē·əl). — *n. Zool.* Any of a suborder (*Fissipedia*) of terrestrial carnivores with separate toes, as [matter omitted]

fist¹ (fist) *n.* **1.** The hand closed tightly, as for striking; the clenched hand; also, grip; clutch. **2.** [matter omitted]

fist² (fist). *n.* A fice.

fla·vor (flā′vər) *n.* **1.** Taste; especially, a distinctive element in the overall taste of something. **2.** Something added, as to food, to increase taste or to impart a specific taste; flavoring. **3.** A special, subtle quality pervading something: a novel that has the *flavor* of Dickens. — *Archaic.* Odor. — *v.t.* To give flavor to. — Also *Brit.* **fla′vour.** [< OF *flaor, fleur,* prob. ult. < L *flare* to blow; *v* sense by analogy with *savor*]

fla′vor·less *adj.*

flea (flē) *n.* **1.** A small, wingless, parasitic insect (order *Siphonaptera*) that sucks the blood of mammals and birds and is capable of leaping for relatively great distances. For illustration see INSECTS (injurious). ◆ Collateral adjective: *pulicene.* **2.** One of several small beetles or crustaceans that jump like fleas, as a beach flea. — **a flea in one's ear 1.** A pointed hint. **2.** An upsetting or stinging rebuke, refusal, or rejection. [OE *flēa, flēah.* Akin to FLEE.] —

flite (flīt) *Dial. v.i. flit·ed, flit·ing* To wrangle; quarrel. — *n.* Abusive quarreling. Also spelled *flyte.*

Labels (pointing to the entries):

- The main entry, *1, p. xvii.*
- Word division, *1, p. xvii.*
- Pronunciation, *2, p. xvii.*
- Part of speech, *3, p. xvii.*
- Run-in part of speech, *3, p. xvii.*
- Homographs, *p. 642.*
- Variant form, *8, p. xviii.*
- Cross-reference, *9, p. xviii.*
- Level label, *p. xx.*
- Definition numbers, *5, p. xviii.*
- Definition dividers, *5, p. xviii.*
- Etymology, *p. xxi.*
- Scientific name
- Currency label, *6, p. xviii.*
- Illustrative phrase
- Run-on derivatives, *11, p. xviii.*
- Collateral adjective, *7, p. xviii.*
- Idiomatic phrase
- Inflected forms, *4, p. xvii.*

182

9, p. xviii.

Variant form, 8, p. xviii.

fly'er (also) See FLIER.

fold-boat (fōld'bōt') *n.* A faltboat (which see).

forb (fôrb) *n.*—*SW U.S.* A weed or other herb that is not grass. [Appar. < Gk. *phorbē* fodder]

Foreign-language label, 6, p. xviii.

force majeure (fôrs mà-zhœr') *French* —Superior and irresistible force.

Locality label, 6, p. xviii.

foreign office The department of government in charge of foreign affairs. Abbr. *F.O.*

Abbreviation

fret·ful (fret'fəl) *adj.* Inclined to fret; peevish or restless. —**fret'ful·ly** *adv.* —**fret'ful·ness** *n.*

—Syn. complaining, impatient, pettish, petulant, restive. —Ant. patient, calm, uncomplaining.

Synonym and antonym list, 13, p. xix.

Phrasal entry, 1, p. xvii.

friend·ship (frend'ship) *n.* **1.** The state or fact of being friends. **2.** Mutual liking and esteem. **3.** [matter omitted]

—Syn. *Friendship, amity,* and *comity* characterize the relation between persons, nations, etc. In *friendship* there is an affectionate desire to give sympathy and aid. *Amity* refers to the absence of discord rather than to positive affection or regard. *Comity* is applied to nations or parties more often than to individuals and denotes a courteous respect for the wishes or rights of others.

Discriminated synonyms, 13, p. xix.

friv·ol (friv'əl) *v. Informal v.i.* **1.** To behave frivolously [matter omitted]

Style label, p. xx.

gamp (gamp) *n. Brit.* A large heavy umbrella: a humorous usage. [matter omitted]

Usage note, 12, p. xix.

got·ten (got'n) Past participle of GET. ◆ *Gotten,* obsolete in British, is current in American English along with *got.* In the informal senses of obligation and possession only *got* is used: *I've got to go, He's got a fine library.*

Abbreviation

GPM or **gpm** or **g.p.m.** Gallons per minute.

Combining form, p. 269.

-graph *combining form* **1.** That which writes or records: *seismograph.* **2.** [matter omitted]

Biographical entry, 1, p. xvii.

Hal·lam (hal'əm) Henry, 1777–1859, English historian.

Geographical entry, 1, p. xvii.

Hamilton River A river in southern Labrador, flowing 600 miles, generally east, to Hamilton Inlet, a bay of the Atlantic.

Related phrase

-hood *suffix of nouns* **1.** Condition or quality of; state of being: *babyhood, falsehood.* **2.** [matter omitted]

Prefix, p. 1063.

Suffix, p. 1338.

hyper- *prefix* **1.** Over; above; excessive: *hypercritical.* **2.** *Med.* Denoting an abnormal state of excess: *hypertension:* opposed to *hypo-*. [matter omitted]

Field label, 6, p. xviii.

6. The *instrument* under which Cromwell took his title gave him no unnecessary executive authority.
7. The only army which the law *recognized* was the militia.
8. He was so frightened that he had no *stomach* for more mysteries.
9. The children showed the effects of *low* nutrition.
10. The hour was morning's *prime*.

B. How many definitions can you think of for the word *pipe*, both noun and verb? Write as many as you can, then look up the word in an unabridged dictionary, comparing your list of definitions with those you find in the dictionary.

a. Order of Definitions

If you will compare the two dictionary treatments of the word *factor*, given on pages 176–77, you will find that the order of definitions is quite different. The definition which comes first in the unabridged dictionary is the sixth in order in the abridged dictionary. Where in the unabridged dictionary is the first definition in the abridged dictionary?

The problem of determining the order of definition faces the compiler of every dictionary. Some dictionaries list the older meanings first and proceed historically to the more recent. Others begin with the most common meanings. You must know what order your dictionary follows. Find in the preface of your dictionary the statement which explains this.

b. Changes in Meaning

The dictionary can trace for us the changes in meaning which words undergo over a long period of time. If we look up the word *deer* in *Webster's Third New International Dictionary*, we find as the earliest meaning (one which is no longer current), *Animal, especially quadruped mammal.* In the course of centuries the word has become more particular or specialized in its meaning. Conversely, the first recorded meaning of the word *frock* is *An outer garment worn by monks or friars*. Now the word is applied to any dress or gown. This word has developed in a direction opposite to that taken by *deer*, which has become more general in meaning.

EXERCISE III

Trace the changes in meaning that have taken place in the following words, and in the case of each, determine whether the development has been in the direction of generalization or specialization. Use an unabridged dictionary in preparing this exercise.

| business | ordeal | starve | wade |
| butler | quarantine | undertaker | zest |

Changes in meaning are not limited to those proceeding from a specific meaning to a more general, or from a general meaning to a more specific. Certain words which, at the outset of their history, denote thoroughly respectable ideas, in the course of time acquire disreputable meanings and finally come to stand for an unpleasant or not wholly praiseworthy thing or idea. The word *villain* originally meant *farm laborer, person of ignoble birth*. By gradual stages the word came to signify ignobility of character instead of occupation.

Other words have changed in the opposite direction. The word *marshal* meant originally *groom* or *stable servant*; today it may be used to denote an officer in a royal household or one of high rank in the army. Still other words which originally referred to specific, concrete objects are now used as names for abstractions. Our modern word *dreary* once meant *bloody*. The opposite change, from abstract to concrete, has also occurred in many words.

EXERCISE IV

Trace the changes in meaning that have taken place in the following words, and in each instance point out what the direction of the change has been, in the light of the discussion given in the preceding paragraphs.

boor	doom	humor	pioneer
counterfeit	fame	imp	steward

4. SYNONYMS AND ANTONYMS

We often find that we are using a certain word so frequently that it becomes monotonous. If you have used the word *advance* four or five times in one paragraph, you will want to find a word such as *proceed* or *progress* to substitute for it. Such substitute words are called *synonyms*, and in most dictionaries they appear after the definition of each word.

Two words rarely have exactly the same meaning. An accurate reader and writer differentiates carefully between nearly synonymous pairs of words. The unabridged dictionaries and the better abridged dictionaries usually point out such differences with great care. There are in addition such special reference works as *Webster's Dictionary of Synonyms*, *The Roget Dictionary of Synonyms and Antonyms*, Fowler's *Modern English Usage*, and Bergen and Cornelia Evans' *Dictionary of Contemporary American Usage*, each devoted either wholly or in part to helping the writer with problems of synonymy. See also Chapter IX, page 333 and Chapter X, **L4c.**

EXERCISE V

A. Consult the preface of your dictionary and read the section on synonymy. Note particularly what is said about the order in which the synonyms are given, the punctuation within the synonymy, the type faces used in this section and their significance, and any system of cross references which is employed.

B. Find suitable synonyms for the following words:

discern	peremptory	propensity
empty	praise (verb)	soar

C. These pairs of words are at times interchanged in use. Be able to point out the distinction in meaning between the two members of each pair, and use each word correctly in a sentence.

gift	present	serene	tranquil
mortal	fatal	expand	distend
exemption	immunity	inert	sluggish
observation	observance	elevate	exalt
arrest	check	grotesque	bizarre
mutual	common	dominate	domineer

D. What is an *antonym?* Find suitable antonyms for the following words:

countenance (verb)	impromptu
facility	parsimonious

5. LABELS

Immediately preceding the definition of many words is found what dictionary makers call a *label.* This indicates that such a word or a particular meaning of it is somewhat restricted in actual use. There are three kinds of labels: *subject labels, geographical labels,* and *usage labels.*

Subject labels are generally applied to technical words or

to technical meanings of a word and show the department of knowledge to which it is confined. The noun *stop* has special meanings in the fields of machinery, music, phonetics, finance, and sailing; and each of its definitions peculiar to these fields is prefixed with the appropriate label.

The geographical labels show the particular region where a word, a meaning, or a pronunciation occurs most frequently. Words such as *floorwalker*, which is used chiefly in the United States; *dogie*, which is used only in the Western United States; or *petrol*, confined to British use, are so labeled in an accurate dictionary.

The usage labels are often misunderstood. The one most frequently misinterpreted is the label *colloquial*. If you will consult any dictionary for the meaning of this word, you will find *colloquial* means simply *pertaining to*, or *characteristic of*, *conversation*. The second edition of *Webster's New International Dictionary* was careful to add to its definition, "Colloquial speech may be as correct as formal speech." If a word or a particular meaning of a word is marked *colloquial* in a dictionary, this label means merely that the word is used in informal conversation rather than in formal writing, and you may feel perfectly free to use it in this way. Some dictionaries no longer use *colloquial* as a label because of its liability to misinterpretation.

Another common usage label is *dial.* for *dialect* or *dialectal.* This is applied when a word is used in several localities, so many, in fact, that it would be awkward to assign it to any particular one. Again this label is not necessarily a condemnation. It merely states that a word or meaning not characteristic of the whole English-speaking world is used in a particular manner in certain regions. Notice also such labels as *illiterate*, *substandard*, *nonstandard*, *slang*, *obsolete*, and *archaic*. If you are uncertain of the meaning of any of these, look them up.

6. DERIVATION

The English language is derived from a number of different sources. Many of our common words were in the language when the invading Anglo-Saxon tribes made their homes on the island of Britain. But the English-speaking people have always been great word borrowers; consequently Latin, French, Scandinavian, Italian, German, Dutch, Greek, and almost every other known language have contributed something to our word stock.

That branch of language study which concerns itself with the origin and derivation of words is known as *etymology*; the *etymology* of any particular word shows the elements of its formation and the origin and derivation of these elements. If we look up the word *draw* (verb) in the dictionary, we shall find its etymology given as OE *dragan*. This means that *draw* is a native or Old English word, that it was in the language spoken by the Anglo-Saxon tribes that came to England in the fifth and sixth centuries. The Old English word is recorded without comment, so we may assume that the meaning of *dragan* in Old English was about the same as its modern descendant.

A longer and more complicated history is illustrated by the word *energy*. The dictionary shows that it is derived from Late Latin *energia*, which in turn came from the Greek *energeia*, a noun made from the adjective *energos*, "active"; finally, *energos* was composed of the prefix *en-*, "in," and *ergon*, "work."

At times two or more elements coming from different languages have combined to make a single English word. In the word *eatable*, the French suffix *-able* has been added to the English verb *eat*. English and Latin are combined in *speedometer*. Even such a strange combination as Persian and Latin is to be found in the word *asafetida*.

EXERCISE VI

A. Consult the preface of your dictionary and make a list of the usage labels it employs. Look up the following words in your dictionary. What limitations does the dictionary place upon their usage in the English language?

donate	glabrous	manageress	reluct
feisty	goober	mesotron	scarlatina
floozy	hoosegow	pugree	whammy

brass (high-ranking military officers)
brass (excessive assurance)
pinto (a horse)
scant (adverb)

B. Read everything in the preface of your dictionary which explains how the etymologies are presented. Where, in respect to the complete word treatment, do they appear? Are there any situations where the word itself is not given in the etymology, but only the language from which it is derived? Familiarize yourself with the abbreviations used to indicate the various source languages, and find out where these abbreviations are listed.

C. Consult your dictionary for the origin of the following words. Be able to tell from which language they are derived, what they meant when they were taken into the English language, and what change in meaning they have since undergone.

adobe	flank	landscape	quartz
asterisk	flannel	moose	skin
finger	kismet	peninsula	umbrella

7. WORD FORMATION

When we looked up the etymology of the word energy we found that this word was put together centuries ago by the Greeks, who placed the syllable *en*, meaning *in*, before *ergon*, their word for *work*. They made a word where none had existed before.

In our present-day language we still do the same thing. As soon as the term *pop art* had acquired definite meaning in the art world, we began to characterize a person who produced it as a *popster*; and this in turn led to *op art* as a shortening of *optical art* and the corresponding term *opster*. The explorations of outer space have given rise to a totally new vocabulary. Such terms as *retrorocket*, *cosmonaut*, and *Lunik* put word-forming elements into new combinations. *Gantry* has acquired a new meaning. *Count down*, *space walk*, and *soft landing* are new compounds, the first having shifted from a verb to a noun function, and the latter having given rise to the verb construction *to soft land*. By means of such word-forming processes, we often make a single word answer the purpose of a whole clause or phrase.

The extent to which this process of word-derivation has taken place in English is truly astonishing. From such a familiar root word as *bear*, at least thirty-six other words have been formed, ranging all the way from *barrow* to *birth* to *overburdensome*. The Latin root *ced*, "go from," with its participial form *cess-*, and the related French form *cease*, have been even more prolific, producing eighty modern English words.

Some dictionaries will not give separate definitions for all words so formed, but expect the user to look up the prefix or suffix and then the main word, that he may put together his own definition.

EXERCISE VII

A. Consult your dictionary to determine how each of the italicized prefixes in the following list modifies the meaning of the word to which it has been attached.

| anteroom | extralegal | semisolid | transoceanic |
| disable | omnipotent | superhuman | ultraviolet |

B. Consult your dictionary to determine how each of the italicized suffixes in the list below modifies the meaning and changes the grammatical function of the word to which it has been attached. Look for the treatment of the suffix as a whole rather than for the individual word; that is, look up *-able* as a separate entry rather than in connection with *perishable*. Do likewise with the others.

| perish*able* | bak*er* | steril*ize* |
| marri*age* | botan*ist* | amaze*ment* |

C. Look up the word *acronym* in your dictionary. In the light of the definition given there, explain the origin of the following: *UNESCO, DDT, radar, Sea-bee, cortisone.*

8. PRONUNCIATION

Second only to the service performed by the dictionary in supplying meaning, is the information given about pronunciation. This is difficult to convey accurately in print and is frequently misunderstood. With a little practice you can learn to interpret correctly the dictionary treatment of pronunciations.

You must first realize that dictionaries have changed considerably with respect to the kind of pronunciation that is indicated in them, but that this change is not always understood by people who use them. Some thirty years ago it was not unusual for a dictionary to record the pronunciation which would normally be used by a public speaker with a view to being clearly understood by his hearers. Such a person, addressing a large audience, would have been likely in pronouncing the words *evil* and *forest* to give the second syllables the values of the vowels of *bit* and *bet* respectively. Electronic voice amplification has made unnecessary the cultivation of a somewhat artificial style of platform pronunciation; and as a result most dictionaries now indicate what has been appropriately described as the language of well-bred ease—the pronunciations characteristic of the unstudied, informal conversation of educated speakers. Even though the pronunciations indicated are those of words spoken in isolation rather than in running context, editors seek to avoid anything that smacks of "overpronunciation," with its unnatural emphasis upon normally unstressed syllables and the preservation of vowels that are reduced in idiomatic and correct English speech.

It is even more important that you understand clearly the meaning of each of the symbols employed to indicate pronunciation. To help you in this, most dictionaries provide a key, either at the foot of the page or on the inside cover. Refer to this first. The value of each symbol is indicated in terms of the sound you use in a series of common words. Suppose you are doubtful about the pronunciation of the y in *xylene*. The key tells you to use in it the stressed vowel sound of *ice*, not of *if*. It does not tell you how to pronounce the *i* in *ice*, which does indeed vary in different parts of the country.

If, as in some dictionaries, there is a section in the preface which is devoted to pronunciation, by consulting it you can learn more about the pronunciation of the symbols. For example, from the preface of *Webster's Third New International Dictionary*, you would discover how northern and southern American pronunciations of the vowels of *out* and *loud* differ from each other; where, in the English-speaking world, the *r* is "dropped"; and the various pronunciations given to the vowel of *fast*.

An especially important symbol in many dictionary keys

is the inverted e or schwa [ə], used to indicate the neutral sound of a vowel in unaccented syllables. It has the value of *a* in *around, e* in *taken, i* in *cabin, o* in *gallop, u* in *circus.* This method of indicating the unstressed vowel is considered useful in that it avoids suggesting unnatural or exaggerated pronunciations of these vowels.

In addition to the exact quality of the sounds which make up a word, we also need to know the amount of stress which the various syllables of a word normally receive. Stress is quite as important as sound quality in our scheme of pronunciation; this is illustrated by a word such as *increase.* If the first syllable is accented (*in'crease*) the word is a noun; if the second syllable receives the stress (*increase'*), we interpret the word as a verb.

You must also recognize that most dictionaries indicate at least two degrees of stress, primary and secondary. These are most often differentiated by the heaviness of the type of the acute accent mark. Thus, a word like *convocation* will be transcribed as follows, with primary stress on the third syllable and secondary stress on the first: *kon' vō kā' shən.*

There is a widespread belief that when a number of pronunciations are given for any word, the first of these pronunciations is to be greatly preferred over the others, that it is more correct than those which follow. If the first pronunciation is so much more correct than those which follow it, why should the dictionary even take the trouble to record a second and at times a third pronunciation?

Actually the supposed superiority of the first pronunciation has no foundation. According to the General Introduction of the *American College Dictionary* (p. xix), "Any pronunciation in this dictionary is a good pronunciation and may be safely used. If the second or third pronunciation is your natural pronunciation, it is the one to use."

Moreover, no really scientific and accurate dictionary claims to set up a single standard of correctness for all the words in the English language. Since the editor conceives of his task as that of compiling a record of usage, and since, as the Webster editors tell us, "at present uniformity of pronunciation is not to be found through the English-speaking world," there will be many times when numbers of variant pronunciations will have to be listed. You may be certain that if a pronunciation were not acceptable, it would not have been included in a reliable dictionary.

EXERCISE VIII

A. Consult your dictionary to discover how many degrees of accent are marked and whether the accent marks precede or follow the syllables to which they apply.

B. How does your dictionary mark the accent of the following words? When the word in question is used as both noun and verb, note the position of the stress in both functions.

accent	detour	finance	protest
address	dictator	irrefutable	recall
ally	discourse	perfume	resource
defect	divan	pretense	robust

C. What change in grammatical function occurs in the following words when the accent changes?

adept	frequent	refuse
compress	invalid	subject

D. There is frequently some question about the proper pronunciation of the following words. Look them up in your dictionary and find out what pronunciations are recorded. Remember that there is no disapproval attached to the label *colloquial*.

abdomen	either	often
acetic	gape	patronage
advertisement	granary	pumpkin
aggrandizement	harass	quintuplet
alien	hygienic	ration
amateur	indisputable	reservoir
apparatus	inquiry	robot
apricot	interesting	romance
bouquet	isolate	route
calf	lever	student
centenary	literature	tissue
clematis	mobile	tomato
comparable	mustache	Tuesday
creek	naphtha	version
decadence	nascent	yolk
decorous	new	zenith
drama	obesity	

E. Consult your dictionary for the pronunciation of the following words. See whether your pronunciation is included among those given.

blatant	impious	perforate
cavalry	incognito	respite
chasm	incisive	sagacious
eccentric	irrelevant	schism
exigency	indict	status
garrulous	Italian	superfluous
heinous	orchid	victuals

F. Most dictionaries devote special sections to the pronunciation of foreign personal and place names. Consult the preface of yours and familiarize yourself with any symbols representing non-English sounds. Practice making such sounds until you can produce them with some degree of ease. Then determine the pronunciation of the following words:

Casals	Edinburgh	Boulogne
Gauguin	Novgorod	Popocatepetl
Genghis Khan	Majorca	Versailles
Maupassant	Goethe	Van Gogh
Giotto	Tschaikowsky	Balzac

9. SPELLING

(See also Chapter VIII.)

The dictionary is our guide also in matters of spelling. For those words in the language which are spelled in more than one way, it records the variants. As we have already seen, it tells us whether compounds are spelled solidly as a single word or as two, or if they are hyphenated. We are shown how words are divided into syllables, enabling us to separate them properly at the ends of lines. Irregular spellings of noun plurals and verb participles and past tense forms are indicated. Finally, foreign words not yet anglicized and therefore demanding italics (underlining in manuscript or typescript) are identified.

Many of the variant spellings you will find in the dictionary reflect differences between British and American practice. For example, *humour* is British, *humor* American. Find out how your dictionary treats these differences. There may be a section in the preface listing British spelling preferences. In the body of the dictionary, the British variant may be given under the American spelling, or the British spelling may have a cross reference to the treatment of the word under its American spelling. It is desirable to use accepted American rather than British spellings where the conventions of the two countries are not the same.

Otherwise, when two spellings are given for any word, you must interpret the dictionary treatment just as you did in the case of variant pronunciations. One form must appear first in the treatment; the editor places first that form for which he has the most evidence. The second spelling would not be there at all if it did not have the support of good usage. Look in the preface of your dictionary to see how it deals with variant spellings.

EXERCISE IX

A. What is the preferred spelling of the following words? In each case indicate, if possible, the status of the alternate spelling: British, simplified, etc.

aeon	eon	inflexion	inflection
caliber	calibre	judgement	judgment
canceled	cancelled	mold	mould
catalog	catalogue	practice	practise
defense	defence	staunch	stanch
enclose	inclose	vapour	vapor

B. Which of the following foreign words are not yet anglicized and thus require italics (underlining)?

bar mitzvah	petit four
cap-a-pie	picador
chef-d'oeuvre	sine die
déjeuner	virtuoso
mochila	Weltanschauung

C. Find out how syllabic division is indicated in your dictionary and whether there is any discussion of the problem in the preface. Without first looking up the words in the following list, indicate what seems to be the proper division; then look them up in your dictionary. In how many instances do your divisions correspond to those in the dictionary?

bookmark	feeble	oblige
chasm	formulate	pressure
dabble	hearty	situation
exasperate	magic	telegraph
favor	multiply	transact

10. GRAMMAR

The dictionary offers three kinds of grammatical information:

1. Immediately after the pronunciation of any word, the dictionary tells you what part of speech that word is. Learn the symbols and abbreviations your dictionary employs in indicating the parts of speech. If any word may perform the function of more than one part of speech, that is also indicated in its treatment. Verbs are also labeled *transitive* or *intransitive* in most dictionaries.

2. After the part-of-speech entry, irregularities in inflectional forms are noted: irregular plurals such as *mice*, irregular past tenses such as *went*, irregular comparatives such as *better*. If there are alternate forms for any word, such as the plural of *formula*, which may be either *formulas* or *formulae*, this is also indicated.

3. When there is uncertainty about the use of a word, the dictionary often makes a definite statement about it. For example, in connection with the troublesome use of the pronoun *none*, the Webster dictionaries say, "As subject, *none* with a plural verb is the commoner construction."

EXERCISE X

By reference to an unabridged dictionary, answer the following questions dealing with problems of grammar. Note any differences between colloquial and formal English which you may find and remember that the term *colloquial* is not used in a derogatory sense.

1. What is the plural of *stigma*?
2. Is the verb *try* ever used with *and* followed by the infinitive (*Try and get it*)?
3. What is the past tense of *sink*?
4. Are there any circumstances when *towards* is more likely to be used than *toward*?
5. What part or parts of speech is the word *like*?
6. Some writers insist that there is no such word as *enthuse*. Are they justified in this?
7. What is the past tense of the verb *light*? of the verb *plead*?
8. May one say "I have got" for "I have"?
9. What is the plural of *gladiolus*? Is *gladiola* singular or plural?
10. Does *whoever* occur as the object of a verb as well as the subject?
11. What are the principal parts of the verb *strive*?
12. Is *neither* ever used with a plural verb?
13. What is the plural of *partridge*?
14. Can *go* be used as a transitive verb?
15. How do you spell the plural of *bus*?
16. Is *loan* used as a verb?
17. What is the past participle of *hide*?
18. Is the verb *can* used to indicate permission?
19. Is *where* ever used as a pronoun?
20. What is the past tense of *dive*?

CHAPTER VI. Grammar

LIKE the dictionary maker of today, the grammarian is a scientist. First, he observes the language to see how it behaves; he gathers facts about it. Then he classifies the results of his observations just as the botanist sorts out his plants, or the geologist his rocks. Finally, from his classifications he draws certain general conclusions, which we call *laws* or *rules*. Grammar, then, is a descriptive statement of the way a language is structured and how it works.

1. PARTS OF SPEECH

Perhaps the best way to approach the grammar of your own language is to look at it as if it were a foreign language, entirely new to you, about which you were trying to learn something.[1] During the war in the Pacific many an American soldier was suddenly faced with learning to communicate in a strange language. For instance, a pilot then might have parachuted to safety on an unknown island and had to depend on the natives for his survival. To communicate with them, he would have had to learn their language. If you had to do this, how would you go about it?

Undoubtedly, you would begin by pointing to certain objects and then, using signs, would indicate that you wanted to know the names for these objects. You would point to a tree, a table, a hut, and so on. After a while you would begin to include two or more of the same objects within

[1] Actually, you know English grammar already in the sense that you unconsciously follow the rules almost all the time. But the purpose now is to bring this knowledge to the conscious level and to observe the rules by which the language works.

the scope of your questions. You might even put your hat on your head, take off your coat, or light a fire, in order to find out what names were given to these various actions.

Through such a procedure you would, consciously or unconsciously, have begun to probe into the noun and verb systems of this unfamiliar language. By comparing the word for one hat with that for many hats you would begin to find just how the idea of number was indicated. By putting first a hat on your head, then a hat on a native's head, then motioning to him to put a hat on his own head, and then on yours, you would be learning something about the functions of person, subject, and object in relation to certain verbs.

After each conversation with the islanders you would look through the material you had collected, and attempt to put together into a single class those words which behaved fundamentally in the same way, had the same or similar forms or perhaps indicated the same general kinds of ideas. The classes or classifications which you arrived at as a result of this comparative process might well be called parts of speech.

The parts of speech, then, are classes of words in any given language which have been sorted out according to (1) certain changes that take place in their *form*, such as the addition or alteration of endings; (2) certain *functions* they perform in the sentence, such as that of description or the indication of *who* might be acting; and (3) certain modifications in *meaning*.

For the English language, such attempts at classification have given us eight parts of speech: noun, pronoun, adjective, verb, adverb, preposition, conjunction, and interjection. Since these parts of speech represent merely human endeavors toward a satisfactory classification, you will not be surprised to learn that we have not always recognized the same number of classes and that we have not always given these classes the same names. For example, grammars of the sixteenth century did not recognize the adjective as distinct from the noun. At various other times articles, infinitives, participles, and expletives have all been recognized as separate classes. The newest grammarians, as we shall see, use still other classifications.

Though the language changes from century to century, and though grammarians constantly try to find better methods of analyzing and describing it at any one time, we need to master a terminology which will enable us to discuss the various ways in which speech is put together. Just so we learn the terminology pertaining to an automobile: you would not be content to say, "The thing that I work with my foot that stops the car," instead of *brake*. If you are to deal with problems of language, you must distinguish a noun from an adjective as readily as you would distinguish the battery of a car from the generator.

The definitions still most widely known today for the various parts of speech are as follows:

1. A **noun** is the name of a person, place, thing, quality, collection, or action.

2. A **pronoun** is a word used in place of a noun.

3. An **adjective** is a word used to modify (i.e., describe, limit, or qualify) a noun or pronoun.

4. A **verb** is a word that asserts action, state, or being.

5. An **adverb** is a word that is used to modify a verb, adjective, or another adverb.

6. A **preposition** is a word that shows a relationship between its object (usually a noun or pronoun) and some other word in the sentence.

7. A **conjunction** connects words, phrases, or clauses.

8. An **interjection** is an exclamatory word or phrase which

expresses feeling or emotion and which has no grammatical relationship to the rest of the sentence (if there is one).

The	old	horse	ambled	up	the	street.
Adjective or Article	Adjective	Noun	Verb	Prep.	Adjective or Article	Noun

The	captain	quickly	ordered	him	from	the	room.
Adjective or Article	Noun	Adverb	Verb	Pronoun	Prep.	Adjective or Article	Noun

We	came	early	but	did	not	mind	waiting.
Pronoun	Verb	Adverb	Conj.	Verb	Adverb	Verb	Noun

Oh,	is	that	you?
Interjection	Verb	Pronoun	Pronoun

Notice that a great many English words may function as any one of several parts of speech without changing their spelling or pronunciation. The classification of such a word depends on the way it is used at any given time: its *function*. In the following sentences the word *down* is used in five different functions and is consequently classified as a different part of speech in each instance.

1. It was second *down* and five yards to go. (Noun)
2. The *down* grade was very steep. (Adjective)
3. He will *down* the ball on the goal line. (Verb)
4. The runner was knocked *down*. (Adverb)
5. The team marched *down* the field. (Preposition)

THE NEW ANALYSIS

During the past half century the traditional definitions of the parts of speech have been criticized as being vague and inconsistent in method.[1] It has been pointed out that the definitions of *noun* and *verb* are based on meaning, those of

[1] See Otto Jespersen, *The Philosophy of Grammar*, Chap. IV, and C. C. Fries, *The Structure of English*, Chap. V.

adjective and adverb on function, that of the pronoun on both function and meaning, while the difference between preposition and conjunction, which both act as connectives, is not made clear. The use of meaning as a criterion has been shown to be less satisfactory than either form or function, since the latter two can be studied more objectively.

Grammarians today, therefore, though generally retaining the traditional names for the parts of speech, have redefined them. They divide all words into two broad types: *form-words* and *function-words*. The form-words (nouns, some pronouns, adjectives, verbs, and adverbs) are so called because words of these classes undergo systematic changes in form by which each may be identified. The function-words are all the others, including some traditionally classified as pronouns, verbs, and adverbs; and they are so called because (unlike the form-words) their forms do not change and their grammatical functions are more prominent than their meanings.[1]

The classes of form-words are of unlimited membership: new nouns, verbs, etc. may be and are added to the vocabulary without the least difficulty. But the classes of function-words are virtually fixed as to membership: complete (and relatively short) lists of them can be made for any period in the history of the language. The new definitions of the parts of speech, expressed simply and broadly, would be as follows:

1. A **noun** is a word which may add an affix to show plurality or possession; also, certain specific affixes (such as -al, -ous) can be added to nouns but not to other parts of speech.

2. A **pronoun** is a sub-type of the noun and, like it, has specific forms to show plurality and possession; some pro-

[1] Fries, Chap. VI, treats function-words fully.

nouns may also show gender, person, and the difference between subject and object by means of changes in form.

3. An **adjective** is a word which may add an affix to show a differing degree of comparison; the uncompared form will also fill both slots in the *frame-sentence* (a sentence containing a blank, or *slot*, which can grammatically be filled only by the part of speech under consideration), "The _____ man was very _____."

4. A **verb** is a word which may change its form to show differences in number, tense, or mood; also, certain affixes (such as *re-*, *-able*) may be added to verbs but not to other parts of speech.

5. An **adverb** is a word (commonly formed from an adjective plus *-ly*) which will fill the one-word slot in the sentence, "He came _____."

These five are the form-words. The function-words include not only (6) **prepositions** and (7) **conjunctions**,[1] but two new classes: the *determiner* and the *intensifier*. These will now be defined somewhat more fully.

8. A **determiner** is any word which will fill the slot in the frame-sentence, "_____ good one is very good," or, in the plural, "_____ good ones are very good." Thus *a*, *the*, *my*, *your*, *his*, etc., *some*, *many*, *few*, *all*, *each*, *every*, and the numerals are determiners. This class obviously includes certain sub-classes: the former articles (*the*, *a*, *an*), which some grammarians keep separate from adjectives; the numerals and certain enumerating words also adjectival in function; and the possessive forms of the personal pronouns, which, being possessive, are construed like adjectives. Determiners resemble adjectives in that they modify nouns—indeed, as

---

[1] In any classification, *interjections* are a class apart, since they do not take part in the structure or syntax of the sentence.

the name *determiner* suggests, they are markers of nouns; but unlike adjectives they cannot undergo comparison.

The sub-classes of the determiner, though similar in function, are not merged: when two or more determiners are used together before a noun they must come in a fixed sequence required by English word-order. We must say "*the three* men, *all the* men, *all three* men"—we cannot say "*three the* men, *the all* men." For this reason some grammarians call words like *all* "pre-determiners," because they must have first position in the series of modifiers preceding the noun:

All	the	six	tall	worried	Chicago	students
pre-det.	**article**	**num.**	**adj.**	**participle**	**attributive**	**noun**

9. An **intensifier** is a word which may modify an adjective or an adverb, but not a verb; thus it will fill the slot in "He was _____ good," and "He worked _____ slowly," but not in "He worked _____." Examples of intensifiers are *very, rather, pretty, quite, too* (in the sense of *excessively*). Traditionally these have been classed with adverbs despite their inability to modify verbs. Word-order requires that the intensifier come before the word modified. It is the recognition of the role played by word-order in modern English sentence structure, largely unrealized and neglected in grammars of the past, that has led modern grammarians to re-classify English words and redefine the parts of speech.

EXERCISE I

What part of speech is each word in the following sentences? (Note any differences of classification that may occur.)

1. We need to oil the car.
2. The snow drove by in sheets.
3. Do you plan to buy it tomorrow?
4. This oil will stand about in pools for weeks.

5. Because of the cost of the material, she had to alter the pattern.
6. You must eagerly help her in buying whatever she wants.
7. Oh, how can one ever forget!
8. The company was composed of relatives, neighbors, and a few strangers.
9. Such conditions are worse and more common than we realize.
10. I prefer the green hat to the yellow.

2. NOUNS

In the Old English stage of the language (about 500–1100 A.D.), the noun had many different forms to show three grammatical properties: gender, number, and case. But gender was lost during the Middle English period (1100–1500) and case greatly reduced. The inflectional system has become much simplified in Modern English.

a. Gender. Gender is that property which indicates the sex of the object.

English recognizes three genders: masculine (male), feminine (female), and neuter (without special sex-defining characteristics). *Boy* is a masculine noun, *mare* is feminine, and *table* is neuter.

In English we need only make sure that any *pronoun* which we use will agree in gender with its noun antecedent (the noun to which it refers); that is, we must refer to a table as *it*, not as *he* or *she*. The native speaker would hardly ever do otherwise, so gender raises no problems for him.

b. Number. Number is that property which indicates whether one thing or more than one is named.

English has two numbers, singular and plural. In general, the plural number of a noun is indicated by the addition of -s or -es to the singular. A few nouns form their plurals in other ways, e.g., *oxen, leaves, geese, sheep.*

When we must form the plurals of nouns taken from other languages, notably those which have been borrowed from Latin and Greek, we are faced with this question: Shall the noun retain its foreign plural suffix (*-i, -a, -ae,* etc.), or shall the English plural suffix be adopted? Our practice in this matter is not consistent; some nouns such as *spatula* take only the native English suffix (*spatulas*); others, such as *stimulus,* retain only the ending appropriate to the language from which they were adopted (*stimuli*); a third group, illustrated by *formula,* may employ either ending (*formulas, formulae*). Further, there is a strong tendency today to naturalize Latin and Greek words by treating a plural form as the singular (this *data,* that *media,* etc.) and even by pluralizing these new singulars (*phenomenas, medias,* etc.). Some of the first group have become established. If you are in doubt about any particular word, consult your dictionary.

Observe that our practice in forming the plural of compound nouns is also not consistent, for example: *fountain pens, aides de camp, passers-by, menservants, brothers-in-law, stepbrothers.* Note that in compound nouns ending in -ful, *three bags full* may mean something quite different from *three bagfuls.* The first form calls up a picture of three bags simultaneously filled, whereas the second centers the attention upon the amount that would fill the bags, though it may not actually be in them. Both derivation and frequency of use affect our practice here.

A special group known as *collective nouns* is composed of those words, singular in form, which are the names of a group or class. *Family, government, crowd* are collective nouns. (For their use, see **G9a.1.**)

c. Case. Case is that property which indicates functional relation to other words in a sentence.

In older stages of English, nouns (and also pronouns and adjectives) changed their forms in a variety of ways according to whether their function was that of *subject*, *direct object*, *indirect object*, or *modifier*. The word *stone*, for example, had these forms among others:

nominative	sē	stān	the stone	(subject)
genitive	þæs	stānes	of the stone	(modifier)
dative	þæm	stāne	to the stone	(indirect object)
accusative	þone	stān	the stone	(direct object)
instrumental	þȳ	stāne	with the stone	(modifier)

This system of indicating different syntactic functions by a change in form is called *case*,[1] but it has virtually disappeared from Modern English. The same functions can all be indicated today, of course, but by other means: by *word-order* (position in the sentence), or by *function words* (e.g., prepositions). The only case-form which survives in nouns is the so-called genitive or possessive form (e.g., *John's*), which always functions as a modifier.

Modern English shows *subject* by position before the verb and *object* by position after it. Except in questions, the subject-verb-object pattern of word order is the standard one in English; the noun or pronoun which precedes the verb is thereby known to be its subject, and that which follows the verb, its object (if it can take one). Thus the form of a noun does not change with its function as subject or object; only its position changes.

John	hit	the	ball.
Subject	**Verb**	**Determiner**	**Object**

The	ball	hit	John.
Determiner	**Subject**	**Verb**	**Object**

[1] Case is found also in Latin, Greek, Modern German, etc.

If the verb is a copula or linking verb, which cannot take an object, a noun (or pronoun) which follows it and refers to the same person or thing as the subject is called a *predicate noun* (or *pronoun*) or a *subject complement*. (See Glossary of Grammatical Terms, **G15**.)

The genitive or possessive case relationship may be expressed in the old way by inflection (addition of *'s*) or in the new way by the function word (*of* before the noun or pronoun):

INFLECTION	FUNCTION WORD
warrior's weapons	weapons *of the warrior*

The former is also known as the *inflected genitive* and the latter as the *periphrastic genitive* (that is, roundabout, formed by a phrase).

Likewise the indirect object relationship may be indicated either by means of word order (subject-verb-indirect object-object) or by using the preposition *to* or *for*.

I	gave	Tom	the	book.
Subject	**Verb**	**Indirect Object**	**Determiner**	**Direct Object**

I	gave	the	book	to	Tom.
Subject	**Verb**	**Determiner**	**Direct Object**	**Preposition**	**Object of the Preposition**
					Periphrastic Indirect Object

Certain other relationships can be shown only by prepositions or function words. The noun following or governed by the preposition is called the *object of the preposition*, and the two together form a *prepositional phrase*.

> I went *with the man.*
> We came *into the room.*
> They stayed *in the room.*

The so-called periphrastic genitive is a prepositional phrase

G2c GRAMMAR

exactly like these in every way. (Certain other functions of case are given in the Glossary of Grammatical Terms, **G15**.)

The following sentences illustrate various functions just named:

The	bird	flew.
Determiner	**Subject**	**Verb**

George	was	our	carpenter.
Subject	**Verb**	**Determiner**	**Predicate Noun**

The	bird	swallowed	every	worm.
Determiner	**Subject**	**Verb**	**Determiner**	**Direct Object**

That	horse's	head	was	quite	white.
Determiner	**Possessive**	**Subject**	**Verb**	**Intensifier**	**Predicate Adjective**

I	sold	him	a	book.
Subject	**Verb**	**Indirect Object**	**Determiner**	**Direct Object**

I	sold	my	book	to	him.
Subject	**Verb**	**Determiner**	**Direct Object**	**Preposition**	**Object of the Preposition**

EXERCISE II

A. Consult your dictionary for the feminine forms corresponding to the following nouns of masculine gender: *emperor, Joseph, administrator, earl, fox, hero, host, alumnus.*

B. What are the plurals of the following nouns? If in doubt, consult your dictionary: *piano, potato, tooth, child, brother, knife, antelope, vertex, plateau, seraph, nucleus, nebula, grouse, synthesis, apparatus.*

C. Label each of the nouns in the following sentences as *subject, direct object, indirect object, predicate noun, possessive,* or *object of the preposition:*

1. James made one comment concerning Ruskin's book.
2. The book was a large volume.
3. God's mercy prolongs the life of man.

4. With the talents of an angel, a man may be a fool.
5. Sidney gave the soldier some water to drink.
6. The Temple of Victory stands upon a hill.

3. PRONOUNS: CLASSES

The pronouns are divided into a number of different classes, depending partly upon the nature of their antecedents and more particularly upon the functions performed by the pronouns themselves. The classes of pronouns are personal, relative, interrogative, demonstrative, indefinite, reflexive, intensive, and reciprocal.

a. Personal Pronouns. Person **is the property which indicates to whom reference is being made, the speaker** (I, we), **the person addressed** (you), **or some third person or thing** (he, she, it, they). **Personal pronouns are so called because they have different forms for the various persons.**

They also have distinctive forms for each of the three genders in the third person singular; and, with two exceptions, the form used for the subject (or nominative) case functions is different from that used for the object functions.

The personal pronoun declension is traditionally given as follows:

	SINGULAR			PLURAL		
	Subj.	Poss.	Obj.	Subj.	Poss.	Obj.
1st Per.	I	my, mine*	me	we	our, ours*	us
2nd Per.	you	your, yours*	you	you	your, yours*	you
3rd Per.						
masc.	he	his	him	they	their, theirs*	them
fem.	she	her, hers*	her			
neut.	it	its	it		all genders	

Note that the starred forms in the possessive column

213

function as real pronouns, taking the place of nouns (These are my *books*; These are *mine*). The others are not pronouns but noun modifiers; as we have seen, modern grammarians classify them among the determiners.

b. Relative Pronouns. A relative pronoun, as its name indicates, is used to relate or connect the different clauses of a sentence to one another.

Did you see the man *who* came yesterday?

There are three relative pronouns (*who, which,* and *that*) and certain compound forms based upon the pronoun *who* (*whoever, whosoever*). In addition, *what, where, as, but* sometimes serve in relative functions. The relative pronouns have no distinctive forms in number or gender. What changes in form do occur, serve only to indicate case relationships, and the relative pronoun *that* does not even show these. The remaining two pronouns are declined as follows:

SUBJECT	who	which
POSSESSIVE	whose (of whom)	whose (of which)
OBJECT	whom	which

Although the relative pronouns have no gender inflection, the choice of pronoun is determined in part by the nature of the antecedent. The relative pronoun *who* is used only to refer to persons, the pronoun *which* to animals and inanimate objects, and the pronoun *that* may refer to any of these.

c. Interrogative Pronouns. The interrogative pronouns are used in asking questions.

The interrogative pronouns are *who, which, what,* and compound forms based upon them (*whoever, whichever, whatever,* etc.). The forms of interrogative *who* and *which* are the same as for relative *who* and *which*. *What,* like the relative pronoun *that,* is not declined.

d. Demonstrative Pronouns. The demonstrative pronouns, this **and** that, **indicate or point out.**

They have the plural forms *these* and *those* but no others.

e. Indefinite Pronouns. The term indefinite **applies to meaning rather than function.**

This class of pronouns includes *one, none, any, some, anyone, someone, no one, everyone, everybody, nobody, all,* etc. The pronoun *one* and the compound forms built upon it and upon the element *-body* assume the same possessive inflection as nouns do (*one's, someone's, everybody's*), and *one* may be pluralized when it is used in an expression such as "the worst ones." The number of *none* is discussed in Glossary of Usage, page 356; certain problems of number affecting other indefinite pronouns will be considered later in this chapter, G9b. Some of these words (*one, none, any, some, all,* etc.) may also function as modifiers of nouns, in which case they are classified as determiners.

f. Reflexive Pronouns. A reflexive pronoun is generally the direct object of a verb and has as its antecedent the subject of that verb.

John hurt *himself*.

The forms of the reflexive pronoun are as follows:

myself	ourselves
yourself	yourselves
himself, herself, itself	themselves

g. Intensive Pronouns. Intensive pronouns have the same forms as reflexive pronouns.

An intensive pronoun, as its name indicates, serves to intensify or emphasize its antecedent. It is not limited to any single function in respect to the verb; it may act as subject, object, or prepositional object, but it is in the same construction as its antecedent.

> I broke it *myself*.
> I gave it to John *himself*.
> Mary *herself* said so.

For a more detailed discussion of situations in which intensive pronouns are used, see -*self*, page 361.

h. Reciprocal Pronouns. A reciprocal pronoun denotes interchange of the action indicated by the verb.

> The two brothers saw *each other*.
> The members of the company shouted at *one another*.

For further comment on the use of *each other* and *one another*, see *each other*, page 347.

EXERCISE III

Classify and give the construction of each of the pronouns in the following sentences.

1. I spoke to Mr. Jones, who is the manager.
2. Are you looking for someone?
3. What are the various opinions about this?
4. She cut herself with the knife that you gave her.
5. Anybody can do that.
6. We lost each other in the woods.
7. Many like to play the violin because they think it has the sweetest tone of all instruments.
8. He lost it himself, but blames no one.
9. The jury, which was confused, asked them for instructions.
10. She will have none of this.

4. ADJECTIVES

The adjective occupies a unique position among the four major parts of speech (i.e., noun, pronoun, verb, and adjective) in that inflections for person, number, gender, and case are altogether lacking, though a full array of them existed in the earliest (Old English) stage of the language.

Comparison. The adjective is regularly inflected only to indicate the degrees of comparison, that is, the relative quality, quantity, or intensity of whatever the adjective expresses.

POSITIVE	warm	comfortable	happy
COMPARATIVE	warmer	more comfortable	happier, more happy
SUPERLATIVE	warmest	most comfortable	happiest, most happy

Notice that in place of the -er and -est inflections attached to *warm*, we use the function words *more* and *most* when comparing the adjective *comfortable*. This is called *periphrastic* comparison. In current usage, short words generally assume the inflectional ending while long words require periphrastic comparison. The ability to take -(e)r and -(e)st is, however, very important, since it is a formal marker of the adjective. (See also **G13**.)

5. VERBS

The properties of the verb are person, number, tense, mood, and voice. The first two of these need little comment, since they are qualities or properties which have to do with the subject rather than with the verb itself. In certain languages the verb ending does reflect these qualities of the subject. In English only the third person singular form of the verb (in the present tense indicative) is distinct from all the others; it is characterized by the ending -s or -es (*I go, you go, he goes*). The only exceptions to this pattern are the frequently used auxiliary or helping verbs, *shall, will, can, may, must* (*I, you, he can*).

a. Tense

(See also **G11**.) It is traditional to recognize six tenses of the verb in English. They are present, past, future, present perfect, past perfect, and future perfect. These are formed (for example in the verb *see*) as follows:

PRESENT:	I see
PAST:	I saw
FUTURE:	I will see, I shall see
PRESENT PERFECT:	I have seen
PAST PERFECT:	I had seen
FUTURE PERFECT:	I will (shall) have seen

The first two tenses, since they are formed only from the principal parts of the verbs themselves are called *simple tenses*. The last four, since they require an auxiliary along with some one of the parts of the main verb, are known as *compound tenses*.

1. The Future

The formation of the various tenses is quite regular except for the future, where the speaker or writer is forced to choose between two possible auxiliaries, *shall* and *will*. Besides, there are differences between American and British practice in this respect, as well as the further problem of the contracted colloquial forms, *I'll, you'll*, etc. American practice recognizes two kinds of future, the informal, or simple, future and the formal, or emphatic.

The informal, or simple, future uses will and represents the subject as a free agent.

I will go	We will go
You will go	You will go
He (She, It) will go	They will go

The contracted forms *I'll, you'll, he'll* are more informal and less emphatic.

The formal, or emphatic, future uses shall **and represents the subject as being under obligation or constraint (especially in the second and third persons).**

I shall go	We shall go
You shall go	You shall go
He (She, It) shall go	They shall go

The emphatic future is used chiefly to express prophecy, determination, or authority on the part of the speaker; and in legal enactment, judicial decisions, commands. (Note, however, that *I will'* go, *you will'*, etc., with heavier stress upon the auxiliary *will* than upon the main verb, is also used to express determination or authority on the part of the speaker.)[1]

For a discussion of the use of the auxiliaries *should* and *would*, see *should*, pages 362–63.

2. Time and Tense

Since the terms *present tense*, *past tense*, and *future tense* are regularly used in speaking of the verb, there is danger of concluding that the grammatical function of tense corresponds point by point to the idea of time. This conclusion is not correct. Note these three points:

A single tense may represent varying times of action:

1. PRESENT TENSE—PRESENT TIME: I take off my hat.
2. PRESENT TENSE—PAST TIME: Then he comes in and tells me what I am supposed to do. (In narrative, the so-called historical present.)
3. PRESENT TENSE—FUTURE TIME: I leave for Boston this evening.
4. PRESENT TENSE—NO STATED TIME BUT REPETITIVE ACTION: I eat cereal every day.

[1] This discussion of the future owes much to an article by Professor Amos J. Herold, "The Future Tense in Modern English," *English Journal* (College Edition), XXV (October, 1936), 670–677.

A single time of action may be represented by more than one tense:

1. PAST TIME—PAST TENSE: Then he came in and told me what I was supposed to do.
2. PAST TIME—PRESENT TENSE—see 2 in the preceding division.
3. PAST TIME—PRESENT PERFECT TENSE: I have already told you what to do.

Certain times of action may be represented by verb constructions not always included in the regular verb conjugation:

1. PAST TIME: I used to take off my hat.

2. FUTURE TIME: I am going to take off my hat.
                     I am to go to the theatre.
                     I am about to write a letter.

Furthermore, when we use the simple present tense, we hardly ever have reference to an action which is actually taking place here and now.

Suppose one says:

I *eat* cereal in the morning.
Of course I *wear* a necktie.
I *drive* from my home to the campus in seven minutes.

It is obvious that the speaker is neither *eating* nor *driving* as he speaks, and although he may be wearing a necktie, it is clear that his reference is to a much larger block of time than merely the present moment. If he were to refer to present action, he would be much more likely to say:

I *am eating* cereal.
I *am wearing* a necktie.
I *am driving* from my home to the campus.

In other words, the *simple present* tense is used to indicate habitual action, or action without reference to any precise time. To indicate what is happening here and now, the speaker is obliged to use a tense form which is expanded. This expanded present (*I am driving*), composed of the present tense of the verb *to be* and the present participle of the verb, is usually called the *progressive present,* because it refers to action in progress or going on.[1]

The third possibility, *I do eat* (the *emphatic present*), is generally felt to show more emphasis than either of the preceding forms. It may refer either to a specific action or to a habitual or a timeless one.

The conjugation of the present tense may then be represented as follows:

SIMPLE PRESENT	PROGRESSIVE PRESENT	EMPHATIC PRESENT
I eat	I am eating	I do eat
You eat	You are eating	You do eat
He eats	He is eating	He does eat

Notice also the corresponding past tense forms: *I ate, I was eating, I did eat.*

When we turn from the simple declarative statement to questions and denials, instead of having three possible forms of the present tense, we now have only two: *am I eating, do I eat, I am not eating, I do not eat.* Notice that *do I eat* and *I do not eat* must now perform the interrogative and negative function for both the simple and the emphatic present, and *am I eating, I am not eating* are the interrogative and negative forms for the progressive present.

3. The Perfect Tenses

In general the term *perfect* means that an action has been completed or perfected. In actual practice, the three

---

[1] Some grammarians apply the term *aspect* to this kind of construction in preference to *tense,* indicating that the main idea expressed is not so much the time of the action as whether the action is (as here) uncompleted ("durative aspect") or completed ("punctual aspect").

perfect tenses are most often used to indicate completed action but usually with reference to some other time, either mentioned or implied in the rest of the sentence.

To illustrate, let us begin with a sentence having the verb in the simple past tense: *I saw him*. If we wish to indicate that something else was finished and done with before the action reported in this first statement was performed, we would use the past perfect tense:

> I had been in Omaha ten days before I saw him.
> **PAST**   **PAST**
> **PERFECT**

Our practice in respect to the future is exactly the same. We may begin with such a future statement as *This will occur*. A second expression of time made with reference to the first, in other words a "before-future" action would be expressed as

> I shall (or will) have gone before this will occur.
> **FUTURE PERFECT**   **FUTURE**

> I shall (or will) have gone before this occurs.
> **FUTURE PERFECT**   **PRESENT**
>   **USED AS FUTURE**

Finally, we come to the third of the perfect tenses, the present perfect. Just as the past perfect indicates a before-past action or one made with reference to the past, and the future perfect indicates a before-future action, so the present perfect indicates a before-present action:

> I have come to Hollywood to see a picture made.
> **PRESENT**
> **PERFECT**

The past tense, *I came to Hollywood . . .* also indicates an action prior to the present. Notice that the present perfect is used only when there is a specific or implied reference to the present; when a definite time in the past is given, then the past tense is always used.

I came to Hollywood (*yesterday*) (*last month*) (*last year*) to visit a studio.

I have (*just*) (*now*) come to Hollywood to visit a studio.

Such a sentence as "I have come to the United States last year," typical of ones frequently spoken by foreigners who have not an idiomatic command of the English tense system, violates the general practice of not using the perfect with a definitely marked past event.

b. Mood

(See also **G12**.) Mood (or *mode*, as it was formerly called) shows how an act is conceived, whether as a fact, a possibility, a desirability, or a command. Mood is indicated either by certain changes in verb form or through the employment of function words.

The number of moods recognized by grammarians has varied from time to time; the maximum number is generally four: imperative, infinitive, indicative, subjunctive.

1. Imperative. The imperative mood expresses a command, suggestion, request or entreaty:

Come here! Be careful. Don't bump your head.

The imperative consists of the uninflected present stem of the verb (*Come!*) and is thought of as being in the second person, singular or plural, in terms of the person or persons addressed. The form is always the same, and normally the subject is unexpressed.

2. Infinitive. The infinitive (no longer generally recognized as a mood) was so named because the action indicated is not limited by definite notions of time, nor of persons acting or involved in the action.

It seems, rather, to occupy a place in infinity. *To come* says nothing about who is coming, how many are coming, when the coming is to occur; it is the action of coming in a timeless, personless sphere. (See also **G14** and page 262.) The infinitive in English has developed a variety of uses:

To hesitate is to be wise. (Substantive or noun use, subject of verb.)

I like *to eat* candy. (Substantive use, object of verb. Verbal use, governing *candy*, which in turn is the object of the infinitive.)

He had a question *to ask*. (Adjective use, modifies *question*. Notice that this is not equivalent either in structure or meaning to *He had to ask a question*.)

The task is not easy *to perform*. (Adverbial use, modifies *easy*.)

I may *go*. (Verbal use with *may*.)

They allowed her *to sing*. (Objective complement; *her* functions as the subject of the infinitive and is in the object case.)

Notice that the infinitive appears with *to* except when used with the modal auxiliaries. Thus when used with *can* (and *could*), *do*, *may* (and *might*), *must*, *shall* (and *should*), *will* (and *would*) it is without *to*; when used with *dare* or *need* it may be with or without *to*; when used with *ought* it is seldom without *to*.

3. Indicative. From the name given to this mood, we understand that it refers to an action or state conceived as a fact; it indicates.

It is the mood to which all the verbal examples given on pages 217–222 belong.

> I *drive* a car.
> We *bought* groceries.

4. Subjunctive. Since we have called the indicative the fact mood, it would be equally appropriate to call the subjunctive the contrary-to-fact, **the** hypothetical, **or the** imaginative **mood.**

In earlier stages of English the subjunctive had a variety of special forms that were used with considerable regularity.

In modern English, however, most of these have disappeared, and of those that remain, most are relics that appear only in fixed idiomatic uses. Even in the most formal usage the old subjunctives are now rare.

Some of the idiomatic survivals are the following:

1. Expressions introduced by *if* (expressed or implied):

> If *I were* only a man! *Were I* in your place, . . .
> If *it were* possible . . . *Were it* mine to choose, . . .
> If *it be* true . . . *Be that* as it may, . . .
> If he *mistake* not . . . If the situation *permit* . . .

2. Expressions introduced by *though* (expressed or implied):

> Though *he die* a thousand deaths, . . . *Be it* ever so humble, . . .

3. Expressions introduced by *that* (expressed or implied):

> We order that it *be paid.* I move (that) Joe *be delegated* to go.

4. Exclamatory wishes:

> Long *live* the Queen! Heaven *forbid!* So *be* it! So *help* me God!

Notice that we are not free to substitute other words in these exclamatory expressions; we could hardly say "Long sleep the President!" or "God refuse!" We are limited to those from the past which still have some actual currency.

In other situations the indicative often takes the place of the subjunctive:

> If the situation *permits*, I shall go.
> If it *is* true, I will be much surprised.

The exceptions are (to some extent) *I were* and *it were.* "If *I was you*" is not acceptable in standard English, spoken or written; yet it is perfectly acceptable in many other sentences, such as "He saw that if *I was* right, he must be wrong."

The situation is similar with *it was* and *it were*: both are acceptable but under different conditions. For example:

INDICATIVE: If *it was* broken, why didn't you repair it?
SUBJUNCTIVE: If *it were* broken, shouldn't you repair it?

In the first we know that the object was actually broken; in the second we are only imagining the possibility and its consequence. Yet even in current formal usage this distinction is not always preserved, and *was* is very frequently used in hypothetical situations: "If this *was* possible, he could change his legal status."

To express the situations formerly expressed by the subjunctive, and where the indicative is not adequate, modern English uses verb phrases (which, since they fall into established patterns, are also called phrasal verbs).

OLDER USAGE	PRESENT USAGE
If this *were* only possible!	If this *could* only *be* possible!
If the account *were* true, . . .	If the account *should be* true, . . .
Though this *were* true, . . .	Though this *might be* true, . . .
Though it *be* known, . . .	Though it *may be* known, . . .
Be it so!	*May* it *be* so!
Long *live* the Republic!	*May* the republic *live* long!

c. Voice

English has two voices, *active* and *passive*, which represent the subject either as acting or acted upon. The passive voice is formed by using the auxiliary *be* in combination with the past participle of the verb. Though Latin and some other languages had many single-word passive forms, all the forms of the English passive are compounded or phrasal.

Note that *book*, which functions as the object of the

verb in the active voice in the illustrations which follow, becomes the subject of the verb in the passive sentences.

	ACTIVE	PASSIVE
PRESENT:	I take the book (subject acting)	The book is taken (subject acted upon)
PROGRESSIVE PRESENT:	I am taking the book	The book is being taken
PAST:	I took the book	The book was taken
FUTURE:	I will (shall) take the book	The book will be taken
PRESENT PERFECT:	I have taken the book	The book has been taken
PAST PERFECT:	I had taken the book	The book had been taken
FUTURE PERFECT:	I will (shall) have taken the book	The book will have been taken

If we wish to express, in a passive sentence, the subject of the corresponding active sentence, we may use a prepositional phrase composed of *by* and the object form—in the sentences just given, *by me*.

d. Participles and the Gerund

Other parts of the verb are the participles (present and past) and the gerund or verbal noun, together sometimes called *verbals*.

1. A participle is a word formed from a verb base + -(e)d or -ing which may simultaneously have the functions of a verb and an adjective.

Rowing is the present participle derived from *row*; *rowed* is the past participle. Like a verb, a participle may take either a direct object or both direct and indirect objects. Like an adjective, it may modify a substantive or be modified by an adverb.

I was *rowing*. (Participle used in verb phrase, but it may also be regarded as a predicate adjective.)

The *straining* runner overtook him at last. (Participle used as pre-substantive adjective.)

Giving us a worried look, he began to speak. (*Giving* is a participle modifying *he*. At the same time it governs the direct object *look* and the indirect object *us*.)

The boat approached, swiftly *rowed*. (The past participle *rowed* modifies *boat* and is modified by the adverb *swiftly*.)

2. The gerund or verbal noun is a verb form ending in -ing, **used as a noun.**

Like any other noun, the gerund may be modified by an adjective. It resembles a verb in that it may take an object and may be modified by an adverb.

Rowing is *exercising*. (Two gerunds, the first acting as subject and the second as predicate noun.)

I hate *rowing* a heavy boat. (Object of a verb and has an object, *boat*.)

Good *rowing* takes practice. (Gerund modified by an adjective.)

We are in favor of *leaving* early. (Considered as a noun, *leaving* is the object of the preposition *of*; it is also modified by the adverb *early*.)

e. Principal Parts

Most of us *do* use hundreds of verbs in our daily conversation, yet we rarely give conscious attention to their formation, simply because the great majority of English verbs are regular. They form their past tense and their past participle by adding *-ed*, and make no alteration in the chief vowel (*look, looked, looked; row, rowed, rowed*). Such verbs as *look* and *row* are called regular.

Certain verbs, instead of adding endings to form the past tense and past participle, change the vowel (*begin;*

began, past tense; *begun,* past participle); certain others not only change the vowel, but add an ending as well (*ride, rode, ridden; bring, brought, brought*); a few have the same form throughout (*put, set, cut,* etc.). Though verbs which do make internal changes are few in number, it is important to recognize that in some cases there are alternate forms for one or more of the principal parts. Most modern dictionaries show that either *sang* or *sung* may be used as the past tense of *sing.* Whenever in doubt about the acceptable form of any verb, use your dictionary.

f. Transitive and Intransitive Verbs

Those verbs which can take a direct object to complete their meaning are *transitive* verbs.

He *reads* the book.

Verbs which by virtue of their meaning do not permit a direct object are called *intransitive.*

He *stands.*

Notice, however, that the verb *stand* in the sense of *endure* or *tolerate* does take an object and is transitive in those meanings.

I can't *stand* it.

Confusion sometimes arises when transitive and intransitive verbs are similar in sound and meaning, as is the case with *sit* and *set, lie* and *lay.* These particular verbs, in fact, are so often confused that their incorrect use is usually taken as a sign of illiteracy. See Glossary of Usage, **Us3.**

g. Linking Verbs

Certain intransitive verbs, though they necessarily take no object, may require a complement (see page 88). These are called *linking verbs* (or *copulas*) because they link the complement to the subject.[1]

1. When the complement is a noun or noun-equivalent, it refers to the same person or thing as the subject:

> Jane *was* a good student.
> The table *seems* an antique.
> This *is* it.

Only one kind of difficulty is likely to arise here: when the complement is a pronoun it should logically be in the subject case to agree with the subject; yet because it comes after the verb, where objects usually come, we are tempted to put it in the object case. This explanation applies to such expressions as *It's me* and *That's him*. (On this matter, see **G10**, *Problems of Case*.)

2. When the complement is an adjective or adjective-equivalent, it modifies the subject.

Notice the linking verbs in these sentences:

> He *became* exhausted.
> Mary *appears* older.
> The work *is* tiring.

With some of these sentences difficulties do arise because the language itself is at present undergoing change: new meanings are being developed for certain verbs, and the forms of some adverbs are gradually changing. To avoid the common confusion on this matter one may note:

---

[1] This type of complement is called the *subject complement* or *subjective complement* (and in older terminology, the *predicate nominative*).

Certain verbs are almost always linking verbs.

Be, become, seem, appear are the chief of these. (See the examples given above.) As linking verbs these regularly take an adjectival complement.

A number of other verbs may function either as linking verbs or as simple intransitives.

These especially refer to the senses: *look, sound, taste, smell, feel,* etc. When used as linking verbs they are followed by adjectival complements; when used as simple intransitives they may be followed by adverbs but not by adjectives. Compare:

SIMPLE INTRANSITIVES	LINKING VERBS
1. Elsie *looked* carefully (she used her eyes keenly)	1a. Elsie *looked* careful (she appeared to be a careful person) so we hired her.
2. Their antennae *feel* delicately (they have a sensitive touch)	2a. Their antennae *feel* delicate (they appear fragile to the touch)
3. He *smells* well (he has a keen nose) but his sense of taste is poor	3a. He *smells* good (he has a pleasant odor)

All these sentences are technically correct, but it is incorrect to use the forms of the second column intending the meanings of the first.

These verbs are quite distinct from each other in their meanings. In the simple intransitive the verb expresses an action performed by its subject (an act of *looking, touching, smelling*); in the linking verb it expresses an action received by its subject (that is *smelled, looked at,* or *touched*) and performed by someone else, unnamed. (Thus the linking verb construction is very much like the passive, since in both the actual object is expressed as the grammatical subject and the actual subject does not need to be mentioned.) Once a writer has decided whether he wants to use such verbs as simple intransitives or as linking verbs, he should have little further trouble: the latter require an adjective complement; the former do not. (Such a verb used in either function may or may not have adverb modifiers.)

Some verbs that formerly were simple intransitives have recently been developing the linking function.

Since such new functions begin in the spoken language, they tend to retain a colloquial flavor and are therefore inappropriate for formal writing. An example is the word *act*. The simple intransitive construction *He acts madly* means *he behaves as if he were insane*, and the verb is correctly followed by an adverb; but the colloquial American linking verb construction *He acts mad* means *he appears by his actions to be insane* (or *angry*), and the verb is properly followed by an adjective. A good dictionary will usually indicate the status of such usages. If they are labeled *colloquial* or *informal*, avoid them in formal writing.

Some adjectives and adverbs are identical in form and therefore ambiguous after intransitive verbs.

Some of our oldest and best established words have the same form for adjective and adverb: *tall, fast, long, big, little, small*, etc. Others, though they also have a distinctive adverb form in -*ly*, preserve the shorter form which may be either adjective or adverb: *short, broad, wide, quick, slow, smooth, rough, strong, weak*, and many more. (For further discussion see **G6**, *Adverbs*, which follows.)

EXERCISE IV

A. Indicate the person, number, tense, mood, and voice of each of the verbs in the following sentences:

1. The house was struck by lightning.
2. If the baby does not thrive on raw milk, boil the milk.
3. That will do.
4. He is not listening, for he has fallen asleep.
5. It was moved that the minutes be approved.
6. My father convinced me that nothing was useful which was not honest.
7. I am pleased that you should have remembered my birthday.
8. Will you give me a light?
9. Eating is a pleasure.
10. If you should miss the train, you will have to wait an hour.

B. Consult an unabridged dictionary for the principal parts of the following verbs. Remember, if two forms are given for the same principal part, both are acceptable. Remember also the label *colloquial* is not a condemnation of any form.

dive	bite	awake
spring	beat	strive
hang	get	break
show	light	dream

6. ADVERBS

The function of the adverb has already been described as that of modifying verbs, adjectives, or other adverbs. In terms of meaning the following classes have been traditionally recognized:

> ADVERBS OF TIME: *then, quickly, suddenly, early*
> ADVERBS OF PLACE: *there, here, yonder, over, up*
> ADVERBS OF MANNER: *sweetly, badly, brightly*
> ADVERBS OF DEGREE: *very, quite, not, rather*

However, other classifications are, of course, possible; as we have seen (page 207), because the so-called adverbs of degree do not modify verbs, some modern grammarians separate them as *intensifiers*.

The adverbs given in the foregoing list will show how much the ending *-ly* has become associated with the adverbial function though it is not used on adverbs alone.[1]

Remember that not all adverbs have the *-ly* ending. For example, although *rapidly* is found only with the *-ly* form, the adverb *fast* has not adopted it. Certain English adverbs have two forms, one identical with the corresponding adjective (*loud, soft, quick, slow*) and the other formed with the *-ly* suffix (*loudly, softly, quickly, slowly*). Either form is grammatically correct; we usually choose the form that sounds better. In an imperative sentence, *go slow, come quick*, the shorter form is generally used; in longer and more leisurely sentences, the longer form is employed. When in doubt, consult your dictionary to find the acceptable forms.

Adverbs may undergo comparison in the same two ways as adjectives: with the inflections *-er* and *-est*, and with the function words *more* and *most*. Nowadays, however, very few are inflected; the majority use *more* and *most*, and some cannot be compared.

7. PREPOSITIONS

(See also Chapter IV, **W5h.**)

The notion that a sentence should never end with a preposition has been current for over two hundred years. It arose in part from the rhetorical theory that a sentence must always end with a strong word (noun, pronoun, verb, adjective, adverb). Moreover, from its etymology (*pre*,

---

[1] At least one modern grammarian accepts as adverbs only those which end in *-ly*. (See James Sledd, *A Short Introduction to English Grammar* [Chicago, 1959], pp. 79–80.)

"before" + *position*), the word preposition was held to mean *that which comes before*. Therefore it was concluded that something must always come *after* the preposition.

Whatever the reasons for the belief, it clearly does not apply to the English language, nor has it ever been observed in general practice. Two things should be pointed out here:

a. In many sentences the relative construction necessary to avoid ending the sentence with the preposition is unnatural and lacks force.

NATURAL: We had interesting things to talk *of*.
CLUMSY: We had interesting things *of which* to talk.
NATURAL: It is not a good gymnasium to play basketball *in*.
CLUMSY: It is not a good gymnasium *in which* to play basketball.
NATURAL: What a foolish thing to think *about*.
CLUMSY: What a foolish thing *about which* to think.

b. In many instances the function of adverb and preposition cannot be clearly separated, and the so-called preposition is really a verbal particle which cannot be displaced without altering the meaning of the sentence.

This is the answer I worked *out*.
Here is the quotation he brought *in*.
Did he break the teapot when he knocked it *over*?

8. CONJUNCTIONS

Conjunctions or connecting words may be divided into two classes according to the kind of elements they connect.

1. Coordinating conjunctions connect words, phrases, or clauses of equal rank: *and, or, but*.
2. Subordinating conjunctions introduce clauses subordi-

nate to the rest of the sentence: *as, since, because, for, so, unless,* etc.

> *Since* I know he is in earnest, I believe he will succeed.

3. There is also a group of adverbial connectives (also called *conjunctive adverbs*), including the words *however, moreover, nevertheless, also, therefore, consequently,* etc., which may be used to link the independent clauses in which they occur to the preceding clause. They differ from the true coordinating conjunctions in that they introduce a clause which, though *grammatically* independent, is *logically* subordinate to or dependent upon what has gone before.

I know he is in earnest; *consequently,* I believe he will succeed.

See also *so,* page 363.

EXERCISE V

Select and classify the conjunctions in the following sentences:

1. He lost the race although he made a good run.
2. I missed the target because I was excited.
3. He likes to visit libraries and wander about them for hours.
4. It seems that he ought to go at once.
5. He finally arrived, but it was too late.
6. I will not write unless I hear from you.
7. Because I am over twenty-one, I am ineligible.
8. I know it is true, for he told me so.
9. She was quite disturbed when I told her about it.
10. If you hear from them, let me know at once.

SYNTAX

We have now studied the forms and functions of the various parts of speech and have interpreted them in terms of meaning. Nouns, pronouns, verbs, and adjectives have been treated for the most part as if they were quite separate and unrelated, as if they had little to do with one another. This, of course, is not at all the case; on the contrary, in real language situations the parts of speech seldom occur in isolation but constantly act and react upon one another to form a unified whole.

The study of the ways in which the various parts of speech function with respect to one another is called *syntax*. After careful observation, grammarians have formulated certain laws or rules of syntax, with some of which you are familiar, as, for example, "A subject agrees in number with the verb it governs." Such rules are valuable, but at times they are so very general that they do not help us in particular problems.

9. *PROBLEMS OF NUMBER*

a. Subject and Verb. A subject agrees in number with its verb. (Note however that, with the exception of the forms of to be, **the only verb forms that differ in singular and plural are of the third person, present indicative. Others are identical in singular and plural.)**

Nobody would be likely to say, "The sidewalk are covered with snow" or "The men has come." Subject and verb are side by side, and the relation is obvious. But when some phrase or clause of a different number comes between subject and verb, an inattentive speaker or writer may be thrown off the track. Such errors as "The sidewalk between the armory and the dormitories are covered with snow" or "The men you sent for to repair the furnace has come" may result. If the subject is clearly held in mind and the rule applied, such errors may easily be avoided.

On the other hand, occasional confusion may arise over the application of the rule. We may begin a sentence with a collective noun such as *family, committee,* or *board* and hesitate just a moment, wondering whether to use the singular or plural form of the verb. Or we may puzzle over such a sentence as, "The wages of sin (is) (are) death." Note the following exceptions to the general rule:

1. A collective noun takes a singular verb when the group is thought of as a unit and a plural verb when the individual members of the group are thought of separately.

By ten o'clock the family *were* all here. (Considering them as having arrived separately.)

The family *goes* to church at ten o'clock. (Thinking of going to church at a definite time as a group action.)

This rule applies also to such nouns as *number, part, rest, remainder.*

> A number of tickets *were* sold but not called for.
> The greatest part of his youth *was* spent in study.
> The greatest part of his days *were* spent in study.

The pronouns none and any **may be in either number, according as the singular or plural idea is uppermost in the speaker's mind.**

None of us *seem* to have thought of it. (The whole lot of us failed to think.)

None of us *seems* to have thought of it. (No single one of us thought.)

I'll take any of you who *want* to go. (I expect a group.)
I'll take any of you who *wants* to go. (I expect one person.)
None but the brave *deserves* the fair.

The pronouns either and neither, **though formerly like** none **and** any, **today require a singular verb.**

(See *either, neither*, page 347.)

> Neither of your officers *is* safe.
> *Is* either of you going to the fair?

2. A compound subject (two or more subjects joined by and) **or several subjects without a connecting conjunction require a plural verb.**

> The students and faculty *join* in the chorus.
> A boat, a book, a shady nook, *are* better to me than gold.

When several coordinate subjects represent the same person or when they are felt as forming a distinct collective idea, the verb is in the singular.

> Your guide and mentor *tells* me of your progress.
> The sum and substance of the argument *is* this.
> The tumult and the shouting *dies*. (KIPLING)

The noun determiner every, **even when it modifies a compound subject, requires a singular verb.**

> At the camp every boy and girl *is* taught to swim.

3. When a singular subject is associated with other words (with, together with, as well as, no less than, in addition to, **etc.), the verb is generally singular.**

The captain with his soldiers *makes* the charge.

The mayor, as well as the members of the council, *was* re-elected.

In sentences like these there is a conflict between the grammar (since the subject is singular) and the broader meaning (since we are really talking about a number of things or people), as with a compound subject. Such sentences therefore often seem clumsy and should be rewritten.

4. Two or more singular subjects separated by such disjunctives as not only . . . but, either . . . or, neither . . . nor **are generally followed by a singular verb.**

Either a cow or a horse *was* in the field; he could not tell which.

Not only the father but also the mother *refuses* to give permission.

5. When one of two subjects separated by a disjunctive is singular and the other is plural, the verb agrees with the nearer.

Either the governor or his advisers *are* responsible.
Not only the actors but the playwright *was* disappointed.

6. When a subject and a predicate, connected by some form of the verb to be, differ in number, the verb generally agrees with the subject.

Books *are* his only concern.
His only concern *is* his studies.

7. Introductory there **and** here **are generally followed by a singular verb if the subject is singular and by a plural verb if the subject is plural.**

There *are* many things to think about.
Here *is* one thing to remember.

When a compound subject, the first member of which is singular, is introduced by there **or** here, **a singular verb may be used.**

There *was* a bed, a dresser, and two chairs in the room. (Rated as "established" by *Current English Usage* [Chicago, 1932], p. 325.)
Here *comes* an old man and his three sons. (SHAKESPEARE)

8. In mathematical calculations either the singular or the plural of the verb may be used.

Two times three (*is*) (*are*) six.
Eight and six (*makes*) (*make*) fourteen.

b. Pronoun and Antecedent. The general rule is that a pronoun agrees in number with its antecedent.

The boys gave *their* skates to the poor children.
Someone has left *his* books in my room.

1. A collective noun requires a singular pronoun of reference when the group is thought of as a unit and a plural pronoun when the individual members of the group are thought of separately.

> The army guards *its* plans carefully.
> The mob threw up *their* caps and cheered.

2. In formal literary English it is now customary to use a singular pronoun in referring to the indefinite pronouns each, every, everyone, everybody, someone, somebody, anyone, anybody.

> Each is anxious to do *his* part.
> Everyone should guard *his* health carefully.
> Anybody may come when it suits *him.*

3. For the use of the singular demonstratives with kind, sort, see kind, **page 352.**

In conclusion it may well be pointed out that all the special problems considered in **G9** (*Problems of Number*) come about as a result of a conflict between form and meaning. Usually such a conflict arises when a form, singular in number, conveys a plural idea (the reverse situation does occur, but less often); and we are uncertain whether the other words in the sentence should agree with the form or with the essential nature of the idea. It is interesting to note that in situations where there is such a conflict, meaning generally prevails over form.

EXERCISE VI

Decide whether the singular or the plural form should be used in the following sentences:

1. A number of us (goes) (go) to the concerts regularly.
2. Everybody is happy because (he) (they) (has) (have) been excused from classes.
3. Neither Duke nor Pitt (is) (are) likely to win the title.
4. The value of these houses (varies) (vary) from ten to fifteen thousand dollars.

5. All that we can promise (is) (are) reasonably good results.

6. The golf team, which (has) (have) five members, (wins) (win) the tournament every year.

7. My friend and colleague (does) (do) me great honor.

8. Everybody was here, but (he) (they) all went home early.

9. There (has) (have) been many attacks against the share-the-wealth plan.

10. This is a matter of importance to every man and woman who (owns) (own) property.

10. PROBLEMS OF CASE

Most problems of case need only to be considered in relation to the pronoun, since the noun has a single form for subjects and objects and since the possessive form functions adjectivally.

a. Case forms of the personal pronoun

1. In formal literary English the subject form of the personal pronoun is generally demanded in the predicate after forms of the verb to be.

> If it were *he*, I could not stay.
> It is *they* who have deceived us.

Note that no question arises with the second person pronouns, since *you* is both the subject and object form.

In informal, colloquial language, the object forms of the personal pronoun are considered acceptable when used predicatively after forms of the verb to be.

FORMAL: It is *I*. That is *he*. I had no thought of its being *he*.
INFORMAL: It is *me*. That's *him*. I did not think it was *him*.

Although the Oxford Dictionary sanctions *him, us,* and *them* in such a situation quite as readily as *me*, there is evidence of considerably more resistance in American usage *against it is him, them* than against *it is me.* Therefore, *it is him, them* should be used with caution, if at all.

It is me and similar uses of the personal pronouns seem to have arisen from the strong tendency to place the object case form of the pronoun after a verb, regardless of what the verb might be. For a discussion of the importance of word order in connection with matters of case, see **G2c.**

2. In comparisons in formal literary English, the words than and as are considered as conjunctions, and the pronoun following one of them therefore has the same case form as that with which it is compared.

SUBJECT: You are stronger than *I*.
He skates as well as *they*.

OBJECT: The news pleased him no less than *me*.
The noise annoyed us as well as *them*.

3. The object of a preposition and the direct and indirect objects of the verb require the object form of the pronoun.

He gave it to John and *me*.
He took *us* boys to the circus.

Because so much stress is laid upon the form of the pronoun in expressions like *John and I decided to go, we boys are going,* one sometimes gets the notion that *John and me* and *us boys* are incorrect in all situations. This is not true. Remember that the form of the pronoun is always determined by its function in the sentence.

CORRECT: He gave it to John and *me*. (Here *me* is part of the object of the preposition *to*.)
INCORRECT: John and *me* are going to the circus. (Since the pronoun here is part of the subject of the verb, *I* should be used.)

4. The subject of an infinitive is in the object form.

John wanted *him* to go.
Tom ordered *them* to let him know at once.

The object form of the pronoun is employed after the infinitive to be when the infinitive has a subject.

> They took him to be *me*.
> Harry imagined the culprit to be *him*.

Here the infinitive acts merely as a connecting link or equals sign (=) joining the subject of the infinitive to the pronoun which follows. Since the subject of the infinitive is already the object of the verb (see rule 4), the pronoun following the infinitive also takes the object form.

5. An appositive should be in the same case as the noun with which it is in apposition.

(See Apposition, page 256.)

> He nodded to both of us, Jane and *me*.
> All the family, Mother, Father and *I*, will be at home.

b. Interrogative and Relative Pronouns

Only the pronoun *who* and compound forms built upon it have different forms for subject and object uses.

1. Interrogative whom regularly appears as the direct or indirect object of a verb or the object of a preposition only in the most formal literary English.

> W*hom* shall we choose for this great office?
> To *whom* was the responsibility entrusted?

In colloquial English, interrogative *who* is regularly used as direct object when it comes before the verb, or when the preposition governing the pronoun does not precede it.

> W*ho* are you looking for?
> W*ho* did they find?

In a sentence employing an interrogative pronoun, the normal sentence order (subject-verb-object) is so altered that the object appears *before* the active verb. The strong sense of a pattern calling for the subject form of a pronoun in a pre-verbal position here gives rise to the use of *who*.

2. Do not use relative whom **for** who **in the following situations:**

When a parenthetic expression like *I think, I consider, he says* intervenes between the relative pronoun and the verb it governs:

WRONG: We feed children *whom* we think are hungry.
RIGHT: We feed children *who* we think are hungry.

When the pronoun is the subject of a clause which in its entirety functions as the verbal object:

WRONG: Try to determine *whom* are the guilty ones.
RIGHT: Try to determine *who* are the guilty ones.

The object of the verb *determine* is the complete clause, whose subject is *who*.

Note that the case of a relative pronoun is regulated by its use (as subject or object) in *its own clause*.

c. The Genitive or Possessive

1. The inflected genitive of nouns is chiefly used with animate objects and less frequently with nouns that denote lifeless things.

RARE: the table's leg, the mountain's foot, the room's door.
COMMON: the leg of the table, the foot of the mountain, the door of the room.

When the inflected form is used with the names of things, they are usually thought of as having life, e.g., *duty's call, the ocean's roar.* There are also a number of fixed combinations employing the inflected form: *heart's content, week's pay, money's worth, boat's length.* Notice that we frequently use the noun attributively, making it equivalent to an adjective: *table leg, mountain top.*

2. The possessive pronoun whose **is frequently used to refer to neuter antecedents when the periphrastic of** which **would result in an awkward construction.**

In actual practice the use of *whose* has never been confined to persons.

This is the chapter *whose* contents cause much discussion.
Soon we came to a river on *whose* bank stood a deserted factory.

Note that when *of* is already a part of the construction, the insertion of *of which* would be exceedingly clumsy.

FAULTY: This is a book of the contents of which he was quite ignorant.
REVISED: This is a book of whose contents he was quite ignorant.

3. A noun or pronoun preceding and governing a verbal noun is usually in the possessive form.

> What was the reason for *John's* leaving so soon?
> What was the reason for *their* leaving so soon?

With nouns, the use of the common or uninflected form preceding the verbal noun is not unusual; it may occur in both formal and informal English.

> What was the reason for *John* leaving so soon?

With personal pronouns, however, the use of the object form preceding the verbal noun is limited to informal speech and writing.

FORMAL: What are the chances of *my* being discovered?
INFORMAL: What are the chances of *me* being discovered?

In certain instances the choice of the case form is a useful guide to the emphasis which the writer or speaker wishes to give the construction.

> Imagine *him* dancing.

If in this sentence *him* is interpreted as the object of *imagine*, and *dancing* is therefore construed as a present participle modifying *him*, the meaning or emphasis suggested is *Imagine him' dancing* (i.e., the very idea that he should dance) or *Imagine him dancing'* (i.e., not walking, running, or some other activity).

Imagine *his* dancing.

If in this sentence *dancing* is interpreted as a verbal noun, the object of *imagine*, and *his* is therefore construed as a pronoun modifier of the verbal noun, the meaning suggested is, *Imagine what his dancing* (not his walking or running) *would be like*, or *Imagine his* (not John's or Mary's) *dancing*.

EXERCISE VII

A. In each of the following, select the correct case form. Explain your choice.

1. He sat down beside Jane and (she) (her).
2. The police were not certain (who) (whom) was the culprit.
3. The committee and (we) (us) counted all the votes.
4. The man (who) (whom) they believed set the fire had suddenly disappeared.
5. John is more ambitious than (she) (her).
6. Everybody expected you and (me) (I) to come late.
7. This concerns you no less than (them) (they).
8. (We) (Us) voters must take action.

B. In each of the following, select the preferable form for formal writing. Explain your choice.

1. She approved of (me) (my) doing the work.
2. (Who) (Whom) have you selected for class president?
3. There is some talk of the (governor) (governor's) running for re-election.
4. Since it was (he) (him) it made no difference.

5. (Who) (Whom) do you think is the sports editor?

6. There are many motives in a (man's) (man) committing perjury.

7. Nobody knows to (who) (whom) it was sent.

8. Was there any hope of (his) (him) getting the job?

11. PROBLEMS OF TENSE

(See also G5a.)

a. The tense of verbs in coordinate constructions within a single sentence or unit of writing should be consistently maintained.

WRONG: The ghosts *decide* to accomplish their good deed by changing the dull life of the bank president to a gay one, and they *proceeded* to do so.

RIGHT: The ghosts *decide(d)* to accomplish their good deed by changing the dull life of the bank president to a gay one, and they *proceed(ed)* to do so.

WRONG: By cutting classes in order to enjoy a more extended Christmas vacation, they *missed* work and thus *lose* out in the end.

RIGHT: By cutting classes in order to enjoy a more extended Christmas vacation, they *miss* work and thus *lose* out in the end.

b. The tense of the verb in a subordinate clause should be in logical agreement (not necessarily the same tense) with the verb in the main clause. Do not shift about in time among past, present, and future.

WRONG: As time *rolls* on and on, the common people *began* to *demand* and *secure* a few of the rights that *belonged* to them.

RIGHT: As time *rolled* on, the common people *began* to demand and to *secure* a few of the rights that *belong(ed)* to them.

Notice the verb *belong*. For this use of the present tense, see G11e–f.

WRONG: If I *were* (or *was*) there, I *would have disagreed*.
RIGHT: If I *had been* there, I *would have disagreed*.

Notice that the auxiliary verbs *must* and *ought* require expanded forms in situations where they must be put into the past tense.

WRONG: She *held* no jurisdiction over the children and *must* have a guardian for them.
RIGHT: She *held* no jurisdiction over the children and *had to have* a guardian for them.

c. Guard against an unnecessary use of the conditional auxiliary would in the following:

Where the condition has already been suggested by some other word or construction.

FAULTY: If the great inventors *would have* stopped to daydream, they could have accomplished little.
REVISED: If the great inventors *had* stopped to daydream, they could have accomplished little.

FAULTY: By observing the reveries of our neighbors, we *would be* able to judge their character.
REVISED: By observing the reveries of our neighbors, we *are* able to judge their character.

Where the intended meaning is wholly indicative and not conditional.

FAULTY: Something happened which again *would focus* the eyes of the people upon this extraordinary person.
REVISED: Something happened which again *focused* the eyes of the people upon this extraordinary person.

Where would appears as the result of attraction to another verb in the sentence.

FAULTY: If they had been born three thousand years ago under the same financial circumstances, they would still have been as unequal as they *would be* today.

REVISED: If they had been born three thousand years ago under the same financial circumstances, they would still have been as unequal as they *are* today.

d. Do not use the present perfect tense to indicate an action completed in some remote past. It suggests the recent past.

FAULTY: The South *has suffered* so much during the Civil War that it *has been* slow to recover.

REVISED: The South *suffered* so much during the Civil War that it *has been* slow to recover.

e. Use the simple present to indicate actions or conditions unlimited by definite time boundaries.

FAULTY: We *had* no better example of these conditions than the United States as it was one hundred years ago.

REVISED: We *have* no better example of these conditions than the United States as it was one hundred years ago.

f. Occasionally the "timeless present" is attracted into some other tense by another verb in the sentence.

"Galileo discovered that the earth *moved*" is undoubtedly satisfactory, although a severe critic might insist that *moves* be substituted.

EXERCISE VIII

Improve the following sentences by altering the tense of the verbs whenever it seems necessary:

1. Always being somewhat serious-minded, I have done very well in high school.

2. These young people were of an inquisitive nature and thus decide to delve into the past to discover the causes of the misfortunes current today.

3. If there is to be censorship of thought at universities, the word university would become a misnomer.

4. As far back as 1900 world citizenship has been stressed.

5. A democratic government does provoke a restless energy in its citizens, but this energy might not be of benefit to democracy.

6. If the two opponents campaigned on the same platform, the results would have been doubtful.

7. He will be on hand every time a person of note will talk upon politics.

8. Peter O'Toole and Audrey Hepburn carry off the leading parts very well, and the supporting cast also contributed toward the success of the picture.

9. Throughout one's high school career there are, without a doubt, many times when the subject being studied required more thought than it got.

10. *Holiday* impressed me as being a magazine which would attract anyone who was interested in travel.

12. *PROBLEMS OF MOOD*

(See also **G5b**.)

a. After as if **and** as though **both the indicative and the subjunctive occur, but the indicative occurs more frequently when the verb is in the negative.**

NEGATIVE: As if I *wasn't* old enough!
DECLARATIVE: I feel as if I *were* coming down with a cold.

Note that in all these choices *were* occurs only on the formal level while *was* occurs on both formal and informal levels.

b. In the reporting of motions and resolutions and in the indirect imperative, the subjunctive is the only form employed.

Resolved, that the secretary *be* instructed to deliver the following communications to the trustees.

The terms of the treaty provide that each nation *pay* its contractual obligations.

13. PROBLEMS OF DEGREE

a. The comparative degree of an adjective or adverb is used when speaking of two things and the superlative degree when speaking of three or more.

(See also **G4**.)

For example:

> John is *taller* than Henry.
> John is the *taller* of the two boys.
> John is the *tallest* of the boys in his class.

From the very earliest period of our language the desire for emphasis has led to the use of the superlative when speaking of two things, and this usage may be found frequently in literary English.

We must consider whether Homer was not the *greatest* poet, though Virgil may have produced the *finest* poem. (JOHNSON)

Feeling against the superlative with two is strong, however, and seems to be increasing. Cautious writers had better use the comparative with two and reserve the superlative for more than two.

The superlative with two is very common in colloquial English.

b. According to strict logic, those adjectives and adverbs which indicate absolute qualities or conditions are incapable of comparison.

Presumably, if a thing is *unique* (that is, the only one of its kind) or *round* (that is, perfectly circular), nothing else can be *more* unique or *more* round. Yet, as everybody knows, in the course of time many of these absolute words tend to lose their absolute character, chiefly because of a desire on the part of speakers and writers to give emphasis to their language. One needs only to cite the Preamble to the

United States Constitution, "in order to form a more perfect union," to show that this may happen in serious writing as well as in speech. It is a tendency which is often criticized. It will be the better plan for you to choose the word which indicates exactly the quality you have in mind.

LOGICAL: It was a *unique* experience.
ILLOGICAL: The material for her dress was *most unique*.
LOGICAL: The material for her dress was *most unusual*.

14. THE SPLIT INFINITIVE

Avoid split infinitive constructions when they result in awkwardness or incoherence.

AWKWARD: It would be inappropriate *to* in any way, shape, or manner *question* the remarks of the previous speaker.
BETTER: It would be inappropriate *to question* in any way the remarks of the previous speaker.

There are circumstances when the split infinitive is necessary, if the meaning is to be clear. This is particularly true when the infinitive follows another verbal construction. Suppose we begin with a sentence such as "He wished to forget his past," and decide that we must modify the infinitive *to forget* with the adverb *utterly*.

If the adverb is placed before the infinitive, "He wished utterly to forget his past," we have a squinting construction; the adverb *utterly* looks both ways, and the sentence is not immediately clear.

If *utterly* is placed immediately after the infinitive, "He wished to forget utterly his past," it intrudes between verb and object and produces a clumsy rhythm.

If *utterly* is placed after the verbal object, "He wished to forget his past utterly," it loses force because of its distance from the verb and sounds like an afterthought.

In this instance the best solution is, "He wished to utterly forget his past."

The split infinitive has been used steadily (though not frequently) by English and American authors since the fourteenth century. To mention only a few, Goldsmith, Coleridge, Irving, Hawthorne, Dickens, Arnold, Whittier, Lowell, Browning, George Eliot, Theodore Roosevelt, Woodrow Wilson, all have used it. Obviously, therefore, it cannot be utterly condemned. Neither can it be accepted without qualification; in practice, each individual case must be decided upon its own merits. Before committing thoughts to paper, you should put the adverbial modifier in all the possible places—before, after, and within the infinitive. If the split infinitive is the least ambiguous of all the possible constructions and if the adverbial modifier seems to have the proper emphasis in only that position, then the split infinitive should be used. Sentence rhythm may sometimes affect your decision.

Note that the passive and perfect infinitives regularly permit the insertion of adverbs between the infinitive of the auxiliary and the past participle of the main verb.

> PASSIVE INFINITIVE: He deserves to be *well* treated.
> PERFECT INFINITIVE: He appears to have *just* arrived.

15. GLOSSARY OF GRAMMATICAL TERMS

Absolute. A construction composed of a participle with its noun or pronoun subject or object, or both. It is attached to, though not a part of, an independent clause. When a subject is present, the construction is sometimes called a *nominative absolute* from the case form of the pronoun.

WITHOUT SUBJECT EXPRESSED:
Taking everything into consideration, the decision was just.

WITH SUBJECT EXPRESSED:

He having gone, the party proceeded merrily on.

WITH SUBJECT AND OBJECT EXPRESSED:

The rain having washed out the bridge, we turned back.

Abstract Noun. A noun denoting a quality, a general idea, or something that cannot be perceived by the senses: *affection, courage, weakness, justice.* See also **Common Noun.**

Accusative Case. The name sometimes given to the direct object construction.

Active Voice. The construction of the verb that indicates that the subject is acting, rather than being acted upon. See **G5c.**

Adjective. A word used to describe, limit, or qualify a noun or pronoun. In the new analysis, a word which may add an affix to show a differing degree of comparison; the un-compared form will also fill both slots in this frame sentence: "The _____ man was very _____." See **G4** and **G13,** also **Descriptive Adjective, Limiting Adjective.**

Adjective Clause. A clause that modifies a substantive. See page 94.

I saw an automobile which I liked.

Adverb. A word used to modify (i.e., describe, limit, or qualify) a verb, an adjective, or another adverb. In the new analysis, a word (commonly formed from an adjective plus *-ly*) which will fill the one-word slot in the sentence, "He came _____." See **G6.**

Adverbial Clause. A clause that modifies a verb, an adjective, or an adverb. See pages 94–95.

I will leave Boston when my check comes. (Modifies verb *will leave.*)

He was older *than his brother was.* (Modifies adjective *older.*)

We are working harder *than they are.* (Modifies adverb *harder.*)

Adverbial Noun.   A noun used adverbially: He went *home.*

Agreement.   A functional or formal correspondence between two parts of speech; e.g., a verb and its subject agree in number, when both of them are singular or both are plural.

Antecedent.   Literally, "that which goes before." It is the name given to the word or group of words to which a pronoun refers.

While *John* was running, he slipped and fell. (*John* is the antecedent of *he.*)

This is the *farm* which we saw in the distance. (*Farm* is the antecedent of *which.*)

Apposition.   When one substantive is in coordinate relation to another and denotes the same person or thing, the two are said to be in apposition, or either one is in apposition to the other.

Mr. Jones, the *grocer,* has sold his business. (*Grocer* and *Mr. Jones* are in apposition.)

Appositive.   That which is in apposition; the second of the two substantives in apposition is sometimes called *the appositive.*

Archaism.   A word, expression, or construction which is still in occasional use but is recognized as belonging to an older period of the language.

Article.   The definite article is the word *the.* The indefinite article has the forms *a* and *an.* The articles are also considered a sub-type of the adjective, and in the new analysis they are classed as determiners.

Aspect.   See footnote, page 221.

Auxiliary Verb.   The name given to the active verb of a verb phrase, since it *helps* the infinitive or participial form of the main verb. *Be, do, have, shall, will, can, may, must, ought,* and sometimes *dare* and *need* act as auxiliaries.

Case. That property of a substantive by means of which its relationship to other words in a sentence is indicated. See **G2c.**

Clause. A single subject-predicate sequence which may be a complete sentence or part of a complete sentence. See page 85. Clauses are classified as independent and subordinate, and as noun, adjective, and adverb clauses.

Cognate Object. An object (of an otherwise intransitive verb) whose meaning closely resembles the meaning of the verb: He dreamed a *dream.*

Collective Noun. The name of a group or class: *family, committee, board,* etc. See **G9a.1–2.**

Colloquial. Pertaining to spoken rather than to written language; the colloquial is usually less formal than the written. See **D5.**

Common Noun. A name which may refer in common to any one or to all the members of a group of persons, places, or things: *city, dogs, newspaper,* etc. See also **Proper Noun.**

Comparative Degree. In comparison of adjectives and adverbs, that degree marked by addition of the inflection *-er* by use of the function word *more* before the ⌐ ̄ or adverb. See **G13.**

Comparison. That function of an adje ̄ to indicate degrees of superior ̈ intensity. See page 217. ̄ parison are recognized: ̗ lative.

Complement. The name given which completes the though

verb. See also *Subject Complement, Object Complement,* page 89.

> Jane was a *good student.* (Subject complement.)

Complex Sentence. A sentence consisting of one independent clause and one or more subordinate clauses. See Chapter III, S5.

Compound Sentence. A sentence consisting of two or more independent clauses joined by a coordinating conjunction. See Chapter III, **S4.**

Compound Subject. A subject composed of two or more nouns or noun equivalents, the last two joined by *and,* all governing the same verb.

> *Bread, butter, and cheese* were on the table.

Concrete Noun. The name of a person, place, or thing that can be perceived by the senses: *flower, glass, whisper, iron,* etc. See also **Abstract Noun.**

Conjunction. A part of speech which connects or joins words, phrases, or clauses. See **G8.**

Conjunctive Adverb. An adverbial connective which may be used to link the clauses of a sentence. See page 236.

Coordinate. Grammatically equal, in the same rank or order, as, for example, the two independent clauses of a compound sentence.

Coordinating Conjunction. A conjunction used to connect grammatical elements of equal rank. See page 235, also **Subordinating Conjunction.**

Copula. See **Linking Verb.**

Dative. The name regularly given to the indirect object in such inflected languages as Latin and German, occasionally used with reference to this construction in English.

Declension. The inflection of substantives according to a definite sequence of their case, number, and gender forms. Example: *I, my (mine), me; we, our (ours), us.* To decline a noun, pronoun, or adjective is to give these forms in regular sequence. The term is more appropriate to Latin, or other highly inflected languages, than to English.

Degree. That characteristic of adjectives and adverbs which is indicated by the function of comparison. The three degrees are positive, comparative, superlative. See **G4, G13.**

Demonstrative Adjective. A term sometimes applied to *this, that,* etc. when they are used to modify substantives.

this book, *that* horse.

Demonstrative Pronoun. A pronoun which indicates or points out. See **G3d.**

Dependent Clause. A clause grammatically subordinate or incapable of standing alone. See Chapter III, **S5.**

Descriptive Adjective. An adjective which modifies the noun to which it is applied by describing rather than limiting or qualifying its essential meaning: the *red* dress.

Determiner. Any word which will fill the slot in the frame-sentence, "_____ good one is very good," or, in the plural, "_____ good ones are very good." Thus *a, the, my, your, his, some, many, few, all, each, every,* and the numerals are determiners. See page 206.

Direct Address. The name applied to the construction in which a person is addressed directly: *John,* close the door.

Direct Object. The person or thing directly affected by the action of a transitive verb. See **G2c.**

Disjunctive. Expressive of disjoining (separation), as the conjunctions *either . . . or, neither . . . nor, but, although.*

Expletive. A word which "fills out" a sentence pattern which would otherwise be incomplete. English expletives are *it* and *there:*

> *It* was the third of May.
> *There* remains one piece of evidence.

The pattern of the English declarative sentence requires something in the subject position before the verb. In the examples, the actual subjects are *the third of May* and *one piece of evidence.*

Finite Verb. A simple verb, or a member of a verbal construction or verb phrase, which is governed by the subject and agrees with it in number and person. It indicates a specific action or state within definite boundaries of time and therefore contrasts with the infinitive and the participles. In the sentence *He is going, is* is the finite verb, and *going* is a participle. To be complete, a clause conventionally requires a finite verb. See S3a.

Form-word. A word (noun, some pronouns, adjective, verb, or adverb) belonging to a class in which members undergo systematic changes in form by which each may be identified.

Frame-sentence. A sentence containing a blank, or *slot,* which can grammatically be filled only by the part of speech under consideration. See page 206.

Function Word. A word (a preposition, conjunction, determiner, or intensifier) which has little or no independent meaning of its own, so called because the forms of words in its class (unlike form-words) do not change and their grammatical functions are more prominent than their meanings. It is used chiefly to indicate relations between other words: The roof of the house.

Future Tense. That tense of the verb that uses the auxiliaries *shall* and *will* to show future time. See G5a.1.

Genitive Case. See Possessive Case.

Gerund. A verbal form ending in -ing, which is used as a noun. See **G5d.2**.

Govern. To hold in a certain relationship. For example, a verb is said to govern its object.

Group Genitive. When a phrase is felt to be a unit in terms of meaning, it may be given the genitive's inflection as a group. As early as the fifteenth century we find "The Archebishoppe of Caunterburys barge," and today such expressions as "the Chairman of the Board's decision," "the head of the home's income." Historically (and logically) the first noun, not the second, should be inflected, since it names the real possessor; yet if it were, this would destroy the unity of the phrase. The alternative is the repetitious and clumsy "the decision of the Chairman of the Board," etc. The group genitive is acceptable within limits: the decision should rest on whether it is less awkward than another way of expressing the same idea. Such group genitives as "The girl on the corner with a flower in her hat's look was one of surprise" are grotesque and quite unacceptable for formal use.

Imperative. The mood of the verb employed in giving a command, making a request, etc. In English it is identical in form with the Indicative. See **G5b.1, G12b**.

Indefinite Pronoun. A pronoun indicating not one particular thing but any one or more of a class of things: *some, any, everyone*.

Independent Clause. A clause capable of standing alone, or one which makes an independent assertion. See Chapter III, **S5**.

Indicative. The mood of the verb which indicates or states an action conceived of as fact. See **G5b.3, G12a**.

Indirect Object. The person or thing indirectly affected by the action of the verb: I gave *him* the ball. See **G2c.**

Infinitive. That form of the verb which consists of the present stem, frequently preceded by *to*, which indicates the action of the verb conceived of in a timeless, personless sphere. *To come* is an infinitive, as is just *come* in such a verb phrase as *will come*. See **G5b.2.**

Inflection. A change in the form of a word (without altering the part of speech) by means of which a change of meaning or of relationship to some other word or group of words is indicated. The *-s* in *dogs* and the *-ed* in *played* are inflections.

Intensifier. A word which may modify an adjective or an adverb, but not a verb; thus it will fill the slot in "He was _____ good," and in "He worked _____ slowly." Examples of intensifiers are *very, rather, pretty, quite, too.* See page 207.

Intensive Pronoun. A pronoun which serves to intensify or to emphasize its antecedent: I saw him *myself.* See **G3g.**

Interjection. An exclamatory part of speech (word or phrase) expressing emotion, pain, greeting, etc., which has no grammatical relationship to the rest of the sentence (if there is one).

> alas, ouch, oh dear, nonsense, hello, pst, ugh!

Interrogative Pronoun. A pronoun used in asking a question. See **G3c.**

Intransitive Verb. A verb which by virtue of its meaning does not permit a direct object: He goes. See **G5f.**

Limiting Adjective. An adjective which modifies the noun to which it is applied by limiting rather than describing or qualifying it.

> the *two* dolls, *yonder* tree

Linking Verb. A term applied to such verbs as *be, seem, appear,* etc., viewing them primarily as furnishing a connecting link between subject and predicate (also called *copula*). See **G5g.**

Mood (Mode). The construction or function of the verb that indicates how an act is conceived, whether as a fact, a possibility, a desirability, a command, etc. See **G5b.**

Nominal. Pertaining to a noun.

Nominative. The case name for the subject of a sentence or a predicate noun. See page 210.

Nominative Absolute. See **Absolute.**

Nominative of Address. A noun used in direct address is also sometimes considered to be in the nominative case, although the grammars of some languages use the term *vocative* for this function.

Noun. A part of speech, the name of a person, place, thing, quality, collection, or action. In the new analysis, a word which may add an affix to show plurality or possession. See **G2.**

Noun Determiner. See **Determiner.**

Noun Phrase. In transformational and generative grammar, the noun or noun-equivalent which forms the subject of a sentence, with all its modifiers, if any. See **ApI.**

Number. That property of a substantive or verb which indicates whether the reference is to one or more than one. See **G2b.**

Object. See **Direct Object, Indirect Object.**

Object Complement. That portion of the sentence completing the predicate by telling something about the direct object. See page 89.

> We think him *a good chairman.*

Part of Speech. The grammatical classification of words according to form, function, or meaning. See **G1**.

Participial Phrase. A phrase introduced by a participle.

> We saw the train *rounding the bend*.

Participle. Forms of the verb ending in *-ing, -ed, -en* (or indicated through internal change, e.g., *sung*), which are used in expanded constructions, as *am going, was driven*, or which may be used as adjectives, as *folded* in *folded arms*.

Passive Voice. That construction of the verb which represents the subject as being acted upon rather than acting. See **G5c**.

> The ball *was hit* by John.

Past Perfect. That construction of the verb which represents an action as having been completed before another past action took place, in other words a *before-past* tense. See **G5a, G5a.3**.

Past Tense. That construction of the verb which is usually used to indicate an action as having taken place in the past (sometimes called *preterit*). See **G5a**.

Perfect. The name given to those tenses which appear to indicate completed action as opposed to action going on or continuous. See **G5a.3**.

Periphrastic. A construction which accomplishes by means of a phrase or the use of function words what might otherwise be indicated by means of inflections.

> The roof *of the house*. (Periphrastic genitive)
> The *boy's* hat. (Inflected genitive)

Person. The property of a verb or pronoun which indicates whether the reference is to the speaker, the person spoken to, or a third person or thing. See **G3a**.

Phrasal Verb. A verb construction which forms a unit though containing both finite and infinite parts of the verb. See Chapter III, **S3a**, and **ApIe.**

Phrase. A group of words which contains less than the minimum subject-verb sequence essential for a clause and which acts as a grammatical unit.

The roof *of the house.*
(Prepositional phrase used as an adjective)

Rowing the boat is exercise.
(Gerund phrase used as subject)

We *have come.* (Verb phrase)

Plural. That classification of number which refers to more than one.

Positive Degree. In comparison of adjectives and adverbs, the degree which is not inflected and thus shows no increase in intensity. See **G4, G13.**

Possessive Case. That form of the noun which, when written, usually adds -'s for the singular and -s' for the plural; it is used to indicate a number of relationships, among which possession is one of the most common. Most pronouns also have possessive forms. See **G2c.** (See also **Group Genitive.**)

Pre-determiner. A sub-type of the determiner. See page 207.

Predicate. The active verb of a sentence or clause along with all the words it governs and those which modify it. See Chapter III, **S2–3.**

Predicate Adjective. An adjective which appears in the position of the predicate (i.e., after the verb) but which modifies the subject.

The grass was *green.*

Predicate Complement. See **Subject Complement.**

Predicate Noun. A noun which appears in the predicate position after a linking verb and completes its meaning.

> He seems a *gentleman.*

Preposition. A word that shows the relationship between its object and some other word in the sentence. See **G7.**

Prepositional Phrase. A phrase introduced by a preposition. Prepositional phrases are syntactically equivalent to adjectives or adverbs.

Present Tense. The construction of the verb which indicates action going on now, habitual or eternal action. See **G5–5a, G5a.2.**

Principal Clause. See **Independent Clause.**

Principal Parts. The forms of a verb from which the various tenses are derived. The principal parts are the present stem, the past tense, and the past participle: *pull, pulled, pulled; sing, sang, sung.*

Progressive. The construction of a verb which represents a specific action going on, in contrast to a habitual, an eternal, or a completed action.

> I am eating. (Present progressive)
> I was eating. (Past progressive)

Pronoun. A pronoun is a word used in place of a noun. In the new analysis, a sub-type of the noun which, like it, has specific forms to show plurality and possession; some pronouns may also show gender, person, and the difference between subject and object by means of changes in form. See **G3.**

Proper Noun. The name of a particular person, place, or thing, in contrast to a common noun which merely names one or more of a general class. *Detroit, George Washington, the Drake Relays* are proper nouns. See also **Common Noun.**

Property. A characteristic quality of a part of speech or construction; that which is proper to it. For example, gender is one of the properties of English nouns.

Reflexive Pronoun. A pronoun which is the direct object of a verb and has as its antecedent the subject of that verb. See **G3f.**

He kicked *himself.*

Relative Clause. A clause introduced by a relative pronoun.

the lady *who lived next door*

Relative Pronoun. A pronoun which is used to relate or connect the various clauses of a sentence to one another. See **G3b.**

Simple Sentence. A sentence containing a single independent clause.

Singular. That classification of number which refers to only one. See **G2b.**

Slot. In a frame-sentence, the blank which can grammatically be filled only by the part of speech under consideration. See page 206.

Subject. The word or group of words in a sentence naming the topic about which something is said. See **G2c.**

Subject Complement. An element in the predicate which "completes" the subject in either of two ways: if it is a noun or noun-equivalent, it has the same referent as the subject; if it is an adjective or adjective-equivalent, it modifies the subject. See **G5g.1–2.**

Subjunctive. That function or construction of the verb which conceives of an action as contrary to fact, hypothetical, or imaginative. See **G5b.4.**

Subordinating Conjunction. A conjunction used to connect a dependent or subordinate clause to an independent clause. See Chapter III, S5; G8.

Substantive. A term applied primarily to a noun, but also to any word or group of words equivalent to a noun, as pronouns, noun phrases, or noun clauses.

Superlative Degree. In comparison of adjectives and adverbs, that degree marked by addition of the inflection *-est* or by use of the function word *most* before the adjective or adverb. See **G4, G13.**

Syntax. That division of grammar which deals with the relationship of the parts of speech to one another within the sentence (or between sentences). This relationship is often indicated by inflection, but even more, in modern English, by the sequences of words, or word order. See page 236 ff.

Tense. That property of the verb which has to do with the time of action. See **G5a.**

Transitive. A transitive verb is one which can take a direct object. See **G5f.**

Jack hit the ball.

Verb. A word that asserts action, state, or being. In the new analysis, a word which may change its form to show differences in number, tense, or mood; also, certain affixes (such as *re-*, *-able*) may be added to verbs but not to other parts of speech. See **G5.**

Verb Phrase. In transformational and generative grammar, the verb of a sentence with all its modifiers, if any. See **ApI**.

Vocative. See **Nominative of Address.**

Voice. The characteristic of verbs which indicates whether the subject is acting (active) or being acted upon (passive). See **G5c.**

CHAPTER **VII. Punctuation and Mechanics**

1. WHAT PUNCTUATION IS

HAVE you ever imagined trying to understand someone who spoke in an absolute monotone, who pronounced every word and every syllable of every word with equal stress, and who paused for precisely the same length of time after each word that he uttered? This would undoubtedly be a physical impossibility, but try to imagine it anyway.

Such a person would not be speaking English—or any other language. He would merely be reciting words, and they would convey no more meaning than the words in a spelling list dictated by a teacher. The intonations, stresses, and degrees of pause that we normally, and quite unconsciously, employ as we speak are of prime importance in signalling structural or grammatical meaning. For example, the four words *they, are, coming,* and *here* may be spoken in that order as a plain statement of fact, as a question, or excitedly as an exclamation. It is chiefly the intonation pattern which identifies the kind of sentence for us. Similarly, it is stress and pause which enable us to distinguish in the three-word series *light, house,* and *keeper* a person who keeps a lighthouse from one who does light housekeeping. Try these aloud until you understand clearly the point which has just been made.

Most writing systems are based primarily upon the phonetic quality of the speech sounds in the language. That is, they are designed to distinguish *p*'s from *b*'s, *m*'s from *n*'s, *o*'s from *u*'s. But this is not enough. We need in addition a device or convention which will lend to the written word some of the body and color that pitch, pause, and stress add to the spoken. Such a device—punctuation—performs this service for the written word. Before the words *period*, *colon*, and *comma* came to be applied to the various marks of punctuation, they all signified a sentence, a segment of a sentence, or a pause. That is to say, they began as names for rhetorical units; they implied a recognition of some of the facts of the spoken language.

2. WHAT IT DOES

The purpose of punctuation, then, is to help make clear the meaning of a piece of writing. By putting certain words together and by separating these from other words, punctuation is vital to communication. We can think of the various points as road markers along the highway of written thought. They guide the reader's mind very much as the familiar road signs channel and control the flow of automobile traffic, slowing it down here, speeding it up there, and merging or separating it elsewhere. Too much punctuation, just like too many stop signs, can be irritating; too little, like an unmarked highway, can cause a reader to lose his way and to end in utter confusion.

The kind of difficulty that may arise from faulty punctuation is illustrated by a law passed by the North Dakota legislature some years ago making it illegal to sleep in a hotel in that state. A slip in the text of a regulation providing for hotel inspection escaped everyone's notice, and the regulation was duly passed in the following form:

"No hotel, restaurant, dining room, or kitchen shall be used as a sleeping or dressing room by an employee or other persons."

Eliminate the comma after the word *hotel* and the section makes some sense. However, it took a legislative amendment to get rid of that comma.

This is an extreme example, and the unconvinced may argue that the intent of the statute was clear in spite of the superfluous comma. Not so clear was the Michigan law which provided that "every railroad corporation shall provide a uniform, hat or cap and a distinguishing badge" for each conductor, brakeman, and other employee dealing with the public. Two English departments consulted as to the meaning of the sentence interpreted it quite differently. One maintained that the phrase "must be understood grammatically as meaning either a uniform or hat or cap." The other replied that "although the statement is slightly ambiguous it was intended . . . to indicate that the railroad corporation is to provide three things, viz: (1) a uniform, (2) a hat or cap, (3) and a badge." This shows how carefully punctuation must be watched if we do not want the reader to misunderstand us.

Punctuation performs three fundamental services.

1. It *terminates* utterances and helps to classify them. It is impossible to speak or write ordinary English without using sentences, and it is impossible to speak or write a sentence without giving it an ending. In speech the end of a sentence is marked by an intonation turn and a pause; in writing by a period, a question mark, or an exclamation mark.

2. It *joins* or *links* parts of an utterance and indicates the degree of relationship between the parts. The parts of a sentence may or may not be of equal value or importance. Accordingly, punctuation performs an important service in showing the kind and degree of relationship which the writer has in mind. The semicolon and the comma are the principal linking points.

3. It *separates* introductory or casually inserted elements of a sentence. Very often explanatory details inserted into the subject-verb-object skeleton, which forms the basis for virtually all our sentences, can cause confusion or ambiguity unless they are set off by a punctuation mark. A mark so applied helps to suggest the subordinate nature of the incidental information and to focus attention upon the principal statement. The comma and the dash are chiefly used for this purpose.

A word of caution is necessary here. Although punctuation is intended as an aid to clarity, *unless the structure and grammar are clear and correct to begin with, punctuation cannot give this help.* But if they are clear and correct, punctuation may emphasize the fact. In short, punctuation works hand in hand with sentence structure and may best be considered in relation to it. (See Chapter III.)

Note also that for some situations there is only one right punctuation, but in many others there is a choice. No writer will go far wrong if he follows the principle of *clarity without excess.* Make the marks of punctuation serve your purpose as a writer. Rules are not to be blindly or slavishly followed.

There are some other conventions of punctuation which are more or less mechanical in their application. These include the use of the apostrophe, quotation marks, parentheses, italic type, and capital letters. They are discussed at the end of this chapter and in Chapter XIII.

3. *THE PERIOD*

a. The ordinary declarative or imperative sentence is terminated with a period.

The sun came up bright and early.
Bring me the book that is on the table.

b. The indirect question is terminated with a period.

I asked them why they had come.

c. "Courtesy" questions, actually polite requests phrased as questions, are usually terminated with a period rather than a question mark.

Will you please send me three boxes of your bond paper.
May we have some indication of your plans as soon as possible.

d. The period is used after an abbreviation.

Dr., St., Jr., Mr., Mrs., i.e., P.M., B.C., N.Y.

If in doubt about the proper form of the abbreviation, or how many periods are demanded, consult your dictionary. Names made from initial letters, especially when they refer to organizations or governmental agencies, often omit the period.

HOLC, OEO, NDEA, UNESCO, TVA, BPOE

e. A series of three periods [. . .], sometimes called suspension points, is used to show that material has been omitted from a quotation.

See Chapter XIII, **MS4b.**

4. THE QUESTION MARK

a. The direct question is terminated with a question mark.

Is it cold outside?

b. A sentence declarative in form but interrogative in purpose is terminated with a question mark.

The baby is awake?

In this case the question mark is really a device for indicating voice pitch. Compare:

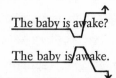

and

c. In sentences part declarative and part interrogative, the nature of the final clause determines whether a period or a question mark is to be used.

At Timothy's it was whispered sadly that poor Roger had always been eccentric about his digestion—had he not, for instance, preferred German mutton to all the other brands?

GALSWORTHY, *Forsyte Saga*

And could he relish just a little pot of their very best prune preserve—it was so delicious this year, and had such a wonderful effect. GALSWORTHY, *Forsyte Saga*

For the punctuation of a declarative sentence ending with a directly quoted question, see Chapter XIII, **MS2d.**

5. THE EXCLAMATION MARK

A declarative or imperative sentence expressing particularly strong feeling is terminated with an exclamation mark.

> I will not do it!
> Come here at once!
> Do I know him!

Notice that in the last sentences the exclamation mark suggests a wholly different stress and pitch pattern than would be indicated by the question mark.

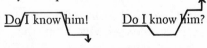

There are sentences which are both exclamatory and interrogative in which the writer may emphasize the aspect he chooses by his choice of end punctuation.

What was that odious word!
What was that odious word?

It is important to know whether you should use a period, a question mark, or an exclamation mark to terminate a sentence. It is equally vital to make sure that these marks are ending a single, complete sentence—not part of one, or something that is more than one. Remember that the basic pattern for a conventional sentence is one and only one, independent subject-predicate sequence (*Dogs bark*) and that the predicate must contain a finite verb. Review Chapter III, **S3.**

WRONG: The usual shouts of leave-taking.
WRONG: But it was the ride home that counted it began with the usual shouts of leave-taking and confusion of seating arrangements.
RIGHT: But it was the ride home that counted. It began with the usual shouts of leave-taking and confusion of seating arrangements.

EXERCISE I

Supply the appropriate punctuation in each of the following sentences:

1. He wanted to know if I had read the assignment
2. "Have you read the assignment " Charles inquired
3. You're coming with me, aren't you
4. I met Mrs Knowlton in the bank this morning
5. "All aboard " the conductor called
6. Do we really know that James can't come
7. It's so nice and snug here—don't you want to stay for a while
8. Will you pass the salt, please
9. "Pooh   You think you're smart, don't you " he shouted in disgust
10. "Pooh You think you're smart, don't you " he queried with the trace of a smile

6. PUNCTUATION THAT LINKS

We have already seen in Chapter III that there are occasions when, in order to indicate a close relationship between two or more independent utterances, we join them in a compound sentence. There are two principal ways of doing this:

1. By using a coordinating conjunction (and, or, but).

Horses gallop, but rabbits hop.

2. By simply putting the two clauses together without any connecting word.

The second of these poses a problem. Clearly some sort of punctuation between the two clauses is necessary. Yet to use a comma as a linking device is, as we have already seen in Chapter III, S8e, open to severe criticism. *Horses gallop, rabbits hop* is an example of the comma splice. *Horses gallop* could be written as one sentence and *Rabbits hop* as another since each pair of words fulfills the grammatical requirements of an independent clause. If, in the total context, they are connected in meaning and if the writer wishes to suggest such a connection, convention has established the semicolon as the means of indicating it. The semicolon, thus, serves as the signal of connection when no coordinating conjunction is present to make the link. Accordingly, the two patterns for connecting clauses of equal rank are:

CLAUSES JOINED WITH	and
A CONJUNCTION	_____, or _____.
	but
CLAUSES JUXTAPOSED;	
NO CONJUNCTION	_____ ; _____.

If you will keep these two basic patterns in mind, you will have no difficulty in understanding some of the modifications in them that will be dealt with in the sections on the semicolon and on the comma.

7. *THE SEMICOLON*

a. The semicolon is used between coordinate clauses when they are not connected by a conjunction.

Nothing could induce him to leave her; nothing could persuade him to go home alone.

The dividing lines are far from sharp; rather, there is a gradual merging today of all populations.

Eccentricity was not always a force; Americans were deeply interested in deciding whether it was always a weakness.

What America eats is handsomely packaged; it is usually clean and pure; it is excellently preserved.

A technician must convince others that his findings or his plans are sound; an administrator must gain support, and money, from his superiors or his board of directors; a writer of travel articles must make people want to travel.

Sometimes, however, a closer linking than that made by a semicolon seems desirable: (a) when the coordinate clauses without a connective are very brief, (b) when they contain little or no internal punctuation, (c) when they are closely related in idea and seem to form parts of series. In such cases the comma may be used.

There are so many of them, they have lots of company, and good company, too, great and small, rich and poor.

New York *Times*

Who was she, what was she, did she exist?

GALSWORTHY, *Forsyte Saga*

He touched it with his finger, he wanted to see its eyes. They opened, they were dark—whether blue or brown he could not tell. The eyes winked, stared, they had a sort of sleepy depth in them.

GALSWORTHY, *Forsyte Saga*

The comma splice, as this construction is called, has been discussed at some length in Chapter III, S8e. Be very careful in using it. Some instructors will not permit it under any circumstances—a justifiable attitude, since approximately one-fifth of all errors in punctuation are comma splices that are difficult or impossible to justify. When used with skill, the comma splice can become a convenient and useful device. In narrative writing, for example, where connections need to be less formally logical than in expository writing, this construction can be made to give rapidity and fluency.

b. The semicolon is placed between coordinate clauses when they are connected by a conjunctive adverb.

A conjunctive adverb is one which modifies some word in the clause in which it occurs but also links that clause with the preceding clause or sentence. The following are conjunctive adverbs: *therefore, however, hence, accordingly, consequently, furthermore, moreover, nevertheless, likewise, otherwise, still.* In current writing, however, these words appear more often at the beginning of sentences or within clauses than as clause connectives.

I know he is in earnest; therefore I believe he will succeed.

He left the building early; otherwise I would have seen him.

Americans spend untold sums on education; nevertheless we must produce more scientists and mathematicians.

I have every reason to suppose that his statement was made in complete sincerity; still I wonder if it was based on well-established fact.

c. The semicolon is used between coordinate clauses connected by a conjunction when the clauses are long and contain much internal punctuation.

For example, to understand any prophet thoroughly, we ought to know the life, character, and pursuits of that prophet, under what circumstances his book was composed, and in what state and through what hands it has come down to us; and, in general, most of this we cannot now know.

ARNOLD, *Essays in Criticism*

He does not languish dumbly; but for a long time there is no answer, save an occasional hiss or growl, to his melancholy cries of love.   ALDOUS HUXLEY, *Sermons on Cats*

Even when the clauses to be connected are relatively short, a semicolon is sometimes used to make the meaning clear or to secure the proper emphasis or sense of separation.

He heard the rapid murmur of their talk; but what they said, he could not catch.

Here he could find his way blindfolded; and freed from the strain of geographical uncertainty, his mind returned to Bosinney's trouble.   GALSWORTHY, *Forsyte Saga*

d. Subordinate clauses in series are linked by semi-colons when they are long or contain internal punctuation. Other long series items may also be linked by semicolons, particularly when there is internal punctuation.

Religious persons are also frequently critical of the colleges —institutions, they think, where one loses one's faith; places which deny the possibility of belief; centers no longer dominated by theology and no longer dedicated to the service of the Lord.

H. M. JONES, *How Much Academic Freedom?*

If you are skeptical, I recommend that you try this exercise —add up, as of the current date, the social workers, planners and reformers; the college presidents, deans and professors; the

editors of magazines, journals and newspapers (not forgetting
college newspapers); almost everybody in Washington, D.C.,
during recent years; and the tens of thousands of miscellaneous
social-minded folks who attend conferences, workshops and in-
stitutes organized for the improvement of the human race.

MARTEN TEN HOOR, *Education for Privacy*

EXERCISE II

A. Observe in the following passage the division into
sentences and point out those which might have been combined or compounded and those compound sentences which
might have been separated. Give reasons, whenever possible,
for the practice which the author did follow.

He wrote operas; and no sooner did he have the synopsis of
a story, but he would invite—or rather summon—a crowd of his
friends to his house and read it aloud to them. Not for criticism.
For applause. When the complete poem was written, the friends
had to come again, and hear *that* read aloud. Then he would
publish the poem, sometimes years before the music that went
with it was written. He played the piano like a composer, in the
worst sense of what that implies, and he would sit down at the
piano before parties that included some of the finest pianists of
his time, and play for them, by the hour, his own music, needless
to say. He had a composer's voice. And he would invite eminent
vocalists to his house, and sing them his operas, taking all the
parts.   DEEMS TAYLOR, *Of Men and Music*[1]

B. Punctuate the following passage in the most appropriate and consistent fashion.

perhaps he is right I too have observed like the old policeman that the students are not so frivolous as they used to be
but I am not convinced that the new seriousness is meritorious
in itself why should it be it is not so important to be serious as
it is to be serious about important things the monkey wears an
expression of seriousness that would do credit to any college

[1] Reprinted by permission of Simon & Schuster.

student but the monkey is serious because he itches the war
which is credited with having brought on the new seriousness
in the colleges merely intensified the conviction of students
that it is important to make money the new seriousness is a
seriousness about the financial future of the individual reflected
in his determination to get some kind of training that will guarantee him what he calls security

C. Although punctuation out of context is frequently
meaningless, the following sentences illustrate some errors
in student papers. Repunctuate the following sentences.

1. But look at countries which have submitted to this philosophy in none of them will you find eliminated that hatred which
is based on racial prejudice.

2. When I asked him why he did not move to a better location
where his efforts would be rewarded. He instantly defended his
old farmland.

3. But after all the superstitions are considered; life seems to
continue without much regard for them.

4. The boys got on the train and the bus came along just then.

5. Have they not the right to run their own factories without
interference.

6. A line was formed and butter tubs were thrown from one
to another and the last man placed them on a warehouse floor-
truck.

7. We all saw the suffering that went on during the depres-
sion, it may not have gone into our own homes but it did come
close to most of us.

8. The constitutional rights of the individual are the most
vital parts of a government for the majority must rule.

9. It isn't what you learn in college that matters, it's the
people you meet and the pleasures you enjoy.

10. Take me for example my train arrived this morning at
8:30 after a thirteen hour trip from New York.

11. The purpose in mind today is basically the same but the
outcome is probably somewhat different.

12. It is not possible for one's ideas to be completely correct,

thus it is better to listen to all ideas, pick out the aspects of each which are true, and form a new and more accurate opinion.

13. Then the meetings would not be as unproductive as at present and the advisers would become something more than mere rubber stamps for the purpose of approving elections.

14. The belief in God is still prevalent in the hearts of men, it may be buried deep under other ideas but nevertheless it is still there.

15. It may be true that those ideals do not move us easily or do not move us far yet I believe that there is scarcely a person who does not have some reaction when his native land is insulted.

D. In a collection of essays or such a magazine as *The Atlantic Monthly* find ten sentences in which semicolons are used. Be able to identify the rule governing the use of each. Are there instances in which commas might have served the purpose? If so, attempt to explain why the writer chose the semicolon instead.

8. PUNCTUATION THAT SEPARATES

Able and efficient readers get meaning from the printed page not by focusing their eyes upon every single word in the line but by taking in groups of words at every fixation. If these groups correspond to units of thought or units of grammatical structure, the reading task is considerably lightened. One service that punctuation performs is to separate word groups in just this fashion.

To illustrate how important separation can be, let us look at a mathematical problem. Suppose you were asked to solve:

two times six minus four plus three

Unless you had some mechanism which kept together those elements which were most closely related and separated those which were remote, you would not be able to tell which of the following solutions was the one intended:

$$2(6) - 4 + 3 = 11$$
$$2(6) - (4+3) = 5$$
$$2(6-4) + 3 = 7$$
$$2 (6 - 4 + 3) = 10$$

What was required to make sense out of this problem was to see how the various parts of it patterned—to apply to it the punctuation of mathematics.

In prose writing the comma is the point which most regularly performs this separative function. In fact, the word *comma* itself is derived ultimately from the Greek verb *koptein*, which means *to strike* or *cut*. Although the rules for the use of the comma are more numerous than for any other single mark of punctuation, they amount to little more than noting and indicating various structural patterns that may occur in English sentences.

9. *THE COMMA*

a. The comma is used with the conjunctions and, but, or, for and nor when they join the principal clauses of a compound sentence.

The time had passed pleasantly that afternoon, and he was surprised to find that it was nearly six o'clock.

The children were put to bed early in the evening, but neither of them went to sleep.

You must come promptly and regularly, or I shall have to employ someone else.

We had invited only six for dinner, for the dining room in our apartment was very small.

Short clauses connected with *and* are often left unpunctuated, especially when the subject of the clauses is the same.

He had a job now and he might get something better.

DREISER, *American Tragedy*

Although the clauses are longer in the following sentence, the comma has not been used.

Her glasses had slipped towards the end of her small nose and her hair had escaped from the tight hat she was wearing over her ears. HERRICK, *Chimes*

The omission of the comma suggests a close relationship in idea between the members of the compound sentence. Omit the comma before *and* only when such a close relationship exists. The conjunction *but* is almost always preceded by some mark of punctuation which serves to emphasize the contrast in meaning between the two clauses.

I find no fault with anyone who has a normal interest in athletics, but the perverted bigness of football produces people with a perverted interest in sport.

Do not confuse a compound *sentence* with a compound *predicate*. A compound predicate does not require connective punctuation, although it is sometimes employed for clarity when the predicate is long or complicated in structure. Compare example *c* with *a* and *b*.

a. He is one who had no youth or has no memory.
b. We have taken the urbanite away from his fireside and convinced him that winter sports are designed for him.
c. She appeared trim and brisk and yet nervous, and gazed at the street end and looked about like a frightened animal.

b. Clauses introduced by the connectives so, then, **and** yet **are sometimes linked to the preceding clause only by a comma.**

She was never out of disgrace, *so* it did not matter to her how she sat. GALSWORTHY, *Forsyte Saga*

It had been snowing, *then* it began to rain.

The annuity was regularly paid up to 1878, *then* Mr. Harle got into difficulties.

The control of atomic warfare is properly an international question, *yet* after all what convinced the western nations of Communist insincerity was not so much Russia's dubious proposals about a meeting at the summit as her open and flagrantly predatory and cynical treatment of the satellite countries.

Use of the comma rather than the semicolon with these three logical connectives is largely the result of newspaper and magazine practice. Sentence rhythm probably also has its effect, since these connectives, like *and*, *but*, etc., are monosyllables and make a less definite break than *however*, *accordingly*, etc.

Clauses beginning with *so*, *then*, and *yet* should be punctuated according to the closeness of relationship, the length of pause one would normally assign to the break between the two clauses, and the amount of internal punctuation contained within the clauses. Note the difference between the following:

A hard little thing underneath; *yet* with her moments, when she gazed on beauty, of an almost burning softness.

GLASGOW, *The Romantic Comedians*

One could understand it and enjoy it; *so* it became the favorite thing at popular festivals, as well as at the Christmas entertainments in the great hall.

W. P. KER, *English Literature*

There was now no reason why he should not take it with him, *so* he put it in his pocket.

S. BUTLER, *Erewhon Revisited*

The size of Congressional districts varies greatly, *yet* the Constitution provides that they should be of equal population.

Recall the warning that has been given about the overuse of *so* as a connective. (See *So*, page 363.) A sentence which uses *so* preceded by a comma is sometimes weak because *so* is not the best connective for the purpose or because such a construction does not throw enough emphasis upon the principal clause. Note the difference in emphasis and relationship suggested by the following:

LOOSE: This problem is insoluble, so let us ignore it.
COMPACT: As this problem is insoluble, we may ignore it.
COMPACT: This problem, being insoluble, may be ignored.

In any case, *so* has a conversational flavor; therefore if you are trying to be formal, use some other word by preference.

c. In some special cases the comma is used in place of the semicolon between coordinate clauses not joined by a conjunction.

(See Chapter III, S8e.)

d. A long introductory clause is separated from the principal clause by a comma.

When the English were converted to Christianity, it was unavoidable that there should be a clash between Christian and pre-Christian ethics in this matter of vengeance.

If a member of the legislature takes a campaign contribution from the owner of a gambling syndicate, can that member cast a roll-call vote to outlaw slot machines?

As the time drew near for their parting, Jessica relaxed somewhat her impersonal discipline.

Short introductory clauses are frequently not set off by commas.

When he arrived we were packing our bags.
After Joe scored they hurried out of the stadium.

An introductory noun clause followed immediately by its verb need not be set off by a comma.

It is not a good policy to place punctuation marks between subject and predicate, since it risks destroying an essential relationship.

What the tourist enjoys most is the unusual scenery.

e. Commas are used after introductory phrases when the phrases are long, when a mark of separation is required to indicate the point at which the main clause begins, or where ambiguity or misunderstanding would result from lack of punctuation.

Keep in mind the number of commas and other marks which the sentence demands, and also the closeness of connection that you wish to suggest between the phrase and whatever it modifies.

In the first of the examples below, the phrase *the following day* would seem to belong with *promise*, rather than with *returned*, if there were no comma. (Another way to make the sentence unambiguous would be to place this phrase after *returned* or at the end of the sentence.)

INTRODUCTORY PHRASES WITH COMMAS:

True to her promise, the following day Hortense returned to Mr. Rubenstein.

To succeed in business, you must advertise.

In those early days, after it became a custom for each family to prepare its own Christmas potion, the quality of the drink depended upon the wealth of the host.

On the floor, perennially flirtatious and recklessly nimble, he seldom failed to remark several agile septuagenarians, whom he had known as dashing blades when he was a boy.

Without thinking, we are making an important confession about ourselves as a nation.

INTRODUCTORY PHRASES WITHOUT COMMAS:

About six miles beyond Belleville the car came to a bend in the hollow where there was a country store.

In the same way an individual noun may turn into a collective.

With better management it will not fail again.

In preparing the wassail of England a great wooden bowl containing cider, beer, or wine as a base was placed on the hearth and above it apples were suspended on strings.

Within each one of these forts the strictest organization of industry was insisted on.

Since the first report we have heard nothing.

An absolute phrase at the beginning of a sentence is usually followed by a comma:

In the nature of things, the tone of a royal borough is one of leisure, stateliness, and a perfect sense of form.

As to publicity, the fat was in the fire.

On the other hand, facts must be faced.

The first package being exhausted, we had to open the second.

f. Certain types of introductory words are frequently followed by a comma:

1. Nouns in direct address.

Mr. Wentworth, I want to congratulate you on your successful meeting.

2. Interjections intended to be only mildly exclamatory.

Oh, he's a pretty bright fellow.

3. Expletives such as indeed, surely, certainly, moreover, furthermore, why, **and** yes **and** no.

Indeed, I should be pleased to go.

Well, it's rather complicated.

No, you haven't the answer yet.

In the use of introductory words, develop a feeling for their connection with the rest of the sentence. *Yes* and *no* may be followed by end punctuation if a marked pause is intended.

> I don't know. Yes, I guess I do.
> Yes. I will.

Words such as *certainly*, *now*, etc., should not be punctuated at all if they are considered as having adverbial force. Notice how the difference in grammatical function is indicated by the punctuation in the two following sentences:

INTRODUCTORY *now*: Now, go and see what can be done.

ADVERBIAL *now*: Now go, and return when you have finished the work.

4. Such as, especially, **and similar introductory words are usually preceded by a comma when they introduce a short series of illustrations and by a dash or a colon when they introduce a long series, or a series of long illustrations.**

He had the opportunity to hear a number of operas, such as *Rigoletto*, *Il Trovatore*, and *Siegfried*.

The student is expected to familiarize himself with as many of the aspects of Modern English as possible: such as the sounds of the language and manner of their formation, the sources of the present-day vocabulary, the most active inflectional patterns, and the pertinent facts of English syntax.

5. The introductory words namely, thus, for example, **and** that is **may be preceded by a comma, a dash, a colon, or a period. When preceded by a comma, no punctuation should follow. When preceded by a dash or colon, a comma may follow.**

> _____, namely
> _____ —namely,
> _____: namely,

g. Parenthetical elements.

Often within a sentence it is desirable to insert clauses, phrases, or words not essential to the basic structure. These are called *parenthetical*. Following the general principle already observed, such material may be punctuated in various ways (with parentheses, dashes, or commas), or left unpunctuated, according to the degree of closeness or separation in the thought. The reader's eye is thus aided to recognize an insertion, and he is prepared for its extraneousness to the main thought.

1. Parenthetical clauses within the sentence are set off by commas.

But bodily health and vigor, it may be said, are not to be classed with wealth and population as mere machinery.

Progress, he insisted, had come not so much from the enactment of new laws as by the repeal of earlier laws.

Yugoslavia has already made an excellent recovery and is destined, we may depend upon it, to an immense development.

There are those, I am sure, who will say that this practice is well enough for a judge removed from the harassments of ordinary office life.

2. A noun used in direct address is set off by commas.

Come, *Mary*, let us go at once.

In conclusion, *Mr. Chairman*, I should acknowledge my appreciation of your confidence in designating me to serve on this committee.

3. Commas are used to set off the words however, moreover, therefore, **and** furthermore **when they occur as parenthetical expressions within a sentence; they are seldom used to set off** also, indeed, likewise, perhaps.

These acts, *however*, were found to be unsatisfactory and ineffectual.

You will *perhaps* recall that I discussed this matter at some length in my letter of March 14.

h. A nonrestrictive clause should be set off by commas; a restrictive clause should not be set off by commas.

The terms *restrictive* and *nonrestrictive* are applied to various types of modifiers: clauses, phrases, and words. (The terms *essential* and *nonessential* are also used.) A restrictive element is one which could not be lifted out of the context without destroying the basic idea of the sentence, whereas a nonrestrictive one could be eliminated and the basic meaning would be the same; hence, it is in a sense parenthetical.

RESTRICTIVE: Our visitor who came yesterday was from the East.

The lack of punctuation here implies that *who came yesterday* is restrictive in its application; that is to say, of a number of visitors we may have had during the past week, we are talking of the one who came yesterday. Or to put it the other way, since the clause and punctuation do show restriction, the implication is that there have been other visitors.

NONRESTRICTIVE: Our visitor, who came yesterday, had little to say.

With the parenthetical type of punctuation here we now understand that there was only one visitor; the purpose of the clause modifier is not to restrict the meaning of *visitor*, but merely to add a bit of information about him.

NONRESTRICTIVE:

Ann Hathaway's cottage, which we visited, was not at all as I had imagined it.

In one leap, which caused the tiny open boat to quiver like a leaf, he had reached her.

RESTRICTIVE:

The belief that atoms are miniature universes is at times questioned.

Mr. Roebuck will have a poor opinion of an adversary who replies to his defiant songs of triumph only by murmuring under his breath.

Men who are intemperate are destructive members of a community.

One of the chief kinds of over-punctuation results from setting off a restrictive modifier and thus separating an essential element. Students should be careful not to produce such statements as, "All men, who commit murder, should be hanged"—which makes a rather broad charge and calls for a fairly drastic disposal of the adult male population.

Note that these modifiers are not only in the form of *clauses. Phrases* and *words* performing the same function are treated below.

1. Phrases within the sentence are set off by commas when they are nonrestrictive or absolute.

NONRESTRICTIVE PHRASES:

Letters were folded and sealed, and the postage fees, *collected either from sender or receiver*, were based upon the number of pages.

The trade agreement with Brazil, *being one-sided*, is a case in point.

ABSOLUTE PHRASES:

Unquestionably, the advantage which the people of Puerto Rico value most highly, *as a consequence of their being a part of the*

United States, is their American citizenship and all that goes with it.

When one looks, *for example,* at the situation in this country, one wonders if, *after all,* we are able to boast.

June, *in the fulness of her heart,* had told Mrs. Small, giving her leave only to tell Aunt Ann.

I did not, *of course,* delude myself that all, *or even many,* of the bad laws I picked out for attention would disappear.

RESTRICTIVE PHRASES:

The bank *on the corner* does more business than the one in the middle of the block.

An essay *written with care* is certain to please the instructor.

2. Nonrestrictive appositives (that is, those appositives which do not distinguish their principals from other persons or things called by the same name) are usually separated by commas. Restrictive appositives are not set off by commas.

NONRESTRICTIVE:

Bryant, *the distinguished New England poet,* was a newspaper editor.

In a series of illustrated articles supplied by Ezra Gulick, *the young hustler,* local pride and patriotism were appealed to tactfully.

RESTRICTIVE:

The historian *Buckle* emphasized this distinction in his history of civilization.

The poet *Bryant* was a newspaper editor.

As a rule, when the general or classifying term comes first and the specific name or instance follows, the apposition is restrictive; when the specific name or term is mentioned first, the apposition is nonrestrictive.

i. Explanatory clauses, phrases, and words occurring at the end of the sentence are set off by commas when they are nonrestrictive; no punctuation is used when they are restrictive.

There is no essential difference between "after-thought" material and material inserted within the sentence, except that the former is often looser or less formal than the latter. It is merely a parenthetical interpolation tacked on at the end instead of being inserted in the middle.

RESTRICTIVE CLAUSE, NO PUNCTUATION:

We all admired the fighting spirit which the opposing team showed.

NONRESTRICTIVE CLAUSE:

The natives labored with a surprising zeal, which effectually aroused our generosity.

EXPLANATORY CLAUSE:

Don't you think you would be more helpless abroad, in case he followed?

PARTICIPIAL PHRASE:

But worry he did, walking toward the park.

ADVERBIAL PHRASE:

That is certainly a surprise, after all these years.

NOUN IN DIRECT ADDRESS:

How do you like him, Father?

APPOSITIVE:

Quaintly equipped with a black silk umbrella and a pith helmet, he was resting beside a prostrate column when two other travelers approached the lonely temple, a man and a woman.

EXPLETIVE:

She wanted time to think it over, no doubt.

Note that in a sentence where the final expletive is in the form of a clause, there is also the possibility of punctuating with a semicolon, as in clauses without a compounding connective.

> I dislike crowds; don't you?
> I dislike crowds, don't you?

The punctuation here should be chosen to indicate the closeness of the relationship between the two clauses.

Adverbial clauses, particularly those introduced by *though* and *although*, often make stronger sentences if they are *not* put in final position. Compare:

a. Aluminum alloys are winning wider acceptance today, *although structural steel has been in successful use for over thirty years.*

b. *Although structural steel has been in successful use for over thirty years,* aluminum alloys are winning wider acceptance today.

c. *Although aluminum alloys are winning wider acceptance today,* structural steel has been in successful use for over thirty years.

Here, *a* is comparatively weak; *b* and *c* are stronger, each emphasizing a different aspect of the idea.

At times it is necessary to separate a final statement from the rest of the sentence so that an ambiguous reading will not result. Note the difference between the following:

We found that the average yearly cost of maintaining a car in New York was $250 more than in any other state in the Union.

We found that the average yearly cost of maintaining a car in New York was $250, more than in any other state in the Union.

j. Commas are used to separate three or more words or phrases forming a coordinate series.

WORDS IN SERIES: The day was dull, dark, soundless.

PHRASES IN SERIES: Wood on the fire, meal in the barrel, flour in the tubs, money in the purse, credits in the country all come as a result of temperance.

1. Two or more words modifying the same word should be separated by commas only when they are coordinate in thought. Non-coordinate modifiers are not separated.

COORDINATE: He had a host of duck-shooting, back-slapping friends.

They grew gigantic, full, deep, double flowers.

NON-COORDINATE: It is based upon sound fundamental principles.

Then there is our peculiar American political party scheme.

Coordinate implies equality in rank, each of the adjectives referring directly to the noun. This is not the case in such groupings as *limited air offensive, poor little old woman,* and *large stone mansion,* where *limited* describes *air offensive, poor* describes the *little old woman, little* refers to the *old woman, large* to the *stone mansion.* The non-coordinate modifiers are cumulative in their effect. A safe practice is to omit the comma when the adjectives suggest age and size, or when they are numerals.

2. When there are three or more words or phrases in series with the conjunction and between the last two, a comma need not precede the conjunction unless clarity demands it.

NECESSARY FOR CLARITY: We had coffee, fruit, and ham and eggs.

In situations of this type the comma before the first *and* is required to show that *ham and eggs* constitutes a single item in the series.

NOT NECESSARY FOR CLARITY: The beasts were two lions, a hart and an ibex.

In situations like the foregoing there is a wide divergence of practice. In general, newspapers with their tendency toward light or open punctuation omit the comma before *and*. Books and magazines show a stronger tendency toward retention of the comma. Whatever style of series punctuation you adopt, follow it consistently within the limits of a single paper. Phrases, especially when they are long, are more frequently punctuated with the comma before the conjunction.

The spectators came on foot, by motor, many by rail, and some by airplane.

Sea on sea, country on country, millions on millions of people, all with their own lives, energies, joys, griefs, and suffering.

k. Clauses in series are separated by commas under the following circumstances:

1. Independent clauses in series with a conjunction connecting the last two members are punctuated with a comma after each clause except the last. A comma is almost always necessary before the conjunction when the members of the series are clauses.

The number of students will be reduced, the number of teachers will be increased, and several new buildings are to be erected.

Independent clauses in series without a final connecting conjunction are usually separated by semicolons, except for those situations which are discussed on pages 277–78. Where there is internal punctuation within the clauses, the semicolon is an absolute necessity.

2. Subordinate clauses in series are separated by commas when they are short, light, and without internal punctuation. Otherwise they are punctuated with semicolons.

We were informed that the convention had been held in the East last year, that it was to be in the West this year, and that next year it would be held in the South.

I am now trying to demonstrate just exactly in what particulars it was false; that instead of these men being peaceful citizens, honest working men, they were not; that they were men who were acting in violation of the law; that they were defying the law and the officers who were trying to enforce the law.

l. The comma often is used to heighten the contrast of coordinate sentence elements, especially when they are long.

Her procedure was to organize history classes for a winter season, then help the members to form permanent literary clubs.

He too looked like a warrior, unlike the stern-faced man in bronze above him.

I speak as a man of experience, not as a theorist.

m. Commas are used to separate items in dates, addresses, and geographical names.

William Alanson Howard was born on April 8, 1813, at Hinesburg, Vermont.

Determined to acquire an education, he attended an academy at Wyoming, New York, for three years and then entered Middlebury College, Vermont, graduating in 1839.

He gave 23 Burbank Avenue, Altadena, California, as his forwarding address.

10. THE DASH

In general the dash indicates abruptness and incompleteness. It also suggests emphasis. In many situations it alternates with the comma or the colon. Be careful not to over-use it. Properly employed it can serve a variety of purposes.

a. The dash is used to mark a sentence as incomplete.

He has only to understand—

b. A dash is used to indicate that the train of thought is abruptly changed or broken off.

She would continue to gather minute data, tabulate, annotate, classify—at present she was occupied with organic compounds.

c. Sometimes to emphasize a contrast, the dash may be used before but:

Wagner changed the face of opera, it is true—but in the Latin lands he never changed its heart.

d. When used to separate parenthetical material from the rest of the sentence, dashes generally indicate a more violent interruption of the normal train of thought than would be shown by commas.

I shall elsewhere, perhaps, be able some day to find an opportunity; but indeed, it is not in my nature—some of my critics would rather say, not in my power—to dispute on behalf of any opinion, even my own, very obstinately.

ARNOLD, *Culture and Anarchy*

If the parenthetic element already has commas internally, it may be set off with dashes to contrast with the commas.

Believing that all literature and all education are only useful so far as they tend to confirm this calm, beneficent, and therefore kingly, power—first, over ourselves, and, through ourselves, over all around us—I am now going to ask you to consider with me further, what special portion or kind of this royal authority, arising out of noble education, may rightly be possessed by women.

RUSKIN, *Sesame and Lilies*

e. A dash is used before a repetition or a modification which has the effect of an afterthought.

> What a faith—in something!
> It was cold—bitter cold.

11. THE COLON

The colon is a relatively formal mark of punctuation. It suggests also that something is to follow, an explanation, a list, an enumeration.

a. When the first of two coordinate clauses serves as an introduction to the second, the colon is used between them.

The building is no longer a passive shell: it is a functioning organization in which the primitive aspect of shelter, as embodied in the original cave, and of symbol, as embodied in the monument, have become secondary attributes of more complicated processes.

Where they are now: whether they have reached their various goals, whether they have grown stalely respectable, or whether they are more crazy than ever, I do not know and do not greatly care to know.

b. The colon is used after introductory clauses and phrases of a somewhat formal or extended nature.

The question is this: Should a corporation enjoying a monopolistic position in the distribution of a necessity be permitted to use that position to give its own opinion a preferred position over any other by attaching that opinion to the necessary product it purveys?

What America eats is handsomely packaged; it is usually clean and pure; it is excellently preserved. The only trouble with it is this: year by year it grows less good to eat.

I think I can testify that the professors are very much like the rest of the population except in two particulars: their professional training and their rather conservative social views.

c. The colon is used before such as, especially, **and similar introductory words when they introduce a series of long illustrations. When** thus, namely, **or** for example **are preceded by a dash or a period, the colon follows the word in question. (See also P9f4–5.)**

_____. For example:

_____— namely:

d. The salutation of a letter is usually followed by a colon, although in informal correspondence a comma is sometimes used.

EXERCISE III

A. The following passage has been copied sentence for sentence, but all punctuation within the sentence has been omitted. Punctuate it as you think it should read.

But epochs of concentration cannot well endure forever epochs of expansion in the due course of things follow them. Such an epoch of expansion seems to be opening in this country. In the first place all danger of a hostile forcible pressure of foreign ideas upon our practice has long disappeared like the traveller in the fable therefore we begin to wear our cloak a little more loosely. Then with a long peace the ideas of Europe steal gradually and amicably in and mingle though in infinitesimally small quantities at a time with our own notions. Then too in spite of all that is said about the absorbing and brutalizing influence of our passionate material progress it seems to me indisputable that this progress is likely though not certain to lead in the end to an apparition of intellectual life and that man after he has made himself perfectly comfortable and has now to determine what to do with himself next may begin to remember that he has a mind and that the mind may be made the source of great pleasure.

MATTHEW ARNOLD

B. Revise, wherever necessary, the punctuation of the following:

1. Because he hasn't any menacing prejudices to hinder his thinking he can create something worth while from many of his ideas.

2. Later, her parents died and she came back to Springfield where she is now going to school.

3. For instance he might have ideas about what a strange world this is.

4. He has a very fine education as is quite apparent but for some unexplainable reason most of his learning has gone for naught.

5. The engine of today as compared to the engine of ten years ago, is a changed mechanism.

6. All members of the legislative body are party members which means that a large portion of the Russian people are unrepresented.

7. Because of my experience and that of other students I believe that the present system should be radically changed.

8. How different real college life at Michigan or any other institution of higher learning is from movie college life.

9. The real reasons are those that dyed in the wool conservatives cannot or do not attempt to find.

10. This organization which was called the I.L.U. had caused many disputes.

11. The privately owned business enterprises would have to be consolidated thereby eliminating competition.

12. Modern faces peer out through old wigs and costumes giving the effect of a Halloween party instead of a serious drama.

13. In fact I believe that ambition and success go hand in hand.

14. This type of work, where a man is on his own initiative and uses his own ideas to carry out his experiments is what I hope to make my life's occupation.

15. While free schools are open to all the average person rarely has an education equivalent to that of the eighth grade.

16. I obtained the following estimate, that in the same year forty-seven percent of all those gainfully employed, with the

exception of farmers or nearly one-half the working population in the cities earned less than $1,000 a year.

17. There are ninety-two of these elements each different from the other.

18. When their market drops the producers immediately slash wages and reduce prices.

19. The cause of, and a direct cure for the common cold is not yet known.

20. However, one should not believe everything he hears as most of it may be untrue.

C. Punctuate the following passages in whatever way seems to you to carry out the intention of the author most effectively.

1. His occupying the chair of state was a triumph of the good sense of mankind and of the public conscience. This middle-class country had got a middle-class President at last. Yes in manner and sympathies but not in powers for his powers were superior. This man grew according to the need. His mind mastered the problem of the day and as the problem grew so did his comprehension of it. Rarely was man so fitted to the event. In the midst of fears and jealousies in the Babel of counsels and parties this man wrought incessantly with all his might and all his honesty laboring to find what the people wanted and how to obtain that. It cannot be said there is any exaggeration of his worth. If ever a man was fairly tested he was. There was no lack of resistance nor of slander nor of ridicule. The times have allowed no state secrets the nation has been in such ferment such multitudes had to be trusted that no secret could be kept. Every door was ajar and we know all that befell.

2. It is well for me that I cannot hear music when I will assuredly I should not have such intense pleasure as comes to me now and then by haphazard. As I walked on forgetting all about the distance and reaching home before I knew I was halfway there I felt gratitude to my unknown benefactor a state of mind I have often experienced in the days long gone by. It happened at times not in my barest days but in those of decent poverty—

that someone in the house where I lodged played the piano and how it rejoiced me when this came to pass! I say played the piano a phrase that covers much. For my own part I was very tolerant anything that could by the largest interpretation be called music I welcomed and was thankful for even five-finger exercises I found at moments better than nothing. For it was when I was laboring at my desk that the notes of the instrument were grateful and helpful to me. Some men I believe would have been driven frantic under the circumstances to me anything like a musical sound always came as a godsend it tuned my thoughts it made the words flow. Even the street organs put me in a happy mood; I owe many a page to them written when I should else have been sunk in bilious gloom.

SOME MECHANICAL APPLICATIONS OF PUNCTUATION

There are other conventions of punctuation which are more or less mechanically applied. A discussion of these follows.

12. THE APOSTROPHE

The word *apostrophe* comes from a Greek root meaning *turning away* or *elision*, and the punctuation mark bearing that name has come to be used where certain vowel sounds are omitted, or where vowels which existed at an earlier period of the language are no longer pronounced. It is chiefly a mark of omission or contraction.

a. Possessives

1. The apostrophe followed by s is used to indicate the possessive (genitive) singular of all nouns, and the possessive (genitive) plurals of those nouns whose common plural form does not end in s.

girl's toy	John's book
men's clothing	children's party

2. The apostrophe alone is added to plural nouns endings in s to form the possessive plural.

dogs' kennel   wolves' cry   foxes' lair
girls' club   Joneses' house

3. The apostrophe and s is used to indicate the possessive singular of the indefinite pronouns.

one's   other's   either's

CAUTION: The personal and relative pronouns do not add the apostrophe to indicate the genitive.

The book is *hers*.
Whose book is it? (*but Who's* coming?)
It's not *yours* or *his*.
Its cover is torn. (*but It's* a torn cover.)
Ours is better than *theirs*.

4. Practice varies in respect to the formation of the possessive singular of proper nouns ending in s.

Charles's   or   Charles'
Jones's   or   Jones'

When the addition of the 's would result in a series of three sibilant sounds, the final *s* is almost always omitted, even in common nouns.

Kansas' son   conscience' sake
Moses' commandment

5. The apostrophe is frequently omitted in the names of organizations when the possessive is implied, and in certain geographic designations.

Citizens League   Teachers College
Merchants Association   Actors Equity Association
Pikes Peak (recommended by the U. S. Geographic Board)

Whenever possible find out what the official spelling is.

b. The apostrophe is used in place of the omitted letters or numbers in writing contracted forms.

aren't	it's (it is)	who's (who is)
can't	ne'er	you're (you are)
don't	o'clock	'59

CAUTION: Do not confuse *its* (possessive pronoun) with *it's* (*it is*) or *whose* (possessive pronoun) with *who's* (*who is*). These are common errors.

c. The apostrophe followed by s is used to form the plurals of letters and symbols.

a's and b's   size 7's

13. QUOTATION MARKS

See Chapter XIII, MS2, for a discussion of the use of quotation marks.

14. PARENTHESES

a. Parentheses are used within the sentence chiefly to enclose brief explanatory items.

The Speaker then recognized Representative Jones (Ohio).

At the time the book was published (1864), it did not have a ready market.

b. Parentheses are used to set off explanatory elements when they are somewhat distantly related to the rest of the sentence.

Entrance examinations were stiffened to hold them back (a boon to tutoring schools); subjects which, like Greek, the public schools refused to teach, were kept in the requirements in the hope of barring the gate.

HENRY S. CANBY, *American Memoir*

c. The question mark enclosed in parentheses is a conventional way of indicating doubt or uncertainty.

The poem was composed in 1453 (?).

This device should not be employed as an excuse for your having failed to verify an ascertainable fact. Use it only when the fact in question is not known or when the most authoritative sources are uncertain about it.

d. The use of the parenthetic question mark as a label for irony or humor is not in good taste and should be avoided.

Use of this question mark implies that your reader will not catch the ironic intent without it. This means that your irony is not clear enough, or not broad enough. In either case, it would be better to rewrite than to punctuate thus.

AVOID: Altogether it was a splendid (?) sight.

15. BRACKETS

Brackets are used to enclose editorial explanation and correction, especially in quoted matter.

In Kurt Marek's *Gods, Graves, and Scholars,* we are told that, "This first impression was enough to convince him [Schliemann], believing literally in Homer as he did, that Bunarbashi was not the site of the ancient city [Troy]."

For additional material on the use of brackets, see Chapter XIII, **MS4a.**

16. ITALICS

The use of italic type is a mechanical device to secure distinctness on the printed page, and it has come to be employed where emphasis or distinctness is desired. Italics have taken over many of the conventional functions performed in earlier times by quotation marks, different sizes of type, or capitals. In hand-written or typewritten manuscripts, italics are indicated by underlining.

a. Book titles, titles of publications, musical selections, and works of art are italicized.

I suppose you have read *The Hucksters.*

The names of ships are generally italicized.

The ship was called *Wanderlust.*

b. Words from other languages not yet naturalized in English are italicized.

It is a *de facto,* not a *de jure* government.

Consult your dictionary to determine whether a foreign word or expression has become a part of the English language or whether it is still considered foreign.

c. Words, letters, and figures spoken of as words, letters, and figures are italicized.

What can you tell us about the derivation of *telephone?*
The plural inflection generally ends in *-s.*
I can't tell his *3's* from his *5's.*

d. Italics are occasionally used for emphasis.

Employ this device with caution.

He avows also that the fortunate individual whom he is describing, by "being accustomed to such contemplations, will feel the *moral dignity of his nature exalted.*"

17. CAPITAL LETTERS

Capital letters serve two uses: to mark the beginning of a structural unit, and to distinguish proper nouns and adjectives.

a. To indicate beginnings

1. A capital letter begins the first word of a sentence.

2. A capital letter is used for the beginning of each line of poetry when it is printed in the traditional way.

3. A capital letter is used to begin the first word of a quoted sentence.

4. A capital letter is generally used for the first word after a colon when the statement following the colon is a rather long complete sentence.

Observe:

We have followed one plan throughout our history with two small exceptions: The first occurred when President Wilson entered upon his second term, and the second, when Mr. Roosevelt was just about to enter his second term.

The reason for his failure was plain: he had not prepared himself.

See **P11** for additional examples of capital letters used after a colon.

b. To indicate proper names

1. The personal pronoun I is always captialized.

2. All nouns referring to the Deity are capitalized, as are all attributive names of the Deity and of Christ.

God, the Lord, the Son of God, the Virgin Mary, the Trinity, the Supreme Ruler, the Redeemer, the Omnipotent

3. The days of the week, the names of months, holy days, and names of festivals are capitalized.

Monday, January, Good Friday, Labor Day, Passover, Yom Kippur

The names of seasons are not capitalized unless personified.

spring, autumn (*but* the nymph Spring)

309

4. Official titles before the name of the bearer are capitalized.

Mayor Lindsay, Governor Green, King Christian.
(*Note, however:* Mr. Lindsay is mayor of New York.)

5. In titles of books, musical selections, magazine articles, etc., the important words are capitalized. Articles, conjunctions, and prepositions are usually not capitalized except when they occur first in the title.

War and Peace
And so—Victoria

See also Chapter XIII, **MSle.**

6. Words denoting family relationship are capitalized when they are prefixed to the name of a person.

When they are used as a substitute for a person's name, practice varies.

I called Mother Brown on the telephone.
I called (Mother) (mother) on the telephone.
She called her mother on the telephone.

7. North, south, east, and west and their compound forms are not capitalized unless a particular and well-defined section of the country is referred to.

First he came to the Middle West, and subsequently he traveled farther west.

8. Nouns and adjectives of races, nationalities, and languages are usually capitalized: Indian, Caucasian, Mongolian, English. White is never capitalized when referring to a race.

9. School subjects are not capitalized unless a particular course is referred to. The names of the various classes are not capitalized.

I took history as a sophomore.
I took History IV in the twelfth grade.

18. THE HYPHEN

a. The hyphen is used to indicate compound words, particularly those coined for the occasion or those which are still in the process of becoming one word.

1. Two or more words used together as a single adjective before a noun are hyphenated.

A well-furnished house; a middle-aged man; a first-class report; a six-foot pole; a long-delayed reply.

2. The hyphen is also used when two or more words or word elements, though separated, modify the same noun.

Did you order a six- or an eight-foot ladder?

He was not certain whether it was pre- or post-natal.

3. The hyphen is used to distinguish the many pairs of words beginning with re- when one of them has a special meaning.

recover	recreation	resign
recover	recreation	resign
re-cover	re-creation	re-sign

4. The hyphen is frequently used to avoid doubling a vowel letter or tripling a consonant letter.

| co-occupy | bell-like | re-echo |

5. The hyphen is frequently used after the prefixes ex- and self-.

With respect to compound words in general, consult your dictionary whenever you suspect a word should be hyphenated.

b. The hyphen is used to indicate syllabic division at the end of a line.

Consult your dictionary whenever you are in doubt about the proper division of a word. Monosyllabic words cannot be separated.

EXERCISE IV

Punctuate the following passages:

1. Leaving this part of the temple we made up to an iron gate through which my companion told me we were to pass in order to see the monuments of the king accordingly I marched up without further ceremony and was going to enter when a person who held the gate in his hand told me I must pay first I was surprised at such a demand and asked the man whether the people of England kept a *show* whether the paltry sum he demanded was not a national reproach whether it was not more to the honor of the country to let their magnificence or their antiquities be openly seen than thus meanly to tax a curiosity which tended to their own honor as for your questions replied the gate-keeper to be sure they may be very right because I don't understand them but as for that there threepence I farm it from one who rents it from another who hires it from a third who leases it from the guardians of the temple and we all must live I expected upon paying here to see something extraordinary since what I had seen for nothing filled me with so much surprise but in this I was disappointed there was little more within than black coffins rusty armor tattered standards and some few slovenly figures in wax I was sorry I had paid but I comforted myself by considering it would be my last payment a person attended us who without once blushing told a hundred lies he talked of a lady who died by pricking her finger of a king with a golden head and twenty such pieces of absurdity Look ye there gentleman says he pointing to an old oak chair there's a curiosity for ye in that chair the kings of England were crowned you see also a stone underneath and that stone is Jacob's pillow I could see no curiosity either in the oak chair or the stone could I indeed behold one of the old kings of England seated in this or Jacob's head laid upon the other there might be something curious in the sight but in the present case there was no more reason for my surprise than if I should pick a stone from their streets and call it a curiosity merely because one of the kings happened to tread upon it as he passed in the procession

2. Thus it happens that your true dull minds are generally preferred for public employ and especially promoted to city honors your keen intellects like razors being considered too sharp for common service I know that it is common to rail at the unequal distribution of riches as the great source of jealousies broils and heartbreakings whereas for my part I verily believe it is the sad inequality of intellect that prevails that embroils communities more than anything else and I have remarked that your knowing people who are so much wiser than anybody else are eternally keeping society in a ferment happily for New Amsterdam nothing of the kind was known within its walls the very words of learning education taste and talents were unheard of a bright genius was an animal unknown and a bluestocking lady would have been regarded with as much wonder as a horned frog or a fiery dragon no man in fact seemed to know more than his neighbor, nor any man to know more than an honest man ought to know who has nobody's business to mind but his own the parson and the council clerk were the only men that could read in the community and the sage Van Twiller always signed his name with a cross

3. I get the feeling that your aunt is a very remarkable woman he said in his slow precise English with its faint trace of accent she should have been what is it you say a career woman yes that is what I see in her a career woman without a career she should have painted all the time lived alone in a big room with a skylight made herself one meal a day out of tin cans walked alone in the fields and wept over sunsets he had risen and stood looking as he spoke at Aunt Palms scene of early spring no he said now reflectively perhaps she should even have lived in a city bought her plants from pushcarts seen sunsets only two weeks out of a year had no children of her own so that she could have really longed for them and maybe then painted them yearningly like Mary Cassatt Fredericka asked as he hesitated yes if that is one of whom I am thinking

NANCY WILSON ROSS,
The Left Hand Is the Dreamer[1]

---

[1] Reprinted by permission of William Sloane Associates.

4. Number one says the voice now two and from high up somewhere two cans of fog let out spurts of vapor which billow slowly
into layers in the air now down and to your left Mac the voice says
and the man on the jib boom finally moves and sends a stream of
fog from his can directly down to the water and across the camera
field save it says the voice and the fog stops coming and the billows
and layers of what has been sent out merge slowly in the air which
is now being set softly in motion by two giant noiseless fans turning slowly one at the water's edge one trained down from the dock
above Jimmie looks through his finder and says something to the
lighting director and the voice picks up again Al can you bring that
closer

CHAPTER VIII. Spelling

WE Americans place a high value upon the ability to spell correctly, and conversely we tend to associate poor spelling with illiteracy. We have, as a people, always been interested in spelling. Noah Webster compiled his blue-backed *American Spelling Book* almost as soon as we were a nation, long before he thought of a dictionary. For a long period the spelling bee was a favorite school and even community activity; and within the past forty years, newspapers, radio, and television have developed it on a national scale. Even so, business and professional men constantly complain that their secretaries are unable to spell, and college professors are equally unhappy over the misspellings of their students. Rightly or wrongly, those who read the papers and reports you write will tend to judge you and your work by your spelling. This chapter will try to help you correct any deficiencies in spelling that you may have.

1. OUR INCONSISTENT SPELLING

The difficulties and contradictions of English spelling are by no means totally chaotic. They stem from the nature of the English language and from certain aspects of its history. English has always had from twelve to sixteen distinct vowel sounds, not to mention a number of diphthongs or vowel combinations. But for centuries the language has been limited to five characters—or seven at most, if w and y are counted—to spell them with. During the twelve hundred years that we have been using the Roman alphabet, we have tried to meet this situation in a number of ways; but no one of them has been carried out consistently. The reduction of vowels in unstressed syllables—as in *ago, agent, sanity, cus-*

tom, focus, outrageous, where *a, e, i, o, u,* and *ou* all represent the same pronunciation—has created another difficulty.

Another cause is to be found in the variety of elements of which our language is composed. Several classes of words retain more or less exactly a type of spelling distinctive of the language from which they have been borrowed; while the words in each class are consistent with each other, they are at variance with those words similar in sound but derived from a different source. Notice such pairs of words as *vane* and *vein* (to say nothing of *vain*), *thyme* and *time, phase* and *faze* (sometimes spelled *feeze* or *feaze*).

A further reason for the inconsistencies of English spelling may be found in the large number of changes in pronunciation that have occurred in the language since 1500, when printing developed and spelling became generally fixed. Even the names which we give to the letters of the English alphabet (*ay, bee, see, dee, ee*) are different from those given to the letters of the Roman alphabet in any other language (*ah, bay, say, day, ay*); this difference indicates the extent to which our sounds have changed. Even though many of our sounds have changed, the spelling of these sounds has not. Therefore we have silent letters such as *b* in dum*b* and *gh* in thou*gh*t, fossilized remains of sound which are no longer pronounced. We have also various ways of spelling the same vowel sound, as in *knead* and *need,* where the spelling once served to indicate a distinction in pronunciation no longer present.

We must finally remember that it is less than two hundred years since writer, printer, and reader began to set much value on spelling the same word in the same way. Until that time a man's spelling was his own concern, his own property; and no one bothered to see if Monday's spelling matched Wednesday's. People seem to have got along well enough under this free and easy system, but it happens not to be ours.

We have glanced briefly at the history of our spelling, not to excuse or justify bad spelling—the conventions of the twentieth century do not permit this—but rather to show why our rules for spelling have such frequent exceptions.

2. WHY WE MISSPELL

The extent of the eye span and the speed of reading have much to do with misspelling. Some of us have a visual memory; we recall or think of words as we *see* them on a printed page, whereas others *hear* them. Naturally, the visually-minded person will have less difficulty with spelling.

A knowledge of other languages also plays an important part. A student conscious of Latin *evitare*, "to avoid," even if he has not met the Latin adjective *evitabilis*, is less likely to spell English *inevitable* as *inevatible*; and certainly Latin *usura* or French *usure* would prevent him from making such a blunder as *usery*.

If every student read a great deal, if he had a photographic memory, if he were at home in those foreign languages which have contributed heavily to the English vocabulary, if he learned a few basic spelling rules, if he had formed the habit of consulting the dictionary for the spelling of those words about which he felt some uncertainty, if he proofread his compositions before handing them in, spelling would no longer be a major problem. Here are many *if*'s, but every student can fulfill some of them.

3. WHAT TO DO ABOUT IT

The preceding section has already suggested a number of ways in which spelling may be improved. Fortunately, the common words that are frequently misspelled do not number more than three hundred, and the majority of these represent only a few major types of spelling error. Sections 4 through 10 contain rules and suggestions which will help correct some of the most frequent mistakes. Learn these so well that you can apply them automatically.

Once you have mastered these sections you can then proceed to analyze your own particular difficulties. After every theme is returned, make a list of the words you have misspelled. Break up this list into the various types of error represented. If most of the words in it represent a confusion of *ei* and *ie*, put most of your effort on this particular problem. Examine the misspelled words in the light of the rule that has been given. Find out if you have been missing the words that fit the rule or the exceptions. In your reading, make a special effort to notice *ei* and *ie* spellings.

If your chief difficulty is in doubling consonants that should be single, or vice versa, approach this problem in the same way. Have you been confusing the consonants at the ends of root syllables before a suffix, or those doubled when a prefix is added? Look up the troublesome words in the dictionary, and see if the etymology and the derivation of the words will not help you to spell them correctly.

Your instructor can do little more than to mark the words which you misspell and to insist that you improve. Devising some means of improvement and carrying it out is your responsibility.

4. HOW WE INDICATE VOWEL LENGTH

Three devices which have developed throughout the history of our language to differentiate vowel length in certain pairs of sounds form the basis for certain of our spelling rules. One of the earliest of these was to double the vowel letter. Thus, a single letter indicated the short or lax sound and the doubled character signalled the long or tense sound.

We still do this in pairs like *bet, beet; fed, feed; stop, stoop; lot, loot.* Today the practice is confined to the letters e and o.

A second way of showing vowel length was to place an unpronounced final e after a syllable when the vowel in it was long, but to close the syllable with a consonant when the vowel was short. Thus we have *mat* contrasting with *mate*, *pet* with *Pete*, *rip* with *ripe*, *cod* with *code*, and *dud* with *dude*. The e has no value in and of itself; it merely signals something about the vowel letter in the preceding syllable.

Finally, a doubled consonant may indicate a preceding short vowel, whereas a single consonant suggests the long-vowel quality usually associated with the name we give to the letter. Thus, *ratted* contrasts with *rated*, *twinning* with *twining*, *bonny* with *bony*, *cutter* with *cuter*. Usually this device is used when a syllable is joined to the one in which the length of the vowel needs to be indicated.

All three devices are centuries old, and each has a certain logic behind it. Unhappily, no one of them has been carried out consistently. Many of our spelling difficulties arise from not knowing which device or practice to apply. Yet understanding just this much about them leads one to see that there is a kind of system and consistency in the use of single or double consonants and whether the final -e is lost or kept.

5. LOSS OF FINAL "E"

Final e is lost before a suffix beginning with a vowel. It is kept before a suffix beginning with a consonant. We have already seen how final e was used to indicate the length of a preceding vowel, as in *hope*. When a suffix like *-ful*, beginning with a consonant is added to *hope*, we still need the e to show that the vowel is long; thus we spell it *hopeful*. On the other hand, a suffix beginning with a vowel can serve the purpose of signalling the long sound, hence the e is no longer needed when we spell such words as *hoping* and *sliding*. Note the following:

	SUFFIX BEGINNING WITH A VOWEL	SUFFIX BEGINNING WITH A CONSONANT
move	mov+ing	move+ment
pure	pur+ity	pure+ly
achieve	achiev+able	achieve+ment
use	us+age	use+ful
state	stat+ism	state+ly

SOME EXCEPTIONS:

1. After c or g, final e is kept before a and o in order to maintain the "soft" sound of the consonant: *noticeable, traceable, vengeance, outrageous.*

2. Final e is dropped after g in such combinations as *judgment, acknowledgment, abridgment.* (British spelling tends to preserve the e here.)

3. A few other common words which do not follow the rule are *argument, awful, duly, truly, hoeing, singeing, dyeing, mileage.*

EXERCISE I

Spell the following combinations, accounting in each instance for your treatment of the final e:

1. refine+ment
2. refine+ery
3. confiscate+ory
4. safe+ty
5. home+less
6. late+est
7. prime+ary
8. hire+ling
9. orange+ade
10. observe+atory
11. lodge+ment
12. abide+ing

6. DOUBLING OF CONSONANTS

Before a suffix beginning with a vowel, a final single consonant preceded by a single vowel is doubled:

DOUBLING OF CONSONANTS   Sp6

In words of one syllable.

It was shown in Section 4 that our spelling system provides for such contrasts as *hop, hope; mat, mate; snip, snipe.*
But when we add suffixes beginning with a vowel, the scheme is likely to break down. We need to be able to distinguish between *hop* + *ed* and *hope* +*ed*, between *hop* + *ing* and *hope* + *ing.* We do this by doubling the consonant after the short vowel:

hope	hoping	hoped
hop	hopping	hopped
mate	mating	mated
mat	matting	matted
snipe	sniping	sniped
snip	snipping	snipped

Also: *stop, stoppage; cub, cubby; bid, biddable; begin, beginner.*

In words of more than one syllable, when the accent falls on the last syllable.

COMPARE:		
bénefit	bénefiting	bénefited
admít	admítting	admítted
díffer	díffering	díffered
defér	deférring	deférred

EXERCISE II

Spell the following combinations, accounting in each instance for your treatment of the final consonant:

1. shin+ing
2. shine+ing
3. sum+ed
4. equip+ing
5. equip+ment
6. occur+ence
7. profit+able
8. droop+ing
9. drop+ed
10. merit+orious
11. drip+y
12. prefer+able

7. "EI" AND "IE" SPELLINGS

These spellings are easily confused. Memorizing this jingle will help:

> Write *i* before *e*
> Except after *c*
> Or if sounded like *a*
> As in *neighbor* or *weigh*.

Words with *ie* not after *c*: chief, fief, besiege, field, fiend, etc.

Words with *ei* after *c*: ceiling, deceive, receive, conceive.

Words with *ei* pronounced as *a* in care: heir, their.

Words with *ei* pronounced as *ay* in way: weigh, neighbor, veil, reign, freight.

Exceptions to this rule are either, neither, height, leisure, seize, foreign, sovereign, forfeit, weird.

EXERCISE III

Complete each of the following words, indicating whether it is spelled with *ei* or *ie*. Be able to account for your choice:

rel__f	rec__pt	p__rce	perc__ve
conc__t	d__gn	w__ld	gr__f

8. CHANGE OF "Y" TO "I"

Final y preceded by a consonant is usually changed to i except before a suffix beginning with i.

cry	cried	crying
happy	happiness	
mercy	merciful	
modify	modifier	modifying
forty	fortieth	fortyish

Final y preceded by a vowel generally retains the y when a suffix is added.

sway	swayed	swaying
obey	obeyed	obeying
buy	buyer	buying

EXCEPTIONS: dai-ly, gai-ety, lai-d, pai-d, sai-d

EXERCISE IV

Spell the following combinations, accounting in each instance for your treatment of the final -y:

1. try+ing	7. study+ing
2. defy+ance	8. crafty+ness
3. eighty+eth	9. sly+est
4. volley+ing	10. vary+ed
5. array+ed	11. pay+ed
6. fancy+ful	12. employ+ed

9. PLURAL OF NOUNS ENDING IN "O"

Nouns ending in o preceded by a consonant usually form their plurals by adding -es:

echo	echoes	potato	potatoes
hero	heroes	embargo	embargoes

EXCEPTIONS: tobaccos, photos, zeros, autos

Nouns ending in eo, io, and oo usually form their plurals by adding -s:

cameo	cameos
radio	radios
kangaroo	kangaroos

Musical terms ending in o add -s to form the plural:

solo	solos
piano	pianos
alto	altos

EXERCISE V

Form the plurals of the following nouns:

tomato	memento	Negro
rodeo	basso	soprano
cargo	punctilio	

10. CONFUSION OF PREFIXES

Some spelling errors arise from the confusion of prefixes which look alike but are so different in meaning that they cannot be affixed to the same roots. Especially troublesome examples are

ante, "before": antecede

anti, "against": antidote

de, "from, down, away": debate

di, "twice": diploma

dis, "separation": dismiss

dys, "hard, ill": dyspepsia

per, "through": perforate

pre, "before": prescribe

11. WORD DERIVATION AND SPELLING

Develop an awareness of the component parts of derivative words. Learn how a word is composed and associate it with as many similar or related words as you can. Notice that *infantile* is composed of *infant* and *-ile*; if you associate this word with such related words as *infancy*, *infantry*, *infanta*, *infanticide*, then the group as a whole, and particularly the shifted accent on the *a* vowel in the last two words, will keep you from such a spelling as *infintile*.

Similarly, the pronunciation of the stressed vowel in *stability* will help you with the spelling of *stabilize*; that of the stressed vowel in *grammatical* will suggest the correct spelling *grammar*. These associations are especially useful in suggesting the spelling of unstressed vowels.

12. PRONUNCIATION AND SPELLING

Do not attempt to correct spelling errors through a conscious distortion of pronunciation.

This suggestion is contrary to advice frequently offered. One is often told to create such artificial distinctions in pronunciation as *beggar, doctor, adviser,* though most modern dictionaries use the same symbol to indicate the phonetic value of all three vowels. We must remember that spelling began as an attempt—and not a very good one— to reproduce pronunciation. To fashion our pronunciation according to what is in origin a somewhat imprecise attempt at reproducing it, is to put the cart before the horse.

Unnatural pronunciations of this kind are not likely to prove very useful in suggesting the spelling of unstressed vowels. It is true, however, that reasonable care in pronouncing combinations of consonants and avoiding the omission of syllables in certain words may help you in overcoming some spelling errors. Note the following:

recoGnize	sophOmore
probABly	libRary
quanTity	goverNment
enviroNment	boundAry
liAble	suRprise

There are other instances of confusion where it is hard to tell if the faulty spelling is the cause of the mispronunciation or vice versa. At all events, straighten them out. Words in this group include

caVAlry	grIEvous
irRELevant	mischIEvous
pERspiration	heighT

13. THE DICTIONARY

The dictionary is your best help. Every good dictionary contains a number of useful spelling rules. These are usually in the preface. Locate them in your own dictionary and form the habit of referring to them when in doubt. (See also Chapter V, **D9.**)

In addition, irregular spellings of noun plurals, verb participles, past tenses, and other inflected forms are usually given in the treatment of the individual word. If you are in doubt about such a spelling, look it up.

We have already seen in section 11 that it is helpful to develop an awareness of the parts which go to make up related words. The dictionary helps you to do this by listing all the derived forms that a word may have. Sometimes the origin of a word, its etymology, will provide useful information: discovering a Latin form such as *cura* will help you to understand why the English derivative is *curable* and not *curible*.

Another useful service the dictionary performs is to indicate whether compound words are written solid, with a hyphen, or as two words. Here you must be careful to distinguish between the hyphen and the dots which are employed in some dictionaries to divide words into syllables. Our spelling of compounds in English is inconsistent. There are no simple rules, and no one can be expected to remember the spelling of every word combination he is likely to use. Form the habit of checking the spelling of every compound you use in your writing.

Finally, most experienced writers use the dictionary to check the spelling of foreign terms and of particularly difficult words. Form the dictionary habit. Looking up words takes a little time but amply repays your efforts by helping you to improve your spelling.

EXERCISE VI

A. By an examination of the derivation, etymology, and meaning of the separate elements of the following words, explain:

1. Why there should be two *m*'s in *committee*.
2. Why there are two *m*'s in *immigrate* but only one *m* in *emigrate*.
3. What in the etymology accounts for the two *t*'s in *battle* and *battalion*.
4. Why *excellent* has two *l*'s and why the last vowel is *e*, not *a*.
5. Why *accord* has two *c*'s.
6. Why *appear* has two *p*'s.
7. Why *readable* takes the *-able* suffix and not *-ible*.
8. Why *tractable* takes the *-able* suffix and not *-ible*.
9. Why *legible* takes the *-ible* suffix.
10. The difference in spelling of *intercede* and *supersede*.

B. Consult your dictionary to determine which of the following combinations are written as one word, which are hyphenated, and which are written as two words:

1. alms house	11. half timbered
2. chop stroke	12. half way
3. country dance	13. ill bred
4. drift ice	14. leap year
5. drop kick	15. make shift
6. eye strain	16. pilot light
7. fool proof	17. pocket veto
8. foot brake	18. port hole
9. foot pound	19. quick trick
10. gear shift	20. stern wheel

14. PREFERRED SPELLINGS

Remember that some words have at least two "acceptable" spellings. In some instances there is a difference be-

tween British and American practice; in others, both forms
are current in America.

Form the habit of always spelling the same word in the
same way. It is better if you spell consistently all of the
words in the same class; that is, if you spell *humor* and
not *humour*, then spell *odor* rather than *odour*.

Consult your dictionary for preferred spelling of the
following pairs:

adviser—advisor	naturalise—naturalize
center—centre	gray—grey
endorse—indorse	mediaeval—medieval
enquire—inquire	reflection—reflexion
analog—analogue	enrolment—enrollment
fledgeling—fledgling	smolder—smoulder
program—programme	caliber—calibre
gipsy—gypsy	shew—show
odor—odour	orthopaedic—orthopedic
pretence—pretense	encase—incase
manoeuvre—maneuver	practise—practice

15. WORDS WITH SIMILAR SPELLING BUT OF DIFFERENT MEANING

Many pairs of words, different in origin, meaning, and
spelling, have come to be pronounced alike or somewhat
alike. Test yourself on the following pairs, and if uncertain
about the meaning or use of any one member of the pair,
look up both of them in your dictionary.

accept	alley	angel
except	ally	angle
advice	already	ascent
advise	all ready	assent
affect	altar	bare
effect	alter	bear
aisle	altogether	baring
isle	all together	barring
		bearing

born
borne

breath
breathe

canvas
canvass

capital
capitol

cite
site
sight

clothes
cloths

coarse
course

complement
compliment

consul
council
counsel

corps
corpse

costume
custom

dairy
diary

decent
descent
dissent

desert
dessert

dual
duel

formally
formerly

forth
fourth

gamble
gambol

holly
holy
wholly

hoping
hopping

instance
instants

its
it's

loath
loathe

loose
lose

manner
manor

metal
medal

morn
mourn

passed
past

peace
piece

personal
personnel

plain
plane

planed
planned

precede
proceed
procedure

precedence
precedents

presence
presents

principal
principle

quiet
quite

rain
reign
rein

right
rite
write

serf
surf

shone
shown

sole
soul

staid
stayed

stake
steak

stationary
stationery

steal
steel

than	villain	weather
then	villein	whether
there	wander	who's
their	wonder	whose
they're	weak	your
to	week	you're
too		
two		

16. WORDS FREQUENTLY MISSPELLED

The most encouraging aspect of the spelling difficulty is that the words frequently misspelled by college students constitute a relatively small group. The following list includes most of these. You will find it useful for drills and practice.

absence	apparent	career
abundance	appreciate	careless
acceptable	approach	carrying
accessible	argument	category
accident	arouse	ceiling
acclaim	article	challenge
accommodate	athletic	changeable
accusing	attended	character
accustom	audience	choose
achievement	authority	coming
acquaintance	bargain	committed
acquire	basis	comparative
across	beginning	competition
actually	behavior	completely
adequate	belief	conceive
advice	beneficial	concentrate
aggressive	brilliance	condemn
allotted	Britain	conscience
analyze	bulletin	conscious
apology	burial	considerably
apparatus	capitalism	consistency

WORDS FREQUENTLY MISSPELLED **Sp16**

continuously
controlling
controversial
convenience
coolly
counsel
criticism
curiosity
curriculum
deceive
decision
definite
dependent
description
desirability
despair
develop
difference
dilemma
disappear
disappoint
disastrous
disciple
discriminate
dissatisfied
dominant
efficient
embarrass
eminent
emphasize
entertain
entirely
entrance
environment
equipped
escape
exaggerate
excellent

exercise
existence
expense
experience
explanation
extremely
fallacy
familiar
fascinate
fictitious
finally
foreign
friend
fulfill
fundamental
further
government
grammar
group
guarantee
handled
happened
happiness
harass
height
heroine
hindrance
humorous
hundred
hungrily
hypocrisy
idea
ignorant
imagine
immediate
incidentally
independence
indispensable

inevitable
influential
ingenious
initiative
inseparable
intelligent
interest
interpretation
involve
irrelevant
jealousy
knowledge
laboratory
laborer
laid
later
leisure
license
liveliest
loneliness
losing
magazine
maintenance
maneuver
marriage
medieval
merely
miniature
mortgage
mysterious
narrative
naturally
necessity
ninety
noticeable
occasion
occurrence
operate

opinion
opportunity
oppose
optimist
origin
paid
pamphlets
parallel
paralyze
particular
performance
permanent
philosophy
physical
plausible
pleasant
politician
possess
possible
practical
practice
preferred
prejudice
prepare
prevalent
privilege
probably
professor
prominent
propaganda
prophecy
prophesy
prove

psychology
pursue
quantity
readily
realistically
receive
recommend
referring
relieve
religion
repetition
response
rhythm
ridiculous
sacrifice
sacrilegious
satire
satisfied
scarcity
scene
schedule
seize
senses
sergeant
separate
shining
significance
similar
speech
sponsor
strictly
studying
subsistence

substantial
subtle
success
sufficient
summary
suppose
suppress
surprising
surround
susceptible
technique
temperament
theory
thorough
together
tragedy
transferred
tremendous
tries
tyranny
unanimous
undoubtedly
unnecessary
unusual
useful
vacuum
valuable
variety
vengeance
warrant
weather
weird
yield

IX. Usage

THERE are many questions of usage which cannot be decided according to rules of grammar or by the application of general principles of propriety in diction. Such disputed points are individual matters, and a judgment on them can be reached only after a painstaking examination of the most competent authorities and, more important still, of the language itself.

It is the purpose of this section to deal with such troublesome questions and to give the student a practical decision in respect to each of them. Because we firmly believe that the English language itself is the final arbiter in these matters, many of our conclusions are supported by actual citations or illustrations from present-day and sometimes earlier English—some from literature, some from newspapers and other forms of nonliterary writing.

More often the judgments here expressed have been based upon the most reliable collections of the facts of the English language. Of these, the *Oxford English Dictionary* is unquestionably the most important, but in all instances Webster's *New International Dictionary* (Second and Third Editions) and Wyld's *Universal Dictionary of the English Language* have been consulted as well. The following works are also essential whenever an investigation of usage is to be made: Margaret M. Bryant, *Current American Usage*; Bergen and Cornelia Evans, *A Dictionary of Contemporary American Usage*; Sir Ernest Gowers' revision of H. W. Fowler, *Modern English Usage*; O. Jespersen, *A Modern English Grammar*; C. C. Fries, *American English Grammar*; and G. O. Curme, *Syntax*. *Current English Usage* by S. A. Leonard is valuable also as a survey of opinion about usage.

1. LEVELS OF USAGE

Some years ago, Professor J. S. Kenyon made the valuable observation that we must notice two groups of distinctions about any item of usage: its *cultural level* and its *functional variety*. As to the first, we must distinguish between what is *standard* and what is *nonstandard*; as to the second, we must distinguish between *formal* expression and *informal*. The purpose of the schools is to teach standard usage; and since most students already have some command of informal expression, the schools must concentrate on the formal.

The informal language of educated or cultivated people, as it is found in their personal conversation and correspondence and in familiar public speaking, is in no sense incorrect or "bad English" merely because it is informal. Certain features of this style, however, are inappropriate to formal situations—to platform or public speech; to public reading; to legal, scientific, or literary writing. For these latter uses only formal standard English is acceptable. The schools seek to give the student a command of this style.

It must be conceded, on the other hand, that during the past generation or two the gap between the formal and the informal styles has narrowed considerably. Or, to put it another way, there is proportionally less formal speaking and writing today than there was in our grandparents' time; the informal style—what has been called "the style of well-bred ease"—is favored far more widely than it was in even the recent past. Presidential messages to the people, "fireside chats," and other such addresses broadcast over radio and television are a case in point. The written style of our "best" magazines—those addressed to the college-educated reader—are another. This does not mean that there is no longer any gap between informal and formal, or that there is no need to teach or to learn the latter. Plenty of room

334

still exists for the improvement of most people's writing and speaking, if only in making them more subject to conscious control, in giving them orderly structure, clarity, force, and attractiveness.

In matters of usage, then, there are two kinds of distinctions to be made: first, that of level; second, that of function. The glossary that follows seeks to indicate to the student, so far as possible, what is at present established as *standard* or *acceptable* for formal use; usages that are appropriate primarily for *informal* speaking (or writing); and those usages, labeled *dialectal, provincial, slang, jargon,* which are nonstandard and not acceptable for formal use, though they are sometimes admissible to informal writing and of course in realistic representation of some types of dialogue. In every case, the main question is one of *appropriateness* to the immediate situation.

Whenever you consult the glossary, read carefully and completely everything that is said about the expression under discussion. Be certain thereafter that you use that expression only if it is acceptable and suits the style at which you are aiming.

Preceding the glossary is a list[1] of the "worst errors of usage," found frequently in the language of the least educated, but not acceptable in current standard speech or writing.

It should be noted that many of these usages were altogether acceptable at other stages in the history of the English language, and that some are, in fact, more logical than the corresponding forms which are "correct" today. Usage does not always follow logic, and logic is therefore not by itself an adequate guide to correctness, which can

---

[1] Based on Charles Carpenter Fries, *American English Grammar* (New York, 1940).

only be established, at any given time, by the actual usage of the cultivated speakers and writers.

From the point of view of the student, then, the important thing is to know what is acceptable current usage. Many points of usage are disputed or variable, but there is no question about those included in this list. Read the list carefully. If you find that you make any of these errors, rid yourself of them as quickly as possible.

2. WORST ERRORS OF USAGE

a. Matters of Number

1. Failure to pluralize nouns of measure:

WRONG: three year ago; five mile away; ten pound of salt
RIGHT: three years ago; five miles away; ten pounds of salt

2. Pluralizing wrongly:

WRONG: farm's; dog's; hat's
RIGHT: farms; dogs; hats

(The apostrophe shows genitive case or contraction. Obviously, this error is limited to writing.)

3. Using was with plural subjects:

WRONG: we was; you was; the men was
RIGHT: we were; you were; the men were

b. Matters of Grammatical Form

1. Incorrect form of demonstratives:

WRONG: them people; one of them kind
RIGHT: those people; one of that kind

2. Case form in reflexive pronouns:

WRONG: He did it hisself. They thought of their own selves.
RIGHT: He did it himself. They thought of themselves.

3. Using adjectives for adverbs:

WRONG: He washed it *good*. She treated him *kind*.
RIGHT: He washed it *well*. She treated him *kindly*.

(See also Chapter VI, **G6**.)

4. Don't with third person singular subject:

WRONG: He *don't* care. It *don't* matter.
RIGHT: He *doesn't* care. It *doesn't* matter.

5. Confusing principal parts of verbs:

Leaving -ed (pronounced -t) off the past tense and past participle:

WRONG: He *talk* to me. We've often *work* after dark.
RIGHT: He *talked* to me. We've often *worked* after dark.

Adding -ed where it does not belong:

WRONG: He was *drowneded*. They *knowed* better.
RIGHT: He was *drowned*. They *knew* better.

(The second occurs in the attempt to regularize an irregular past tense.)

Using the present form for the past tense:

WRONG: I *give* it to him yesterday. I *see* he was ready.
RIGHT: I *gave* it to him yesterday. I *saw* he was ready.

Using the past participle for the past tense:

WRONG: The water *run* down. She *done* him wrong. They *seen* us.
RIGHT: The water *ran* down. She *did* him wrong. They *saw* us.

Using the past tense for the past participle:

WRONG: I've *did* it many a time. The children have *went* home.
RIGHT: I've *done* it many a time. The children have *gone* home.

Ought used as a participle:

WRONG: He hadn't *ought* to tell.
RIGHT: He *ought* not to tell, or He *should* not tell.

See also *Had ought*, page 350.

c. Redundancies

1. Multiple negatives:

WRONG: He's *not* going there *no* more. There *ain't never* been *nobody* like her. He *can't hardly* talk.

RIGHT: He's *not* going there any more. There has *never* been anybody like her. He can *hardly* talk.

2. Double comparatives (and superlatives):

WRONG: *more kinder* people; *most unpleasantest* work
RIGHT: *kinder* people; *most unpleasant* work

d. Miscellaneous Faults

(See the individual articles in the glossary which follows.)

1. **Use of** ain't.
2. **Confusion of** lay **and** lie.
3. **Confusion of** as regards **and** in regard to.
4. **Use of** that there **and** this here.

3. GLOSSARY OF USAGE

The following abbreviations are regularly used throughout the glossary:

Oxford English Dictionary: OED
Webster's New International Dictionary: WD
Wyld, *Universal Dictionary of the English Language*: Wyld
Horwill, *Dictionary of Modern American Usage*: DAU
Mathews, *Dictionary of Americanisms*: DA
Fowler, *Modern English Usage* (Gowers' revision): F
Bryant, *Current American Usage*: B
Evans, *A Dictionary of Contemporary American Usage*: E

A, an. A is the normal form before consonant *sounds* irrespective of spelling: *a cat, a yoke, a united front. An* is the regular form before vowel sounds irrespective of spelling: *an apple, an old man, an hour, an F*. The form *a* is proper before such words as *history* and *hotel*, in which the *h* sound is currently pronounced but was silent at an earlier period. *An historical novel* or *an hotel* is quaintly archaic but has little else than snob appeal to recommend it.

Above. The argument that *above* is either a preposition or an adverb and therefore may not be used as an adjective (i.e., *the above paragraph*) is not valid. (*OED, WD, Wyld, B, E,* and *F* all recognize this use.) This adjectival use of *above* may, at times, be objectionable on grounds of style, since it is most properly classified as legal and commercial jargon. *Preceding* or *foregoing* may serve as substitutes. See Chapter IV, **D6d.**

Ad. A clipped or shortened form of *advertisement*. Appropriate only for informal use.

Aggravate. The *OED* has citations for aggravate in the sense of *exasperate, vex, annoy*, from the seventeenth century to the present time, including the novelists Richardson and Thackeray. Nevertheless in American usage today it is informal only.

Ain't. Not acceptable. Use instead the forms of the verbs *be* or *have* which the situation demands. The first person singular, negative interrogative poses a problem since the alternatives *aren't I* and *am I not* are not entirely satisfactory. *Aren't I* is objectionable because it uses the plural or second person singular verb *are* with the first person singular subject *I*. *Am I not* is felt by many to be awkward or stilted because all the other short, frequently used auxiliary verbs place the contracted informal *n't* between verb and subject in the interrogative, for example: *don't I, can't I, haven't I*. The lack of a satisfactory alternative to *ain't* forces the use of such indirect substitutes as "Isn't that so?" or "Don't you think?"

Alibi. American informal for *an excuse*. In formal writing use *alibi* only in its technical legal sense.

All of. According to *WD* and *E, all* is often followed by *of* and a pronoun, and in recent usage by *of* and a noun. *All of the books* is thus quite as acceptable as *all the books*.

All the farther. *All the farther, all the faster, all the higher,* etc., are dialect and not Standard English when intended to mean *as far as, as fast as, as high as;* use the latter. This idiom seems to have been formed on the pattern of *all the more;* but *all the more* is adjectival, whereas *all the farther,* etc., are adverbial.

All the farther, etc., when used to mean *farther yet* or *even farther, even faster, even higher,* etc., are quite acceptable usages.

Alright. Although this spelling is used unconsciously by some who do not know the conventional spelling and consciously by certain writers who wish to defy the conventions, it cannot be said to have found general acceptance. The conservative spelling is still *all right.*

Among. See **Between.**

And etc. The *and* is superfluous, since *etc.* is already an abbreviation for Latin *et cetera,* "and so forth."

And/or. In origin a legalism, equivalent to *each and every, all and sundry,* and like them often used unnecessarily in ordinary prose. Use it only when the context does not permit *or* to carry the meaning of *and.*

Angle. Although the use of *angle* for *point of view, facet, phase,* is recognized by some authorities as wholly legitimate, students frequently overuse the word. Vary it with some of the words suggested.

Anybody's else. See **Else.**

Anyone. The dictionaries show both one- and two-word spellings for *anyone (any one), everyone,* and *someone.* The dual spelling is useful because it makes possible the distinction between any person indiscriminately and any particular or single person, for example: "Did anyone go?" "Did any one of them go?" For the agreement of *anyone* with a pronoun, see Chapter VI, G9b.2.

Anyplace. Recognized as American informal by several authorities. Use *anywhere* in formal writing.

Anyways. Acceptable as a literary form only when the word means *in any way or manner, anywise,* as for example: "Nor was such interference . . . anyways injurious."—DE QUINCEY. But *anyways* is a provincialism when it means *in any case, at all events.* Use *anyway* in place of it. "Anyway, I am glad you came."

Anywheres. This form is a remnant of the genitive or possessive case, which at one time had an adverbial as well as a possessive use. It is not Standard English. Use *anywhere* in place of it.

Apt. In British English *apt* is used to indicate something which may happen because of habit or inherent tendency; *likely* indicates merely the probability of something taking place. WD: "An impulsive person is *apt* to blunder. An angry dog is *likely* to bite." In American English *apt* is often used interchangeably with *likely* to indicate probability. "Sentences averaging more than 20 to 25 words are *apt* to become involved and confusing." —*Style Book* of the Jackson (Mich.) *Citizen Patriot.*

Around. The use of *around* to mean *about, nearly* is often classified as U. S. informal, but *DAU* and the supplement to the *OED* indicate that it has gained some recognition as literary usage. "The convention adjourned *around* four o'clock."— W. G. MCADOO. Acceptable.

As. (1) *As,* used for *because* or *since* in introducing a clause, has been overworked: "As you are not ready, we must go without you." The objection to it is on grounds of style, therefore, rather than of grammar. WD suggests that *as* assigns a less immediate and explicit cause than *since* or *because.*

(2) *As,* used for *that,* introducing a noun clause after the verbs *know, say, think* ("I don't know *as* I can go") is an old usage which dropped out of the standard language and is now provincial. Do not use it.

As . . . as . . . Many authorities used to hold that *as . . . as* should be used in positive comparisons ("I am as old as he") but that *so . . . as* was required in negative comparisons ("I am not *so* old as John"). An examination of the actual usage of many recognized writers shows that the *as . . . as* construction has been used with negative comparisons as well as positive for the last two hundred years. "He did not do as well as we expected" is classified as established in *Current English Usage.*

As to.   Often overused as in the following: "The question *as to* whether they should remain at work or go on strike was still unsettled." This sentence would be just as clear without the *as to*. It is better omitted. Faulty: "He said nothing *as to* the score." Better: "He said nothing *about* the score." The chief function of *as to* is introductory. It may be used to place at the beginning of a sentence some element that without it would have to be placed in a less prominent position: "*As to* the accuracy of the information, we cannot speak."

Asset.   Although the use of *asset* in a noncommercial sense for *resource, support, source of strength, valuable object, favorable circumstance,* is recognized by WD and by Wyld as legitimate, it is frequently overused. Vary it with the expressions suggested.

Awful.   *Awful* is an adjective, *awfully* an adverb; do not use them in the wrong places.

> WRONG: Awful good food. An awfully lot.
> RIGHT: Awfully good food. An awful lot.

Even when grammatically correct, however, these words, used in their common intensive meaning of *very great* or *extremely,* are clearly informal and therefore inappropriate to formal writing or speech. *Awful* once meant *awe-inspiring* but because of overuse for the past century this sense has been weakened, and the word today is merely an emotional intensive which depends on the context for meaning.

Back of.   Used in both spoken and written American English where British English would employ *behind* or *at the back of.* "Various motives were back of this reversal of policy."—PROFESSOR H. ROBINSON.

Bad.   *Bad* instead of *badly* as an adverb is not acceptable. "He writes *badly*," not "He writes *bad*."

Badly.   Informal as an intensive after the verbs *need, want.* Informal: "I need it *badly*." Formal: "I need it *very much*." *Badly* with such verbs as *feel* and *look* is not in general use; here *bad* is used and is construed as a predicate adjective: "it looks bad; I feel bad."

Balance. Originally, commercial jargon for *remainder, residue, rest.* Now recognized as colloquial by WD and Wyld. DAU and E cite examples to show that this use of the word is coming into literary English. "He spent the balance of his life in travel."—*Dictionary of American Biography.* You may still encounter some objections to this use. Avoid them by employing other words.

Beside. Generally a preposition, meaning *by the side of.* "I rode *beside* him."

Besides (for *over and above, moreover*). Generally used as an adverb: "I don't want to go out; *besides,* it is already too late." As a preposition: "Have you anything to tell us *besides* what we already know?"

Between. (1) Be careful neither to say nor to write: "Between you and *I.*" Right: "Between you and *me.*" *Between you and I* is an overcorrection due to the intensive drill on *you and I* in a nominative case construction; but here the pronouns are objects of the preposition *between.*

(2) The rule that *between* implies two, whereas *among* implies more than two is not absolute. *Between* has been used to apply to more than two for the last thousand years. Concerning the use of *between* and *among* the OED says, "It is still the only word available to express the relation of a thing to many surrounding things severally and individually, *among* expressing a relation to them collectively and vaguely: we should not say 'the space lying among the three points,' or 'a treaty among three powers,' or 'the choice lies among the three candidates in the select list,' or 'to insert a needle among the closed petals of a flower.'"

Blame on. The expression "He blamed it on me" is informal, arising from the use of *blame* as a noun: "He placed the blame upon me." If the verb is used in formal writing, the preposition *for* should be used with it: "He blamed me for it."

Boy friend. This word and its counterpart *girl friend* are Americanisms that fill a need in modern life and are rapidly being adopted in England and elsewhere for informal use. They have no adequate alternatives: since the companionship implied is usually informal, *fiancé* and *fiancée* say too much, *sweetheart* also implies a farther stage of emotional attachment than may have been reached. *Boy friend* and *girl friend* have not achieved literary status, however, and will not suit a formal style.

Bunch. When applied to people—"a nice bunch" (of people)— this is informal. In writing use *group, gathering, assemblage,* or some other word.

Burst. The forms *bursted* and *busted* for the past tense and past participle are several hundred years old, but have now been replaced by *burst* for both functions. *Bust* is perhaps provincial or humorously informal in the United States.

But what. In such a sentence as "I have no doubt but what he will come," *but what* is informal. Literary English demands *that:* "I have no doubt that he will come."

Calculate. An American provincialism, in the sense of *to intend, plan, expect.* Use one of the words suggested in place of it.

Can. According to the conventional rules, *can* means *to be able to* while *may* means *to have permission.* Citations from the OED indicate that throughout the last half century *can* has been moving in the direction of *may.* It has gone so far in England that dictionaries reflecting British usage give *to have permission* as one of the meanings of *can,* without qualification.

Cannot help but. This is a mixed construction arising from a confusion of "I can but do it" and "I cannot help doing it." Though it has some literary authority ("He could not help but see them."—WALPOLE, *Jeremy.* "Professor Raleigh, from whose work on style I quoted above, often writes forcibly and suggestively, but we cannot help but feel . . . that it is more the work of a stylist than a thinker."—JOHN BURROUGHS, *Literary Values*), feeling against it is strong and it had better be avoided.

Can't hardly. A double negative which is no longer in acceptable use.

Can't seem. See **Seem.**

Case. Overused in such expressions as "in this case," "that being the case," "take another case"; the meaning is vague and sometimes ambiguous. Use instead such expressions as "in this instance," "that being so," "take another example."

Claim. "In America the verb *claim* has lost its distinctive meaning of *demand as one's due*, having become a mere synonym for *assert, state.*"—*DAU.* Both the *DAU* and the supplement to the *OED* furnish many citations from reputable American writings. "A citizen of a foreign country claiming to be imprisoned for some act committed with the sanction of his government."—c. a. and m. beard, *The American Leviathan.* This use of *claim* always implies that what is asserted or stated is for some reason open to doubt. If no such implication is intended do not use *claim;* use *assert, state, contend, maintain,* or the like.

Complected. According to the *OED* and *DAU,* American colloquial for *complexioned. WD* labels it *informal; E, not standard.* Do not use it.

Considerable. Used as an adjective meaning *a large quantity of* and applied to material things or used absolutely as a noun meaning *a large quantity, OED* labels this *U. S. Colloquial; E* calls it *questionable.* "They say he has considerable money." "Yes, he has considerable."

Contact (verb; for *to come* or *to bring into contact with*). Although this verb appears without a restricting label both in *WD* and *OED,* there is still much prejudice against it, possibly because it has been overused. Avoid it. Use "get in touch with," "make contact with," "arrange to meet," or the like.

Could of (for **could have**). Do not write this. In normal unemphatic speech the unstressed forms of *have* (verb) and *of* (preposition) are pronounced alike, that is, with a neutral vowel followed by the sound of *v:* [əv]. Hence the spelling *could of* is one way of representing what is actually pronounced, but it indicates that the writer is ignorant of the grammatical construction involved.

Couple (noun). In a literal sense *couple* means *two of a kind, a pair.* In the United States it is often used in the sense of *an indefinite small number, a few.* In Standard English *couple* must be joined to the following noun by *of.*

    U. S. INFORMAL: We were gone a couple of months.

    NONSTANDARD: They gave us a couple chairs.

Cute. This is derived from the word *acute* with the initial vowel cut off. Two hundred years ago the word meant *sharp, keen-witted*, but now it has a meaning similar to *cunning*. It has always been informal and often overused.

Data. The plural of Latin *datum* and formerly always used with a plural verb or pronoun. At present, according to *WD*, it is "not infrequently used as a singular" because of the collective conception of *data* as a unified mass of information. *F* and *DAU* contend however, that the singular use of *data* is confined to America. It is widely used in scientific writing today. "No provision was made for the publication of this data."—PROFESSOR F. J. HASKIN.

Date. In the sense of *appointment, engagement for a specific time*, this is informal. It is informal also as a noun meaning *the person with whom one has a social engagement* or as a verb meaning *to make a social engagement with*.

Definitely. Frequently overused for the purpose of giving emphasis or intensity. If you have acquired this habit, guard against it. Use synonyms, such as *certainly, surely*, etc.

Different than, Differently than. These expressions appear to have arisen from a confusion of *differ from* and *other than*. Though some literary men have used them, they are now very much out of favor and had better be avoided. Use *different from, differently from*. English usage prefers *different to, differently to*.

Don't. An informal contraction for *do not* which, according to *WD* is "Sometimes loosely used for *does not*." The supplement to the *OED* cites a number of examples, all from American English. There is a widespread feeling against *he, she, it don't*. Avoid it, both in speech and writing. (See **Us2b.4**.)

Due to. In origin *due* is an adjective; therefore the argument is sometimes advanced that it may modify only a substantive and that it is incorrect when used prepositionally to introduce an adverbial phrase, for example: "Due to the blizzard, we were obliged to remain in Madison."

J. S. Kenyon asserts that "some highly respectable writers admit" this construction. The supplement to the *OED* considers this use of *due to* more frequent in America than in England, although it seems to have developed as early as the seventeenth century. Notice that this development of *due to* exactly parallels the development of *owing to*, which is always accepted without question as an introductory prepositional phrase.

To avoid the prejudice against this use of *due to*, you may substitute *owing to* or *because of*.

Note that there is no objection whatever to *due* as an adjective in such a sentence as "His cough was due to exposure."

Each other.   The textbook rule that *each other* must be used in referring to two persons and objects, and that *one another* is to be used in reference to more than two, has rarely been observed in the language itself. Both *WD* and the *OED* indicate that *each other* and *one another* are used interchangeably. *F*, *B*, and *E* all concur.

Either, Neither.   Originally used to designate one of two persons or things. Since the seventeenth century, the terms have occasionally been used to designate one of a larger number. To avoid criticism, use *any* or *any one* and *none* or *no one* when your reference is to more than two. QUESTIONABLE: Either of the three books will do. RIGHT: Any of the three books will do. (See also page 238.)

Else.   The possessives *anybody's else*, *everybody's else*, *somebody's else* are old forms which have been generally abandoned. Use *anybody else's*, etc. See also Group Genitive, page 261.

Enthuse (for *to become enthusiastic*).   *E*, "U. S. Colloquial."

Etc.   This is a Latin abbreviation for *and so on*. Do not use it as a vague substitute for details you are too lazy to think of or write down. See **And etc.**

Everyplace.   See **Anyplace.**

Expect.   Informal or provincial when used to mean *suspect*.

Extra.   In the sense of *unusually* has occasionally been condemned, for example: "An extra fine day." This use may be questioned on grounds of taste, since the more recent quotations from the *OED* suggest it is commercial jargon.

Factor. Sometimes overused for *element, circumstance, influence*. See Chapter IV, **W6a.**

Falls. Authorities are agreed that this word is usually plural and requires a plural verb. "The falls are one mile from here."

Farther, Further. In theory *farther* is supposed to indicate distance, and *further* to indicate degree, time, or quantity: "The house is three miles *farther* down the road." "*Further* than this I cannot say." In actual practice *further* and *farther* are interchanged in all uses except that of *in addition* or *more*, where only *further* is permissible.

> UNIDIOMATIC: farther details.
> RIGHT: further details.

Feature (verb). The use of *feature* as a verb in the sense *to exhibit, make a special attraction of,* began as an American colloquialism, but it has been adopted in England also, as the supplement to the *OED* shows. There is still much objection to this use.

Fellow. Informal when used to mean *a person.*

Figure (verb). Like *calculate,* this word is often used to mean *to plan, judge, deduce.* These senses are all informal.

Fine. This word has been used as a general term of approval for the last five hundred years, nor does it seem to have been confined to informal English. Unfortunately it frequently happens that this is one of the few terms of general approval in a student's vocabulary, and he tends to use it on all occasions. If you have the *fine* habit, try first to be somewhat more specific in your expressions of admiration, and if this is beyond you, find some synonyms for *fine*.

Fine used as an adverb meaning *well* is informal.

Fix (noun). Informal for *predicament, plight.*

Fix (verb). American informal for *repair, arrange, prepare.*

Folks. Informal for *relatives, family,* sometimes *parents.* For formal use the more specific words are better.

Former. The first of two persons, things, groups, etc., to which one is making or has made reference; the other is called the *latter*. "John and James are brothers; the *former* [John] is a doctor, the *latter* [James] an architect." Do not use *former* and *latter* with more than two persons, groups, etc.

Funny. Informal in the sense of *strange, queer, odd*.

Get. The *OED* lists thirty-four meanings for this verb used independently and thirty-eight more in combination with prepositions. Many of these are informal, and certain others are provincial. Thus the word is very easy to overuse or to use vaguely. We could hardly do without it in conversation or daily speech, but we had better use it with caution in writing, especially in those senses which are farthest removed from the early meaning of the verb, *to acquire*. Consult the dictionary whenever in doubt. See also **Got, Gotten.**

Girl friend. See **Boy friend.**

Good. No longer correct as an adverb. ARCHAIC: He reads good. RIGHT: He reads well. On the other hand, in "He feels good, It tastes good," etc., *good* is an adjective, following a linking verb, and is perfectly acceptable. (See Chapter VI, **G5g.**)

Good and. Informally used as an intensive: "*good and* cold."

Got. *Have got* is common for *have* in the sense *possess* and has been criticized as repetitious. The construction very possibly arose because of a desire for emphasis. After *have* came to be used more and more as an auxiliary verb, speakers undoubtedly felt that it was weak and unsatisfactory when used as an independent verb; consequently the *got* was added to intensify the meaning. *Have got* for *have* began as an informal usage in the sixteenth century; and according to Jespersen, *A Modern English Grammar*, the nineteenth-century examples show its extension to higher forms of literature. J. Lesslie Hall, *English Usage*, mentions among others Carlyle, Thackeray, Dickens, Lamb, Ruskin, Holmes, as using it.

Have got in the sense *to be obliged* parallels the development of the verb *ought*. Both of them at one time meant *to possess* and in both verbs there was a shift of meaning from possession to obligation and a displacement of the present tense by a past

349

tense form. The dictionaries usually label this use of *have got* *informal,* but an examination of the occurrences of this expression in such writers as Disraeli, Ruskin, Wilde, Shaw, Trollope, and Wells, suggests that the expression is quite firmly established in written English. There is undoubtedly less prejudice against these uses of *have got* in British than in American English.

Gotten. An older form of the past participle of *get.* It is the more frequent form in American English where it is used in the senses *come, become, acquire, receive,* but not *possess, have.* "So, I think the State of Wyoming could not be charged . . . with *having gotten* itself into a position . . ."—SENATOR MCADOO, February 23, 1938.

Graduate from. According to *E,* "He graduated from college" is preferable to "He was graduated from college." It is the form used in most colleges today. *B* also characterizes it as the standard expression.

Guess. American informal for *think, suppose, believe.*

Guy. Used as a noun, this is overworked American informal corresponding to English *chap;* for formal use *person* or *fellow* is preferable.

Had better. In "I *had better* go," *had better* is somewhat more common than *would better* although both do occur.

In writing do not use *better* without an auxiliary verb.

INAPPROPRIATE FOR FORMAL USE: You better come.
REVISED: You had better come.

Had have, Had of, Hadn't of. Nonstandard combinations. Use *had* alone.

WRONG: Had he have come . . . , If he had of come . . .
RIGHT: Had he come . . . , If he had come . . .

Had ought, Hadn't ought. The verb *ought,* like many other auxiliaries, is defective; that is, it does not have all of the principal parts which a normal verb ordinarily possesses. At one time in its history, when *ought* and *owe* were still considered as forms of the same verb and when the verb meant *to possess* as well as *to be under obligation,* the form *ought* was used as the past participle as well as the past tense. It is this old use which still prevails in the forms *had ought* and *hadn't ought*, both of which are now inappropriate to written English.

The status of these expressions in spoken English is more difficult to define. *Had ought*, the affirmative, is probably a provincialism, but because of the American hesitation to use *oughtn't*, the negative *hadn't ought* is common informally. Avoid criticism by saying or writing, "Shouldn't you have . . ." or "Ought you not to have. . . ."

Had rather. *Had rather* and *would rather* are equally acceptable.

Hardly. See **Can't hardly.**

Have got. See **Got.**

Healthy. *WD*: "conducive to health." *OED* indicates it has been used synonymously with *healthful* since 1552.

Help but. See **Cannot help but.**

Himself. See **Self.**

Honorable. A courtesy title used very widely in this country. *DAU* says that it is applied "to (1) the President and members of his Cabinet, (2) members of either house of Congress, (3) state governors and holders of the more important State offices, (4) members of State Legislatures, and (5) almost any other politician or government official, major or minor, to whom one desires to pay a compliment." Conventionally, the word *honorable* should always be preceded by *the* and followed by the initials or first name of the person so addressed or by the title *Mr.*, "The Honorable Charles F. Williams," "The Honorable Mr. Graham." In actual practice the *the* is sometimes omitted when the title and name do not appear in connected context, as on programs and announcements. Some newspapers are hesitant to apply the title to an American at all, viz., "There is no such title as *Hon.* in the United States."—*Style Book,* Washington *Evening Star*

Humans. Sometimes vaguely used as a noun for *human beings, persons, people,* etc. It is properly used as a noun only in a collective sense to indicate the species or human race.

If. There has been some objection to the use of *if* in introducing a noun clause indicating doubt or uncertainty, as, "I do not know *if* I can go," and *whether* has been recommended in its place. The facts of recorded usage do not justify such an objection to *if*, as the construction has been in constant use in both informal and literary English for the last thousand years. In written English *whether* is more common when followed by *or*: "I didn't know *whether* he would go *or* stay."

In. Generally used to indicate a situation already existing within limits of space, time, or circumstance: "He walked *in* the room." *Into* is used to show direction of movement inward: "He walked *into* the room." In a sentence such as "He went *in to* dinner," notice that *in* is an adverb and *to* is a preposition; hence they must be separated in spelling.

In back of. Not appropriate for formal or written English. This is American informal, created after the pattern of *in front of*. In writing, substitute *behind, at the back of, back of*.

In regards to. A confusion of *in regard to*, where *regard* is a noun, and *as regards*, where *regards* is a verb. Substitute either of the two preceding expressions.

Inside of. Informal for *within*, for example: "Inside of the house." When used in reference to time, "Inside of three hours," it is American and British colonial informal. *Of* is wholly permissible in all circumstances when *inside* is a noun and not a preposition: "The inside of the box was also carved."

Kind. In formal English, *kind* preceded by the demonstrative and followed by *of* and a noun, should be in the singular throughout, "*This kind* of man has his use," or in the plural throughout, "*These kinds* of men have their use (or uses)." (The choice here depends upon what is meant.)

Kind of. Informal when used adverbially for *somewhat, in a way, to some extent*.

Kind of a. In formal writing, use *kind of* followed directly by the noun: "That is a *kind of* settlement customary with the ancient Greeks." *Kind of a* . . . is common informally.

Lady. *Woman* is properly used as the feminine form in all situations where *man* would be the normal masculine form. *Lady* is properly the feminine equivalent of *gentleman.*

INAPPROPRIATE: Three ladies came out of the theater just as I passed.

APPROPRIATE: Three women came out of the theater just as I passed.

RIGHT: Her manners and speech were those of a lady.

Latter. See **Former.**

Lay.   Used chiefly as a transitive verb, one which takes an object. The verb *lie* is the corresponding intransitive verb. "Now I *lay* the book on the table." "He *lies* on the bed." The verb *lie* is a strong or irregular verb, and has as its principal parts the forms *lie, lay, lain. Lay* is a weak or regular verb, and has as its principal parts *lay, laid, laid.* Much of the confusion between the two verbs arises from the fact that the past tense of *lie* and the present tense of *lay* are identical. Note the following illustrations of the past tense forms: "I *laid* the book on the table." "He *lay* on the bed."

The few standard intransitive uses include *to lay eggs* ("Is the hen *laying?*"), and *to deal blows* ("He *laid* about him with a club").

Leave (verb).   Some of the transitive senses of this verb are confused with transitive senses of the verb *let* because of overlapping of meaning: *leave* means *to cause or allow to remain* ("He *left* it on the table"), while *let* means merely *to allow* ("He *let* me do it"). However, while *let* is acceptable when followed (as it is here) by an infinitive, *leave* is not:

ACCEPTABLE: He let me do it; let us go; etc.

UNACCEPTABLE: He left me do it; leave us go; etc.

Either *leave* or *let* may be acceptable when followed by an adverb, though their meaning will not be exactly the same:

> *Leave* me alone. (Allow me to be by myself.)
> *Let* me alone! (Set phrase: Stop annoying me!)
> *Leave* me in. (Allow me to remain in.)
> *Let* me in. (Allow me to come in.)

Leave and *let* have a number of other meanings and uses that

353

are seldom confused. For more information on these, consult your dictionary.

Less, fewer.   Historically *less* was used with substances existing in the mass, *fewer* with countable items: "*less* sugar," but "*fewer* apples." Although *less* is sometimes substituted now for *fewer*, you will avoid criticism if you maintain the distinction.

Let.   See **Leave.**

Liable.   Originally used only to indicate the possibility of something undesirable happening, for example: "He is *liable* to break a leg." Since about 1900, there has been a tendency in America to use the word where an Englishman would use *likely*; that is, to indicate something that is probable without reference to its desirability. "Norman Hunter's new record . . . is liable to stand unmolested for many years."—N. Y. *Evening Post.*

This sense is not yet established in formal usage, however. See also **Apt.**

Like.   Originally *like* was a preposition and therefore could govern a noun, but could not introduce a clause; as was a conjunction whose function was to introduce clauses. Examples: "The sun looked *like* a ball of fire." "The sun looked *as if* it were a ball of fire." "Do it *as* I do."

Concerning the substitution of *like* for *as* (not *as if*, however) the *OED* comments, "Now generally condemned as vulgar or slovenly, though *examples may be found in many recent writers of standing.*" So far as written English is concerned, then, the safest course is to use *like* and *as* as illustrated in the preceding paragraph.

In informal English, it is doubtful if anything can stem the tide of the substitution of *like* for *as*, though its frequent use by advertisers gives it the odor of commercial jargon.

Like for *as if* is also inacceptable for writing; informally it is less objected to in England than in the United States.

Like for.   *Like* followed by *for* preceding an infinitive ("We'd *like for* you to come") is a provincialism.

Likely.   See **Apt, Liable.**

Loan (verb). "Loan is in modern (British) English usage a noun only, though it was once a verb also. In America it is still a verb." —Horwill, *DAU. WD* records this verb without any comment. "Carlyle *loaned* me Maurice's novel."—CONWAY, *Autobiography*. Acceptable in American usage.

Locate. According to the *OED*, the transitive use of *locate*, "to settle, establish" ("He *located* the factory near the river") is in acceptable usage both in England and America. The intransitive use ("He *located* at Terre Haute") is found chiefly in informal American English. To avoid criticism, use *settle* in place of the intransitive use of *locate* in formal writing. The loose use of *locate* in the sense of *find* ("I can't locate my books") should be avoided.

Lose out. The word *out* has been used to intensify the verbs *lose* and *win* in American English for the last fifty years. *DAU* shows that *lose out* and *win out* appear in formal literary English. Unless *out* adds something to the meaning, however, it is superfluous and may be legitimately objected to on grounds of style.

Lots of. Informal for *a great deal, much.*

Lovely. A good word, if not overused.

Mad. American informal and British English dialect when used to mean *angry.* This is an old meaning of the word, recorded as early as 1300. In formal use it means *insane.*

May. See **Can.**

May of. See **Could of.**

Mean. American informal when used to mean *ill-tempered, characterized by petty selfishness or malice.*

Might of. See **Could of.**

Mighty. As an adverb, it is informal.

Most. In formal written English *almost* is an adverb meaning *nearly; most* is an adverb meaning *in the greatest degree.* "We are *almost* there." "I am *most* grateful." In American informal and British English dialect *most* is sometimes substituted for *almost.*

Muchly. An unnecessary adverbial form. Do not use.

Must of.   See **Could of.**

Mutual.   Sometimes confused with *common*. WD comments, "That is *common* in which two or more things share equally or alike; *mutual* properly implies reciprocal action." "This intention is *common* to all of us." "The transaction was of *mutual* benefit to buyer and seller." Concerning *mutual friend* and *mutual acquaintance*, OED comments, "Still often used on account of the ambiguity of *common*."

Myself.   See **Self.**

Neither.   For reference to more than two objects, see **Either.**

Since the seventeenth century, *neither* has been used occasionally with a plural verb, usually when a prepositional phrase containing the antecedents of *neither* stands between it and the verb. "Neither of them *declare* themselves eyewitnesses of Christ's resurrection."—CARDINAL NEWMAN.

"After *neither-nor* we still often find the plural verb after singular subjects since there has long been a tendency to give formal expression to the plural idea which always lies in the negative form of statement."—CURME, *Syntax.* "Neither Leopardi nor Wordsworth *are* of the same order with the great poets. . . ."—MATTHEW ARNOLD.

Prejudice against this construction appears to be increasing in the United States, however, the feeling being that *neither* should take a singular verb.

Nice.   Sometimes condemned as a term of general approval. OED writes, "In common use from the latter part of the eighteenth century as a general epithet of approval or commendation, the precise signification varying to some extent with the nature of the substantive qualified by it." No modern dictionary disapproves of the word. Avoid overusing it.

No place.   See **Anyplace.**

Nobody else.   See **Else.**

None.   WD comments, "As subject, none with a plural verb is the commoner construction." The argument that *none* is properly singular because historically it is equivalent to *no one* is false. When we wish to emphasize the singular, we usually say *no one* or *not one*. None may be acceptably used with either a singular or plural verb, the choice depending on which meaning one wishes to emphasize.

Not . . . no.   Although common and acceptable in earlier English, where it was used for emphasis, the double negative is not acceptable today.

WRONG: I could not hear nothing. I didn't have no apples.

RIGHT: I could hear nothing. I couldn't hear anything. I had no apples.

The statement often made that a double negative means a positive, while true in mathematics, is false in language. "I won't never do it again" does not mean "I will do it again"; it means "I emphatically won't do it again." (It is, of course, nonstandard today.) A positive statement such as "She is attractive" is not the equivalent of the doubly negative statement "She is not unattractive." The latter implies that the speaker does not wish to go as far as the former would take him. Both are entirely acceptable; choose according to how positive or outspoken you wish to be in a given situation.

Nowhere near.   Frequently condemned as informal, and even at times called vulgar. In writing, use *not so old as* or *not nearly so old as* for *nowhere near as old.*

Nowheres.   Not acceptable in written English. See **Anywheres.**

Of.   See **Could of, Inside of, Had of.**

Off of.   This expression, formerly in standard use, is now dialect.

DIALECT: He jumped off of the barn.

STANDARD: He jumped off the barn.

One . . . one.   It was once insisted that *one* be consistently used throughout a sentence: "*One* rarely enjoys *one*'s luncheon when *one* is tired." Writers today do not hesitate to insert forms of the pronoun *he:* "One rarely enjoys *his* luncheon when *he* is tired." Do not attempt to use *their* in such sentences, however.

Only.   See Chapter III, **S9b.7.**

Onto.   Frequently condemned either as informal or as a misspelling. There are instances where it is necessary to avoid the ambiguity of *on* or *upon* after certain verbs. Notice that

"He jumped on the deck" and "He jumped onto the deck" are not the same in meaning, nor would "He jumped on to the deck" agree exactly with either. WD records onto without a restrictive label. Notice, however, that the more economical on or to alone will often satisfy the requirements of the situation.

Ought to of. See **Could of.**

Out. See **Lose out.**

Out loud. Frequently condemned as informal, but recorded in the OED with citations from literary sources. Aloud may be used in its place without fear of pedantic criticism.

Outside of. Accepted usage when the phrase means beyond the bounds of. "The sepulchre lay outside of the ancient city." American informal when it means except, besides.

> INFORMAL: I see no one outside of my parents.
> LITERARY: I see no one except my parents.

Over with. Informal for over, concluded, ended.

Per. The argument that per is a Latin word and accordingly must be used only before other Latin words is not in accord with the facts. It has been used with English words ever since 1588. It may be used in phrases relating to conveyance, per express; in phrases relating to manner of statement, per invoice; or in expressions denoting rate or proportion, per foot, per pound. Per usual is humorous slang; a phrase such as fifteen per, omitting the object, is jargon and should be avoided. As per is redundant.

Percent. Although percent is in origin an abbreviation for per centum, "by the hundred," it is not usually followed by a period according to American practice. There is objection on the part of some authorities to the use of percent in situations other than after a numeral: "A high percent was demanded." Here it is preferable to use percentage: "A high percentage was demanded."

Except in commercial writing, write out percent; do not use the sign %. Percent may be spelled as one or two words, but it is now more frequently written solid. Percentage is always written as one word.

Phenomenon. This word, borrowed from Greek, has kept for its plural inflection the -a inflection of the Greek neuter nouns; however, both WD and the OED recognize the native plural *phenomenons* as well. Neither dictionary gives any justification for the use of *phenomena* as a singular. "The phenomena *were* (not *was*) of interest to us."

Plan (on). "In America the word *plan* may mean not only 'devise,' but 'intend, hope.' "—DAU. This use is not colloquial, as is sometimes suggested. In this sense *plan* is followed either by the infinitive with *to*, or by the gerund preceded by *on*: "I plan to go tomorrow." "I plan on going tomorrow."

Plenty. Informal when used as an adverb: "The house was *plenty* large." In American English *plenty* does occasionally appear as an adjective, but only when used predicatively. "In the early days when land had been *plenty*."—JAMES TRUSLOW ADAMS.

Pretty. *Pretty* as an adverb, meaning *fairly, moderately, tolerably*, has been in constant use since the middle of the sixteenth century. Hall, *English Usage*, records two hundred instances from sixty of "the best essayists, scholars, novelists, and historians of the last two hundred and fifty years." It tends to be overused. Vary it with some of the synonyms just suggested.

Prior. The preposition *to* is proper after this word: *prior to*. This expression is rather formal; *before* is usually preferable.

Proposition. Informal or commercial jargon for *proposal, scheme, project, undertaking*. Avoid overuse. As a verb, this is slang.

Proven. This older form of the past participle, archaic in England, is in current use in America. The OED shows a range of citations from 1536 to 1899 and comments, "Properly in passive." DAU has a number of examples from current American writing. Hall points out that *proven* is Tennyson's regular form. There need be no hesitation about the use of either *proved* or *proven*; both are acceptable.

Providing. Some authorities insist on *provided* in a sentence such as "I will come *provided* everyone else does." *Providing*, in this sense, appears as early as the seventeenth century and has been used by George Eliot, Ruskin, and other accepted writers. There is still a slight preference for *provided*.

Quite. Frequently labeled informal in the sense *to some extent, rather,* but the *OED* records instances of this use from the middle of the eighteenth century up to the present time, including Richardson, Fielding, and Ruskin.

Raise. *DAU* comments, "In England one grows farm or garden products, breeds animals, and rears children. In America one raises them all." The citations show that the verb *raise*, "to bring up, foster children," is used frequently by established writers in this country.

Raise as an intransitive verb ("Both leaves of the drawbridge *raise*") is obsolete in England but still appears occasionally in American writing. There is so much prejudice against it that it is preferable to use *rise* in its place.

Real. As an intensive adverb, chiefly American informal. Its meaning has developed in the same path as that of *very*, which was originally an adjective only.

INFORMAL: real good.

FORMAL: very good.

Reason is because. See Chapter III, page 118.

Refer back. This expression appears repetitious, but there are situations which seem to demand its use. If a matter, which has at some previous time been referred to a committee, is brought up for discussion and is again referred to the committee which considered it originally, the simple verb *refer* will not suffice; for the matter has already been *referred* once. *Sent back* might be preferable, but since *refer* is already so firmly fixed in parliamentary language, *refer back* seems to be here to stay, but only in similar instances. The alternative *re-refer* is clumsy.

Reverend. According to the conventional rules, the title *reverend* should always be preceded by *the* and followed by *Mr.* or by the initials or first name of the person so addressed. In this country the practice of omitting *the* is widespread, according to E. C. Ehrensperger, who, some years ago, made a careful study of American practice in this matter. He mentions the

Harvard Alumni Bulletin, the Boston *Transcript,* and many church periodicals, in which *the* is regularly omitted. The omission of the name, initials, or *Mr.* after *Reverend* is provincial. For formal use, do not omit *The.*

Right. With intensive force, "*right* soon" ("*right* good," Southern U. S.) equals *very;* archaic in England and provincial in America. *Right* meaning *straight* with temporal connection ("He went *right* home") is informal American rather than British usage.

Right along (for *continuously*). Informal.

Right away (for *immediately*). Informal.

Seem. The logic of "I can't seem to solve this problem" is often questioned. The difficulty lies in the lack of an infinitive for *can.* To state the idea fully, one would have to say "I seem not to be able to solve this problem," "I seem unable to," or "I do not seem able . . . ," all of them cumbersome. The *can't seem* construction developed because inability is expressed by means of verbs far more frequently than it is through adjectives. It is recognized as acceptable by *WD. E* comments, "It is acceptable in the United States but is not often heard in England."

Seldom ever. No longer acceptable.

Self. The intensive forms *myself, himself, yourself* are properly used to give emphasis: "I *myself* did it." They are frequently substituted, also, for the personal pronouns *I, me, you, he, him*—a practice which some condemn outright. But the problem is too complex to be made the subject of a single rule. The following analysis is taken from R. C. Pooley, *Grammar and Usage in Textbooks on English:*

"As a matter of fact there are five uses of *myself* as the substitute for a personal pronoun, disregarding the reflexive uses. They are:

1. Sole subject of a verb. '*Myself* when young did eagerly frequent doctor and saint . . .' (FITZGERALD). Archaic, poetic, not acceptable in current prose usage.

2. Second member of a compound subject. 'John and *myself* brought the Yule log home.' Frequently heard, but not fully enough established to gain recognition.

3. After comparisons with *than* or *as*. 'Enough to make a better man than *myself* . . . run into madness' (RICHARDSON); 'No one knew this as well as *myself*.' Acceptable informal usage, not at all rare in literature.

4. Sole object of a verb or preposition. 'To *myself* mountains are the beginning and end of all natural scenery' (RUSKIN). Not quite as acceptable in current usage as No. 5.

5. The second or later member of a compound object of a verb or preposition. 'He invited . . . John Wilson and *myself* to visit him for a day or two' (LOCKHART, *Life of Sir Walter Scott*). This use is fully established in literature and current English."

The same conclusions apply to the other persons of the intensive pronoun, *yourself, himself, herself*, etc.

Set.   Because of the similarity of sound and meaning, this verb is often confused with *sit*.

Sit is an irregular or strong verb, and its principal parts are *sit, sat, sat. Set* is a regular or weak verb. Its principal parts are *set, set, set*.

While *set* is both transitive and intransitive, however, *sit* is far more often intransitive (though in a few uses transitive). Following are acceptable uses of both these verbs:

Set, TRANS.: Mary set the book on the table. He set his jaw.

INTRANS.: The sun sets at seven. The hen is setting. The cement set quickly.

Sit, TRANS.: He sat himself down. She sits the horse well.

INTRANS.: Sit in that chair. The house sat on a hill.

The last two sentences are of the kind in which the confusion comes. Never use *set* in these or others like them.

Shall.   See Chapter VI, page 219.

Should, Would.   The following generalizations will help:

1. **Would** expresses a conditional willingness.

I *would* try out for the play if I had time.
You *would*
He, she, it *would*
We, you, they *would*

2. **Would** expresses customary action in past time.
   I would light the fire every evening.
   You would
   He, she, it would
   We, you, they would

3. **Should** expresses obligation.
   I should go because I owe them a visit.
   You should
   He, she, it should
   We, you, they should

4. **Should** and **would** express a kind of future dependent upon a condition.
   I, we would or should be glad to help (if I, we could).
   You would
   He, she, it, they would

Should of. See **Could of.**

Show up. Informal for appear, arrive, be present. Slang for expose.

Sit. See **Set.**

Size. Present-day usage sanctions size used elliptically with a noun following: "a medium-size plate." The OED shows it in use from the eighteenth century down to the present.

Size up. Informal for estimate, judge.

Slow. Has been used adverbially since 1500. Considerations of euphony generally decide between slow and slowly. Slow is more appropriate to abrupt or imperative uses.

So. 1. Student themes frequently lead the instructor to believe that so is one of the few conjunctions in the student's vocabulary. For this reason, many teachers have been led to condemn so in a sentence like: "They had no guest room; so we went to a hotel." So has been used in this fashion for the last seven hundred years, but for the sake of variety it would be well for the student to become aware of accordingly, therefore, on that account, and to avoid an overuse of so.

2. The use of so for so that in the sense in order that is not in the best modern usage.

FAULTY: I waited a few minutes so I would not be too early.
REVISED: I waited a few minutes so that I would not be too early.

3. *So* as an intensive adverb, "so sad," "so fresh," has been in continuous literary use for as long as we have any record and is wholly justifiable if not overused.

Some. American informal or provincial when used as an adverb for *somewhat, a little.*

> I worked *some* today.
> He is *some* better.

Slang when used as an intensive: "He is *some* ballplayer."

Someplace. See **Anyplace.**

Somewheres. Dialect. Use *somewhere.*

Sort of. See **Kind of.**

Sort of a. See **Kind of a.**

Such. When *such* is completed by a relative clause, the relative clause should be introduced by as: "Such words as occur in the first three sentences . . ."

Such used informally with a noun gives intensive force: "*Such* a place!"

Sure. American informal when used as a substitute for *yes, certainly.* "*Sure,* it is true; they all have merit." American informal and English dialect when used as an adverb; formal English today demands *surely.* "That *surely* is a difficult poem."

In your writing use *sure* only as an adjective. "He walked with a *sure* and steady pace."

Swell. In the sense of *very good, excellent,* this is slang (WD).

Take and. Dialect in such an expression as, "I'll *take and* saw this board."

Take sick. Dialect for *become sick.*

Taxi (verb). In accepted usage, (1) "to travel in a taxicab," (2) "to run an airplane or seaplane along the ground or on the water under its own power."

Tend. When *tend* is used to mean *attend, care for,* the *to* is omitted. "He tends the sick."

Terribly. In the meaning *very much, extremely*, this is a "counter word"—much overused. In standard use it still carries the sense of terror or fear.

That there. No longer current in Standard English.

> WRONG: That there dog is a good hunter.
> RIGHT: That dog is a good hunter.

These kind. See **Kind.**

This here. No longer current in Standard English.

> WRONG: This here book is torn.
> RIGHT: This book is torn.

Through. Informal when used adverbially for *finished* in the pre-participial position: "I am through writing." Satisfactory for all occasions when used predicatively after the verb *to be*: "He did not arrive until the speech was half through."

Thusly. Do not use. Use the simple form *thus*.

Too. In the sense of *very* this word has recently acquired wide currency in the United States: "I wasn't too glad to see him. I don't have too much money." This probably began as an expression of light irony, but is now perfectly neutral. Informal; in writing, use *very*, or some other standard word.

Toward, Towards. *Towards* is prevalent in British usage; *toward* is more common in American usage except where emphasis is desired. "His back was *toward(s)* me."

Transpire. WD: "To come to pass; happen; occur;—a sense disapproved by most authorities but found in writings of authors of good standing." "I am fearful of supporting the conference report after what has transpired." It may be objected to on stylistic grounds as jargon. The standard meaning is *to come to light, become known*.

Try and. The use of *and* instead of *to* with the infinitive after *try* goes back to the seventeenth century. It may be found in Milton, Coleridge, Lamb, Thackeray, Arnold, George Eliot, and Charles Kingsley, and in standard current usage in England. However there is considerable prejudice against this construction in American usage.

Type. Such phrases as "a good type of book," "the modern type of hotel," have recently become widespread in the United States with the ellipsis of *of*. This is largely informal; yet one may read (e.g., in the New York *Times*) "Old-type format," "Family-type Burlesque," "New-type spring," and so on. For formal use "new *type of* spring" is preferable.

Ugly. *OED*, definition 6: "Offensive to refined taste or good feelings, disagreeable, unpleasant, not nice." Citations range from 1621 to the present time.

    OED, definition 8: "Cross, angry, ill-tempered."

    Obviously any objection to these extended meanings of *ugly* is not supported by the facts of usage. When you do employ the word in either of these senses, make certain that the context indicates clearly which of the meanings you intend. Do not use it ambiguously.

Unique. Logically, *unique* means the only one of its kind, and therefore it does not admit of comparison, i.e., a thing cannot be *more* or *most* unique, or even *very* unique. *OED* comments, "From the middle of the nineteenth century it has been in very common use, with a tendency to take the wider meaning of 'uncommon, unusual, remarkable.'"

Up. The adverb *up* furnishes great sport to those critics who expect language to be consistent in its logic and who totally neglect the psychological factor. They point out that *up* in combinations, such as *fill up* a glass, *open up* a box, is wholly superfluous because it adds nothing to the meaning of the verb. In the consciousness of the speaker, however, *up* does add emphasis and a sense of finality or completion. Just when *up* is superfluous is at times very difficult to decide. Is *folding* a paper exactly the same as *folding* it up? Is *cleaning* a room exactly the same as *cleaning* it up? It takes the *OED* three full columns to settle some of these questions of meaning, and nowhere does it condemn *up* as superfluous. The tendency to complete or emphasize verbs with *up* seems to be about seven centuries old.

Used to could. Not Standard English. The construction arises from the same situation that is responsible for *can't seem,* namely the lack of an infinitive form of *could*. Say *used to be able*, formerly *was able*.

Very.   According to some authorities *very* must be followed by *much* or *well* or some other adverb when it modifies a participle: "I was very *much* interested." The *OED* definition of *very*, B 2c, reads, "Qualifying past participles used predicatively or attributively=Very much." This clearly indicates that *very* does occur in Standard English as the modifier of a past participle.

A common sense rule would be that *very* may be used alone with any participle that can be used attributively as an adjective. Since we can say *a swollen foot*, it is permissible to say *the foot was very swollen*.

Viewpoint.   Although there has been some objection to the use of this word, it has been in existence for more than a century and is in good usage. "I think, however, if I have the right viewpoint . . ."—SENATOR NORRIS, *Congressional Record*, Feb. 11, 1938.

Wait on.   No longer used in Standard written English in the sense *to wait for*. It is a regional usage in America.

Want (for).   *Want*, "desire, wish for," is normally followed by the direct object, which may in turn serve as the subject of an infinitive but not of an active verb. "I want you to go," not "I want you should go." *Want* followed by *for* preceding the infinitive ("I want for you to come") is a provincialism.

Want in (**out, up,** etc).   In the sense of *want to go in* (out, up, etc.), this is Scottish, Irish, and American colloquial, according to the *OED*. Dialectal would probably be a more accurate classification.

Way.   On the use of the noun *way*, "manner in which something is done," without a preposition, the *OED* comments, "Now somewhat rare, the form with *in* being commonly preferred." "Be happy *in* your own way."

Ways.   "In America the use of *ways* as a singular in such expressions as *a long ways* is not a solecism as it would be in England." —Horwill, *DAU*. "We are a good *ways* apart." Generally informal.

Where. Where in a sentence such as, "I read in the paper where a plane was lost," is no longer used in written English. Use *that* in its place: "I read . . . that a plane was lost." Some modifications of this construction are acceptable informally. Avoid it in writing.

Where . . . at. Examples of *at* after *where* ("Not knowing where she was *at*") are cited by the Supplement to the OED from American writings, but the quotations seem to be primarily informal. Avoid in writing.

Where . . . to. Informal with *from* or *to* at the end of a sentence or clause. "Where did it go to?"

Which. See Chapter VI, **G3b**, and page 246.

While. Frequently overused as a conjunction, meaning "whereas, besides, in addition, on the contrary." Generally, *and* or nothing at all will serve the purpose.

> FAULTY: To the right of us was the river, while the mountains were on our left.
> REVISED: To the right of us was the river; the mountains were on our left.

Who. See Chapter VI, **G3b, G10b.1–2.**

Whose. See Chapter VI, **G3b, G10c.2.**

Will. See Chapter VI, page 218.

Win out. See **Lose out.**

Woods. WD: "More often in the plural and often, chiefly in colloquial use, construed as a singular."

Would better. See **Had better.**

Would of. See **Could of.**

PART THREE

THE LONG PAPER

Part One of this book was designed particularly to help you in the preparation of the fairly short papers which, in most composition courses, are assigned from week to week. In addition you will need practice in handling larger units, if for no other reason than to give you experience in preparing the term papers and course theses which will be required as you go on to more advanced work.

Most composition courses, therefore, include the writing of a long paper, due at the end of the term. In addition to posing more difficult problems of organization, such a paper usually requires you to collect information or opinion from printed sources, to evaluate and digest it, and to adapt it to the purposes of your own writing.

In preparing a paper of this kind, you must observe certain standards of conduct with reference to the handling of the material which you get from outside sources. The most frequent breach of ethics which students commit in writing their long papers has been given the rather high-sounding name of *plagiarism*. Most of you would call it copying.

The word *plagiarism* came into the English language from Latin. In old Roman times *plagiarius* was a term for a kidnapper, one who abducted the child or slave of another. Today *plagiarism* is applied to the stealing of ideas rather than persons. A plagiarist, therefore, is one who copies or appropriates the ideas, words, artistic productions of another person, and, by using them without giving due credit, passes them off as his own. In school this is looked upon as plain cheating. There is essentially no difference between copying from a book in the library or from the examination paper of the student sitting next to you. In either case you are claiming credit for something that is not yours. In the out-of-school world, patent and copyright laws have been devised to prevent this form of dishonesty and to punish offenders.

Now let us face the situation frankly. There are few topics upon which you could write five thousand words without getting material help from outside sources. In preparing your long paper you will have to do this, and in fact, one of the reasons for assigning it is to give you practice in using the library and in finding in it the material that you need. Actually, the proper use of ideas and information from duly qualified sources will strengthen your paper.

It is the improper use of such material which constitutes plagiarism, and the impropriety consists principally in failing to show that such material is quoted, neglecting to indicate where it comes from—which amounts to passing it off as your own. Don't do it. The chances are that you won't get away with it, and even if you do, you will have learned nothing from this practice, nor will it contribute in any way to your self-respect.

In the following pages the process of preparing a long paper is taken up: in Chapter X, use of the library, preparation of the initial and final bibliography cards, and notecard form; in Chapter XI, the development of a plan for the theme and methods of adapting and condensing source material on the notecards; in Chapter XII, outlining the theme; and in Chapter XIII, conventions of manuscript form—in particular, form of quotations, footnotes, and the final bibliography. Thus the paper may be prepared step by step with the study of the chapters following.

X. The Library

BEFORE writing a long paper you should learn about your library and discover what its facilities are. Does it have a reference room where encyclopedias, dictionaries, yearbooks, and works of general reference are kept? Are there special reading rooms devoted entirely to books in particular fields of study or divisions of knowledge, such as mathematics, literature, philosophy, history, and economics? Has your library made any special collections of books on any one topic, such as English gardens or colonial furniture, and are such collections housed in a special building or special room? Are there rooms devoted to magazines and newspapers? And perhaps the most important question: Where is the card catalogue?

1. CARD CATALOGUE

A card catalogue is an index, arranged alphabetically, of all the books in the library. It may include periodicals, bulletins, and pamphlets along with the books, or these may be indexed in special catalogue drawers. Inquiry at the circulation or reference desk should determine what kind of treatment is given to periodicals and pamphlets. Although the card catalogue will locate periodicals for you, it will not index their contents; for this information, the periodical indexes listed in **L3** and **L5** below must be consulted.

The cards are filed according to authors, titles, and subjects. Catalogues vary in their completeness, but you may always be certain that there will be an author card for every book in the library. However, only the principal subjects of a book will be given subject entries (see **L1c** below). If a subject is sought which is not given a heading in the catalogue, a more inclusive, broader subject-heading should be consulted. Thus, if no entire book on Paris is found in the catalogue, *France—Description and travel* will be the next heading to examine.

a. Author, or Main Entry, Cards

The card catalogue contains an author, or main entry, card for every book. The author is sometimes the name of a society or government office responsible for the publication, or sometimes, in cases where authorship cannot be determined, the title must be put in the "author" position (e.g., Bible, *Beowulf*, *The Patriotic Anthology*, etc.). Here is a reproduction of a typical author card from a library catalogue:

E
470.2
F7   **Freeman, Douglas Southall,** 1886–1953.
        Lee's lieutenants, a study in command, by Douglas Southall Freeman ... New York, C. Scribner's sons, 1942–44.

        3 v. illus. (ports.) maps (part fold.) 24 cm.

        "Short-title index": v. 3, p. 781–784. "Select critical bibliography": v. 3, p. [797]–825.

        CONTENTS.—v. **1.** Manassas to Malvern hill.—v. **2.** Cedar mountain to Chancellorsville.—v. **3.** Gettysburg to Appomattox.

        1. U. S.—Hist.—Civil war—Campaigns and battles. 2. Confederate states of America—Biog. 3. U. S.—Hist.—Civil war—Biog. 4. U. S.—Hist.—Civil war—Regimental histories—Army of northern Virginia. I. Title.

     E470.2.F7   973.73   42—24582

     Library of Congress   [66r45h⁵₁]

Items of information on the card are as follows:

1. The series of letters and numbers in the upper left corner is the library call number and is the number which you must give the attendant to get the book, since it indicates where in the library stacks the book is located.[1] If the library has open stacks the reader may locate the book himself.

2. The top line contains the author's name, last name first, followed by his given name or names in their regular order. The date of the author's birth, and of his death if he is no longer living, follows his name.

3. Indented under the author's name is a paragraph giving the full title of the book as found on the title-page (usually not repeating the author's name) and the names of any other people (editors, translators, etc.) credited as responsible for the book's existence. If the book catalogued is not the first edition, the card must specify what edition it is. The reason for this is clear enough. Later editions may represent revisions, and a reference to a certain page or to a quotation from the first edition of the book may not apply to other editions.

4. Following the title, author, or editor credits, and the edition information, the "imprint" is given: the place of publication, name of publisher, and date of publication and/or copyright date. (If any of this information in the main body of the entry, including the edition note, is not found stated on the title-page, it is enclosed in brackets on the catalogue card.)

---

[1] There are two principal systems of classifying books used in American libraries. The Dewey decimal system, beginning with a number somewhere between o and 999 provides one thousand subject categories. The Library of Congress system, using a combination of letters and numbers, is somewhat more flexible and better suited to large libraries.

5. In a second paragraph is given the "collation" or description of the physical makeup of the book: number of volumes or of pages, types of illustration, and height of the book in centimeters. (The end of this line is also used for a "series note," if the book is part of a set or series with another title.)

6. After the collation paragraph may appear a separate note calling attention to unusual or important features of the book, often bibliographies or supplementary sections.

7. Next may appear a "contents note," which lists separate titles found in one volume or titles of each volume of a set or series, as shown in the card illustrated here.

8. The final paragraph of the card gives a listing, or "tracing," of the subject headings (with Arabic numbers) and title or added author headings (Roman numerals) under which the book is to be entered in the catalogue. These not only serve to trace the complete set for the cataloguers but also may direct the searcher to related subject headings.

b. Title Cards

To aid the reader or student who remembers the title of a book but does not know or has forgotten the author, card catalogues contain title cards as well. All books with distinctive titles can usually be found under title card listings. Other titles, such as those beginning *Introduction to . . .*, *Collected Plays of . . .*, or *The Life of . . .* should be searched under the subject or author. In some libraries title cards are confined to a limited number of works, those sought after most frequently.

In sets of "unit cards" produced by printing, multilith, or other duplicator process rather than by typewriter, the title card, like the subject card, is a duplicate of the author card, with the title heading typed at the top. Here is a specimen title card (in library catalogues not all words of a title are capitalized):

```
E
470.2          Lee's lieutenants, a study in command.
F7        Freeman, Douglas Southall, 1886-1953.
               Lee's lieutenants, a study in command, by Douglas
            Southall Freeman ...  New York, C. Scribner's sons, 1942-
            44.
               3 v.  illus. (ports.) maps (part fold.)  24 cm.

               "Short-title index": v. 3, p. 781-784.  "Select critical bibliography":
            v. 3, p. ₁797₁-825.

               CONTENTS.—v. 1. Manassas to Malvern hill.—v. 2. Cedar mountain
            to Chancellorsville.—v. 3. Gettysburg to Appomattox.

               1. U. S.—Hist.—Civil war—Campaigns and battles.  2. Confederate
            states of America—Biog.  3. U. S.—Hist.—Civil war—Biog.  4. U. S.—
            Hist.—Civil war—Regimental histories—Army of northern Virginia.
            I. Title.

            E470.2.F7                   973.73                 42—24582

            Library of Congress              ₁66r45h⁵‡₁₁
```

c. Subject Cards

To assist the student who knows only the general topic
he wants to pursue, all library catalogues include cards with
subject headings. These are usually filed in alphabetical
order with the author and title cards, although they may be
placed in a separate catalogue.

If you were interested in learning something about the
history of the names of various places, you would look in the
catalogue under the general heading Names. This topic might
have under it several subheadings, such as Names, Family;
Names, Geographical; Names, Personal; and so on. On the
subject card below, the general heading is Confederate States
of America; and the subheading, indicating the special aspect
of the Confederacy treated, is Biography. The set of books
on this card is also important to researchers interested
in Civil War biography generally, in Civil War campaigns
and battles, and in the regimental history of the Army of
Northern Virginia. Consequently, four separate subject headings, numbered 1–4 in the last section of the card, are assigned to aid searchers with differing interests in this subject.

The subject card is a duplicate of the author card, with the subject heading added on the top line. Here is an example of a subject card (some libraries type the headings for subjects in capitals, others use red ink to distinguish them from other headings):

```
E
470.2        CONFEDERATE STATES OF AMERICA - BIOGRAPHY.
F7        Freeman, Douglas Southall, 1886-1953.
                Lee's lieutenants, a study in command, by Douglas
            Southall Freeman ...  New York, C. Scribner's sons, 1942-
            44.

            3 v.  illus. (ports.) maps (part fold.)  24 cm.

            "Short-title index": v. 3, p. 781-784.  "Select critical bibliography":
            v. 3, p. [797]-825.

            CONTENTS.—v. 1. Manassas to Malvern hill.—v. 2. Cedar mountain
            to Chancellorsville.—v. 3. Gettysburg to Appomattox.

            1. U. S.—Hist.—Civil war—Campaigns and battles.  2. Confederate
            states of America—Biog.  3. U. S.—Hist.—Civil war—Biog.  4. U. S.—
            Hist.—Civil war—Regimental histories—Army of northern Virginia.
            I. Title.

            E470.2.F7              973.73              42—24582

            Library of Congress        [66r45h5½]
```

2. PERIODICAL DIRECTORIES

The following are the most important books which list and give essential information concerning periodicals:

Ulrich's International Periodicals Directory. Ed. E. C. Graves. 11th ed. 2 vols. 1965–66.

N. W. Ayer and Son's Directory of Newspapers and Periodicals. 1880–date. Annual.

Union List of Serials in Libraries of the United States and Canada. 3d ed. 5 vols. 1965. This directory tells what libraries have what issues of what periodicals.

3. SUPPLEMENTS TO THE CARD CATALOGUE

The card catalogue has in it at least one card for every book in the library. It would be impractical, however, for any library to include in its catalogue the author and the title of every magazine article it possesses. Yet frequently the information to be found in magazines is concise and recent, exactly what a student needs to help him write a theme. It is even less practical to index the contents of newspapers, but newspaper articles may be essential for some topics. Similarly, many libraries find it impractical to index the contents of books of essays separately. Government publications on your subject may be available (free, or for a nominal charge) which your library does not have. You may, therefore, need to consult some or all of the following supplements to the card catalogue.

a. Periodical Indexes

The chief indexes to modern periodicals of reasonably wide circulation are

Readers' Guide to Periodical Literature, 1900–   (here and elsewhere, dates following title of indexes refer to years of magazines indexed). This is published twice a month with biennial cumulated volumes. Entries are given under author, title, and subject. Since the *Readers' Guide* covers those magazines which have the widest circulation (but which must have sufficient intellectual respectability to be subscribed to by libraries), most libraries have it, even if they have no other index.

Social Sciences and Humanities Index (until 1965, called *International Index to Periodicals*), 1907–   . This is a companion series to the *Readers' Guide,* so the two do not overlap in coverage. Until 1955 the coverage of this index included a number of important foreign language and scientific journals. Since then, as its new name suggests, it has been largely restricted to periodicals chiefly concerned with the social sciences and humanities.

Other useful general indexes are

Annual Magazine Subject Index, 1907–49. Reprinted in 1964.
   A now defunct rival to the *Readers' Guide.*
British Humanities Index (until 1962, called *Subject Index to*
   Periodicals), 1915–   . Useful for topics of British interest.
Internationale Bibliographie der Zeitschriften Literatur, 1965-
   . This joins together *Bibliographie der Deutschen Zeit-*
   schriften Literatur, 1896–1964, and *Bibliographie der Fremd-*
   sprachigen Zeitschriften Literatur, 1911–64. It is the most
   comprehensive of all general indexes. The combined series
   has subject headings in German with French and English cross-
   references. Titles are listed in the original language of publication. Many English language periodicals are indexed.

For nineteenth-century periodicals consult

Nineteenth Century Readers' Guide, 1890–99.
Poole's Index to Periodical Literature, 6 vols., 1802–1907.
   This index is somewhat difficult to use because entries are
   given only under key word of title. You will, therefore, have
   to be resourceful in using it. You might imagine yourself to
   be dealing with a particularly inconsistent variety of subject
   index.

There are also a great many other indexes devoted to
articles in special fields of study and interest. They range
from some covering very broad fields, say, agriculture and
biology, or applied science and technology, to others restricted to quite narrow fields, say, cancer research. Many
of the most important specialized indexes are listed in
L5. (For advice on how to discover whether a specialized
index exists for your subject see the introduction to **L5.**)
Not all indexes to periodicals have the word *index* in their
title. Reference guides with *abstracts* or *excerpta* in the title
also usually serve as indexes and provide, in addition, a brief
summary (similar to but shorter than a précis, see **NT2**)
of each article listed.

In using periodical indexes you must familiarize yourself
with the standardized system of volume and page reference

employed by nearly all magazines. All the issues of a magazine for one year (in some cases, six months) constitute a *volume* of that magazine, and at the close of the year those numbers are bound together. All the issues of the first year of any magazine will constitute *Volume 1*, those for the second year, *Volume 2*, and so on. Most magazines begin their page numbers with the first issue of the volume and number continuously until the end of that volume has been reached. Accordingly, references to magazines in some of these indexes and in many other bibliographical sources will be to the volume and page; the year and month may not be mentioned at all. References to weekly magazines will more often give the particular date of issue, since many of them do not number their pages continuously from the beginning of the volume. However, most indexes give the dates; and in requesting magazines, whether unbound or in bound volumes, it is usually sufficient to give the date of the issue wanted, disregarding the volume number.

b. Newspaper Indexes

It is often difficult to find newspaper material on many topics. Fortunately, yearly indexes are issued by two of the finest newspapers in the English language. The (London) *Times* publishes an *Official Index to the Times*, and *The New York Times Index* serves the newspaper of that name. In recent years the *Christian Science Monitor* and the *Wall Street Journal* have also issued indexes. These indexes are, in a way, indexes to *all* newspapers in that they give the approximate date that any newspaper is likely to deal with any event of national or international interest.

c. Essay and Government Document Indexes

For essays published in books, the chief index is

Essay and General Literature Index, 1900–33. Supplements, 1934–   . This does for essays in books what periodical indexes do for essays in periodicals.

The main general indexes to government publications are

Monthly Catalog of United States Government Publications (U. S. Superintendent of Documents), 1895–   . The monthly catalogues are collected into yearly volumes with an index.

Monthly Checklist of State Publications (U. S. Library of Congress), 1910–

The Clearinghouse for Federal Scientific and Technical Information issues indexes of federal research reports and technical translations (look under *Science and Technology* in **L5**). Several books of advice on using government publications exist. One of the best is Schmeckebier, Laurence F., and Eastin, R. B., *Government Publications and Their Use,* rev. ed., 1961.

4. GENERAL REFERENCE WORKS

In beginning your investigation of some topic you will find it convenient to consult an encyclopedia or general reference work for general information on your subject. From such general works you will also extract the titles of books and articles which deal with your subject at greater length.

a. Encyclopedias

Chambers's Encyclopaedia, 15 vols., 1964. Articles are generally brief, though written by outstanding scholars, the majority of whom are English.

Collier's Encyclopedia, 24 vols., 1965. The general level is somewhat more elementary than that of the other encyclopedias listed in this section. The articles are written by competent specialists, however.

Encyclopedia Americana, rev. ed., 30 vols., 1949. Now reissued annually. Try to use the latest issue if possible. The publishers also issue an annual supplement, the *Americana Annual*.

Encyclopædia Britannica, 14th ed., 24 vols., 1929. The fourteenth was the last numbered edition; it is now reissued annually. There is an annual supplement, *Britannica Book of the Year*. Despite the name, the *Britannica* is now owned, edited, and published in the United States. Many authorities consider the eleventh edition of this encyclopedia (29 vols., 1910) superior to anything that has appeared since. This edition is still useful in connection with topics not demanding information that is recent or highly technical.

b. Yearbooks

These give statistical facts chiefly about trade, population, and governmental affairs.

American Year Book, 1910–19, 1925–
Economic Almanac, 1940–
Europa, 1930–   . A survey of economic and social conditions and a directory of European political, industrial, financial, cultural, and scientific organizations.
Information Please Almanac, 1947–
Statesman's Year-Book, 1864–
Statistical Abstract of the United States (U. S. Bureau of the Census), 1878–   .
World Almanac, 1868–

See, in addition, the annual encyclopedia supplements listed in the preceding section.

c. Special Dictionaries

(See also **D1.**)

Allen, F. S. *Allen's Synonyms and Antonyms*, 1921; rev. ed. by T. H. V. Motter, 1938.
Bartlett, John. *Familiar Quotations*, 13th ed., 1955.
Brewer, E. C. *Dictionary of Phrase and Fable*, 1923.

———— *Reader's Handbook* of famous names in fiction, allusions, references, proverbs, plots, stories, and poems. New ed., 1923.

Bryant, Margaret M. *Current American Usage*, 1962.

Craigie, Sir William, and Hulbert, James R. *Dictionary of American English on Historical Principles*, 4 vols., 1936–44.

Evans, Bergen and Cornelia. *A Dictionary of Contemporary American Usage*, 1957.

Fernald, J. C. *English Synonyms and Antonyms*, 1931; rev. ed., 1947.

Follett, Wilson. *Modern American Usage*, 1966.

Fowler, H. W. *A Dictionary of Modern English Usage*, 1926; 2nd ed., revised by Sir Ernest Gowers, 1965.

Harbottle, T. B. *Dictionary of Quotations* (classical), 1906.

Henderson, I. F. and W. D. *A Dictionary of Scientific Terms*, 6th ed. rev. by J. H. Kenneth, 1957.

Kenyon, John S., and Knott, Thomas A. *A Pronouncing Dictionary of American English*, 2nd ed., 1953.

Mathews, Mitford M. *A Dictionary of Americanisms*, 2 vols., 1951. Reissued in 1956 in one volume.

Mencken, H. L. *A New Dictionary of Quotations on Historical Principles*, 1942.

Nicholson, Margaret. *A Dictionary of American-English Usage*, 1957. An adaptation of Fowler's work listed above.

The Oxford Dictionary of Quotations, 2nd ed., 1953.

Roget, P. M. *The Original Roget's Thesaurus of English Words and Phrases*, 1966. The *Roget Dictionary of Synonyms and Antonyms*, 1931, arranged alphabetically instead of topically, is somewhat more convenient to use.

Smith, W. G. *Oxford Dictionary of English Proverbs*, 2nd ed., 1948.

Stevenson, Burton. *The Home Book of Quotations*, 9th ed., 1958.

Webster's Dictionary of Synonyms, 1942.

Webster's Geographical Dictionary, rev. ed., 1964.

Weekley, Ernest. *A Concise Etymological Dictionary of Modern English*, 1921; rev. ed., 1952.

Wentworth, Harold, and Flexner, Stuart B. *Dictionary of American Slang*, 1960.

5. REFERENCE GUIDES TO SPECIAL SUBJECTS

No brief discussion of the use of the library can do more than scratch the surface. You can discover many more reference sources (including, perhaps, the most valuable one for your topic) by consulting one or more of the many guides to reference books which exist. The most comprehensive modern guides in English are

Winchell, Constance M. *Guide to Reference Books*, 7th ed., 1951. With 4 supplements bringing it up to 1963. An eighth edition is in preparation. Earlier editions were compiled by I. G. Mudge. This has been the bible of two generations of American researchers.

Walford, A. J., ed. *Guide to Reference Material*, 1959. Supplement, 1963. This is the British counterpart to Winchell. It is somewhat less comprehensive generally, but is stronger on British reference books and some kinds of bibliographies.

Murphey, Robert W. *How and Where to Look It Up*, 1958. This is intended for less experienced researchers. It is especially useful for nonacademic subjects.

Many brief guides exist (look in the card catalog under *reference books*, subheading *bibliographies*). One popular and inexpensive one may be mentioned:

Barton, Mary Neill, and Bell, Marion V. *Reference Books: A Brief Guide for Students and Other Users of the Library*, 6th ed., 1966. New editions of this work are usually issued every three or four years.

You can reduce the amount of time you spend compiling your preliminary bibliography if you can find a standard bibliography for your subject. Many such bibliographies exist. Most will have to be brought up to date and otherwise supplemented, but this is easier than starting from scratch. Two useful sources to consult in looking for a bibliography are

Besterman, Theodore. *A World Bibliography of Bibliographies*, 4th ed., 5 vols., 1965–66.
Bibliographic Index, 1937–

Also consult the card catalogue (look under the heading for your subject, then the subheading *bibliographies*). Perhaps the greatest time-saver, short of an up-to-date, authoritative bibliography on precisely your subject, is the guide to research for a specific field. Such guides are prepared for most academic subjects for the use of graduate students, teachers, and reference librarians. Several appear in the reference lists that follow. These guides are a species of bibliography and may be located in the same way as other bibliographies. Many are listed in Robert L. Collison's *Bibliographies: Subject and National*, 2nd ed., 1962, as well as Winchell, Walford, and Besterman. Watch for guides to research while checking the card catalogue under your subject. You also might ask an instructor in the subject you are interested in to recommend one.

Finally, remember that the range of reference sources available is changing daily. The growing concern of governments, libraries, industry, and professional organizations of all kinds for bringing about efficient access to a body of knowledge that is growing at a steadily increasing rate, and the recent technological improvements (computers, photoduplication processes) in means of storing and recording knowledge are rapidly bringing about a revolution in indexing. By the time you read this, therefore, important new reference sources may well have come into existence, or important improvements made in old ones. Your safest policy is to assume that the lists in this chapter need to be supplemented.

Agriculture

Bibliography of Agriculture (U. S. Department of Agriculture), 1941–

Biological and Agricultural Index, 1916–   Known as *Agricultural Index*, 1916–64.

Blanchard, J. Richard, and Ostvold, Harold. *The Literature of Agricultural Research*, 1958.

Experiment Station Record (U. S. Department of Agriculture), 1889–1946.

World Agricultural Economics and Rural Sociology Abstracts, 1959–

Yearbook of Agriculture (U. S. Department of Agriculture), 1894–

Art and Architecture

A.L.A. Portrait Index, Library of Congress, 1906. This is an index to portraits contained in printed books and periodicals.

American Art Directory, 1898–   . Formerly *American Art Annual*.

Ars Una, 1909–28. A series of one-volume histories of art, each volume being devoted to the art of a single country.

Art Index, 1929–

Chamberlin, Mary W. *Guide to Art Reference Books*, 1959.

Encyclopedia of World Art, 10 vols., 1959–   . Vols. 11–15 in preparation.

Harper's Encyclopedia of Art, 2 vols., 1937.

Koyl, G. S. *American Architects Directory*, 2nd ed., 1962.

Sturgis, R. *Dictionary of Architecture and Building*, 3 vols., 1901–02.

Who's Who in American Art. 1936/7–   . Published biennially before 1953, triennially after 1953.

Who's Who in Art, 13th ed., 1965. Published biennially.

Biography

Appleton's Cyclopaedia of American Biography, 6 vols. and 6 supplementary, 1887–1900; 1918–31.

Barnhart, C. L. *New Century Cyclopedia of Names*, rev. ed., 3 vols., 1954.

Biography Index, 1946–

Current Biography, 1940–   . With index cumulative to ten years.

Dictionary of American Biography, 20 vols. and index, 1928–37. Supplement One, to Dec. 31, 1935, pub. 1944; Supplement Two, to December 31, 1940, pub. 1958. A one-volume *Concise Dictionary of American Biography* was published in 1964.

Dictionary of Canadian Biography, 2nd ed., 2 vols., 1945.

Dictionary of National Biography, 22 vols., 1885–1949. Supplement, *The Twentieth Century Dictionary of National Biography*, 5 vols. Biographical data about Englishmen who are no longer living. There is also a *Concise Dictionary of National Biography*, which is a two-volume epitome of the larger work.

International Who's Who, 1935–   . Short biographies of persons prominent in Europe, North and South America, Asia, Australia, Africa.

National Cyclopedia of American Biography, 48 vols., 1893–1964; nine supplementary volumes are devoted to the biographies of living persons.

Thorne, J. O. *Chambers' Biographical Dictionary*, rev. ed., 1962.

Webster's Biographical Dictionary, rev. ed., 1964.

Who's Who, 1849–   . Biographical accounts of living British subjects. From time to time deleted entries are gathered together in *Who Was Who*, with dates of death appended.

Who's Who in America, 1899–   . Biennial. A biographical account of living Americans. Three volumes of *Who Was Who in America* have been published covering the period 1897–1960.

Who's Who of American Women, 4th ed., 1966–67.

Similar biographical dictionaries, encyclopedias and yearbooks exist for countries other than England and America.

Classical Literature and Antiquities

Cary, M. *Oxford Classical Dictionary*, 1949.

Hamilton, Edith. *Mythology*, 1942.

Harvey, Sir Paul. *Oxford Companion to Classical Literature*, 2nd ed., 1937.

Peck, H. T., ed. *Harper's Dictionary of Classical Literature and Antiquities*, 3rd ed., 1923.

Smith, W., Wayte, W., and Marindin, G. E. *A Dictionary of Greek and Roman Antiquities*, 3rd ed., 3 vols., 1890–91.

Walters, H. B. *A Classical Dictionary of Greek and Roman Antiquities*, 1916.

Commerce, Economics, Business, Finance

Business Periodicals Index, 1913–   . Part of *Industrial Arts Index*, 1913–57.

Coman, E. T., Jr. *Sources of Business Information*, rev. ed., 1964.

Economic Abstracts, 1951–

Foreign Commerce and Navigation of the United States (U. S. Bureau of the Census), 1821–

Index to Economic Journals, 6 vols., 1961–   . The six volumes issued so far cover the period 1886–1963 for the journals indexed.

Munn, G. G. *Encyclopedia of Banking and Finance*, 6th ed., 1962.

Rand McNally Commercial Atlas and Marketing Guide, 96th ed., 1965. Index, Supplements.

Education

Alexander, C., and Burke, A. J. *How to Locate Educational Information and Data*, 4th ed., 1958.

American Business Education Yearbook, 1944–

Biennial Survey of Education (U. S. Office of Education), 1919–

Cartter, A. M. *American Universities and Colleges*, 9th ed., 1964.

Education Abstracts, 1949–
Education Index, 1929–
Harris, C. W. *Encyclopedia of Educational Research,* 3rd ed., 1960.
Monroe, P., ed. *Cyclopedia of Education,* 5 vols., 1911–13. Reissued in 3 vols., 1925.
Statistics of Education in the United States (U. S. Office of Education), 1958/59–date.
World Survey of Education: Handbook of Educational Organization and Statistics, 1951–   . Triennial.

Engineering and Industrial Arts

Applied Science and Technology Index, 1913–   . Part of *Industrial Arts Index,* 1913–57.
Dalton, Blanche H. *Sources of Engineering Information,* 1949.
Engineering Index, 1884–
Tweney, C. F., and Shirshov, I. P. *Hutchinson's Technical and Scientific Encyclopaedia,* 4 vols., 1935.

History

Adams, J. T., ed. *Dictionary of American History,* 7 vols., 1941; reprinted, 1963. Adams has also compiled several other valuable reference works in American history.
Beers, H. P. *Bibliographies in American History,* 2nd ed., 1942.
Cambridge Ancient History, 12 vols. and 5 vols. of plates, 1923–39.
Cambridge Medieval History, 8 vols., 1911–36.
Cambridge Modern History, 13 vols. and atlas, 1902–26.
New Cambridge Modern History, 9 vols., 1957–
Historical Abstracts, 1955–
Howe, G. F., and others. *Guide to Historical Literature,* 1961.
International Bibliography of Historical Sciences, 1926–
Langer, W. L., ed. *Encyclopedia of World History,* rev. ed., 1952.
Schlesinger, A. M., and Fox, D. R. *A History of American Life,* 13 vols., 1927–48.
Writings on American History, 1902–   . An annual bibli-

ography of books and articles on United States history; by the American Historical Association.

Law

Ballentine, James A. *The College Law Dictionary*, 1948.
Corpus Juris, 1914–   . Annotations from decisions in important cases.
Corpus Juris Secundum, 1937–   . A complete restatement of the entire American law as developed by all reported cases.
Index to Legal Periodicals, 1908–
Roalfe, William R., ed. *How to Find the Law*, 5th ed., 1957.

Literature and the Stage

Annual Bibliography, *PMLA*, April 1919–   . This bibliography is issued annually as a supplement to the journal *PMLA*. It is the essential current bibliography for English and American language and literature.
Baker, E. A. *Guide to Historical Fiction*, 1914.
Baker, E. A., and Packman, J. *Guide to the Best Fiction*, 3rd ed., 1932. Although this is primarily an index of English and American fiction, translations from foreign languages are included.
Bateson, F. W. *Cambridge Bibliography of English Literature*, 4 vols.; George Watson, Supplement, 1957.
Baugh, Albert C., and others. *Literary History of England*, 4 vols., 1948.
Benét, William Rose. *The Reader's Encyclopedia*, 2nd ed., 1965.
Bernhardt, W. F. *Granger's Index to Poetry*, 5th ed., 1962.
Bond, Donald F. *A Reference Guide to English Studies*, 1962.
Book Review Digest, 1905–
Cambridge History of American Literature, 4 vols., 1917–21; reprinted, 1933.
Cambridge History of English Literature, 15 vols., 1907–27; reissued, 1932. Index, 1933, Bibliography.
Clark, B. H. *Study of the Modern Drama*, 1934.
Contemporary Authors, 1962–   . Semi-annual. Lives of less famous authors.

Cumulated Dramatic Index, 1909–49; 2 vols., reprinted 1962. Index to periodical material with appendices covering books on the drama and play texts.

Dobrée, Bonamy, ed. *Introductions to English Literature,* rev. ed., 5 vols., 1950–58.

Firkins, I. *Index of Plays, 1800–1926,* 1927. Supplement: *1927–34,* 1935.

Firkins, I. *Index to Short Stories,* 1923. Supplement, 1929.

Hart, James D. *Oxford Companion to American Literature,* 4th ed., 1965.

Hartnoll, Phyllis. *Oxford Companion to the Theatre,* 2nd ed., 1957.

Harvey, Sir Paul. *Oxford Companion to English Literature,* 3rd ed., 1946.

Kunitz, S. J., and Haycroft, H. *American Authors, 1600–1900,* 1938.

Kunitz, S. J., and Haycroft, H. *British Authors of the Nineteenth Century,* 1936.

Kunitz, S. J., and Haycroft, H. *Twentieth Century Authors,* 1942. First Supplement, 1955.

Logasa, H. *Historical Fiction Guide,* 8th ed., 1964.

Logasa, H., and Ver Nooy, W. *Index to One-Act Plays,* 1900–24. Fourth Supplement, 1958.

Preminger, Alex, and others. *Encyclopedia of Poetry and Poetics,* 1965.

Sharp, R. F. *Short Biographical Dictionary of Foreign Literature,* 1933.

Shipley, Joseph T. *Dictionary of World Literature,* 1943.

Spiller, Robert E., and others. *Literary History of the United States,* 3 vols., 1948; reissued, 1962–63.

Who's Who Among Living Authors of Older Nations, 1931–

Wilson, Frank P., and Dobrée, Bonamy. *Oxford History of English Literature,* 1945–

Medicine

Excerpta Medica, 1947–   . This very comprehensive abstracting index for medicine and related fields is divided into

24 parts. Sections 1–15 were begun in all cases either in 1947 or 1948. Sections 16–24 were added between 1953 and 1966.

Index Medicus, 1960–   . This is the successor of a series of indexes which, under varying titles, go back to 1879.

Kelly, Emerson Crosby. *Encyclopaedia of Medical Sources*, 1948.

Music

Cobbett's Cyclopedic Survey of Chamber Music, 2 vols., 1929–30.

Darrell, R. D., *Schirmer's Guide to Books on Music and Musicians*, 1951.

Feather, Leonard. *Encyclopedia of Jazz*, rev. ed., 1960.

Grove's Dictionary of Music and Musicians, 5th ed., 9 vols., 1954. Supplement, 1961.

Leigh, R. *Index to Song Books*, 1964.

Music Index, 1949–

Scholes, P. A. *Oxford Companion to Music*, 9th ed., 1955.

Sears, M. E. *Song Index*, 1926. Supplement, 1934.

Thompson, O. *International Cyclopedia of Music and Musicians*, 9th ed. by R. Sabin, 1964.

Thompson, O. *Oxford History of Music*, 7 vols., 1931–38.

Mythology and Folklore

Chambers, Robert. *Book of Days*, 2 vols., 1914.

Diehl, Katherine S. *Religions, Mythologies, Folklores: An Annotated Bibliography*, 2nd ed., 1962.

Edwardes, M., and Spence, L. *Dictionary of Non-Classical Mythology*, 1923.

Fraser, Sir James G. *The Golden Bough*, 12 vols., 1907–15. Supplement, 1936. A new edition, abridged and updated by Theodor Gaster, was published in one volume in 1959.

Gray, L. H., and others. *Mythology of All Races*, 12 vols. and index, 1916–32.

Grimal, P. *Larousse World Mythology*, 1965.

Hazlitt, William C. *Faiths and Folk Lore of the British Isles*, 2 vols., 1905; reissued, 1965.

Leach, Maria, ed. *Funk & Wagnalls Standard Dictionary of Folklore, Mythology and Legend*, 2 vols., 1949–50.

Philosophy and Psychology

Baldwin, James M. *Dictionary of Philosophy and Psychology*, 3 vols., 1901–05; 2nd ed., 1910; corrected ed., 1928; reissued, 1960. The third volume also appears under the title: Rand, B. *Bibliography of Philosophy, Psychology and Cognate Subjects*, 1905.

Bibliography of Philosophy, 1934–   . A yearly bibliography of scholarly philosophical literature.

Psychological Abstracts, 1927–   . American Psychological Association. *Psychological Index*, 1894–1935, was merged into this in 1936.

Warren, Howard C. *Dictionary of Psychology*, 1934.

Political and Social Sciences

Bulletin of the Public Affairs Information Service, 1915–
Congressional Quarterly Almanac, 1945–
Hoselitz, Bert F. *A Reader's Guide to the Social Sciences*, 1959.
International Bibliography of the Social Sciences (UNESCO International Committee for Social Science Documentation), 1951–   . Four sections: Economics, 1952–   ; Political Science, 1952–   ; Social and Cultural Anthropology, 1955–   ; and Sociology, 1951–   .
Political Handbook and Atlas of the World, 1927–
Population Index, 1935–
Seligman, E. R. A., and Johnson, A. *Encyclopaedia of the Social Sciences*, 15 vols., 1930–35; reissued in 8 vols., 1937.
Smith, E. C., and Zurcher, A. J. *New Dictionary of American Politics*, 1949.
Sociological Abstracts, 1952–
United Nations Documents Index (United Nations Library), 1950–
United Nations Yearbook, 1946–
White, C. M. *Sources of Information in the Social Sciences*, 1964.

Religion

Attwater, D. *Catholic Dictionary*, 3rd ed., 1958.

Case, S. J., McNeill, J. T., and others. *A Bibliographical Guide to the History of Christianity*, 1931.

Catholic Encyclopedia, 15 vols. and 2 supplementary, 1907–22. Revised and enlarged edition, 16 vols. and 2 supplementary, 1950–59.

Catholic Periodical Index, 1930–

Encyclopedia of Religion and Ethics, 12 vols. and index, 1908–27; reissued in 7 vols., 1931.

Ferm, Vergilius. *Encyclopedia of Religion*, 1959.

Index to Religious Periodical Literature, 1949–

Jewish Encyclopedia, 12 vols., 1901–06; new rev. ed., 1964.

Schaff, P. *New Schaff-Herzog Encyclopedia of Religious Knowledge*, 13 vols. and index. 1908–12; reprinted, 1950. Supplemented by *Twentieth Century Encyclopedia of Religious Knowledge*, 2 vols., 1955.

Universal Jewish Encyclopedia, 10 vols., 1939–43; index, 1944.

Yearbook of American Churches, 1916–

Science and Technology

Asimov, Isaac. *Asimov's Biographical Encyclopedia of Science and Technology*, 1964.

Bibliography and Index of Geology, Exclusive of North America, 1934–

Bibliography of North American Geology, 1919–

Biological Abstracts, 1927–   . In part a continuation of *Botanical Abstracts*, 1918–26; and *Abstracts of Bacteriology*, 1917–26.

Chemical Abstracts, 1907–

Crane, E. J., and Patterson, A. M. *Guide to the Literature of Chemistry*, 2d ed., 1957.

Fry, B. M., *A Guide to Information Sources in Space Science and Technology*, 1963.

GeoScience Abstracts, 1959–   . Replaces *Geological Abstracts*, 1953–58.

Index to Federal Research and Development Reports (Clear-

inghouse for Federal Scientific and Technical Information),
1965–   . For the period 1946–64 consult *Nuclear Science
Abstracts, U. S. Government Research and Development Reports, Technical Abstract Bulletin* and *Scientific and Technical
Aerospace Reports*, for which this is a combined index.

International Abstracts of Biological Sciences, 1954–

International Aerospace Abstracts, 1961–

McGraw-Hill *Encyclopedia of Science and Technology*, rev.
ed., 15 vols., 1966.

Meteorological and Geostrophysical Abstracts, 1950–

Michels, W. C. *International Dictionary of Physics and Electronics*, 2nd ed., 1961.

Newman, J. R. *Harper Encyclopedia of Science*, 4 vols., 1963.

Parke, Nathan Grier. *Guide to the Literature of Mathematics
and Physics, Including Related Works on Engineering Science*,
rev. ed., 1958.

Science Abstracts, 1898–   . Two sections: *Physics Abstracts*
and *Electrical Engineering Abstracts*.

Singer, Charles, and others. *A History of Technology*, 5 vols.,
1961–64.

Technical Translations (Clearinghouse for Federal Scientific and
Technical Information), 1959–

Thewlis, J. *Encyclopaedic Dictionary of Physics*, 9 vols., 1961–
64.

Thorpe, J. F. *Thorpe's Dictionary of Applied Chemistry*,
4th ed., 12 vols., 1937–56.

Zoological Record, 1864–

Note: No duplication has been permitted between the
lists in this chapter. When a source is relevant to more than
one subject, or fits into more than one category, it is assigned
to the one where it seems most likely to be useful.

6. COLLECTING SOURCE MATERIAL

a. Bibliography

Once you know your way about the library and have
chosen the topic for your paper, you are ready to collect

source materials. Where you go first will depend on your subject. Is it on something recent or contemporary? Then newspapers and magazines may have to satisfy you—there may be no book on it. Is it historical? Then you may have to rely on books alone.

In either case, the first thing to do is to make a list of sources in which you are likely to find something of the kind you want. Look up your subject in the card catalogue and the periodical indexes. List any source which seems relevant, but do not collect sources indiscriminately. The library card, read carefully, will often guide you. The date will tell how recent a book is; the number of pages and subject references will suggest its scope; and in other ways you can decide without seeing them that some books are not worth listing or looking at for your present need. The best way to keep a record of the sources you find—in fact, the only good way—is to get cards or slips of paper similar to the library cards, and to put each separate title on one slip. *Do not merely make a list in a notebook.* Using cards or slips may appear slow when you begin, but it pays for itself in the end. As you collect more and more material, you will want to sort it and arrange it in various ways, a procedure easily managed with cards, but intolerably clumsy with a notebook list. Bookstores supply cards in various sizes. On each card you should record all the information you will need to make out call slips later (or to find what you want in the open shelves or the stacks). Pick up copies of call slips for books and periodicals to see what you will need. When you complete this collection of cards, it will form your preliminary bibliography of sources to be examined.

After completing your preliminary bibliography, your next step will be to examine each source listed. Some you will glance at and discard. At the same time you will discard the corresponding bibliography cards. Others you will decide to take notes on. For every source you decide to take any notes on, expand and correct the bibliography card (or make out a new one). Be sure that this final bibliography card is accurate and contains all the information you will ultimately need. (See Chapter XIII, **MS7-8**.) This is the way your final bibliography cards should look.

(a) A BOOK

> 973.9
> S
>
>   Schlesinger, Arthur M., Jr. <u>A</u>
>   <u>Thousand Days: John F. Kennedy</u>
>   <u>in the White House</u>. Boston:
>   Houghton Mifflin Company, 1965.

(b) AN EDITED BOOK

> B
> Brown
>   Stillinger, Jack, ed. <u>The Letters of</u>
>   <u>Charles Armitage Brown</u>.
>   Cambridge, Mass.: Harvard
>   University Press, 1966.

(c) A MAGAZINE ARTICLE

> Bowen, Catherine Drinker. "Journey
> Through the American States."
> <u>Atlantic</u>, CCXVIII (November, 1966),
> 94-103.

(d) A NEWSPAPER ARTICLE

> "Treasury Facing Dilemma on Debt."
> <u>New York Times</u>, November 13,
> 1966, Sec. 3, pp. 1, 9.

b. Reading Notes

In addition to your bibliography cards, keep another set of cards or slips on which to take notes as you read. Be sure to make your notes legible and accurate, and do not forget page references. A quotation without a page reference is almost impossible to find again. Punctuate to show quotation, omissions, your own words, etc.

Turn back for a moment to the author card on page 372.

Suppose you decided to take notes on this book for your paper. You would first make a final bibliography card very much like the author card, using the essential bibliographical information it gives.

Now for each of the notes you take from this book you would make a card like this:

Freeman   *Lee's Lieutenants*

"Beauregard's devotion to the Napoleonic
strategy would not permit abandonment
of all hope of a general offensive. At the
moment, it was possible to undertake on
his extreme right a diversion to confuse
the enemy's attack on his center and
left."   *Vol. I, p. 53*

[Use in Section III : Beauregard's importance as a strategist.]

Note that "Freeman" and the title are all you need to connect this with the bibliography card, which has the information about the book itself. At the bottom, you indicate with a bracketed phrase the subject of your note. If this phrase corresponds to one division of your outline, the sorting of your collected notes will be greatly facilitated. The material on this card is quoted exactly. The volume and page reference follows.

Though the sample note is a quotation, you should not suppose that most of your notes should be quoted. In fact, most will take the form of précis (see Chapter XI, **NT2c**). If you retain any of the characteristic phrasing of the author in your précis, be sure to mark it with quotation marks. Remember, if you quote anything, that the instructions for marking quotations and changes in quotations in Chapter XIII, **MS2, MS4,** apply equally to the notecards, for your theme can be no more accurate than your notecards in this respect. Failure to distinguish between précis (or paraphrase) and quotation on the notecard may cause you to unintentionally commit plagiarism (see the introduction to Part Three) in the long theme, for to represent an author's words as your own (even if you admit that the ideas are his) is to commit plagiarism.

As you collect your materials, remember that *it is easier to discard extra notes than to go back to the source and find a statement which you could now use, but of which you made no record.* Do not depend on memory; write your notes.

7. *USE OF SOURCE MATERIALS*

Your task is not finished when you have amassed a great body of material from books, magazines, and newspapers. You are assigned a long paper to make you do some thinking on your own account. Since you cannot think in a vacuum, the information that you have gathered is the material for your thoughts. This information should appear in your paper, but the paper must be concerned primarily with your ideas and conclusions about this information.

In short, your paper must have a purpose: the discussion and presentation of your own conclusions about a particular problem which you have succeeded in isolating in the course of your reading. You must have a point to prove, an attitude to maintain, a conclusion to present. This point of view must be supported in terms of actual fact. A possible opposite point of view or a possible set of conclusions differing from yours will have to be refuted in terms of actual fact. In other words, your next task is to sift your material, digest it, and put it in order.

XI. Planning and
Note-Taking

1. FIRST STEPS

If a specific subject for your paper has not been assigned, follow the suggestions for choosing a topic which have been given in Chapter I, **T1**, making whatever adaptations may be necessary. The short paper usually covers a single idea or narrow range; the subject for a long paper must be capable of fuller development.

It is still necessary, however, to avoid too broad a subject. If "Adult Education" or "Modern Architecture" may serve as topics for full-length books, they are too extensive for a two- or a five-thousand word paper. You had better select a limited aspect of the topic. In connection with the second of these, for example, you might treat modernism in certain kinds of buildings (churches, schools, private homes), or you could concern yourself with the use of specific materials—glass, or the newer processed woods. Another possibility would be to treat important individuals, such as Frank Lloyd Wright, or groups of architects, such as the Bauhaus school.

Remember also that it is just as desirable to write a long paper on some topic of which you already know a little as it is to base a short theme upon personal knowledge and experience.

a. The Plan

There is no one best way to write a long paper. Obviously, if you could have a ready-made outline and then search out the specific information necessary to develop the paper from it, that would be a great simplification. But how can you make the outline before you have studied the subject and discovered its possibilities? You will need to do more reading and note-taking, in other words, than will appear in the final paper, just because you cannot tell exactly, as you read, what the final limitations of the paper will profitably be. Your reading must be done, in part, to give you a perspective on the subject; after this you can make a final outline from which the paper will actually be written. At the same time, your collection of materials should not be haphazard. As you read and take notes the latent pattern of the subject will gradually emerge. You will become aware of what points are the important ones and why. Keep a record of these; it will save much labor when you come to making the outline.

b. Finding Materials

In the preceding chapter are bibliographies or lists of books sufficient to give you a start in your search for information upon almost any topic you choose. Remember that any bibliography which pretends to cover a dozen or more fields of knowledge in as many pages must be very sketchy indeed. It will serve only as a beginning. In the bibliographical section devoted to the special fields (see **L5**), there is usually one reference to a bibliography or an encyclopedia for every field. An encyclopedia of music will be useful not only for the information which it may give about any one topic—let us say the development of folk music—but it will mention special articles and studies entirely devoted to such a topic. Follow up these references, and do not neglect the newspaper and magazine bibliographies (see **L3** and **L5**). Do not stop collecting information until you find yourself going round in a circle—until the material you come upon merely repeats the information which you already have.

2. *NOTE-TAKING*

It is not usually possible to keep on one's desk all the books and other sources that may be needed in writing a long paper. Nor is this necessarily the most desirable procedure. It is usually more practical and efficient to take what you are likely to need once and for all from each source and to keep your notes in some handy and consistent form (see **L6b**).

Furthermore, the exact words in which your sources are written are usually less important than what they say. To quote them at length word for word would be wasteful, and may indicate that you have not digested them adequately. Quote only those things which are said in a particularly effective way; condense the rest as you read. The most useful devices for restating and condensing are the paraphrase, the synopsis, and the précis.

a. The Paraphrase

Frequently you will find material which is expressed in difficult or technical language. The sentences are involved; the words are abstruse. One of the best ways to understand such passages is to rewrite them in your own words, that is, to *restate* or *paraphrase* them. Examine carefully the two portions of essays which follow and the paraphrases which accompany them:

ORIGINAL I:

The historical and psychological researches of the past century have rendered the theory which lies behind the practice of modern democracy entirely untenable. Reason is not the same in all men; human beings belong to a variety of psychological types separated from one another by irreducible differences. Men are not the exclusive products of their environments. A century of growing democracy has shown that the reform of institutions and the spread of education are by no means necessarily followed by improvements in individual virtue and intelligence. At the same time biologists have accumulated an enormous mass of evidence tending to show that physical peculiarities are inherited in a perfectly regular and necessary fashion. Body being indissolubly connected with mind, this evidence would almost be enough in itself to prove that mental peculiarities are similarly heritable. Direct observation on the history of families reinforces this evidence, and makes it certain that mental idiosyncrasies are inherited in exactly the same way as physical idiosyncrasies. Indeed, mind being in some sort a function of brain, a mental idiosyncrasy is also a physical one, just as much as red hair or blue eyes. Faculties are heritable: we are born more or less intelligent, more or less musical, mathematical, and so on. From this it follows that men are not essentially equal, and that human beings are at least as much the product of their heredity as their education.

ALDOUS HUXLEY, "The Idea of Equality,"
from *Proper Studies*[1]

PARAPHRASE I:

The investigations of historians and psychologists during the past century have made it impossible to accept the theory behind the practice of modern democracy. Men are not equally intelligent; they belong to a variety of types which differ from one another by very small yet actual degrees. Nor are men wholly the product of their surroundings. From the democracies which have grown up during the past century, one may observe that the reform of institutions and the spread of education have not made particular men better or wiser. Also, biologists have collected much evidence which seems to show that physical peculiarities are inherited according to certain definite and inescapable laws. Since body and mind are so very closely connected, one might conclude that peculiarities of the mind are passed on in the same fashion. This conclusion is strengthened by observing the history of certain families. Moreover, since mind is the working of the brain, which is a physical organ, a mental

[1] Reprinted by courtesy of Harper and Row.

peculiarity is just as physical as the color of the hair or eyes. Abilities are inherited—we are born musical, mathematical, and so on. Then it must follow that men are not essentially equal, and that they are at least as much the product of their heredity as of their education or environment.

ORIGINAL II:

Studies serve for delight, for ornament, and for ability. Their chief use for delight is in privateness and retiring; for ornament, is in discourse; and for ability, is in the judgment and disposition of business. For expert men can execute, and perhaps judge of particulars, one by one; but the general counsels, and the plots and marshalling of affairs, come best from those that are learned. To spend too much time in studies is sloth; to use them too much for ornament is affectation; to make judgment wholly by their rules is the humor of a scholar. They perfect nature, and are perfected by experience; for natural abilities are like natural plants, that need pruning by study; and studies themselves do give forth directions too much at large, except they be bounded in by experience.   BACON, *Of Studies*

PARAPHRASE II:

Studies have three uses. They please us when we are alone; they improve our conversation; and they show us how to conduct our affairs. A man with experience of the world but without learning will be able to dispose of particular details, but a learned man is the more able to make plans and to carry them out. To spend too much time on studies results in inaction. To show off your learning is affectation. Never to add the fruits of practical experience to the learning found in books is the tendency of the impractical scholar. Studies bring our natural abilities closer to perfection, and they in turn are aided by experience. That is, our natural abilities have to be cut back and trimmed just as a shrub has to be pruned. And since abstract ideas tend to run away with us, studies need to be restrained and bounded in by experience.

In writing a paraphrase:

1. Read the passage over a number of times before beginning to write your paraphrase. Find out the meaning of all words which you do not understand or which are not unmistakably clear from the context.

2. For every unfamiliar or difficult word, substitute a common word. What, in the first paraphrase, was used in place of each of the following in the original: *untenable, irreducible, idiosyncrasy, faculties?* In any of these instances was more than a single word used as a substitute?

3. Watch out for unusual or older uses of familiar words. What, in the second paraphrase, was used in place of *expert, plot, humor?*

4. Break up sentences which have a complicated or unusual construction. Compare the following sentences with its three-sentence paraphrase:

ORIGINAL III:

But let us suppose a new law to be perfectly equitable and necessary, yet, if the procurers of it have betrayed a conduct that confesses by-ends and private motives, the disgust to the circumstances disposes us, unreasonably indeed, to an irreverence of the law itself; but we are indulgently blind to the most visible imperfections of an old custom.

PARAPHRASE III:

A new law may be wholly just and necessary. If those who are responsible for it, however, have clearly acted in the light of their selfish interests, we are so disgusted that we quite illogically do not respect the law. On the other hand, even though an old custom may be unreasonable, we close our eyes and follow it tamely.

5. Make certain that your paraphrase reflects the essential plan of the original. Read the last sentence of the selection from Bacon. Compare it with the paraphrase. What words

in the paraphrase indicate its author's conception of the relationship of the various elements in Bacon's last sentence?

6. Caution: a paraphrase should leave out no idea that is in the original, nor should it add any idea which is not there. All it changes are the words and the sentence structure in which the ideas are expressed. Note also that no paraphrase should be inserted in your paper without some indication (e.g., "In Bacon's view") that it is a paraphrase and not your own statement.

EXERCISE I

A. Look up the derivation of *paraphrase* in your dictionary. What does the prefix *para-* mean? What would be the difference between a paraphrase and a translation?

B. Write paraphrases of the following selections, following the suggestions given above:

1. Whether equality can properly be included among the essentials of the western European political tradition is a question which cannot easily be answered. On the one hand it is one of the cherished objects of the progressive movement, and is now so deeply embedded in the popular consciousness as to make it hard to challenge with impunity. On the other, its realization is in practice almost entirely confined to the narrow sphere of equality before the law, a right which, since one of the primary purposes of law is to protect inequality, is understandably regarded by radicals as at the best purely formal and at the worst a piece of window dressing. The precise form which the idea of equality takes differs considerably even within the progressive movement, ranging from the demand for equality of opportunity as a means of eliciting inequalities of talent and character, to the ideal of absolute economic equality and complete absence of social distinctions which Communism postulates as the fore-ordained end of history, and which democratic Socialists, while rejecting it in practice, regard as an ideal which should be approached as closely as possible. For most people the real basis of the idea of

equality is the obvious community of human nature, a fact which impresses itself most vividly in the common fate of death.

From *The* [London] *Times Literary Supplement,*[1]
March 27, 1948

2. Yet hence arises a grave mischief. The sacredness which attaches to the act of creation, the act of thought, is transferred to the record. The poet chanting was felt to be a divine man: henceforth the chant is divine also. The writer was a just and wise spirit: henceforward it is settled the book is perfect; as love of the hero corrupts into worship of his statue. Instantly the book becomes noxious: the guide is a tyrant. The sluggish and perverted mind of the multitude, slow to open to the incursions of reason, having once so opened, having once received this book, stands upon it, and makes an outcry if it is disparaged. Colleges are built on it. Books are written on it by thinkers, not by Man Thinking; by men of talent, that is, who start wrong, who set out from accepted dogmas, not from their own sight of principles. Meek young men grow up in libraries, believing it their duty to accept the views which Cicero, which Locke, which Bacon, have given; forgetful that Cicero, Locke, and Bacon were only young men in libraries when they wrote these books.

Hence, instead of Man Thinking, we have the bookworm.

Hence the book-learned class, who value books, as such; not as related to nature and the human constitution, but as making a sort of Third Estate with the world and the soul. Hence the restorers of readings, the emendators, the bibliomaniacs of all degrees.

RALPH WALDO EMERSON, *The American Scholar*

3. The general story of mankind will evince, that lawful and settled authority is very seldom resisted when it is well employed. Gross corruption, or evident imbecility, is necessary to the suppression of that reverence with which the majority of mankind look upon their governors, and on those whom they see surrounded by splendor, and fortified by power. For though men are drawn by their passions into forgetfulness of invisible rewards

[1] The Times Publishing Company Limited. All Rights Reserved.©

and punishments, yet they are easily kept obedient to those who have temporal dominion in their hands, till their veneration is dissipated by such wickedness and folly as can neither be defended nor concealed.

It may, therefore, very reasonably be suspected that the old draw upon themselves the greatest part of those insults which they so much lament, and that age is rarely despised but when it is contemptible. If men imagine that excess of debauchery can be made reverend by time, that knowledge is the consequence of long life, however idly or thoughtlessly employed, that priority of birth will supply the want of steadiness or honesty, can it raise much wonder that their hopes are disappointed, and that they see their posterity rather willing to trust their own eyes in their progress into life, than enlist themselves under guides who have lost their way?

There are indeed, many truths which time necessarily and certainly teaches, and which might, by those who have learned them from experience, be communicated to their successors at a cheaper rate; but dictates, though liberally enough bestowed, are generally without effect, the teacher gains few proselytes by instruction which his own behavior contradicts; and young men miss the benefit of counsel, because they are not very ready to believe that those who fall below them in practice, can much excel them in theory. Thus the progress of knowledge is retarded, the world is kept long in the same state, and every new race is to gain the prudence of their predecessors by committing and redressing the same miscarriages.

SAMUEL JOHNSON, *The Rambler*

b. The Synopsis

The paraphrase results in no reduction in the size of the original. It is a satisfactory method of recording short statements, single paragraphs, and comments of a somewhat incidental nature.

If you have read a long article or a chapter in a textbook, it would scarcely be feasible to reproduce it either verbatim or in your own words. You will want to condense it. Often the answer to an examination question may require a summary of some reading or of a portion of a lecture. Likewise, in making your initial survey of the topic on which you plan to write your long paper, you will want some fairly brief notes which will serve to acquaint you with the general area. For these purposes, you must learn how to make short abridgements competently.

The most familiar and least difficult form of condensation is the *synopsis*, a brief or condensed statement. In present use the term is most often applied to a summary of material that is narrative rather than reflective, story rather than essay. We speak of the *synopsis* of a motion picture. A theatre program has a *synopsis*, in acts and scenes, of the whole play. Here is the synopsis of the first act of Shakespeare's *As You Like It*.

A duke of France, dispossessed of his lands by his younger brother Frederick, has retired with a few faithful followers to the nearby Forest of Arden. Rosalind, his daughter, remains at the court of her treacherous uncle as a companion to her cousin Celia, whom she loves. The two girls are spectators at a wrestling match in which Charles, the court wrestler, is defeated by an unknown but attractive newcomer. After learning that the victorious Orlando is the son of a former enemy, Duke Frederick gives him no encouragement to remain at court. Meanwhile Rosalind and Orlando have fallen in love. Orlando is so sorely smitten that he is unable to thank Rosalind for the chain she gives him. Because her virtues and accomplishments have made Rosalind so popular among the people, Frederick banishes her from the court. Celia, his daughter, loves her cousin so much that she follows her into exile.

In writing a synopsis:

1. Leave out everything that does not directly advance the plot of the story. In the foregoing account of the first act of *As You Like It*, neither LeBeau, the courtier, nor the

account that he gives of the three wrestling matches prior to that between Charles and Orlando are mentioned since they are of no importance for the rest of the story.

2. Do not omit any detail that is necessary to understand or account for later happenings in the story. Orlando's inability to speak to Rosalind when she gives him the chain is an important detail, since it accounts for his subsequent action in pinning love verses to the trees of the Forest of Arden, and leads Rosalind, disguised as a boy, to test his affection for her.

3. Jot down on a piece of paper those incidents which you think are important enough to be included in your condensation. Read the selection through a second time, making a second list of important incidents. Then compare these lists and decide on a final list of incidents. Using the revised list as an outline, write your synopsis.

EXERCISE II

1. Write a synopsis of a short story or of a chapter in a novel which you have recently read.

2. Write a synopsis of a motion picture or of a play which you have recently attended.

3. Write a synopsis of the account of some recent athletic contest which has been described at some length in your college paper. In such a case it will be helpful, of course, for you to have seen the contest; but base your synopsis on the account that has been written of the game, and not on what you saw.

4. Write a synopsis of the following narrative:

THE GREAT FIRE OF LONDON

2 SEPTEMBER, 1666 (Lord's day). Some of our maids sitting up late last night to get things ready against our feast to-day, Jane called us up about three in the morning, to tell us of a great fire

they saw in the City. So I rose and slipped on my night-gown, and went to her window, and thought it to be on the back-side of Mark Lane at the farthest; but, being unused to such fires as followed, I thought it far enough off; and so went to bed again and to sleep. About seven rose again to dress myself, and there looked out at the window, and saw the fire not so much as it was and further off. So to my closet to set things to rights after yesterday's cleaning. By and by Jane comes and tells me that she hears that above 300 houses have been burned down to-night by the fire we saw, and that it is now burning down all Fish Street, by London Bridge. So I made myself ready presently, and walked to the Tower, and there got up upon one of the high places, Sir J. Robinson's little son going up with me; and there I did see the houses at that end of the bridge all on fire, and an infinite great fire on this and the other side the end of the bridge; which, among other people, did trouble me for poor little Michell and our Sarah on the bridge. So down, with my heart full of trouble, to the Lieutenant of the Tower, who tells me that it begun this morning in the King's baker's house in Pudding Lane, and that it hath burned Mt. Magnus's Church and most part of Fish Street already. So I down to the water-side, and there got a boat and through bridge, and there saw a lamentable fire. Poor Michell's house, as far as the Old Swan, already burned that way, and the fire running further, that in a very little time it got as far as the Steelyard, while I was there. Everybody endeavoring to remove their goods, and flinging into the river or bringing them into lighters that lay off; poor people staying in their houses as long as till the very fire touched them, and then running into boats, or clambering from one pair of stairs by the water-side to another. And among other things, the poor pigeons, I perceive, were loath to leave their houses, but hovered about the windows and balconies till they some of them burned their wings, and fell down. Having stayed, and in an hour's time seen the fire rage every way, and nobody, to my sight, endeavoring to quench it, but to remove their goods, and leave all to the fire, and having seen it get as far the Steelyard, and the wind mighty high and driving it into the City; and everything, after so long a drought, proving combustible, even the very stones of churches, and among other things

the poor steeple by which pretty Mrs. —————— lives, and whereof
my old schoolfellow Elborough is parson, taken fire in the very
top, and there burned till it fell down: I to Whitehall (with a
gentleman with me who desired to go off from the Tower, to see
the fire, in my boat); to Whitehall, and there up to the King's
closet in the Chapel, where people come about me, and I did
give them an account dismayed them all, and word was carried in
to the King. So I was called for, and did tell the King and Duke
of York what I saw, and that unless His Majesty did command
houses to be pulled down nothing could stop the fire.

SAMUEL PEPYS, *Diary*

c. The Précis

By definition a précis is a concise or abridged statement
of any kind of material. In business, legal, and diplomatic
circles, the subject matter of which précis are required falls
into three broad classes: reports, correspondence, and minutes of evidence. To illustrate: The report of a commission
investigating a Federal project might consume several thousand pages. A member of the President's cabinet is to make
a speech, utilizing the essential facts of this report. Having
neither the time nor the opportunity to study the several
thousand pages of the document, he directs one of his
secretaries to prepare a précis for him. This précis must contain, greatly condensed, all the essential facts and conclusions of the original report. Précis of evidence are equally
useful to lawyers and judges, while précis of correspondence
are regularly prepared for members of the diplomatic service.

The précis writer must be careful to say in about thirty
words what the original says in one hundred; in addition,
in those thirty words he must give the very meanings and
attitudes expressed in the full version. The précis must be
just what its name implies: *precise*.

Your notes on a chapter of assigned textbook reading
are also a kind of précis. Notes made solely for use in pre-

paring a long paper should be in the form of a précis. Class lecture notes are again a type of condensation which must include the essentials of the lecture. How often have you looked at notes that were "cold" and have been unable to make anything out of them? That was, of course, because you had failed to catch the essentials but had instead put down unrelated facts or comments in a helter-skelter fashion. Your condensation had not been *precise*.

Examine carefully the following three selections and the précis which have been made from them.

ORIGINAL I:

Consider, for one thing, what has been the most widely read literature of the past two generations. Is it not a conspicuous fact that among the most popular novels four or five are by writers who never try to make us laugh, or at least, who never succeed? Twenty years ago the "best-selling" English novelists were Miss Marie Corelli and Mr. (now Sir) Hall Caine. Today three out of four of our best sellers are writers who depend for their effect scarcely at all upon humor of situation or character. I do not forget that Dickens, the permanent best seller of English literature was a humorist as well as a tragic sentimentalist. But, taking a general view of popular literature, we shall be safe in affirming that it is easier to become a best seller with a book that does not contain a single laugh than with a book that, in the language of the reviewers, contains a "laugh on every page." A novelist may leave out the laughter of life, indeed, and appeal to the public, not only for his own time, but for all time, as Defoe does in *Robinson Crusoe* and Richardson does in *Clarissa*, but no novelist has ever succeeded in becoming immortal through laughter alone. Sterne has his sentimental interludes. As regards Cervantes, again, we are constantly reproached by some of his most enthusiastic admirers if we do not share his sorrows with Don Quixote, instead of laughing at his misfortunes. It is the same with nearly all the masterpieces of comedy. They are most ardently appreciated, not for comic, but for serious reasons. If you take up a book on Aristophanes or Rabelais or Molière, you will almost certainly find that it sets out to explain his serious purpose rather than to echo his hilarity. (301 words)

ROBERT LYND, "Objections to Laughter"[1]

PRÉCIS I:

For the past two generations three out of four "best-selling" English novelists have depended very little upon humor of situation or character. This was true of Marie Corelli and Hall Caine, twenty years ago. It still holds today. Dickens, both a humorist and tragic sentimentalist, was exceptional. Generally it is easier to become a best seller through a book without a laugh than with one on every page. Novelists like Defoe and Richardson gained immortality though they ignored laughter. No writer has become immortal through laughter alone. Most comic masterpieces, including those of Aristophanes, Cervantes, Rabelais, and Molière, are appreciated for serious reasons. (102 words)

ORIGINAL II:

The primitive society is the closest to laboratory conditions the student of man can ever hope to get. Such groups are usually small and can be studied intensively by few people at slight expense. They are ordinarily rather isolated so that the question does not arise as to where one social system begins and another ends. The members of the group have lived their lives within a small area and have been exposed continually to the pressure of the same natural forces. They have had an almost identical education. All of their experiences have much more in common than is the case with members of complex societies. Their ways of life are comparatively stable. Commonly there is a high degree of biological inbreeding so that any member of the society chosen at random has about the same biological inheritance as any other. In short, many factors can be regarded as more or less constant, and the anthropologist is free to study a few variables in detail with real hope of ferreting out the connections between them. (176 words)   CLYDE KLUCKHORN, Mirror for Man[2]

---

[1] Reprinted by courtesy of The Atlantic Monthly.
[2] Reprinted by courtesy of the McGraw-Hill Book Company.

413

PRÉCIS II:

Primitive society is the anthropologist's laboratory: stable, small, isolated. Environmental factors, including natural forces, education, and range of experience are much the same for everyone. Inbreeding insures similarity of biological inheritance. So many constant factors leave only a few variables, which the anthropologist may study in detail, hoping to establish connections between them. (53 words)

ORIGINAL III:

Wire-tapping got its start in New York in 1895 when a former telephone worker who had joined the city police suggested that it might be a good idea to listen in on wires used by criminals. William L. Strong, who was mayor at the time, gave the project his blessing and for years after that wire-tapping flourished secretly. It was something the public of that period wouldn't worry about, anyhow, because in the nineties the telephone was not generally regarded as a household fixture. In those days police wire-tappers just walked into the telephone company's offices, asked for the location of the wires they were interested in, and got the information without fuss. Lines were usually tapped right in the cellar of the house or at an outside wall box.

There was an uproar when people got wind of the prevalence of wire-tapping. An investigation of public utilities in 1916 called attention to it. Those, of course, were war days, and eavesdropping of all kinds was widely encouraged. The government was tapping thousands of lines. A complete central-office switchboard had been set up in the New York Customs House, with taps running into it from all parts of the city. Every time a suspected alien lifted his receiver a light showed on this board and a stenographer, with headset clamped on, took a record of the conversation.

Inevitably it was claimed that wire-tapping violated a citizen's rights, and a large section of the press cried out against the practice, but nothing ever came of it. The furor, however, made the wire-tapper's job more difficult, because the Telephone Company, finding itself in an uncomfortable position, refused from then on to coöperate with the police in helping them locate suspect wires. (289 words)   MEYER BERGER, "Tapping the Wires," *The New Yorker*[1]

PRÉCIS III:

Wire-tapping got its start in New York in 1895 when a former telephone worker suggested that the police listen in on criminals. In those days police wire-tappers just walked into the telephone company's offices and learned the location of the wires they were interested in without fuss. Lines were usually tapped right in the cellar of the house or at an outside wall box.

Later, during World War days, when eavesdropping was widely encouraged, the government tapped thousands of lines. A complete central-office switchboard had been set up in the New York Customs House, with taps running into it from all parts of the city. Every time a suspected alien lifted his receiver a light flashed and a stenographer, with headset clamped on, recorded the conversation.

When people got wind of the prevalence of wire-tapping, the press denounced it, but nothing happened. The furor, however, made the wire-tapper's job more difficult, because the telephone company refused from then on to coöperate with the police. (164 words)   *Reader's Digest*[2]

Notice in these selections that the proportion between original and précis is somewhat different in each case. Précis II is the most condensed; it has less than one-third but more than one-fourth as many words as its original. Précis I is somewhat less reduced, where Précis III has more than one-half as many words as the article it represents.

Some authorities fix upon one-third of the number of words in the original as the most desirable proportion for

[1] Reprinted by courtesy of *The New Yorker*. Copyright, 1947, *The New Yorker Magazine, Inc.*

[2] Reprinted by courtesy of *Reader's Digest*.

a précis, but the length of the original material and the kind of subject matter have much to do with the amount of reduction possible. Observe that of the three précis chosen for illustration, the one which succeeds in attaining the greatest compactness follows least closely the wording of the original passage, while Précis III, the least compact, lifts many sentences bodily from its source. The point is clear; unless you use your own words, you will find it difficult to be both concise and accurate. The style and content of the original and your needs (for supporting detail, for example), will also affect the amount of reduction possible.

In writing a précis:

1. Read over the article carefully. Be sure that you understand everything that is said. Try to formulate a statement of the intent or purpose of the passage.

2. After you have read the passage through and have a conception of its intent, make notes of the important points. Here, for example, are the notes upon which Précis II was based:

> Primitive society approaches laboratory conditions.
> Groups are small, isolated, stable.
> Environment similar: nature, education, experience.
> Heredity similar because of inbreeding.
> Many constant factors; few variables.
> Can concentrate on connections between variables.

3. Expand the notes into your précis, striving for as much economy of phrasing as possible. It is preferable to write the first draft of the précis from your notes without looking at the original. This procedure will help you to put the précis into your own words. After you have written your first draft, then compare it with the original and make whatever alterations seem necessary to give the exact shades of meaning demanded.

4. (a) Use a single word in place of a phrase whenever possible. Note that in Précis I, *comic* replaces *of comedy*. (b) Try to use adjectives in place of phrases and clauses. Again in Précis I, *immortal* replaces *not only for his own time, but for all time*. (c) Use phrases in place of clauses or sentences. What in the original of Précis II is the equivalent of *similarity of biological inheritance* in the précis?

On your notecards you will, of course, not be seeking to write a fully developed précis. Be sure that you have all the information needed to write one, however. Do not lose the connections the writer suggests between his thoughts. Do not summarize so generally that you reduce the source's statements to platitudes. Do not forget to pick up dates of events, full names and identifications of people mentioned, and definitions of key terms. If a source attributes an opinion to someone else, be sure to pick up the attribution with the opinion. If the date of publication of a source (as picked up on your final bibliography card, see **L6a**) is significantly different from the date at which the work was written, you may need to pick up the date of writing on a notecard. Keep asking yourself these questions: "What supporting details will I need to convincingly answer the question my thesis will ask?" "What background information will my readers need to understand what I will want to say?"

EXERCISE III

Write précis of the following selections, putting to use the suggestions just given:

1. About this time, our club meeting, not at a tavern, but in a little room of Mr. Grace's, set apart for that purpose, a proposition was made by me that, since our books were often referred to in our disquisitions upon the queries, it might be convenient

to us to have them all together where we met, that upon occasion they might be consulted; and by thus clubbing our books to a common library, we should, while we liked to keep them together, have each of us the advantage of using the books of all the other members, which would be nearly as beneficial as if each owned the whole. It was liked and agreed to, and we filled one end of the room with such books as we could best spare. The number was not so great as we expected; and, though they had been of great use, yet, some inconveniences occurring for want of due care of them, the collection, after about a year, was separated, and each took his books home again.

And now I set on foot my first project of a public nature, that for a subscription library. I drew up the proposals, got them put into form by our great scrivener, Brockden, and, by the help of my friends in the Junto, procured fifty subscribers of forty shillings each to begin with, and ten shillings a year for fifty years, the term our company was to continue. We afterwards obtained a charter, the company being increased to one hundred: this was the mother of all the North American subscription libraries, now so numerous. It is become a great thing itself, and continually increasing. These libraries have improved the general conversation of the Americans, made the common tradesmen and farmers as intelligent as most gentlemen from other countries, and perhaps have contributed in some degree to the stand so generally made throughout the colonies in defense of their privileges.

FRANKLIN, *Autobiography*

2. We can add a worthwhile vocational course to our school curriculum, however, if we keep it in its proper perspective and if it meets the tests we have set for it. Unique among our school offerings, vocational courses can be directly related to our narrow community. Such are the programs some schools conduct in cooperation with local business and industry, wherein students receive paid on-the-job training as part-time apprentices. The number of such vocational programs is limited only by the willingness of industrialists and businessmen in the community to co-operate with the school—a matter which resolves to some extent the anti-democratic nature of vocational training for the few.

Many schools have worked out released-time programs with local employers, but should we not take care that such programs do not provide the employers with cheap labor and thus do some adults out of their jobs? I think we should also be careful they do not take time away from the fundamental disciplines. Care, too, must be taken that the number of such on-the-job trainees does not exceed the annual job demand.

JOHN KEATS, *Schools Without Scholars*[1]

3. Idealism must always prevail on the frontier, for the frontier, whether geographical or intellectual, offers little hope to those who see things as they are. To venture into the wilderness, one must see it, not as it is, but as it will be. The frontier, being the possession of those only who see its future, is the promised land which cannot be entered save by those who have faith. America, having been such a promised land, is therefore inhabited by men of faith: idealism is ingrained in the character of its people. But as the frontier in America has hitherto been geographical and material, American idealism has necessarily a material basis, and Americans have often been mistakenly called materialists. True, they seem mainly interested in material things. Too often they represent values in terms of money: a man is "worth" so much money; a university is a great university, having the largest endowment of any; a fine building is a building that cost a million dollars—better still, ten millions. Value is extensive rather than intensive or intrinsic. America is the best country because it is the biggest, the wealthiest, the most powerful; its people are the best because they are the freest, the most energetic, the most educated. But to see a materialistic temper in all this is to mistake the form for the spirit. The American cares for material things because they represent the substance of things hoped for. He cares less for money than for making money; a fortune is valued not because it represents ease, but because it represents struggle, achievement, progress. The first skyscraper in any town is nothing in itself, but much as an evidence of growth; it is a white stone on the road to the ultimate goal. CARL BECKER, *Kansas*[2]

[1] Reprinted by courtesy of the Houghton Mifflin Company.
[2] Reprinted by permission of Holt, Rinehart & Winston, Inc.

4. For my part, I could easily do without the post office. I think that there are very few important communications made through it. To speak critically, I never received more than one or two letters in my life—I wrote this some years ago—that were worth the postage. The penny-post is, commonly, an institution through which you seriously offer a man that penny for his thoughts which is so often safely offered in jest. And I am sure that I never read any memorable news in a newspaper. If we read of one man robbed, or murdered, or killed by accident, or one house burned, or one vessel wrecked, or one steamboat blown-up, or one cow run over on the Western Railroad, or one mad dog killed, or one lot of grasshoppers in the winter,—we never need read of another. One is enough. If you are acquainted with the principle, what do you care for a myriad instances and applications? To a philosopher all *news*, as it is called, is gossip, and they who edit and read it are old women over their tea. There was such a rush, as I hear, the other day at one of the offices to learn the foreign news by the last arrival, that several large squares of plate glass belonging to the establishment were broken by the pressure,—news which I seriously think a ready wit might write a twelvemonth or twelve years beforehand with sufficient accuracy.

HENRY THOREAU, *Walden*

5. If the father has fallen from authority, who has superseded him? The mother? Not at all. The popular impression to that effect has no basis except the fact that the power of the mother has increased *relatively* to that of the father. But this is due to the fall of the father rather than to any notable rise of the mother. No, the new domestic polity is neither the patriarchy nor the matriarchy, but the *pediarchy*.

That the children should encroach upon and eventually seize the authority of the parents is not so strange as might at first occur. After all, it is only the domestic manifestation of the most characteristic social and political movement of modern times, the rise, namely, of the proletarian masses. Within the family the children constitute the majority, the unpropertied, the unskilled, and the unprivileged. They are intensely class-conscious, and have come to a clearer and clearer recognition of the conflict of interest that divides them from the owners and managers. Their methods have been similar to those employed in the industrial revolution —the strike, passive resistance, malingering, restriction of output, and occasionally direct action.

Within the family, as in the modern democracy, the control is by public opinion. It is government of the children, by the children, and for the children. But this juvenile sovereignty is exercised indirectly rather than directly. The officeholders are adults, whose power is proportional to their juvenile support. The real (though largely unseen and unacknowledged) principle of domestic politics is the struggle for prestige among the adults. Some employ the methods of decadent Rome, the *panem et circenses*; others, the arts of the military hero or of the popular orator. But all acknowledge the need of conciliating the juvenile masses.

RALPH BARTON PERRY, "Domestic Superstitions"[1]

6. Once, from eastern ocean to western ocean, the land stretched away without names. Nameless headlands split the surf; nameless lakes reflected nameless mountains; and nameless rivers flowed through nameless valleys into nameless bays.

Men came at last, tribe following tribe, speaking different languages and thinking different thoughts. According to their ways of speech and thought they gave names, and in their generations laid their bones by the streams and hills they had named. But even when tribes and languages had vanished, some of these old names, reshaped, still lived in the speech of those who followed.

After many centuries a people calling themselves Americans held the land. They followed the ways of the English more than of any others, especially in their speech. Yet they gathered together in their blood and in their manner of life something of all those who had lived in the land before them. Thus they took as a heritage many names of the past. Adding more names, they gave to their children with every generation the heritage richer than before.

A few hundred were great names, known to all Americans, of states and cities, mountains and rivers. But most of them were

[1] Reprinted by courtesy of *The Atlantic Monthly*.

little names, known only to those who lived near by, of ponds and swamps and creeks and hills, of townships and villages, of streets and ranches and plantations, of coves and gulches and meadows. These little names arose by so many thousands that at last they were numbered by millions.

GEORGE STEWART, *Names on the Land*[1]

[1] Reprinted by permission of Random House, Inc.

XII. Organizing the Paper

IF your paper is to be successful it must be planned. You may seem to write short papers altogether without plan, and you may even do some without an outline, because their limited scope permits you to plan them in your head—almost without knowing it. Besides, some simple subjects virtually plan themselves: if you are explaining how something is manufactured, you will naturally follow the raw material through a series of processes until the product is finished. But the longer the paper you write, the more deliberate and considered must be your plan. You can hardly do without an outline. Review the discussion in Chapter I, **T2–5**, of classification, outlining, and the thesis sentence before reading the materials on outlining in this chapter.

1. OUTLINING

It is instructive to see how another writer has used the outline. Let us take an essay on education, isolate the *topic sentences* (see Chapter II, ¶7) from each paragraph, and discover the underlying pattern, if such there be.

WHY NOT TEACH SOME OF THESE THINGS?[1]

1. "What shall I teach?" A great many of us who teach have wondered about this very matter.

2. I do not think that there is in general any clearly defined understanding in America as to the real end of education.

3. Firsthand experience in public-school teaching furnishes one with many illustrations of the fundamental absurdity of the assumption that we educate for culture.

[1] Claire Williams, "Why Not Teach Some of These Things?" Reprinted by courtesy of *The Forum*.

4. Others seem to assume that the end of education is to train youth to earn its living. That seems to me also a mistaken assumption.

5. I think that the end of education is to improve slowly, steadily, decade by decade, the quality of the populace.

6. Before we set out to educate, we should decide exactly what things schools can teach which will tend to grade up the population.

7. The gap in mental development between the civilized man and the savage is most easily estimated by observing the difference in language.

8. In normal cases the power to express thought measures the power to think.

9. For the welfare of the state, then, its people should be able to think. To do this they must be in command of language, which is the instrument of thought.

10. It would be much more efficient to train children to speak well at the start than to have them waste time and strength trying to unlearn habits ineradicably established.

11. I emphasize the value of this early training in language, not only for the sake of correct speech, but for another reason: in infancy, knowledge of things advances at the same pace as our knowledge of language.

12. The more children know by seven, the better their chances are to learn a reasonable amount by the time they are seventeen.

13. Next, I should teach formal manners.

14. If a state is to have a civilized population, its children must be taught to behave like civilized beings.

15. About the most important thing the child has to learn is that the world is full of other people, whose rights he must observe, and with whom he must be scrupulous in the fulfillment of his obligations.

16. Next I should include in my school a great deal of physical training.

17. It does lie within our power to do a great deal toward perfecting our pupils' physiques.

18. A child should study drawing to learn how to use his hands

with precision and neatness and to help him retain the faculty of observation.

19. I should require some sort of handwork to give pupils practice in the use of tools.

Having assembled the topic sentences, we read over this summary and decide what the purpose of the essay is. It appears clear that the author is considering what subjects should be taught in the schools; the idea is readily confirmed by a glance at the first topic sentence: "What shall I teach?"

In analyzing the essay, then, let us first ask ourselves, "What subjects does this author want the schools to teach?" Paragraphs 7–11 all deal with the teaching of language, and paragraph 12 continues the argument begun in the preceding paragraph, so we can tentatively set down as one division of the essay a note which would read something like this:

¶s 7–12 LANGUAGE

Next notice that paragraph 13 and the two following deal with manners and forms of behavior. A second division of the essay could be set down then as follows:

¶s 13–15 MANNERS

We may next note that paragraphs 16 and 17 select physical training as one of the subjects to be taught, that paragraph 18 is devoted to drawing, and finally that paragraph 19 deals with manual training. Following the example of the preceding paragraphs, we might add to our notes:

¶s 16, 17 PHYSICAL TRAINING

¶ 18 DRAWING

¶ 19 MANUAL TRAINING

Since all these subjects have to do with the development of physical and mechanical skills, it would be possible to consider them under one head and to organize them as follows:

DEVELOPMENT OF SKILL:

    Physical exercise
    Drawing
    Manual training

All of the things which our author believes should be taught in the schools have now been covered, but the first six paragraphs of the essay still remain to be organized. Paragraph 1 is an introductory statement of the topic of the essay, a *thesis sentence* (see Chapter I, **T5**). Paragraph 2 states that there are a number of opinions about the aims of education. Paragraphs 3–5 illustrate this point by showing how varied such opinions actually are. Therefore, we might make a temporary note something as follows:

No agreement as to aims of education.
    Culture not the chief end
    Training for earning a living not the chief end
    Education should improve the quality of the populace

This is not the only possible organization for these statements; we might put Paragraph 2 with the opening paragraph and call them both introductory:

I. No agreement in America as to certain phases of education.
    A. What shall be taught?
    B. What is the end of education?

Notice that we might then place as subsections under *B* paragraphs 3, 4, and 5.

    B. What is the end of education?
        1. We do not educate for culture.

2. We do not educate to train students to earn a living.

3. We should educate to improve the quality of the populace.

It is precisely this rearrangement of statements that gives outline-making its value. In the course of it, the path of the author's argument is impressed upon you ever more clearly; you come to see just how one statement follows or depends upon another. Moreover, if one statement does not logically depend upon something which has gone before, or if there is a serious break in the writer's train of thought—which may weaken the validity of his conclusion—the processes involved in making the outline will certainly bring the weak points to light. The procedure is reversed, of course, when you make an outline for a paper that you are going to write; but the effect of clarifying the pattern is the same.

Now that we have assembled topic sentences in various ways and have tried a number of possible groupings, the final step is to join the main headings into a connected outline. We may make two distinct types of outlines from this essay, the *sentence outline* and the *topic outline*.

2. SENTENCE OUTLINE

I. In the American educational world there is little or no agreement on certain of the most vital problems.

A. Many teachers are not certain about what should be taught.

B. There is not a clearly defined understanding as to the real end of education.

1. Culture is not the primary aim.

2. Training youth to earn its living is not the chief end.

II. The end of education is to improve the quality of the populace.

III. We must teach those subjects which will accomplish this end.

   A. Training in language works toward this end.
      1. The power to express thought measures the power to think.
      2. Knowledge of things advances at the same pace as the knowledge of language.
   B. Training in formal manners improves the quality of the populace.
      1. It teaches children to behave like civilized beings.
      2. It gives children a sense of the rights of other people.
   C. Development of physical and mechanical skills is also necessary.
      1. Physical training will perfect the children's physiques.
      2. Drawing will help a child use his hands with precision.
      3. Manual training will give children practice in the use of tools.

3. TOPIC OUTLINE

   I. Disagreements in the educational field
   A. Uncertainty about what to teach
   B. Mistaken notions of the real end of education
      1. Culture
      2. Earning a living
   II. Education to improve the quality of the populace

III. Subjects which will lead to improvement

    A. Language

        1. Power to express thought
        2. Early knowledge of things

    B. Formal manners

        1. Improvement of behavior
        2. Development of consideration for others

    C. Development of skills

        1. Physical exercise
        2. Drawing
        3. Manual training

The preceding outlines illustrate the two types most commonly used. They differ in that the *sentence outline* phrases each item so as to make a complete sentence, whereas the *topic outline* gives each item little more than a label or title. The sentence outline is more useful for outlining material which you are reading, as may be seen from the way in which this one was derived, and is more satisfactory for long or complicated papers. The topic outline, because it is simpler, is more satisfactory when used as a preliminary outline or as an outline for a short paper.

The topic outline shown here is not highly developed. It is the kind you might be able to make after you have begun to read your sources and when the pattern has begun to emerge, but before you are ready to write. You should make such a preliminary outline, with wide spaces between the divisions into which you can insert the details of evidence, fact, or illustration that will best serve your argument.

The advantage of making your outline early is that it will guide you in reading and note-taking. You may find after making an outline that in some division of your subject you need to read further. An outline also gives you a pattern by which to sort your notes. Keep enlarging and improving your outline with all necessary subdivisions until you have finished your reading. Then go over it carefully and correct any inconsistencies or faults of structure. Decide what details you will use and discard the others. The resultant corrected outline is ready for presentation to your instructor, if that is required, and in any case it is ready for use in the writing of your paper.

For both sentence and topic outlines the scheme of organization is the same:

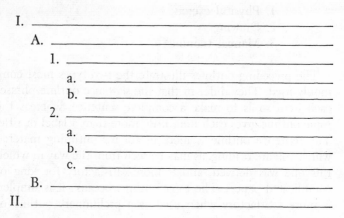

If you need subdivisions beyond the third degree you may use (1), (2), (3), etc., and (a), (b), (c), etc., for subseries under these. These subdivisions are ordinarily not needed in outlines.

4. SUGGESTIONS FOR OUTLINING

Observe the following precautions:

a. Make certain that all the members of one subdivision are of the same degree of importance.

Suppose that the topic outline had read:

III. C. Development of skill
      1. Physical exercise
   D. Drawing
      1. Manual training

Such an arrangement would have been faulty for two reasons:

1. As *drawing* is one means of developing a physical or mechanical skill recommended by the author, it should not have been placed in an equal or coordinate position with *development of skill.*

2. *Manual training* is not a form or subdivision of drawing, therefore it should not be placed in a position inferior or subordinate to *drawing.*

Look at the topic outline again and see how these items are arranged.

b. Strive for parallel phrasing in coordinate parts of the outline. Notice the following:

   B. Formal manners
      1. Improves behavior
      2. Consideration for others

Notice that *Improves behavior* consists of a verb and its object while *Consideration for others* is just a phrase. If we should place a verb in item 2, the two will be parallel:

      1. Improves behavior
      2. Develops consideration for others

c. In general, see that there are two or more parts under each heading. Notice the following:

III. Education to improve the quality of the populace
   A. Subjects which will lead to improvement

If the topic outline had been organized in this fashion, there would have been no second topic of equal rank with A to place under *III*. When you meet such a situation, reconsider your divisions; sometimes you can improve the organization if you either combine the minor heading with the major heading under which you have placed it, or elevate it to the rank of a second major heading. *But do not distort your outline.* If a single subdivision is the most natural, or if only one subtopic demands inclusion, leave the outline so. Do not bring in extraneous material merely to balance the outline; the outline is not an end in itself, but a means toward a better composition.

XIII. Manuscript
Preparation

THE suggestions which follow are designed to help you to make the best possible initial impression upon the reader. A paper that is untidy, hard to read, or amateurish in form makes a poor impression even though it is well written. Experience has shown that a manuscript must meet certain standards to make it readable.

1. FORMAT

a. Write or type your manuscript on paper 8½ x 11 inches in size.

b. If the manuscript is handwritten, use only black or blue-black ink. Write legibly.

Avoid breaks between the letters of a word and do not run words together. Make your capital letters sufficiently distinct from lower-case letters. Make your marks of punctuation carefully, so that the reader will be able to distinguish between a period and a comma, between a colon and a semicolon, and between a hyphen and a dash. Place the apostrophe mark between letters, not above letters.

c. If the manuscript is typewritten, double-space it. Correct it carefully before handing it in.

Be sure to leave enough space after punctuation marks: one space after a comma or semicolon; two spaces after a colon, period, question mark or exclamation mark; no space between the quotation marks and the material quoted (punctuation normally inside the closing quotation marks); two spaces after the closing quotation marks; no space before or after a hyphen (when not used for word division at the

8½" wide

2" above title

capitalize all words in title except to

double space between lines

2 spaces after period, colon, question mark

no space after opening quotation marks

no space either side of hyphen

11" down

3 spaces between title and beginning

one space after commas

punctuation inside closing quotation marks

1" margin

A Visit to Alaska

During the past summer, which had threatened to be drab, I suddenly had an opportunity which has changed my whole outlook: to make a trip to Alaska. Why should a chance occurrence have so great an effect? Because Alaska, "our last frontier," proved to be the most hope-stirring place that I have ever seen. Now I know I must go back; that is where my future lies.

end of a line). If your typewriter is not supplied with a dash, use a double hyphen for a dash. Leave at least an inch margin at the left side. Do not crowd words at the right of the page or at the bottom. The title should be written at least two inches from the top of the first page, with the body of the composition beginning no less than three spaces below it. On subsequent pages there should be an inch margin at the top. The pages should be numbered at the top; Arabic numerals are preferred.

d. Use uniform paragraph indentation.

Indentation in a handwritten manuscript varies with the size of the handwriting, but it should be clearly perceptible to the reader. A distance of one-half to one inch is enough for most handwriting. Five spaces is the usual amount for typewritten manuscripts. Every paragraph begins on a new line. If the last sentence ends before the right-hand margin of the page is reached, do not leave the rest of the line blank unless you intend to begin a new paragraph with your next sentence.

e. Put your title in conventional form.

Every word in a title is to be capitalized except short prepositions, articles, and conjunctions: do not capitalize *the, a, an, and, but, if, for, in, to, into,* etc.

Words of more than four letters should be capitalized: *After, Under, Unless, Though, Whenever,* etc.

Any word in first position must be capitalized: *The, A, An, And, So, In,* etc. Do not end the title with a period, and do not underline it.

Refer also to Chapter I, **T12**.

2. *QUOTATION MARKS*

In general, quotation marks are used to enclose all matter that is *directly* quoted, whether from a written or spoken

MS2a

source. Indirect quotations are not punctuated with quotation marks.

Don't forget to *close* the quotation. This is a common error in student writing.

DIRECT QUOTATION: "I was looking for you," he said.
INDIRECT QUOTATION: He told her that he had been looking for her.

a. The punctuation after the introductory statement preceding a quotation varies with the closeness of the structure, the formality of the statement, and the length of the quotation.

1. A short emphatic quotation requires no punctuation after the introductory word.

He shouted "Thief!" and took up the chase.

2. A short quotation, informally introduced, is punctuated with a comma after the introductory word.

The elder girl said casually, "It is so quaint living down here in the Square."

3. A long quotation, formally introduced, is punctuated with a colon after the introductory word.

After quiet was restored the speaker proceeded: "During the past month I have consulted with a large number of individuals on the increasingly difficult problem of railroad transportation."

b. When the explanatory statement, such as he said, **follows the quotation, the quotation is concluded with a comma, question mark, or an exclamation mark; the explanatory phrase begins with a small letter, stands outside the quotation marks, and ends with a period.**

"It is my mother," he said in a low voice.
"Can't you see it?" she asked.

"Take it away at once!" he commanded.

c. When the explanatory phrase comes between parts of the quotation, the first portion of the quotation is followed by a comma, but the explanatory statement is followed by whatever mark of punctuation would normally follow the first portion of the quotation.

EXPLANATORY STATEMENT AT THE BEGINNING: Stephen replied, "Oh, I know the old proceedings were bad enough, but I am trying to improve them."

EXPLANATORY STATEMENT IN THE MIDDLE: "Oh, I know the old proceedings were bad enough," replied Stephen, "but I am trying to improve them."

EXPLANATORY STATEMENT AT THE BEGINNING: He said, "Then I'll see you tomorrow. Can you be ready at nine?"

EXPLANATORY STATEMENT IN THE MIDDLE: "Then I'll see you tomorrow," he said. "Can you be ready at nine?"

EXPLANATORY STATEMENT AT THE BEGINNING: James said, "We'll just go down to Hampstead; the horses want exercise, and I should like to see what has been going on down there."

EXPLANATORY STATEMENT IN THE MIDDLE: "We'll just go down to Hampstead," said James; "the horses want exercise, and I should like to see what has been going on down there."

d. Relative position of quotation marks and other marks of punctuation.

1. The dash, question mark, and exclamation mark are placed within the quotation marks when they apply to the quotation only, and outside the quotation marks when they apply to the whole statement.

He said, "Are you coming?"

Did he say, "I am going now"?

"Summer courses—out here on the lake—history and art and cooking and swimming—" Beatrice chimed in enthusiastically.

437

"You think you are sufficient in yourself"—then he stopped suddenly and began again, "Some day you will see that you have been mistaken."

2. The comma and the period normally precede the closing quotation mark.

"I don't feel natural when I express them your way," she admitted, "in words."

At times placing the period within the quotation marks seems illogical, but the practice is general, possibly because it looks better on the printed page.

According to Johnson's opinion, "the first Whig was the Devil."

3. The colon and semicolon always follow the quotation marks.

A judge, like a marshal or a postmaster, is just so much "recognition"; another piece of patronage.

e. A quotation within a quotation is indicated by single quotation marks.

"But he did say," Charles pointed out, " 'I won't come if I don't finish my work,' so apparently he hasn't finished it!"

f. When the quoted material consists of several paragraphs, quotation marks are placed at the beginning of each paragraph and at the end of the quotation.

g. When someone's exact phraseology is included within an indirect quotation, quotation marks are frequently placed around the directly quoted material.

A distinguished Conservative statesman tells us from the town hall of Tamworth that "in becoming wiser a man will become better"; meaning by "wiser" more conversant with the facts and theories of physical science.

h. In formal writing it is customary to enclose slang in quotation marks.

Gentlemen, if I may say so, this plan appears to be completely "cockeyed."

Do not employ this in informal writing. Moreover, do not enclose colloquialisms or nicknames in quotation marks in any kind of writing. Students frequently overuse quotation marks in this way. Unfamiliar technical terms may be enclosed in quotation marks, but present practice favors italics for these, or underlining in handwritten and typewritten manuscripts. Underlining is the printer's sign for italics.

i. Words mentioned but not used may be enclosed in quotation marks.

The word "and" occurs three times in this context.

Italics are also frequently used, especially in linguistic practice, to indicate that a word is being mentioned rather than used. See Chapter VII, **P16c.**

j. Titles of literary, musical, and artistic works may be enclosed in quotation marks, but present practice favors italics.

3. *QUOTED MATERIAL*

Short quotations, from a few words to two or three lines, need not be separated from the main text except by being enclosed in quotation marks.

In the course of the trial the defendant cried out repeatedly that he was "an innocent man," the victim of public hysteria. "Ten years ago," he declared at one point, "this case would never have come to court." The prosecution objected and the remark was stricken from the record.

In a published book, long prose quotations are usually centered and often set in smaller type. In typed or handwritten papers, indent the entire quotation five spaces, and, in a typed paper, use single-spacing. A long prose quotation centered and set off in this fashion need not be enclosed in quotation marks, provided the language of the text shows that it is a quotation and proper credit is given in a footnote. Quotations must follow the original word for word, and punctuation must be reproduced exactly. Omissions may be indicated by the use of suspension points. (See also **MS4.**)

The Burlington and the Union Pacific and all the Eastern industrial power which these two names represented in Nebraska were still in control. Mr. Olney, the Burlington's General Counsel, had been made Attorney General by Mr. Cleveland. He wrote the frightened Mr. Perkins:

> The [Interstate Commerce] Commission . . . is, or can be made, of great use to the railroads. It satisfies the popular clamor for a government supervision of railroads. . . . Further, the older such a commission gets to be, the more inclined it will be found to take the business and railroad view of things. . . . The part of wisdom is not to destroy the Commission, but to utilize it.[6]

Poetry quoted in a text should appear line for line just as it was in the original. If the line of poetry is too long to be written on a single line of the page, the leftover portion should be indented. Maintain the stanza divisions of the original.

> And she paused on her way to gather the fairest among them,
> That the dying once more might rejoice in their fragrance
>   and beauty.
> Then, as she mounted the stairs to the corridors, cooled by
>   the east wind,
> Distant and soft on her ear fell the chimes from the belfry
>   of Christ Church.
>
>   --Longfellow, <u>Evangeline</u>

4. INSERTIONS AND OMISSIONS IN QUOTED MATERIAL

a. Brackets are used to enclose editorial explanation and correction, especially in quoted material.

We find in Hodgson's diary, "The period from March through July [1847] was one of unparalleled political activity."

Be sure, however, that your insertion does not falsify the meaning of the original.

1. The Latin word sic (meaning "thus") may be inserted to show that you are quoting accurately even though the spelling, grammar, or logic may seem inaccurate to the reader.

According to a historian of the late nineteenth century, "Macauley's [sic] command of words in *The History of England* was better than his command of ideas."

2. Brackets may be used to change verbs to appropriate forms and pronouns to the proper person as grammar requires.

QUOTATION: Americans as a people are adventurous, practical, hard-working.

ALTERED QUOTATION: According to a nineteenth-century observer, "Americans as a people [were] adventurous, practical, hard-working."

b. Ellipsis, or omission of words, is indicated by use of a series of three periods [. . .], sometimes called suspension points.

Sometimes it is unnecessary to reproduce all of a quotation to make it serve your purpose. Suppose, for example, that the following sentence, by Jacques Barzun, supported a point that you were making in a paper. "If the relation of the artist to the local community is difficult, despite the ease of communication between them, the relation of all the nation's artists to a central government bureau must be a source of endless trouble, aggravated by the equal relation of all the taxpayers to that same agency." You feel, however, that all that is really germane to your purpose is the initial subordinate clause and the main clause. By using suspension points, you might quote the sentence as follows: "If the relation of the artist to the local community is difficult . . . the relation of all the nation's artists to a central government bureau must be a source of endless trouble. . . ." Note that when the omission comes at the end of a sentence, a fourth period is used.

5. PARAGRAPHING QUOTED MATERIAL

a. In dialogue or conversation each quotation from a new speaker is usually paragraphed, along with that portion of the sentence which introduces the speech or announces the speaker.

Once I asked him the name of the ship on which he was captain.

"It was in 1943," he said vaguely. "Wartime."

"What was the name of the ship?"

"Number Four."

"What kind of a ship was Number Four?"

"It was a barge, a munitions barge. It was towed between Wilmington and the Navy Yard, and I was captain."

A few modern writers vary from this standard practice, but the student will do well to master it just because it is standard. Unless innovation has positive value, avoid it.

b. In quotations within connected narrative, if the quotation demands emphasis, it is paragraphed separately; if the unity between the quotation and the context is more important, the quotation is not made a separate paragraph.

Uttering cries of consternation, Ray's parents rushed after him. They found their son, still enfolded in the big boa and sagging under its weight, quietly laughing as he stroked and soothed it. A few moments more, and he had induced it to cast off and crawl peaceably into its cage.

"Oh, Ray, what a frightful sight!" his mother exclaimed weakly, as she sank into a chair.

Ray grinned. "That's a very gentle, good-tempered snake, Mama," he explained. "If ever a snake had an excuse to lose its temper and strike, that one did, the way Pop was punishing its tail."

"I never did care for snakes," John Ditmars growled, wiping beads of perspiration off his pale forehead.

L. N. WOOD, Raymond L. Ditmars[1]

I got out of bed quietly so as not to wake Molly, dressed and went down the back way over to the Thomas house. There was no one stirring but I knew which room Joe's was. The window was open and I could hear him snoring. I went up and stuck my head in.

"Hey," I said, "killing frost!"

He opened his eyes and looked at me and then his eyes went shut. I reached my arm through the window and shook him.

"Get up," I said. "We got to start right away."

CAROLINE GORDON, "The Last Day in the Field"[2]

The cruellest thing he heard this man say was to a boy who was rather thick and fat but conscientious. "You can't draw," he said roughly. "Take my advice and go home. You'll make more money driving a wagon."

DREISER, The Genius

c. When a quotation is introduced by a portion of a preceding sentence, paragraphing the quotation separately gives it emphasis.

Seeing Grant talking with a group of men over by the kitchen door, he crossed over slowly and stood listening. Wesley Cos-

---

[1] Reprinted by permission of Julian Messner, Inc.
[2] Reprinted by permission of Charles Scribner's Sons.

grove—a tall, raw-boned young fellow with a grave, almost tragic face—was saying:

"Of course I ain't. Who is? A man that's satisfied to live as we do is a fool."

HAMLIN GARLAND, Up the Coulé

Holly turned her head, pointed with her little brown fist to the piano—for to point with a finger was not "well-brrred"—and said slyly:

"Look at the 'lady in grey,' Gran; isn't she pretty today?"

Old Jolyon's heart gave a flutter, and for a second the room was clouded; then it cleared, and he said with a twinkle:

"Who's been dressing her up?"

GALSWORTHY, The Forsyte Saga[1]

6. DOCUMENTING SOURCE MATERIAL

In preparing your long paper you have gathered information of various kinds, some of which you want to use directly. The question is how best to present it. Let us suppose that your paper is concerned with the cost of shipbuilding and that you want to prove that without government subsidy the shipbuilders in the United States could not compete with those of other nations. You have secured some comparative figures on material and labor costs in Great Britain, West Germany, Holland, Japan, and the United States. You cannot merely use these figures without reference to your sources of information without committing plagiarism. Omitted reference to your sources also implies that any source is as good as another, which is not true; or that you had some reason for hiding the source from the reader, which would annoy him and put you under suspicion. The only effective course is to refer to your sources. This may be done in any of three ways:

---

[1] Reprinted by permission of Charles Scribner's Sons.

1. In an indirect quotation, you may give both the information and your source for it in the text of your paper, somewhat as follows:

According to figures published in Business Week in an article entitled "Ship Subsidies Bump the Ceiling" (November 15, 1958, pp. 45-46), the cost of labor in U.S. shipbuilding is equal to the cost of materials, whereas in most foreign shipyards the labor cost is only 15%, and 85% for materials. Furthermore, the hourly pay scale in the U.S. runs anywhere from seven times as high as that of Japan to three or three and a half times as high as that of Britain.

2. In an indirect quotation, give the information in the text of your paper, mentioning the source in a footnote:

In the U.S. the cost of labor in shipbuilding is equal to the cost of materials, as published figures show, whereas in most foreign shipyards the labor cost is only 15%, and 85% for materials. The hourly pay scale in the U.S. also runs anywhere from seven times as high as that of Japan to three or three and a half times as high as that of Britain.[3]

---

[3]"Ship Subsidies Bump the Ceiling," Business Week, November 15, 1958, pp. 45-46.

3. In a direct quotation, give the information in the text of your paper, mentioning the source in a footnote:

According to an article published in Business Week, "In Japan the average hourly wage rate for shipyard workers is about 35¢. German and Dutch yards pay about 60¢, with British yards going up to around 90¢. In the U.S., it ranges from around $2.50 to $2.90 an hour. Generally, the cost of building ships in the U.S. is split 50-50 between labor and materials. In foreign yards, the ratio runs closer to 85% for materials and 15% for labor."[3]

---

[3]"Ship Subsidies Bump the Ceiling," Business Week, November 15, 1958, pp. 45-46.

7. FOOTNOTES

Three common purposes of footnotes are these:

1. To separate borrowed material from your own and to acknowledge the former. This is simple honesty and forestalls any suspicion of plagiarism.

2. To permit the reader to verify for himself or to read further in a source. Thus you also disclaim responsibility for errors in the material you are using.

3. To make a necessary explanation without interrupting the body of the paper. You may even wish to disagree, in the footnote, with the quoted material.

Sometimes footnotes may serve other purposes as well; for example, providing cross reference within the paper or giving additional quotations.

a. Footnotes are indicated by Arabic numerals placed a little above and to the right of the item to which they refer.

Usually the number is placed at the end of the sentence to which the footnote refers unless the sentence is so long that it eventually gets away from the precise item to be explained. When a footnote is used to give the source of quoted matter, the number should appear at the end of the quotation. If the footnote refers to the title of a work, it should be placed immediately after the title.

EXAMPLES:

De Neve had accepted the governorship of California rather under protest, and his resignation was now on file with the commanding general.[5]

Durant came out from New York "dressed in the style of a frontier dandy. He wore a slouch hat, velvet sack coat and vest, corduroy breeches and top boots, all his clothing being of a costly character."[3]

Mr. Krutch's book, <u>Samuel Johnson</u>,[2] is a bold attempt to follow in the track of one of the world's greatest biographies.

Unless the footnote refers to something within a sentence, it is placed after all marks of punctuation. Number the footnotes consecutively throughout the paper.

b. In the footnote itself the number appears first, so indented that it is on a line with the paragraph indentation. It is not followed by a period or any other punctuation.

In published books and articles the number preceding the footnote is superior (above the line), just as is the reference number in the text itself. Follow the same practice for your footnotes, whether typed or handwritten. (See *Typical Footnote Entries*, page 449.)

c. In a theme or class paper the footnote should appear at the bottom of the page on which the passage to which it refers ends.

The note or notes should be separated from the text itself by a line at least two inches long, with at least one and preferably two spaces above and below the line.

EXAMPLE:

. . . He lived in the Wittelsbacher Palais[1] in semi-state, entertained lavishly at Leopoldskron,[2] built a few fantastic houses, still patronized the arts, went to Italy, travelled.

----

[1]Long the residence of his grandson, Ludwig III, and later the seat of the Communist Government in April, 1919.

[2]Now Professor Reinhardt's palace near Salzburg.

d. The basic province of the footnote referring to source materials is the immediate reference, which gives the author's name in normal order, title, facts of publication, and page of the source.

This information is similar to but not exactly like that of the bibliographical entry; the form of presentation also differs in detail. The bibliographical entry would look like this:

Mencken, H.L.   The American Language.   4th ed.   New York: Alfred A. Knopf, 1936.

The footnote entry would look like this:

[3]H.L. Mencken, The American Language, 4th ed. (New York, 1936), p. 54.

TYPICAL FOOTNOTE ENTRIES (*First reference; these correspond to* Typical Bibliographical Entries, *page* 454.)

[1]Douglas S. Freeman, Lee's Lieutenants (New York, 1942), I, 53.

[2]Charles W. Ferguson, "A Sane Approach to Style," Saturday Review, September 26, 1959, p. 12.

[3]"A Vigorous Liberal--Joseph Grimmond," New York Times, October 13, 1959, p. 16.

[4]Carlton J.H. Hayes, Marshall W. Baldwin, and Charles W. Cole, History of Europe (New York, 1956), I, 15.

[5]Nathan Glazer, "The Immigrant Groups and American Culture," Yale Review, XLVIII (March, 1959), 383.

These models will be found adequate for most occasions. If an ampler treatment of footnotes is desired, consult *The MLA Style Sheet,* rev. ed. (New York, 1951), pp. 11–18; *PMLA,* LXVI (1951), 3–31; or the manuals published by various government departments.

e. After a footnote has referred to any source once, a number of abbreviations are permissible in subsequent references to the same source.

When two or more successive footnotes refer to the same place in the same work, it is not necessary to repeat the author and title in the second footnote; use the word *ibid.* (Latin *ibidem,* "in the same place") as a label. If the same work but not the same page is referred to, write: "*ibid.,* p. 231." Note that in modern practice *ibid.* and other Latin abbreviations used in footnoting are not italicized (or, in handwriting or typewriting, underlined); in traditional practice, however, these abbreviations are italicized. If *ibid.* begins the footnote, capitalize it.

If you are referring to a work for the second time but

references to other works have come between the first and the second reference, you may simply give the last name of the author followed by the page reference. Or you may give the last name of the author followed by *loc. cit.* (*loco citato*, "in the place cited"), if the reference is to the same page. If several intervening references occur, it is better to give the page reference again rather than *loc. cit.*

EXAMPLES (*Following footnotes on pages 448–49*)

    ⁴Mencken, p. 163.

    ⁵Douglas S. Freeman, <u>Lee's Lieutenants</u> (New York, 1942), I, 53.

    ⁶Mencken, <u>loc. cit.</u>

If there have been a great many references between the first and second citations of a work, it is better to give again a shortened form of the title.

f. Other established abbreviations and terms which may be used in footnotes are

cf., "compare."
ed., "editor" or "edition."
e.g. (*exempli gratia*), "for example."
et al. (*et alii*), "and others."
f. (after a number), "and the following page."
ff. (after a number), "and the following pages."
   (f. and ff. are frequently italicized.)
fig., "figure."
id. (*idem*), "the same."
i.e., "that is."
l., "line."
ll., "lines."
n., "note."
n.p. or n.p.n., "no page" or "no page number."

op. cit. (*opere citato*), "in the work cited." This abbreviation
is frequently used in referring to a work the second time,
when references to other works have come between the first
and second reference. You may simply give the name of the
author followed by *op. cit.* Thus footnotes 7, 8, 10, 11 (page
452) could be "Freeman, *op. cit.*, p. 392; Ferguson,*op. cit.*, p.
14; Hayes, Baldwin, and Cole, *op. cit.*, I, 18; Glazer, *op. cit.*,
p. 396." This abbreviation differs from *loc. cit.* in needing
to be followed by a page number, since it specifies only the
work, not the place.

pp., "pages."

passim, "here and there." This term is used after the title of a
book or article to indicate references in various places.

q.v., "which see."

sic, "thus." Sometimes inserted in a quotation [*sic*] to indicate
that an expression, an error, or a misspelling exactly repro-
duces the original. (See **MS4.1.**)

tr., "translator."

viz., "namely."

vol., "volume."

The section devoted to abbreviations in a good abridged
or unabridged dictionary will furnish other abbreviations.
Notice that some are conventionally italicized, others not.
In modern practice, however, a number of common abbreviations of Latin words (e.g., A.D., P.M., P.S., cf., etc.,
i.e., per cent, viz., vs.) are not italicized because familiarity
has added them to English stock. Again, in modern practice, some of the more familiar scholarly abbreviations (e.g.,
ibid., id., loc. cit., op. cit., q.v.) are not italicized.[1] (The
footnote citations in this text follow traditional practice in
italicizing these abbreviations.) Except in a formal, scholarly
piece of writing, these footnote abbreviations are not usually
numerous.

[1] See *The MLA Style Sheet*, rev. ed. (New York, 1951), p. 19. See
also MS7e.

TYPICAL FOOTNOTE ENTRIES (*Second reference*)

[7]Freeman, I, 75.

[8]Ferguson, p. 14.

[9]New York *Times*, p. 16. ⟵──────────── (Correct only if no other article from this newspaper was used.)

[10]Hayes, Baldwin, and Cole, I, 18.

[11]Glazer, p. 396.

[12]*Ibid.*, p. 397. ⟵──────────────── (Successive footnote to same source but another page.)

[13]*Ibid.* ⟵──────────────────── (Successive footnote to same source, same page.)

The modern ideal for footnotes is to make them as brief and concise as is consistent with their giving the necessary information. A long paper written by a student, showing proper footnote form, is reproduced on page 460 ff.

8. BIBLIOGRAPHY

In preparing bibliographical entries, the following points should be remembered:

1. Whereas footnotes come in the order dictated by the subject of your paper and often include commentary and discussion as well as references to sources, a bibliography refers only to sources and must be alphabetical. Even a long bibliography subdivided topically will list the items under each topic according to the alphabet.

2. The form should follow the pattern of complete references, naming author, title, edition (if other than the first), place of publication, publisher, date of publication, and number of volumes included in the work. In a very complete bibliography the number of pages in the preface and in the work proper are also added. Some manuals recommend including the name of the publisher only for books which have appeared within the last twenty years.

3. The author's surname must precede his initials and be separated from them with a comma. As you have seen, the bibliographical entry corresponding to the footnote entry on page 448 looks like this:

Mencken, H.L. The American Language. 4th ed. New York: Alfred A. Knopf, 1936.

When there is more than one author, the name of the first must be treated as above; for the others practice varies: the surname may come before the initials, or the initials first as in footnotes. Whichever form you choose, follow it consistently throughout the bibliography.

4. If the author is not known or is unacknowledged, the title alone is entered in its proper alphabetical position.

5. The titles of volumes and the names of periodicals are italicized (in handwriting or typewriting, underlined). (See *Typical Bibliographical Entries*, page 454.)

6. The title of a complete unit which forms part of a volume (for example, one of a collection of essays, or an article in a magazine) is put in quotation marks, followed by the name of the volume, the latter italicized. (See *Typical Bibliographical Entries*, page 454.)

If the source material on which the paper is based is highly variable in its reliability and accuracy, a short critical note after each item, giving the writer's estimate of the value of the work, may be desirable. A bibliography having such notes is called an *annotated* or *critical bibliography*.

ANNOTATED BIBLIOGRAPHY:

Billington, R.A. Western Expansion. 2nd ed. New York: The Macmillan Company, 1960. Noteworthy for its exceptionally full bibliographies; comprehensive and brisk.

Robbins, R.M. Our Landed Heritage: The Public Domain, 1776-1936. Lincoln, Neb.: University of Nebraska Press, 1962. This work offers solid coverage from the legislative standpoint.

Van Every, Dale. The Frontier People of America. 4 vols. New York: William Morrow and Company, 1961-64. Written for a popular audience rather than for a scholarly one.

Making correct footnotes and a bibliography is an exacting task, a real test of your accuracy. Every period, comma, parenthesis must be in the right place according to the pattern you are following; and you must follow your pattern with absolute consistency. You can avoid many errors in footnote and bibliography form, when following the pattern described in this chapter, by noticing that the two sorts of entries differ in three basic ways:

1. The bibliographical entry is broken into several sentence units—each terminated with a period. The footnote consists of one sentence unit terminated with a period. (This basic difference underlies difference in the use of commas, parentheses, and capitalization.)

2. The bibliographical entry, unlike the footnote, is intended to be alphabetized. Consequently, the author's name is inverted, and the first line of the entry begins at the margin while subsequent lines are indented. The footnote gives author's name in normal order and follows the opposite indentation pattern.

3. The bibliographical entry is intended to identify a work; the footnote is intended to identify a cited passage. Hence the fuller description of the volume in the bibliographical entry. Hence the greater precision of page references in the footnote.

TYPICAL BIBLIOGRAPHICAL ENTRIES:

Ferguson, Charles W. "A Sane Approach to Style." Saturday Review, September 26, 1959, pp. 12-14, 34-36.

Freeman, Douglas S. Lee's Lieutenants. 3 vols. New York. Charles Scribner's Sons, 1942.

Glazer, Nathan. "The Immigrant Groups and American Culture." Yale Review, XLVIII (March, 1959), 382-397.

Hayes, Carlton J.H., Marshall W. Baldwin, and Charles W. Cole. History of Europe. Rev. ed. 2 vols. New York: The Macmillan Company, 1956.

"A Vigorous Liberal--Joseph Grimmond." New York Times, October 13, 1959, p. 16.

9. *REPRESENTATION OF NUMBERS*

The following practices of treating numbers have found most general agreement.

a. Dates, street numbers, page, chapter, and division numbers are never spelled.

> On October 16, 1966, I came to New York.
> My address is 92 Haley Court.

1. In formal social correspondence, dates are regularly spelled out.

2. To designate the day of the month, June 1, April 2, September 3, July 4 are preferred to June 1st, April 2nd, September 3rd, July 4th.

3. Street names with numbers up to ten are usually spelled out.

> 33 Fifth Avenue   the Tenth Avenue district

Those with higher numbers usually use figures followed by *st, nd, rd,* or *th.* When house numbers are used with such street names, leave ample space between the house number and the street name.

> 164   128th Street

b. For any one composition or article, set a sensible limit (ten, one hundred, or one thousand) below which you will spell out all numbers and above which you will use figures.

One hundred is perhaps the figure most frequently used, but the frequency and size of the figures have a great deal to do with the choice. Follow your scheme consistently. It is permissible to write out in full any number that can be expressed in two words: *fifty thousand, one billion.*

1. Use a hyphen in compound numbers from twenty-one to ninety-nine.

fifty-six   two hundred (and) thirty

2. Use a hyphen between the numerator and denominator of a fraction unless either part is written with a hyphen.

six-sevenths   six sixty-sevenths

c. Avoid sentences which have in them some numbers spelled out and others written in figures.

UNDESIRABLE: A total of seventy-five items was chosen for consideration by the 260 judges.

UNAVOIDABLE: We found that the three pages contained 15,396 letters.

d. Never begin a sentence with a numeral.

Revise the sentence so that it begins with a word, or spell out the number if it is not too large.

FAULTY: 254 days were required for the journey.

REVISED: Two hundred and fifty-four days were required for the journey.

OR: The journey required 254 days.

e. If a great many numbers must be cited within a short space, express them in figures.

Of the 121 disputed words, 48 were nouns, 36 were verbs, 29 were adjectives, and 8 were adverbs.

The prices of the three articles were $8.32, $10.41, and $11.64 respectively.

f. Do not spell and record in figures the same number except in legal and commercial papers.

Observe the following business forms:

RIGHT: I enclose a check for eight dollars ($8.00).

RIGHT: It is hereby agreed that the minimum rate shall not apply

until five hundred (500) cubic feet have been purchased at the maximum rate.

g. Round numbers and those mentioned by way of illustration should be spelled out.

He ran about seventy-five yards.

The test is valid in ninety-nine cases out of a hundred.

10. ABBREVIATIONS

Formal writing permits very few abbreviations. Thus you should avoid them in your themes. Certain very common abbreviations are acceptable, but even these should be used with caution. For example, the abbreviations listed in **MS7f** are permissible in footnotes. Certain other abbreviations are permissible in one use but not in another.

RIGHT: I went to consult Dr. Klein.
WRONG: I went to see the Dr.

RIGHT: The train leaves at 9:15 P.M.
WRONG: I am leaving this P.M.

The abbreviations that are most generally permissible are the courtesy titles *Mr.*, *Mrs.*, *Messrs.*, *Rev.*, *Hon.*, when used with proper names; the abbreviations for academic degrees: *Ph.D.*, *M.A.*, *D.C.L.*, *LL.D.*; also A.D., B.C., A.M., P.M.

Avoid the use of the ampersand (&) in your themes; write *and*.

An increasing tendency in the United States today is to omit the period that formerly indicated the abbreviation. This is especially true in places where the period would be followed by another punctuation mark:

ESTABLISHED	NEWER
Dec. 5th, 6 A.M.	Dec 5th, 6 AM.
pencils, erasers, ink, etc.,	pencils, erasers, ink, etc,
Gadgets, Inc., Chicago.	Gadgets Inc, Chicago.

Names and other words made from initial letters or syllables now frequently omit the periods:

USA, NATO, OK, Springfield STC, BPOE.

Such omissions, however, are largely a matter of typographical style and had better be left to publishers. As a student, you need to demonstrate that you can use correctly the established conventions of abbreviation.

11. PROOFREADING

No theme should be handed in without having been subjected to at least one rereading. It is best not to reread the theme immediately after writing it. Let it grow cold; errors in spelling and punctuation will then catch your eye more easily; awkward repetitions and ambiguous sentences will stand out. Moreover, if you type your themes, your instructor will not be inclined to accept the plea of a typographical error as an excuse for faulty spelling.

A few of the most common correction signs are indicated below.

1. If you decide that a new paragraph should begin with a sentence which is now a part of some other paragraph, place the sign ¶ or *Par.* in the margin and also before the word with which the new paragraph is to begin. If a paragraph division is to be removed, write *No* ¶ or *No Par.* in the margin.

2. If you find it necessary to insert new material in the context, write it above the line where it belongs and indicate the point at which it is to be inserted by placing a caret (∧) below the line.

The train sped out of Los Angeles, and climbed swiftly up over the Rockies, the old Santa Fe Trail, ∧ and across the state of Kansas.

This scheme for inserted material is for not more than a line. For a greater amount of material to be inserted, put it on a separate page and mark it with the number of the page followed by the letter a. Then indicate the place of insertion on the original page, and at the bottom of the original write, "p. __a follows."

3. Cancel words by drawing single lines through them and placing the sign ℒ (delete) in the margin. *Do not use brackets or parentheses to indicate omissions.*

4. If your paper, after a rereading, requires alterations more violent than the foregoing instructions will take care of, you should rewrite it.

5. If you cannot make all of the necessary alterations in proofreading in your paper by using these correction symbols, you should rewrite it.

The sample research paper that follows
was written by Margaret T. Sorensen,
a student at the University of Minnesota.

Sentence Outline

Thesis Sentence: The downtown area of the city should be maintained as the city center and can be if the traffic problem is
solved and the special character of the area is developed.

I.   The downtown area should be maintained as the city center
     because it satisfies certain needs of the people and the
     city.

     A.   It offers a wide variety of goods, businesses, and
          entertainment facilities.

     B.   It contributes significantly to the financial sup-
          port of the whole city.

II. If the downtown area is to maintain its position as the
     city center, the traffic problem must be solved by im-
     proving street systems, parking, and public transportation.

     A.   Street systems can be improved by construction of
          new freeways or improvement of old ones, or by sol-
          ution of the problems of congestion, pedestrians,
          and slow movement.

     B.   Parking can be improved by experimenting with new
          kinds of parking facilities and by devising ways of
          parking closer to entrances of businesses.

     C.   Public transportation can be improved by making bus
          transportation better and by giving some government
          assistance to help cities develop better transporta-
          tion systems.

III. If the downtown area is to maintain its position as the
     city center, the special character of the area should be
     developed by promoting the activity of downtown, providing
     public gathering places, and encouraging variety in
     buildings.

Downtown Is Challenged

What will be the city center of the future--the downtown
area, traditionally the center, or the newer suburban "center"?
Downtown merchants and businessmen worry increasingly about this
question as more and more suburban shopping complexes spring up.
Obviously, these newer "centers" would not increase in number as
they do unless they met the needs of many people, providing a
source for such purchases as groceries, informal clothing, and
other common items. As an article in House and Garden points
out, however, the suburban center cannot satisfy all needs.
Many people choose the downtown area for certain characteristics
that it alone seems able to provide, such characteristics as
"variety, convenience, entertainment, and cultural facilities,
[as well as] the opportunities for social privacy. . . ."[1]
There seems no reason to believe, therefore, that the suburban
center will ever completely replace the downtown area as the city
center. As Hal Burton declares, "the suburban stores are here to
stay--but so are the stores downtown."[2] I shall try to show that

---

[1]"How to Bring Suburban Joys to Town," House and Garden,
CXXV (May, 1964), 168-69.

[2]Hal Burton, ed., The City Fights Back (New York, 1954),
p. 145.

the downtown area of the city should be maintained as the city center and can be if the traffic problem is solved and the special character of the area is developed.

The key to the attraction which downtown holds for people appears to be variety. A survey of the opinions of 700 out of a metropolitan population of 518,319 was made in 1952 in Columbus, Ohio, to determine where people preferred to shop-- in the suburbs or downtown. The conclusion was that they pre- ferred downtown shopping, the major reason given being that the downtown area offered a wider variety of goods. A secondary reason was that several errands could be accomplished at one time because of the number of different businesses within a relatively small compass.[3] Further, a wider choice of enter- tainment facilities is offered downtown.

The great variety of goods and facilities provided by the downtown area, then, would seem to be one strong reason why it should be maintained as the city center. Only a downtown area, centralized as it is, drawing upon people both from close in and from the suburbs, can support this variety. The suburban shop- ping area usually attracts only those people who live fairly close to it, a limited number, hence the improbability that it could ever support such variety. Statistics show that unless the population of a metropolitan area is at least 750,000, the

---

[3]C.T. Jonassen, Downtown Versus Suburban Shopping (Columbus, 1953), p. 58.

suburban center is not very successful.[4]

Another reason the downtown area is important and should be maintained is that it contributes ten to twenty-five percent of the real-estate tax revenues to the city.[5] If the downtown area did not provide this tax money, the burden would fall directly on the citizens.[6] It therefore seems evident that though providing variety and revenue to the city are not the only reasons for maintaining the downtown area in its present role, these two reasons alone are sufficiently important to call for action by the citizens.

Unless two considerable problems are solved, however, there is little likelihood that the downtown area can maintain its position as the city center. The handling of traffic must be improved and citizens must capitalize on the special character of the downtown area. Since most people depend on some kind of transportation to get downtown, the present handling of traffic is quite inadequate. A municipal planning expert quite vividly describes the importance of transportation to the city when he says:

> A city . . . is like a human being. The center of
> the city is its heart. The streets and the transport-

---

[4]Burton, p. 149.

[5]Charles T. McGavin, "The Parking Problem," in Community Planning, ed. Herbert L. Marx, Jr. (New York, 1956), p. 48.

[6]Ibid.

ation systems are its arteries. If these arteries clog
up, you have heart trouble. . . .[7]

In addition to making it easier for people to get downtown
and back again, attempts must be made to take full advantage of
the special character of the downtown center, its compactness
and variety, to get the most out of it. Although people, when
deciding where to shop, are influenced more by concrete problems
such as transportation, they are also influenced by the character
of a shopping area. If the downtown did not have its own
attractions not found in the suburban center, it would probably
not have survived as long as it has. Jane Jacobs expresses this
very well when she says that the city center attracts by creating
an atmosphere of "gaiety, wonder, and . . . cheerful hurly-burly."[8]
The suburban center is flatly practical by comparison.

The first thing necessary, then, is to provide a street
system that will allow fast access to the downtown area and away
from it again. Streets leading in, and those within the area itself, are often too congested at present, over-difficult to move
in. The suburban shopping centers grow in striking proportion
to the number of cars appearing on the streets. It has been estimated that if the present rate of increase of automobile ownership continues, there will be approximately ninety million pri-

---

[7]Burton, p. 24.

[8]Jane Jacobs, "Downtown Is For People," in The Exploding
Metropolis, ed. by editors of Fortune (New York, 1958), p. 158.

vate autos by 1982.[9] This is probably why ideas advanced for improved street systems are largely directed toward private transportation rather than public; however, improvements made for the one type of transportation will also benefit the other.

The most frequently advanced suggestion for increasing the efficiency of the private vehicle has been to build new freeways or to improve older ones. David Carlson speaks of the automated freeway, a system of electric signaling to control the speed of and spacing between cars, which is able to take one safely to the downtown area at speeds of up to 150 miles an hour.[10] He points out that this type of freeway would be exceedingly expensive, however.[11] Use of reversible lanes to accomodate rush-hour traffic is another automated method for improving freeways. This method has worked successfully on a section of Chicago's Outer Drive, an eight-lane highway, where there are movable partitions that can be raised or lowered according to the traffic need.[12] If freeways in general are the best answer to the traffic problem, architects and city planners believe strongly that they should be constructed in such a way that they would fit

---

[9]Burton, p. 62.

[10]David B. Carlson, "Can Transportation Systems Put Our Cities Back Together Again?" Architectural Forum, CXIX (October, 1963), 64.

[11]Ibid.

[12]Burton, p. 88.

well into the over-all appearance of the city, perhaps passing through buildings, and having shops, restaurants, and parking garages as a part of their structure.[13]

Once the driver of the private vehicle is downtown, he faces the problems of congestion, pedestrians, and slow movement; but proposals have been made to solve these problems, also. Probably the most exciting proposal is to build up into space, in layers, to separate automobiles from the pedestrians and from other slow movement. A plan of building into space, consisting of six layers and stretching out the length of the transportation network, has been suggested for Dallas, Texas. The first layer would be for busses and trucks; the second, for self-parking; the third, for autos and shuttle busses; the fourth and the fifth, for pedestrians; and the sixth, for recreation.[14] This plan has the advantage of making economical use of expensive downtown real estate.

Another proposal is to ban curbside parking. If there were no curbside parking, traffic would not be slowed up waiting for a car parking; also, one, and possibly two, additional lanes of traffic would be made available. Philadelphia banned curbside parking downtown shortly before the busy season of Christmas in

[13]Donald Canty, "The Fight to Tame the Urban Freeway Takes a Positive New Turn," Architectural Forum, CXIX (October, 1963), 70.

[14]"Downtown Snarl," Architectural Forum, CXIX (October, 1963), 79.

1952 as an experiment to see if this would alleviate some traffic congestion. This plan worked so well that the ban was made permanent.[15]

Some other proposals for making traffic move more smoothly are to forbid private cars from stopping to pick up or drop off passengers, to synchronize traffic lights during the rush hours, to eliminate truck traffic during rush hours, and to have busses load and unload at the middle of blocks rather than at intersections.[16]

Possibly a greater deterrent to downtown shopping than poor street systems is the parking problem. As Hal Burton has observed, freeways can help the downtown area because they can get the drivers into the downtown area very quickly. But, if there is no place to park when the driver reaches the area, the freeways have not really helped.[17] Then, again, if the driver is able to find a parking place, it often may either be too far away from the stores or, if it is close enough to the stores, too expensive.

These parking problems have been considered by the merchants of the downtown area, and the solutions proposed vary. The underground garage has been used in several cities such as Los

---

[15]Sam Stravinsky, "Mass Transportation," in Community Planning, pp. 34-35.

[16]Burton, p. 88.

[17]Ibid., p. 77.

Angeles, San Francisco, and Pittsburgh, where the lawns of downtown parks provide camouflaged roofs.[18] Midtown Plaza in Rochester, New York, erected a three-story underground garage that
provides 2,000 parking spaces.[19] Another proposal, fringe parking, requires that the driver park in lots outside the downtown
area and then take some kind of public transportation to downtown. City planner Edmund Bacon, of Philadelphia, intends to use
this method of parking, since he believes the "inner city" is for
pedestrians.[20]

Since people do not care to walk "more than 750 feet from
their cars for any purpose,"[21] merchants have devised plans for
allowing the shopper to park as close to entrances as possible.
In Philadelphia, a garage and store were combined; the two bottom floors are for shopping, and the top floor is for parking.
Both the customers and the merchants have benefited from this
plan.[22] In Los Angeles, the I. Magnin Co. successfully used a
two-entrance plan. This plan calls for attractive front and
rear entrances, but parking is provided in the rear, since the

---

[18]Ibid., p. 63.

[19]Victor Gruen, "Who Is to Save Our Cities?" Harvard Business Review, XLI (May, 1963), 112.

[20]"Modern Living," Time, LXXXIV (November 6, 1964), 70.

[21]McGavin, p. 49.

[22]Ibid., p. 51

land is unusable for any other purpose.[23] In Allentown, Penn

sylvania, the "park and shop" plan has resulted in better busi-

ness, too.[24] When business began decreasing considerably, down-

town merchants decided that the decrease was due to the parking

problem and formed a corporation to buy certain lots near their

stores. When a driver parks in one of these lots, he pays

twenty-five cents for two hours and is given a ticket that is

validated by a corporation merchant when the customer makes a

purchase of one dollar or more. For each additional member

store the driver shops in, his ticket is validated for two ad-

ditional hours of parking.[25] These three parking plans are rela-

tively cheap and convenient for the customers (and are profitable

for the merchants, since their business increases); hence they

are quite desirable. No matter which parking plan is decided

upon by merchants or by the city, additional parking must be

provided downtown.

Many studies have been made, and some of the resulting ideas

put into practice, to aid the driver of the private car. The

viewpoint has been expressed that "the automobile . . . can do

the job [transportation] alone if the nation will get on with the

completion of its highway system."[26] However, a highway system

---

[23]Ibid., p. 52.

[24]Burton, p. 199.

[25]Ibid.

[26]Carlson, p. 65.

is never "complete," since it "often generates enough new traffic to choke itself. . . ." Moreover, if people who use public
transportation were to start using private cars, congestion as it
is now would seem simple compared to then.[27]

Nevertheless, public transporation has been declining.
Passengers find it inconvenient to use--the service is not frequent enough and does not provide comfortable seating, particularly during the morning and the evening rush hours. In New
York, travel by subway is very inconvenient. Some people who
are due at work at 9:30 a.m. must leave home at 7:30 in order to
secure a place to sit. Even so, they may have a seat only until
they reach the express stop, where they will have to struggle
with the waiting crowd to have a seat for the rest of their
trip.[28] Some of this inconvenience could be eliminated if the
transit companies could afford more equipment. Their financial
burdens, however, do not allow for any extra spending. In addition to regular business taxes, transit companies are still required to pay the street-use tax introduced in the latter part of
the nineteenth century to pay for street repairs caused by
tracks. Now, however, few cities have tracks in the streets,
and the general maintenance of the streets is paid for from oil
and gas taxes from all street users; consequently, taxing the

---

[27]Ibid.

[28]Richard J. Whalen, "A City Destroying Itself," Fortune,
LXX (September, 1964), 241.

transit companies for this street-use tax seems unnecessary and unfair.[29] Then, too, sixty percent of every dollar transit companies take in must be paid out in wages. When wages and expenses increase at the same time, transit companies naturally want to increase fares immediately. Most state and local laws, however, do not permit an increase in fares at that time; so great a deficit accumulates by the time companies can raise the fares that any improvements planned have to be forgotten.[30]

The financial burdens of public transit companies utilizing busses, rather than subways or trains, should be stressed because it appears that in the future busses will be the main source of public transportation. Mass transportation has generally declined over the past ten years, with rail rapid transit declining the most.[31] Approximately seventy-five percent of all mass transit passengers are now carried by busses.[32] It is believed that except in cities where there are over 100,000 persons going in or out of the downtown area in the rush hour (New York, Chicago, Philadelphia, and Boston), "express bus service on exclusive rights of way" would be the best way of transporting

---

[29]Chamber of Commerce of the United States, Transit's Crisis . . . Businessman's Concern (Washington, 1953), p. 9.

[30]Ibid., p. 8.

[31]Carlson, p. 65.

[32]Ibid.

people to the downtown area.[33] A city can use for busses exclusively those streets not presently used to capacity and can thereby avoid the high cost of rail construction.[34]

Mention has been made earlier that, if cars were ever to completely replace busses, downtown congestion would be paralyzing. This is one good reason, then, why bus transportation is necessary and desirable. Another is that busses can carry more passengers than a car and thus help the downtown area in two ways--more business for the merchants and fewer parking facilities needed by the city. A third reason is that busses can be very convenient. Shoppers like to get near the downtown stores, and busses can provide this service. Midtown Plaza in Rochester, New York, has bus stops arranged close to all the Plaza entrances.[35]

Since public transportation is not only desirable but also necessary for the preservation of the downtown area, it seems reasonable that some government assistance should be given to aid cities in developing the necessary systems. Possibly the Transit Aid Bill passed by Congress in July of this year is a beginning.[36] This bill provides $375 million in grants to cities

---

[33]Ibid.

[34]Ibid.

[35]Gruen, p. 113.

[36]"Transit Aid Bill Passed by Congress," Minneapolis Star, July 1, 1964, n.p.n.

and states over the next three years to enable them to buy land, parking facilities, busses, rail cars, signal equipment, stations, and terminals.

Convenient transportation, public and private, will encourage people to use the downtown. However, if the downtown area is not attractive and does not have a pleasant atmosphere, people might still consider using the suburban shopping center. The suburban center is on less expensive land than that in the downtown area; consequently, builders of many centers can afford to build their centers as parts of a beautiful landscape. Although the downtown area cannot be planned in this manner, it has a special character of its own that, when properly developed, can make it more exciting than any suburban shopping center.

The character of the city is activity, crowds, and movement. Many people comment that they do not care to go downtown because it is too busy; it is this very busyness within a compact area, however, that makes the downtown area appealing and exciting to most city dwellers. The difference between a boring and an enjoyable city center is that the enjoyable one offers many activities, such as "festivals and public ceremonies."[37] Jane Jacobs stresses the idea that the street can be used as a magnet to attract people when it is filled with activity. She advocates the placing of benches, sun umbrellas, or anything else

_____

[37]Jacobs, p. 167.

in front of stores to encourage shoppers to linger.[38] Emphasizing this same idea of street activity, Victor Gruen suggests the use of outdoor cafés, bandstands, street concerts, dances, or exhibits--anything to promote gaiety and variety.[39]

Another effective way to promote activity is to provide spaces in the downtown area that will serve as public gathering places; such spaces have been provided in some cities and probably will appear in more cities in the future. Midtown Plaza in Rochester, New York, has one square block free from traffic so that people can gather for political rallies, art exhibits, and other activities. This square can be used all year, since it is covered, skylighted, air-conditioned, and heated.[40] Kalamazoo, Michigan, provides its people with a mall free from traffic and supplied with flower beds, playground equipment, and benches. This mall serves the dual purpose of being pleasant for the people and, by encouraging people to linger, profitable for the merchants along it.[41]

Providing variety in buildings is another way the downtown area can add to its character and make it attractive to the people. Redevelopment of downtown areas at present seems to mean

---

[38]Ibid., p. 162.

[39]Ibid.

[40]Gruen, p. 113.

[41]"Can Cities Save Downtown Areas?" U.S. News & World Report, XLVII (November 16, 1959), 74.

that all the old buildings will be torn down and replaced with new ones. However, old buildings help give the downtown character. Since old buildings are preferred to stark new ones by some people, the downtown area should not be torn down and then rebuilt "to satisfy the pages of architectural magazines" but to satisfy the needs of the people.[42] Jane Jacobs thinks, for example, that a Buddhist temple in San Francisco is "crazy, eccentric, and lovable . . . ," and that "a look at this temple is better than a trip to a psychologist."[43] She adds that certain stores--art stores, tailor shops, antique stores--are appropriate in older buildings and lend a certain personality to the city.[44]

In spite of competition from suburban centers, then, if the downtown area is able to work out a solution to the traffic problem and is able to develop its special character, it should be able to maintain its position as the center of the city.

---

[42]Philip M. Klutznick, "Five Challenges to Our Cities," Architectural Forum, CXX (May, 1964), 107.

[43]Jacobs, p. [12] of photo inserts.

[44]Ibid., p. 163.

BIBLIOGRAPHY

Burton, Hal, ed. The City Fights Back. New York: Citadel
    Press, 1954.

"Can Cities Save Downtown Areas?" U.S. News & World Report, XLVII
    (November 16, 1959), 74-77.

Canty, Donald. "The Fight to Tame the Urban Freeway Takes a
    Positive New Turn." Architectural Forum, CXIX (October,
    1963), 69-73.

Carlson, David B. "Can Transportation Systems Put Our Cities
    Back Together Again?" Architectural Forum, CXIX (October,
    1963), 63-67.

Chamber of Commerce of the United States. Transit's Crisis . . .
    Businessman's Concern. Washington, D.C., 1953.

"Downtown Areas." In Community Planning. Ed. Herbert L. Marx,
    Jr. New York: The H.W. Wilson Company, 1956. Pp. 41-46.

"Downtown Snarl." Architectural Forum, CXIX (October, 1963),
    78-83.

Gruen, Victor. "Who Is To Save Our Cities?" Harvard Business
    Review, XLI (May, 1963), 107-115.

"How to Bring Suburban Joys to Town." House and Garden, CXXV (May,
    1964), 168-69.

Jacobs, Jane. "Downtown Is For People." In The Exploding Metro-
    polis. Editors of Fortune. New York: Doubleday & Company,
    Inc., 1958. Pp. 157-184.

Jonassen, C.T. Downtown Versus Suburban Shopping. Columbus:
    The Ohio State University Press, 1953.

Klutznick, Philip M. "Five Challenges to Our Cities." Archi-
    tectural Forum, CXX (May, 1964), 106-108.

McGavin, Charles T. "The Parking Problem." In Community Plan-
    ning. Ed. Herbert L. Marx, Jr. New York: The H.W. Wilson
    Company, 1956. Pp. 46-53.

"Modern Living." Time, LXXXIV (November 6, 1964), 60-75.

Stavinsky, Sam. "Mass Transportation." In Community Planning.
    Ed. Herbert L. Marx, Jr. New York: The H.W. Wilson Company,
    1956. Pp. 34-40.

"Transit Aid Bill Passed by Congress." Minneapolis _Star_, July 1, 1964, n.p.n.

Whalen, Richard J. "A City Destroying Itself." _Fortune_, LXX (September, 1964), 239-244.

APPENDIXES

Appendix I

DIAGRAMING

A useful method of clarifying the relationships of the various elements of a sentence to each other is to *diagram* the sentence. Especially when sentences are so long and involved that it is difficult to analyze them in the abstract, a diagram can be of immense help.

In one form of diagraming now widely practiced it is recognized that every complete clause or simple sentence (S) is composed of two parts: a subject part and a predicate part. In the subject part a noun (N) or noun equivalent (NEq) is always present (except in imperative sentences, where it is implicit), sometimes alone, sometimes with modifiers. In the predicate part a simple verb (V) or a phrasal verb (PV) is always present, with or without complements and modifiers.

Any N or NEq *with or without* modifiers is called a *noun-phrase* (NP); and NP's function not only as the subject part of the S, but as complements in the predicate part.

Any V or PV *with or without* modifiers and complements is called a *verb phrase* (VP); VP's function in the predicate part of the S. (Note that *phrase*, as used here in NP and VP, may refer to a single word.)

There are several methods of diagraming. The traditional one involves placing each word of the sentence being diagramed along a horizontal, vertical, or diagonal line, depending on its relation to the other words. Another method is to place each word in a box, again depending on its relation to the other words; this method results in a set of boxes, each enclosed in another box, except the last, which encloses the entire sentence. The method of diagraming we shall use here is made in the form of lines branching like the limbs of trees. Because on paper or on a blackboard it is easier to draw downwards, these "trees" are usually inverted. The first branching is always from S to NP and VP; further branchings indicate as many levels of structural relationship as the sentence to be diagramed requires. A point at which branching occurs is called a *node*.

a. The simplest tree diagrams the two-word sentence composed of N and V—for example, Birds fly.

①

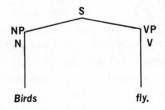

Birds   fly.

The words of the sentence are written out in their normal order, one below each final branch; their part of speech or grammatical construction is labeled at the node above.

The NEq's are diagramed like the N. They are pronoun (Prn), verbal noun (VN), infinitive (Inf), and noun clause (NCl). Diagram 2 shows the one-word NEq's; diagrams 3

②

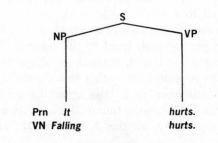

Prn   *It*   hurts.
VN *Falling*   hurts.

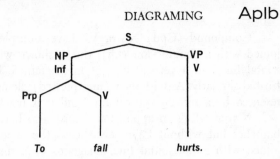

and 4 show the multi-word NEq's. Note that each additional word requires an additional branch and that each additional relationship requires one more level of branching.

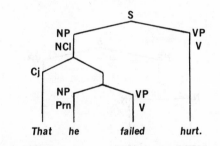

b. Closely joined pairs or groups of the same part of speech require multiple branching.

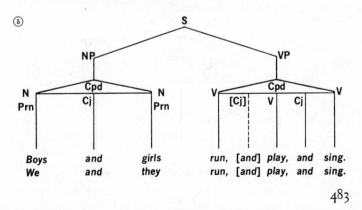

1. Compound (Cpd) N's or V's have multiple branches joined with a conjunction (Cj); this is shown with a horizontal line and a vertical line, as in diagram 5. NEq's are treated similarly. Any implicit (unexpressed) element is represented by a broken vertical line, and it is bracketed.

2. N's or NEq's in apposition (App) also have multiple branches but without Cj's; nevertheless the appositives are joined with a horizontal line. Diagrams 6, 7, and 8 show increasing degrees of complexity in the App's.

A similar situation develops for the object complement; see the method of diagraming this in **ApIe.6,** below.

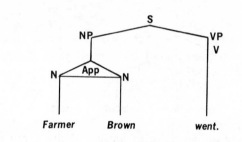

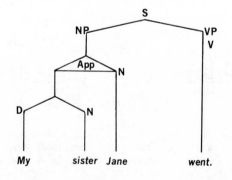

⑧

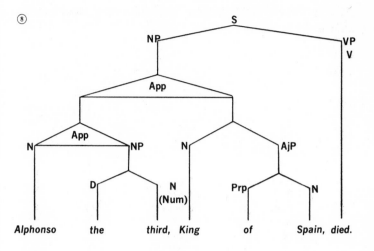

Alphonso the third, King of Spain, died.

EXERCISE I

Diagram the following, making trees and labeling them as in the examples just given:

1. He disagrees.
2. Schwartz the plumber came.
3. Worrying helps.
4. Washington, father of his country, spoke.
5. To discuss clarifies.
6. Laughing or joking amuses and refreshes.
7. That he answered counts.

c. When the NP contains an N and one or more modifiers, the tree is branched to show their relationship.

1. One-word modifiers of an N (or some NEq's) include the following:

Pre-Determiner (PreD)   Adjective (Aj) (one or more)
Determiner (D)   Participle (Ppl)
Numeral (Num)   Attributive (Att)

485

Any of these will fit diagram 9. (Multi-word modifiers are shown under **ApId** below.)

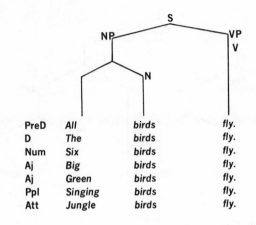

PreD	*All*	*birds*	*fly.*
D	*The*	*birds*	*fly.*
Num	*Six*	*birds*	*fly.*
Aj	*Big*	*birds*	*fly.*
Aj	*Green*	*birds*	*fly.*
Ppl	*Singing*	*birds*	*fly.*
Att	*Jungle*	*birds*	*fly.*

2. When the N has two or more modifiers, English word-order requires that they follow the sequence as shown. That is, a PreD must precede all others, a D must precede all except a PreD, and so on. (One cannot say *Six the birds fly, Jungle singing birds big fly,* etc.) An entire series of these modifiers modifying one N is diagramed in 10. Those few English Aj's which may follow their N are diagramed as in 11.

If two or more Aj's modify a N, word-order also requires that they follow the sequence of size, shape, quality, material. (One cannot say *a wooden yellow crooked big house;* one must say *a big crooked yellow wooden house.*)

3. When a modifier of the N is itself modified, its branch must be further divided. In diagram 12 the Aj is modified by an intensifier (Int).

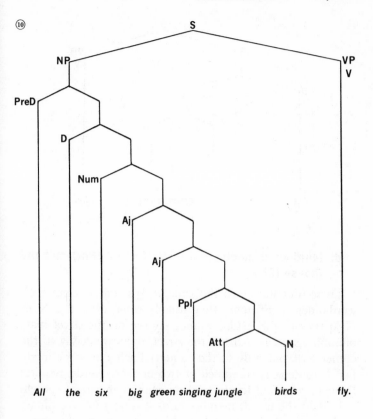

(10)

All the six big green singing jungle birds fly.

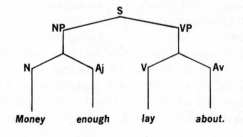

(11)

Money enough lay about.

⑫

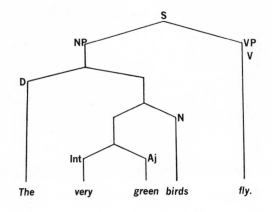

The	very	green	birds		fly.

d. Multi-word modifiers are the Phrase (Phr) and the Clause (Cl).

These function much the same as Aj's and Av's but their word-order is different: they usually come after the N or NEq they modify. (One cannot say *the on the street man;* one must say *the man on the street;* one cannot say *to the corner walk* but *walk to the corner.*) Each Phr or Cl modifier, because it is composed of two or more words, requires branching beyond the level of its equivalent part of speech.

1. If *in the woods* modifies *birds* it is an adjective phrase (AjP); if *in summer* modifies *blue* it is an adverb phrase (AvP); each is composed of a preposition (Prp) and its object (usually N or Prn), with or without modifiers. The whole Phr *blue in summer* modifies *birds,* hence is an AjP. An S containing both modifiers is diagramed in 13.

Note that these same phrases might be made to modify the V, but this would alter the meaning and structure of the sentence, hence also of the diagram, as in 14. (Note also that *in the woods* is equivalent first to an Aj when modifying a N, then to an Av when modifying a V.)

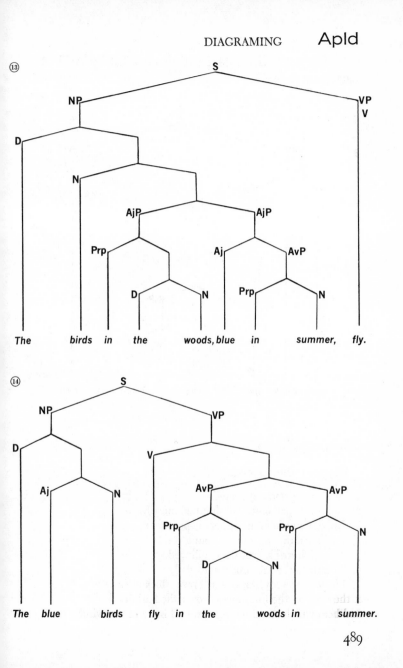

(13)

S

NP — VP / V

D — N

AjP — AjP

Prp — D — N

Aj — AvP

Prp — N

The   birds   in   the   woods, blue   in   summer,   fly.

(14)

S

NP — VP

D

Aj — N

V

AvP — AvP

Prp — D — N

Prp — N

The   blue   birds   fly   in   the   woods in   summer.

489

2. When NP is composed of N modified by AjCl, it is diagramed as in 15.

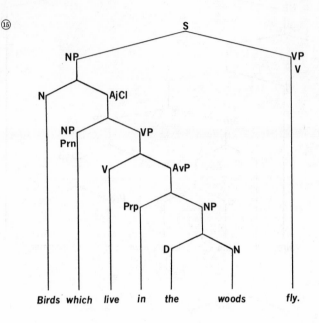

EXERCISE II

Diagram the following:

1. A dear old lady appeared.
2. All the eager children shouted merrily.
3. Broken windows and doors gaped open.
4. Every candidate, old or young, orated.
5. Twelve horribly wet days followed.
6. The distant rumbling comes daily.
7. Patriots aplenty, loyal and brave, flocked in.
8. Houses on the hill look out over the harbor.
9. Trees which stand on high ground bend in the wind.

e. Phrasal Verbs, Direct Objects, Indirect Objects, and Complements

So far, the VP has been seen only in terms of single-word V, but it can, of course, have multi-word V, also called *phrasal verbs* (PV); further, V can have complements (N, NEq, NPhr, NCl) and other following words or word-groups.

Note that the infinitive without *to* (Inf) is treated like any other V, but with *to* it is treated as a phrase (InfP).

1. The multi-word VP may be entirely verbal, in which case it is normally composed of a V, which chiefly carries the meaning, preceded by auxiliary verbs (Aux) and/or modals (Mod) that chiefly carry the syntax. The diagrams show the following PV's:

$$16, \text{ Aux } + \text{ Ppl}$$
$$17, \text{ Mod } + \text{ Inf}$$
$$18, \text{ Aux } + \text{ Ppl } + \text{ InfP}$$
$$19, \text{ Mod } + \text{ Aux } + \text{ AuxPpl } + \text{ VPpl}$$

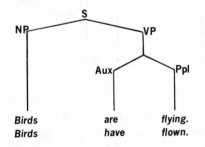

Note that word-order requires the sequence Mod, Aux, V. (One cannot say *flying have should been*.)

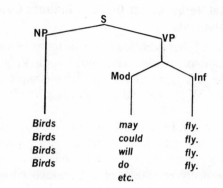

(17)

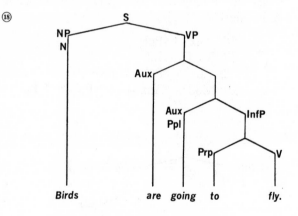

(18)

2. The VP may be composed of V and one or more modifiers (Av, AvP, or AvCl). The simplest form of this is when VP is composed of V + Av, as in diagram 20; but the contrary word-order is also possible, as in diagram 21. When the Av, still modifying the V, comes at the beginning of the S, the diagram must preserve the actual word-order by sending a branch from VP across the NP line, as

Aple

⑲

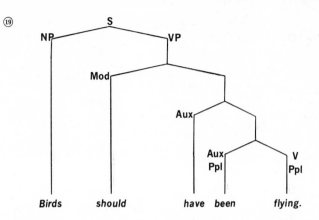

Birds should have been flying.

⑳

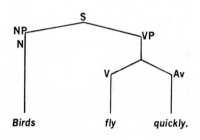

Birds fly quickly.

㉑

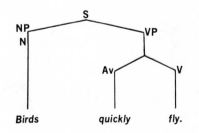

Birds quickly fly.

㉒

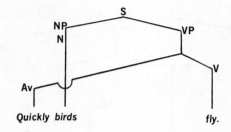

Quickly birds   fly.

㉓

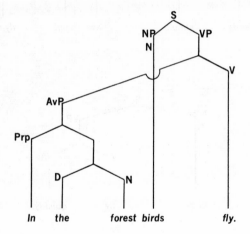

In   the   forest birds   fly.

㉔

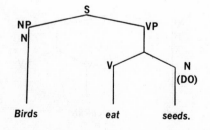

Birds   eat   seeds.

in diagram 22. Diagram 14 illustrated AvP modifiers following the V; when one comes at the beginning of a S, a branch from VP must also cross over the NP line, as in diagram 23.

3. A V taking a one-word direct object (DO) is diagramed as in 24.

In S's where DO comes before the subject part, its branch must cross over the NP line to preserve word-order, as in diagram 25.

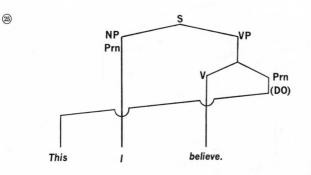

When the DO is a Phr, it is diagramed as in 26.

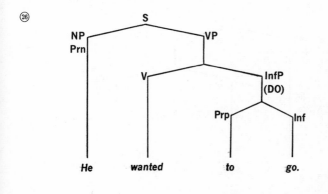

495

When the DO is a Cl, it is diagramed as in 27, 28, and 29. In 27, note that *what, whatever, whom, whomever,* and such words are the objects in their own Cl; hence a crossing-over branch must be put into the diagram.

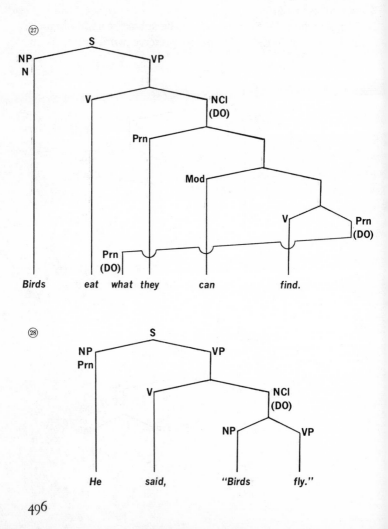

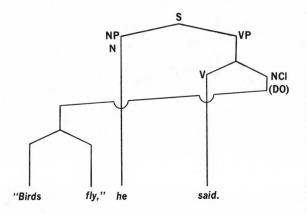

(29)

"Birds   fly," he   said.

A Cl of direct discourse is often the DO; 28 and 29 show this in both possible word-orders.

4. A S in which V takes indirect object (IO) as well as DO is diagramed as in 30.

Note that the periphrastic equivalent of this one-word IO, the AvP *to the birds*, is diagramed like any other AvP (as in 31).

(30)

We   give the   birds   seeds.

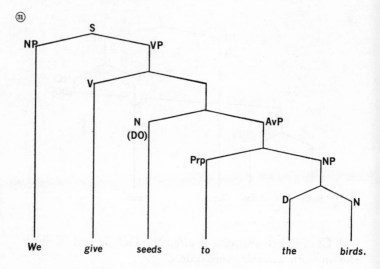

When the IO is a Cl it is diagramed as in 32.

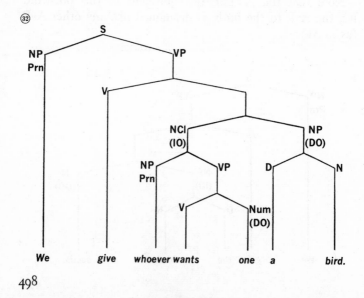

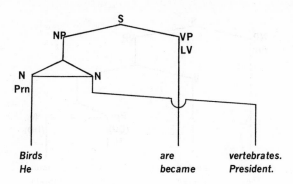

5. When the V has a complement (Cmp) which is a N or NEq meaning the same as the subject, the S is diagramed as in 33.

An Aj Cmp modifying the subject N is diagramed with a similar tree, though the last label is different, as in 34.

Because such a N or Aj refers to the NP but is placed after the VP, it is often called a *predicate* N or Aj. The cross-over lines in diagrams 33 and 34, however, indicate its true relationship.

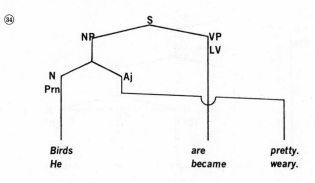

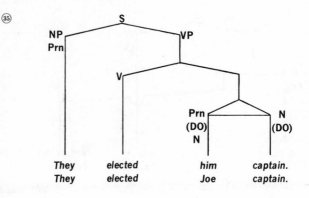

6. A S in which V has a DO and an object Cmp both referring to the same person or thing is diagramed as in 35, 36, and 37. In these, as in **ApIb.1,** above, the two words concerned are joined with a horizontal line. When they are joined by a Cj or CjP, this construction is treated as before, being indicated with a vertical line from the horizontal one.

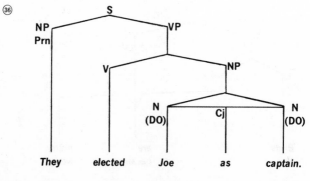

③⑦

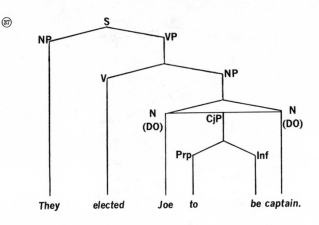

```
                        S
      NP                            VP
       |                    V              NP
       |                    |
                          N              CjP              N
                         (DO)                            (DO)
                                   Prp        Inf

     They      elected      Joe      to      be captain.
```

EXERCISE III

Diagram the following:

1. He is going to donate a million.
2. Jets could land safely.
3. We longed to go immediately to the mountains.
4. The cheerful old man should have been easily pleased.
5. These things alone are of true value.
6. Whatever you want you can buy.
7. This family eats all kinds of meat.
8. "I appoint you permanent secretary," she insisted.
9. To give us what we need and deserve would be simple justice.
10. Apes are primates in the table of classification.

f. Some special situations require more complex diagrams, but in these situations the same principles are followed to preserve word-order and show structural relationships.

1. Interrogative sentences with inverted V and Subj require both branches to cross over, as in diagrams 38 and 39.

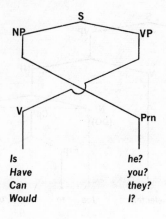

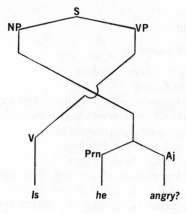

Interrogative S's beginning with the particle *Do* are diagramed as in 40.

Interrogative S's beginning with *Who, What, Which,* and a one-word verb are diagramed like declarative S's. (Example: "Who killed the bird?")

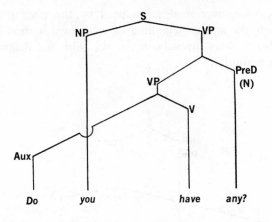

Interrogative S's beginning with When, Where, Why require inversion of V and Subj, and also modify V, hence require complex crossing-over, as in diagram 41.

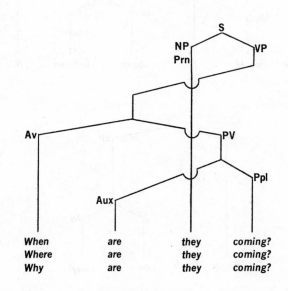

2. Crossing-over is also produced by the placing of an emphatic Av at the beginning of a S, since it modifies V and also requires inversion of V and Subj. See diagram 42 for an example.

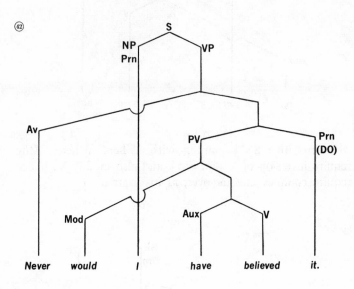

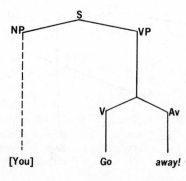

3. Imperative sentences are diagramed with the implicit subject in brackets and attached to the NP node with a dashed vertical line. A simple example is diagram 43. More complex ones would develop only the VP.

4. In compound sentences (CpdS), each clause is diagramed as a S and joined to the other (or others) by a horizontal line. The Cj is at the bottom of a vertical line descending from this, as in diagram 44.

(44)

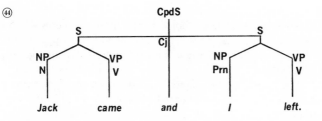

Sentences more complex than these are diagramed as the combinations of features diagramed above.

EXERCISE IV

Diagram the following:

1. Has the truck come?
2. Why did he do it?
3. Faithfully have we followed you!
4. Who is going to perform on this stage tonight?
5. Go and catch a falling star.
6. Gather your belongings and get out!
7. Surely we are not being shadowed?

EXERCISE V

Diagram the following:

1. John bought a coat.
2. John and Mary bought a cloth coat and a straw hat.
3. Mr. Jones, the banker, found a badly battered hat in the garden.
4. Finding the hat was clearly an accident.
5. The hat that was found belonged to my older brother.
6. Mr. Jones decided to return the hat after he discovered its owner.
7. Many thousands of acres are devoted to the production of fruit.
8. To those who seek a home in the industrial centers or in the rural communities, Jackson County offers a rare opportunity.
9. The railroads and truck lines transport the fruits, grains, and vegetables.
10. The great cement plants manufacture a highly necessary product, and hundreds are afforded employment in this outstanding industry.
11. Plowing his way through the line, he gained six yards on the first play.
12. His parents said they would expect him in the evening.
13. The house in which I was born is no longer in a desirable part of the city, but we hate to sell it because we have lived in it for so many years.
14. His bright blue eyes sparkled as he greeted his guests with a smile.
15. The Joneses, by the way, did not accept your invitation.
16. After a short recess, the class resume their activities, and the teacher keeps them busy.
17. Will you buy me the book that I saw on the shelf yesterday?
18. He said that concrete is the best material for highways in countries where the temperature does not vary.
19. Many of us left before the performance was over.
20. The guests having departed, we went to the kitchen and washed the dishes.

Appendix II

BUSINESS LETTERS

Every business letter contains six parts:

        a. The heading
        b. The inside address
        c. The salutation
        d. The body of the letter
        e. The complimentary close
        f. The signature

a. The Heading

The heading contains two essentials, the writer's address and the date. The address is usually placed on two lines and the date below it.

The position of the heading depends on the letter style. In the specimen letter on page 513 (A) the heading, in block form, is at the right; in the letter on page 514 (B), it is flush with the left margin.

Most commercial correspondence, at least that from a firm to an individual, is written on letterhead stationery, illustrated on page 508. If there is no letterhead, the heading is typewritten in block form.

When printed letterhead stationery is used, the date may be blocked at the left margin, about one-half inch below the last printed line, or it may be placed toward the right, where the full heading would normally come:

AMERICAN HERITAGE PUBLISHING CO., INC.

551 FIFTH AVENUE · NEW YORK 17, NEW YORK

March 1, 19--

[THIS LETTERHEAD REPRODUCED WITH THE PERMISSION OF THE AMERICAN HERITAGE PUBLISHING CO., INC.]

Punctuation of the parts of the letter may be *open, mixed,* or *closed. Open* punctuation omits punctuation at the ends of lines in the heading, inside address, salutation, and complimentary close. Letter B on page 514 illustrates this; businessmen prefer it.

Mixed punctuation requires a colon after the salutation and a comma following the complimentary close.

To *close* punctuation, add commas and periods to the lines of the heading and inside address, as in Letter A, page 513. Every part of the letter is enclosed in punctuation marks.

Write the names of states, months, the words *Street* and *Avenue* in full.

b. The Inside Address

Each line of the inside address is blocked at the left margin of the letter.

Punctuation depends on the writer's taste but, once the system of punctuation is chosen, it must be consistent throughout the letter.

The usual position of the inside address is four spaces below the heading. In extremely formal correspondence it may be placed four lines below the typewritten signature, at the left margin.

In writing the inside address, follow the form used by the organization to which you are writing. If *Corporation* or *Company* is abbreviated on its stationery, you may also abbreviate it.

A title of respect should be used with the name of any person addressed in the letter. *Mr., Miss, Mrs.,* or *Messrs.* are appropriate for general use. Special titles such as *Dr.* or *Reverend* belong only to persons who have earned them in their professions.

c. The Salutation

Write the salutation two lines below the inside address, flush with the left margin of the body of the letter, regardless of letter style.

Dear Mr. Blank is the form used most commonly in business. *Sir* is archaic; *Dear Sir* is impersonal, but it may be used in writing to someone with whom you have had no previous correspondence. *Gentlemen* is the appropriate salutation in a letter to a firm, unless its management is made up entirely of women; then *Mesdames* is correct.

Except in *open* punctuation, a colon follows the salutation with a comma after the complimentary close.

d. The Body of the Letter

The three letters illustrated represent the letter styles most widely used in business: *Modified Block* with indented paragraphs; *Modified Block* with blocked paragraphs; *Block,* with all parts flush with the left margin.

The standard paragraph indention for general business use is five spaces.

Use single spacing with double spacing between paragraphs for letters of more than fifty words. Double space shorter letters in modified block style with indented paragraphs only for attractive placement on the page. Single spacing may be used with any letter style. Block style appears with increasing frequency in business correspondence.

Follow the rules of good writing in composing your business letter. Decide, before you begin to write, what the significant point is and what facts you must include to make that point. Phrase the facts in precise form, presenting them in concise sentences and short paragraphs. Use simple, clear English. Use a courteous tone in your letter, one that is considerate of the reader. Avoid clichés, negative words, and participial endings such as "Trusting that we may hear from you again, I remain."

When you have related the facts and made your point, close with a courteous complete sentence.

e. The Complimentary Close

The complimentary close expresses the writer's courtesy to the reader and terminates the letter smoothly. Some forms for the closing are

> Yours truly
> Very truly yours
> Yours very truly
> Sincerely yours
> Yours sincerely
> Cordially yours

Yours truly, a formal closing, goes with the salutation *Dear Sir* or *Gentlemen*. *Sincerely yours*, a less formal closing, would go with *Dear Mr. Blank*. The trend in American business correspondence is toward the less formal in both salutation and complimentary close.

Use *Respectfully yours* in a job application letter or in a letter addressed to a superior in position.

In a modified block letter, place the complimentary close two lines below the body of the letter, either aligned with the date or placed slightly to the right of center. See Letter A, page 513. In a block letter, place the complimentary close at the left margin (see Letter C, page 515).

Begin the complimentary close with a capital letter. Punctuate it so that it is consistent with the other parts of the letter.

f. The Signature

The typewritten signature is placed four lines below the complimentary close. This allows the sender enough space to write his signature in ink. The typewritten signature completes the letter and helps the reader to understand what may be an illegible handwritten name.

The position and form of the signature follow the letter style chosen, as illustrated in the specimen letters.

g. The Envelope

The envelope address conforms to the style of the inside address except that a three-line address is always double spaced. Use single spacing for addresses of four or more lines. The ZIP code follows the name of the state on the bottom line.

The general position of the envelope address is in the lower right quarter of the envelope. Begin it five spaces to the left of center horizontally and one line below center vertically on a standard business envelope (3½ in. x 6½ in.). Begin it ten spaces to the left of center on a legal size envelope (4 in. x 9⅜ in.). An envelope address is illustrated on page 516.

The return address is placed in the upper left corner. It duplicates the style of the printed letterhead. If it is not printed on the envelope, it is typewritten in block form.

A

Heading

593 Oakland Avenue,
Fort Wayne, Indiana 46808,
June 3, 19--.

Inside Address

Miller Publishing Company,
956 Bowdoin Street,
Springfield, Illinois 62707.

Salutation

Gentlemen:

Body

Since I am leaving Fort Wayne permanently and moving to Missouri, I should like to request that my copy of the Garden Magazine be sent, henceforth, to 619 Water Street, Joplin, Missouri 64801.

I should like, also, to take this opportunity of telling you how much I enjoyed Mr. Herbert L. Atkinson's article on growing dahlias, which appeared in the August number. I wonder if you would be so kind as to give me his address, since I would like to ask him about a few points which were not fully discussed in the article.

Complimentary Close

Very truly yours,

Signature

Andrew C. Johnson

Andrew C. Johnson.

Modified Block Style;
Indented Paragraphs;
Closed Punctuation

B

MILLER PUBLISHING COMPANY

Letterhead   956 BOWDOIN STREET · SPRINGFIELD, ILLINOIS 62707

Date   June 9, 19--

Inside Address   Mr. Andrew C. Johnson
                  619 Water Street
                  Joplin, Missouri 64801

Salutation   Dear Mr. Johnson

Thank you for notifying us so promptly of your change
of address. The November issue of the <u>Garden Magazine</u>
is off the press today, and it should reach you at
your new address in a day or so.

You will not be able to communicate with Mr. Atkinson
by mail for at least three months. He left last month
Body   for Guatemala, where he is to be engaged in gathering
specimens of plant life from the jungle. The last
mail, which was to reach his party at Belize, was sent
from the office ten days ago.

We do not know what his address will be after he returns to this country, but as he keeps in constant communication with us, any letter addressed to him in care
of this office will be certain to reach him.

Complimentary Close   Sincerely yours,

Signature   *Charles F. Stockton*

                                 Charles F. Stockton

Modified Block Style;
Blocked Paragraphs;
Open Punctuation

C

Heading
35 High Street
Cleveland, Ohio 44115
February 1, 19--

Inside Address
Mr. Andrew C. Johnson
619 Water Street
Joplin, Missouri 64801

Salutation
Dear Mr. Johnson:

Body

Your letter of October 20, 19--, concerning my article
in the Garden Magazine, has just been forwarded to me.

The questions you raise about the texture of the soil
are very interesting indeed, and I should like to talk
with you at length about them.

I am to lecture in Joplin before the Garden Club on
February 25. Could we arrange to meet for a visit
after the lecture?

I shall be at my present address for the next two
weeks. I am looking forward to hearing from you.

Complimentary Close
Sincerely yours,

Signature
Herbert L. Atkinson

Herbert L. Atkinson

Block Style;
Mixed Punctuation

35 High Street
Cleveland, Ohio 44115

Mr. Andrew C. Johnson

619 Water Street

Joplin, Missouri 64801

Return Address in Block Form; Business Size Envelope for Letter C

INDEX

INDEX

WHEN several page references follow an entry, and the references are of unequal importance, the most important references are indicated by boldface type. Exercises are located on pages which follow the abbreviation *ex*. An *n*. following a page reference indicates that the reference is to a footnote. An x following a page reference indicates that the subject referred to in the entry is exemplified on that page but not discussed.

INDEX

Adverbs, 203, 204x, 206, 233–4, 235, 252–3, 255, 288–9
agreement with verb, 147
choice of, 144–5, 166–7
classes of, 233
comparison of, 234, 252–3
confused with adjectives, 232, 337
conjunctive, 94–5, 236, 258; *ex.* 95–6
definitions of, 203, 206, 255
in imperative sentences, 234
-ly ending in, 234
of degree as intensifiers, 207, 233–4
position of, 110–16, 253–4
prepositional, 235
punctuation of introductory, 288–9
single-word modifiers, 114–16
use of, after intransitive verb, 231–2
weak qualifying, 166–7
with two forms, 234
affect, effect, 136
Affix, 205–6 (*see also* Prefixes and suffixes)
Afterthought, introduced by dash, 300
aggravate, to mean *vex,* 339
agree in/on/to/with, 153
Agreement, 107–10, 146–8, 256 (*see also* Consistency, Shift)
defined, 256
in gender, 208
in tense, 248–9; *ex.* 250–1
logical, between words, 146–8
of appositive pronoun with accompanying noun, 244
of demonstrative adjectives *this* and *that,* 352
of pronoun with antecedent, 108–9, 240–1; *ex.* 241–2
of pronouns in case, 243
of subject with verb, 108, 237–40, 336, 337; *ex.* 241–2
ain't, not acceptable, 339
Alertness to possible subjects, 4–5

alibi, 339
all of, with nouns, pronouns, 339
all ready, already, 136
all right, alright, 340
all the farther, etc., 340
all together, altogether, 136
All-purpose terms, 143–4
Allusion, 148–9
allusion, illusion, 136
almost
position of, 114
v. *most,* 355
also, 123–4
as conjunctive adverb, 236
in parenthetical insertion, 290
amazing, overused for emphasis, 145
Ambiguity, structural, 110–16, 117–19; *ex.* 116–17
Ambiguous reference of pronouns, 108–9, 113
among, between, 343
Ampersand (&), avoided in formal writing, 457
and
as coordinating conjunction, 235, 283–4
punctuation with, in series, 296–7
used between loosely related clauses, 121–2
used to excess, 121
and etc., redundant, 340
and/or, 340
angle, as general term, 143, 340
angry at/with/about, 153
Animate objects, possessive with, 245
Annotated bibliography, 453
Antecedent, 93–4, **108–9**, 213, 215, **240–1**, 256
agreement of pronoun with, 240–1
defined, 256
to be kept clear, 108–9
Antonym, 186; *ex.* 187
any, number of, 238
anybody, anyone, number of, 241

INDEX

INDEX